AF529131

POPULATION ECOLOGY AND FAMILY PLANNING

(A Demographic Anthropology of Himalayan Population: Kinnaura)

POPULATION ECOLOGY AND FAMILY PLANNING

(A Demographic Anthropology of Himalayan Population: Kinnaura)

RAJESH K. GAUTAM
GAUTAM K. KSHATRIYA
A. K. KAPOOR

SERIALS PUBLICATIONS
NEW DELHI (INDIA)

© Rajesh K. Gautam, Gautam K. Kshatriya, A. K. Kapoor

First Published – 2010

ISBN: 978-81-8387-314-7

All rights reserved with the Publisher, including the right to translate or reproduce this book or parts there of except for brief quotations in critical articles or reviews.

Published by

SERIALS PUBLICATIONS
4830/24, 1st Floor, Ansari Road
Darya Ganj, New Delhi-110002 (India)
Phone : 23245225. Fax : 91-11-23272135
E-mail: serials@satyam.net.in

CONTENTS

ACKNOWLEDGEMENTS

First of all we would like to express our deep gratitude to all the Kinnaura respondents of Kinnaur District, Himachal Pradesh, who readily provided all necessary information required for this book. The credit of genesis of this book goes to ICMR (Indian Council of Medial Research) New Delhi who funded the project entitled "Determinants of Genetic and Socio-cultural Aspects of Health vis-à-vis Role of Health Providers among the Tribals of Himalayan, Coastal and Desert Regions" at the Department of Anthropology, University of Delhi.

We are grateful to the Co-Investigator Prof. Satwanti Kapoor and Dr. U. Dutta for valuable guidance and direction during the course of project and writing of this book. Our sincere gratitude is also due to all the faculty members, supporting staff and colleagues research fellows of the Department of Anthropology, University of Delhi, Delhi for their suggestions and help. The authors owe special thanks to the project fellows Dr. Swapan Koley and Dr. Sunita Devi as they were part of data collection in Kinnaur.

We are extremely thankful to district authorities— DC (Deupty Commissioner), CMO (Chief Medical Officer) for instructing their officers to help in collection of data on Kinnaura as part of ICMR Project. As a part of ICMR team our thanks are due to Medical Officers (CHCs/PHCs), Paramedical Staff, Aganwadi Workers, Teachers, Pradhan, and various functionaries of GOs (Government Organizations) and NGOs for their support and help in outreach areas. Thanks are also due to the caretakers of various rest houses as it would have been difficult to carry out investigation in the Kinnaur District without their services.

Our thanks are also due to Prof. N. K. Sethi, Advisor, Planning Commission of India and Former Director of National Institute of Health and Family Welfare (NIHFW), Munirka, New Delhi for providing material support during the course of early phase of work. Dr. V.K. Tiwari faculty in-charge computer center in the Institute (NIHFW) had always been kind and helpful during thesis writing and analysis of the data, we are thankful to him. Dr. Y. L. Tekhre of Department of Social Science (NIHFW) always took extended all the possible helps during the course of present task. The authors are grateful to Dr. Anupam Basu (Reader), Dr. T.Bir (Reader), Mr. Pardeep Kamboj (RA), Mr. Ramesh Chand (ARO) and Mr. Prahalad Singh (SPA) of NIHFW for extending their coordination and help during early stage of thesis.

Dr. Prasanna K. Patra, Dr. Devender Biswal, Dr. Rajeev Kamal, Dr. Sanjay, Dr. Sudeep Ghosh, Dr. Rajesh Khanna, Dr. (Ms) Navneet Kaur, Dr. Aruna, Dr. Abhilasha and other colleagues, fellows and friends deserves for special thanks.

Authors are also grateful to Prof. and Head A.N. Sharma, Department of Anthropology Dr. H.S. Gour University, Sagar (M.P.) Prof. Kalpana Saini, Dr. KKN Sharma, Dr. Chandra Lekha Parmar, Dr. Safia Khan, Mr. Vishvajeet, Dr. Ajay Gharami (Fellow, ICSSR), Dr. Ashish Gupta (Doctoral Fellow and Guest Lecturer), Mr. Pritam Choudhari and other fellow Teachers and Scholars and students of Department of Anthroplogy, Dr. H.S. Gour University Sagar, Madhya Pradesh for their help and support for present endeavour. Dr. Dipak Adak of Anthropological Survey of India, Field Station Sagar owes special thanks for his critical comments. Dr. Manoj Jain of Registrar General of India, New Delhi owes thanks for catalysing the whole process of writing. Dr. Rama Shanker, Faculty of Department of Computer Science, Dr. H.S. Gour University Sagar owes our deep gratitude for extending his support related to computer hardware and softwares.

Last but not least we are grateful to Dr. Satyanaryan of An.S.I. Sagar for proof reading of book. The publisher and his staff owes our thanks for bringing the book timely.

Dated: May, 2008

Rajesh K. Gautam
Gautam K. Kshatriya
A. K. Kapoor

PROLOGUE

A layman has no concern with the term 'population'. In many cases he even didn't has exact number of his 1st or 2nd degree relatives. For a literate person the term 'population' or 'jansankhya (जनसंख्या)' is a scientific term dealt by demographer (population scientist), statistician and economist, he can tell the numeral of population of particular region like his own country or province and even some times he may have idea about smaller units like districts or village; whereas for a demographer the population is a problem by which he earns his bread and butter. Now, politicians have more concern with it, for them population is power. In democracy the number plays big roles. For policy planners the estimates of population and its different segment are essentially required, without estimate of population the policy maker may be handicapped. The study of population at various strata helps them in planning for future of region and nation as a whole. Therefore significance of population studies have vital role in the human welfare and development. The anthropological approach to population studies have further increased the importance of discipline by micro level analysis and reaching to the grass root level of the problem. The human biology, nature and behaviour can not be merely numerical game and could not be better understood by any other way than the anthropological approach. We are sure; you will find a new dimension throughout the book. It is expected that it would be beneficial for larger walk of people viz. students' of anthropology, biology, demography, economics, geography, political science, population studies, sociology, medicine, public health, health management etc. Today corporate world is more conscious about such kind of study for implementation of their own agenda and programme and they can also use its findings and estimates and even they can sponsor similar studies at broader perspectives.

Chapter 1

INTRODUCTION

POPULATION = the whole number of people or inhabitants in a region or country.
ECOLOGY= pattern of relations between organisms and their environment.
HUMAN ECOLOGY = pattern of relations between man and their environment.
DEMOGRAPHY= study of human populations esp. its size, density, distribution and vital statistics.
ANTHROPOLOGY= the science of human beings; especially : the study of human beings in relation to distribution, origin, classification, and relationship of races, physical character, environmental and social relations, and culture.

Anthropology and Demography are related by definition, history, and methodology as well as conceptually and theoretically. Demography is defined as the study of human populations (Demos = People, and graphy = to sketch or to study) largely in quantitative or numerical terms. The term demography was first coined by a Belgian, Achille Guilard in 1855, from the Greek word 'demos' means 'people'. He defined it as the natural and social history of the human species or the mathematical knowledge of populations, of their general changes, and of their physical, civil, intellectual, and moral condition. The discipline of study of human populations is also known by the term 'Population Studies'. Hence the science of Demography and Population Studies are more or less similar. The discipline is primarily concerned with size, distribution, structure and change of population. The three principal component of change in total population are birth, death and migration. Birth is a biological process by which a species multiplies its members by the reproduction of the individuals of similar kind and perpetuate the existence by replacing old members by death. Death is also a biological process; it is demise of an individual. By death a living being dissolve in nature. The third component- migration is a process or phenomenon of moving of individuals or mass from one geographical or territorial boundary to another or new location. Demographically birth is positive factor, responsible for numerical growth in population, whereas death is negative factor, which reduces population in number. Migration is also a negative factor for a particular territory from where migration is taking place.

Moreover, Population characteristics also include units like ethnic characteristics, social characteristics and economic characteristics. Caste, creed, religion, race, nationality, mother tongues are part of ethnic characteristics as well as shade light into social characteristics. Other examples of social characteristics are marital and family status, place of birth, literacy, and educational attainment. Economic characteristics include economic activity, employment status, occupation, industry, and income. It would be worth mentioning here that these days, demographic data have widely been used in planning and developmental programmes. It provides useful information on the pressure of populations upon resources, depopulation, family limitation, eugenics, assimilation of immigrants, urban problems, manpower, and maldistribution of income and so on.

Demographic studies may be synchronic, examining population structures or characteristics at a given moment, or diachronic, as when they study processes of change in population composition and distribution over time. Demography establishes reliable estimates of total population numbers and composition, and of rates of fertility and mortality, as well as the interrelationships which exist between different variables such as age, sex, social class, ethnic origin, migrant status and vital rates. Studies of this kind of data are available within given historical and geographical contexts, which gives rise to a number of sub-specialties within the discipline. Paleodemography, for example, is the study of prehistoric populations, and borrows heavily from the methods of Archaeology in order to reconstruct the demographic structures of early populations and to study the processes of population growth and redistribution, which accompanied, for instance, the evolution of agriculture or of urban life. Historical demography, working with historical materials such as census data, parish records and legal and administrative documents, attempts to rediscover the demographic structures and processes of past populations and critically assesses and reformulate theories of the relationship between, for example, population size, family structure and industrialization. The broad area of social demography is concerned in general with the relationships between population and social processes, and has links both with ecology and with sociological and anthropological theories concerning population and social structure.

On the other hand, Anthropology is defined as the study of human being in time and space, or the study of human development and culture of these sample populations. Historically, the two fields (Anthropology and Demography) derive from similar origins, although they have developed in different directions with only spasmodic interchange over the last four centuries. Theoretically both have often interwoven and overlapped but usually not too explicitly. Anthropologists have been interested in examining the demographic determinants and consequences of cultural process. Demographers have looked for the cultural causes and effects of demographic process. Thus it should not surprise that both fields have imported and exported theory and data to each other. After these interchanges and similarities both are separate disciplines with clear-cut scope and boundaries. There are definite reasons that why anthropologist do demographic study, ranging from the meta-scientific to the practical, from national needs to personal interests.

At the most abstract level anthropologists are concerned with the discovery, classification, and explanation of mankind. The growth of anthropological knowledge is dependent upon recognizing generalizations about society and recognizing the limited uniformity of human condition. This ability to abstract generalities from specifics is particularly important, for the large variability of human patterns has severely restricted the numbers of generalities discovered. In this context culture and population, as two of the few human universals, represent one area of anthropological research with many implications and applications within the discipline. In this way Demographic Anthropological studies tend to bring about more meaningful information at the grass root level for understanding the differences between the groups and planning effective developmental strategies. Censuses and large scale surveys viz. National Family Health Survey (NFHS), Sample Registration Survey (SRS), Rapid Household Survey (RHS) etc. bring an overall picture of population characteristics despite micro differences among different groups. The demographic anthropology, however, fills up this gap through studying small groups. This is very important to understand the problem at grass root level. In the context of India, the sub-division of populations by caste, tribe, class, community etc. provides tremendous heterogeneity in terms of social, cultural and biological aspects and in this way; demographic anthropology contributes effectively in population studies maintaining their distinct identity.

As already stated above the demographic studies focus largely on three readily observable human phenomena; i.e. change in human population size, its composition and distribution. In the process it encompasses five demographic events viz. fertility, mortality, marriage, migration and social mobility. Fertility and mortality are the components, which are not merely independent but are also correlated and inter dependent with different social, economic, political and ecological variables including health indicators. Vital statistics of fertility and mortality viz. birth, deaths and abortions are measures by different parameters. The main sources of demographic statistic in India are Population Censuses, National Sample Surveys, National Health Survey (NFHS), Civil Registration of Vital events and ad-hoc demographic studies.

DEMOGRAPHIC TRANSITION: ANTHROPOLOGICAL PERSPECTIVE

The theory of demographic transition states that how the equilibrium of fertility and mortality regulates the growth of population. There are already defined five phases of demographic transition, as cited below:

(1) The high stationary stage, characterized by high birth rates and high death rates;

(2) The early expanding stage, with falling birth rates but rapidly decreasing mortality;

(3) The late expanding stage, with falling birth rates but rapidly decreasing mortality;

(4) The low stationary stage, with low birth rates balanced by equally low mortality; and

(5) The declining stage, with low mortality and deaths exceeding birth.

According to this theory, in the first phase, the high fertility rates are almost balanced by high mortality rates. In the second phase, with initiation of development parity between births and deaths is disturbed, and mortality decreases as a result of a wide variety of interlinked causes including advances in medicine, technology, and available resources ensuing into population explosion. In the later phase, the rate of population growth declines to a new "steady level" as the birth rate decreases. This decrease in the birth rate is caused partially by higher consumption expectations and the development of new social values.

There have been several problems with the concept of the demographic transition. The first have been determining the societies where high mortality and fertility are roughly equal. Anthropologists who have actually tried to find such societies have not been successful. Even, Paleoanthropologists have been showing that the transition between hunting and gathering and agriculture has been a gradual process characterized by societies with moderate fertility rates, not uniformly high rates as presumed by the theory. Ethnographic data indicate a wide variety of mortality and fertility rates for present-day non-industrialized societies.

A second problem is that transition theory was originally formulated to explain data from Western Europe. The characteristics stage or rates need not be universal. Anthropologists have been showing that demographic characteristics are neither geographically nor temporarily uniform. They concluded that availability of resources seems to determine population size and characteristics.

Third problem is that the transition theorists argue that mortality drops as a result of the diffusion of new medical techniques, and that fertility declines after industrialization. This is true; only for Western Europe. Simultaneously it appears that the population decrease of in pre-industrial societies resulted from cultural contact with western civilization and the consequent of epidemics, wars and slave trades.

The fourth problem concerns with fourth phase of transition where low fertility is balanced by low mortality. Transition theorist tended to look toward modern industrial societies with capital-intensive economies. Anthropologists however have now pointed out numerous examples of " primitive isolates" which are neither industrial nor capital intensive but which meet the transition theorists' criteria of low fertility and mortality.

It is apparent from the above discussion that anthropologists have presented challenge to the transition theorists. This is not to imply that transition theory should be totally rejected or even that the concept of the demographic transition has been proved wrong. Rather the concept has certain clear advantages: parsimony, simplicity and predictability. It still summarizes a huge body of data. Though, it leaves many questions un-answered. Still, its importance in population studies cannot be ignored.

GLOBAL POPULATION SCENARIO

The World

Today, there are more than 6 billion human beings on this planet. This number is multiplication of merely 2,000 people that existed 60,000 years ago. This was critical point, when there were only 2,000 humans in existence, though there seem to be more people at 100,000 years ago but they were limited to Africa. At 40,000 years ago the Neanderthals were the main occupants of Europe. Around 20,000 years ago there were no people in America. Around 10,000 years ago there were a few million people in the world (Wells, 2003). The total population of human being was around 1 billion around the year 1820.

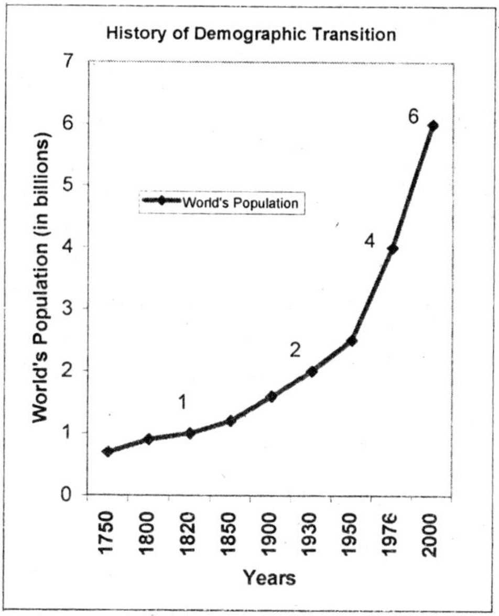

Figure 1: History of World's Demographic Transition

Source:

1. United Nations (1982). Demographic Indictors of the Countries, as assessed in 1980, Department of International Economic and Social Affairs, New York.
2. United Nations Population Fund (1993). The State of the World population. 1993. UNFPA, New York.

The population doubled to 2 billion in 110 years in the year 1930. Then it took just 46 years in getting doubled to 4 billion by 1976. We crossed the threshold of the "New millennium" with 6 billion population (Figure 1), and according to Population Reference Bureau (2002) each individual was sharing an area of 0.008 sq. mile. The projected population for the world would be 9.1 billion by 2050 (Figure 2) on the basis of present vital statistics, viz. crude birth rate (CBR) of 21, crude death rate (CDR) of 9 and total fertility rate (TFR) of 2.8. However, if TFR would have remained constant at higher level (4.18-4.78), the world's population would have crossed

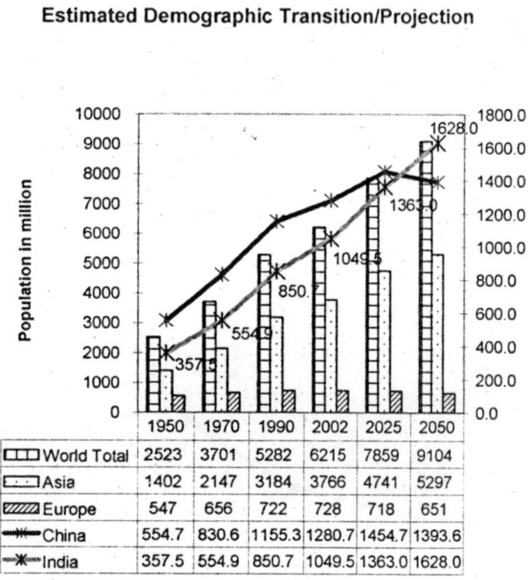

	1950	1970	1990	2002	2025	2050
World Total	2523	3701	5282	6215	7859	9104
Asia	1402	2147	3184	3766	4741	5297
Europe	547	656	722	728	718	651
China	554.7	830.6	1155.3	1280.7	1454.7	1393.6
India	357.5	554.9	850.7	1049.5	1363.0	1628.0

Figure 2: Demographic Transition and Population Projection in Major Parts of the World.

Source:

1. United Nations (1998): World Population Prospects: The 1996 Revision. New York.
2. Population Reference Bureau (2002): 2002 World Population Data Sheet of the Population Reference Bureau, Demographic Data and Estimates for the Countries and Regions of the World.

15 billion. If it remains constant at 2.03 the world's population would be 8-10 billion by 2050. And, According to O'Neil and Balk (2001) it may decrease to 5 billion-upto year 2100 if TFR declines to 1.56 (Figure 3) In 1950, 33 % of world's population

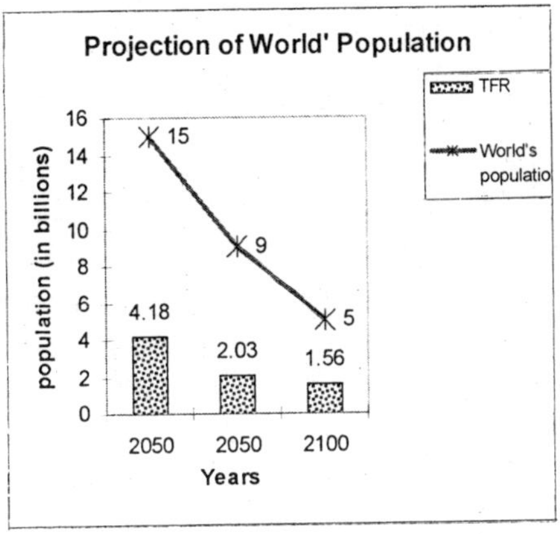

Figure 3: Projection of World's Population on the Basis of Fertility Transitions.

Source: O'NEIL, B. AND BALK, D. (2001): World Population Futures, *Population Bulletin;* 56 (3), p. 3-40.

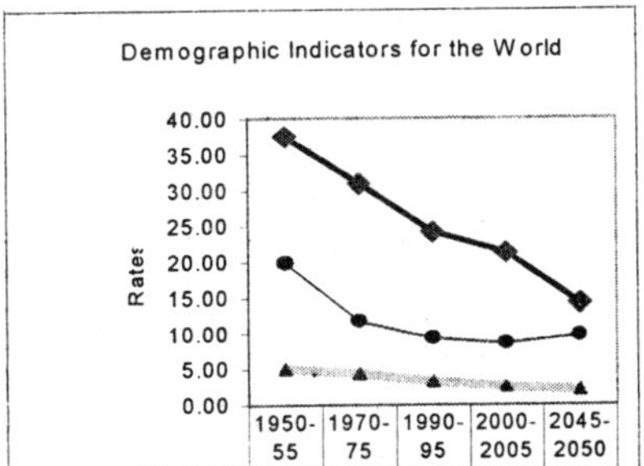

	1950-55	1970-75	1990-95	2000-2005	2045-2050
Fertility Rates	5.00	4.40	3.30	2.60	2.09
Death rates	19.8	11.7	9.3	9	9.7
Brth rates	37.4	30.9	24.1	21.3	14.2

Figure 4: History and Projection of Transition of Vital Demographic Indicators of World

Source:

1. UNITED NATIONS (1998): World Population Prospects: The 1996 Revision. New York.

lived in developed countries (North America and Europe), which in 1990 decreased to 20%. On the other hand, percent share of developing countries in world's population increased from 67 % in 1950 to 80 % in 1990. The demographic indicators and its projections for the World is shown in Figure 4. It is clear from these figures that fertility and birth rates are declining globally and it will continue further also, while death rate will increase slightly from 9 to 9.7 by 2045-2050.

India

India is in the second position with 1.05 billion population in mid-2002 and it would be in the first position with 1.628 billion population in 2050. While China is currently in first position with 1.281 billion population, it would be in the second position with 1.394 billion population in the year 2050. China and India are currently home of 38 % world's population (Figure 5). Today, every sixth person in the world is an Indian. In 1901 India's population was 0.238 billion. It became 0.846 billion in 1991, 1.027 billion in 2001 and 1.068 billion in mid-2003. Reasons behind this rapid growth of population are faster decline in death rate from 42.6 in the year 1911 to 8.5 in year 2000, and slow decline in birth rate from 49.2 in 1911 to 25.8 in the year 2000. The changes in death rate are mainly due to eradication of epidemics and famine, control over communicable diseases, advancement in medical facilities, health-seeking behaviour of people and green revolution. Sudden rise in life expectancy at birth due to better health care and other socio-economic development is also among the cause of the rapid growth of the population. During 1901-1911 the life expectancy at birth for Indians was 22.6 years for males and 23.3 years for females, which increased to 63 and 64 years respectively in the year 2001 (ESCAP, 2001). A comparative picture of life expectancy at birth for major regions of the world during 1950 to 1995 is shown in Figure 6. The demographic indicators for India show that fertility and birth rates are declining and these will continue to decline further (Figure 7).

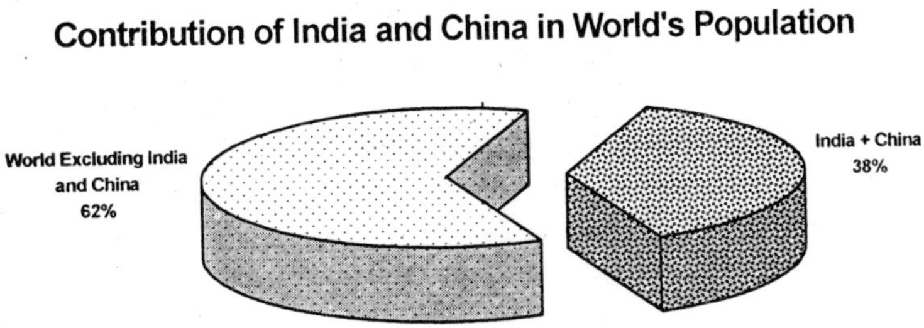

Figure 5: Contribution of India and China in the Total World's Population

Source: POPULATION REFERENCE BUREAU (2002): 2002 World Population Data Sheet of the Population Reference Bureau, Demographic Data and Estimates for the Countries and Regions of the World.

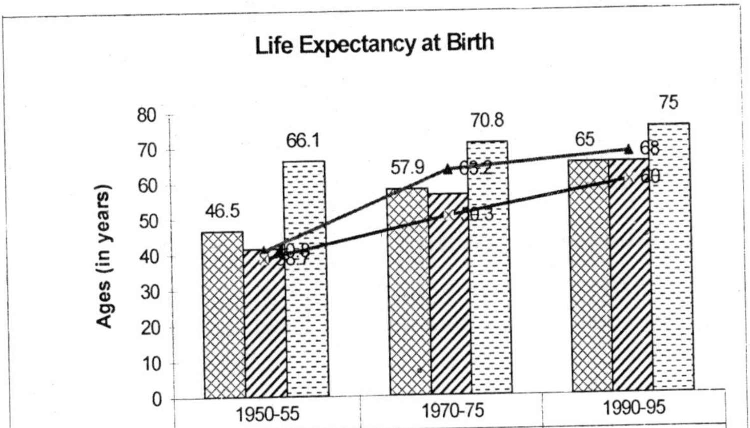

	1950-55	1970-75	1990-95
World Total	46.5	57.9	65
Asia	41.3	56.3	65
Europe	66.1	70.8	75
China	40.8	63.2	68
India	38.7	50.3	60

Figure 6: Life Expectancy at Birth

Source:

1. UNITED NATIONS (1998): World Population Prospects : The 1996 Revision. New York.

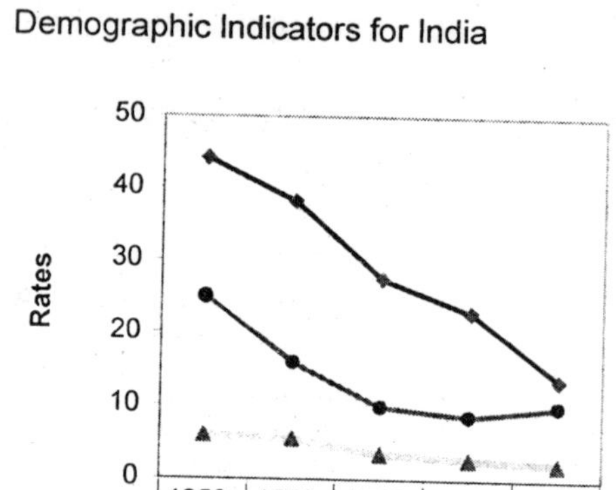

	1950-55	1970-75	1990-95	2000-2005	2045-2050
Fertility Rates	5.97	5.43	3.39	2.74	2.10
Death rates	25.0	15.8	9.8	8.5	9.9
Brth rates	44.10	38.20	27.50	22.9	13.6

Figure 7: History and Projection of Transition of Vital Demographic Indicators of India

Source:

1. UNITED NATIONS (1998): World Population Prospects: The 1996 Revision. New York.

Highlands of the World

Most of the world's population (33.5% or 1.88×10^9 people) lived within 100 vertical metres of sea level. The population living at 2,000-2500 m is (1.3×10^8) comparatively less (Cohen and Small, 1998), but mountainous areas in this planet are among major ecosystem, provide a variety of prospect to examine the structure of human population, which is conditioned by the physical environment. One of the reasons for this potential is the diversity of high altitude environments that exists in different parts of the world. The delimiter line for deciding high altitude is 2,500 m. Though there is not a single factor, but one should consider other variables also in deciding the delimiter for high altitude. Three principal high altitude areas of the world are- (i) the Andes mountains of South America, (ii) the high lands of northern Ethiopia and (iii) the Himalayan highlands (Baker, 1978).

Andes

Andes are mountain system of South America extending along west coast from Panama to Tierra del and are one of the great natural features of the Earth. The Andes consist of a vast series of extremely high plateaus surmounted by even higher peaks that form an unbroken rampart over a distance of some 5,500 miles (8,900 kilometres)—from the southern tip of South America to the continent's northernmost coast on the Caribbean. This mountain system contain the highest peaks in the Western Hemisphere. The highest of them is Mount *Aconcagua* (22,831 feet [6,959 metres]) on the border of Argentina and Chile. Some historians believe that the name Andes originated from the Quechuan word anti ("east"); others believe that it was derived from the Quechuan anta ("copper"). It perhaps is more reasonable to ascribe it to the anta of the older *Aymara* language, which connotes copper colour generally.

Human presence in the Andes is relatively recent; the oldest human remains dates back to 10,000 to 12,000 years, although habitation probably dates too much earlier times. The shortage of oxygen at high altitude, especially above 12,000 feet, is so physiologically demanding that it imposes deep adaptative changes even within the cells of the body. The highest altitude in the Andes at which people have resided permanently is 17,100 feet (shepherds in southern Peru) and, as temporary workers, 18,500 to 19,000 feet (Carrasco Mine, in the Atacama Desert, Chile). From Patagonia to the southern limits of the Bolivian Altiplano, the Andes are sparsely populated; a few small groups of shepherds and farmers live on the lower slopes of the cordillera. Farther to the north, from Bolivia to Colombia, the largest population concentrations and most of the important cities of these countries are found in the Andes. In Peru and Bolivia, a significant proportion of the inhabitants live above 10,000 feet. Roughly half the population of Bolivia are *Aymara*- and *Quechua*-speaking Indians; most of the remainder are Spanish-speaking *mestizos* (or mixed). In the Lake Titicaca district live remnants of the ancient Uru people. Population is distributed mainly between the high páramos, where, except for a semi nomad population of shepherds, the principal occupation is mining, and the lower narrow valleys, where the people practice agriculture. In Peru, mining is the most important human activity above 11,500 feet, but the great majority of the Andean population is engaged in agriculture and raising sheep, goats, llamas, and alpacas; a growing proportion of people have become employed in industry and commerce. A group of Aymara-speaking Indians live in the south around Lake Titicaca, but the largest native population is Quechua-speaking; Quechua speakers constitute the great majority of the highland population. The inhabitants of the Ecuadorian Andes are mainly Quechua speakers and mestizos; in the south there are small groups of Cañaris and, in the north, Salasacas. Agriculture is the main occupation; some Indian peoples engage in ceramics and weaving. In Colombia the largest proportion of the population lives between 5,000 and 10,500 feet. Only a tiny fraction of the country's population is Indian, these groups living on the Altiplano of the Cordillera Oriental and in the Cordillera Central and the southern mountains. The zone of coffee plantations at about 3,000 to 6,500 feet is the most densely populated area (Encyclopædia Britannica 2003).

Ethiopia

Ethiopia, an another highland on this planet is called the landlocked country on the Horn of Africa. It shares frontiers with Eritrea to the north, Djibouti to the northeast, Somalia to the east, Kenya to the south, and The Sudan to the west and northwest. Its total area is 437,794 square miles (1,133,882 square kilometres). Lying completely within the tropical latitudes, the country is relatively compact, with similar north-south and east-west dimensions. The capital is Addis Ababa ("New Flower"), located almost at the centre of the country. Ethiopia is one of the oldest countries in the world. Its territorial extent has varied over the millennia of its existence. In ancient times it remained centred around Aksum, an imperial capital located in the northern part of the modern state, about 100 miles (160 kilometres) from the Red Sea coast. The present territory was consolidated during the 19th and 20th centuries as European powers encroached into Ethiopia's historical domain. Ethiopia became prominent in modern world affairs first in 1896, when it defeated colonial Italy in the Battle of Adwa, and again in 1935–36, when it was invaded and occupied by fascist Italy. Liberation during World War II by the Allied powers set the stage for Ethiopia to play a more prominent role in world affairs. Ethiopia was among the first independent nations to sign the Charter of the United Nations, and it gave moral and material support to the de-colonization of Africa and to the growth of Pan-African cooperation. These efforts culminated in the establishment of the Organization of African Unity and the United Nations Economic Commission for Africa, both of which have their headquarters in Addis Ababa (Encyclopædia Britannica, 2003).

Ethiopia's topography, one of the most rugged in Africa, is built on four geologic formations. Rocks of Precambrian origin (more than 540 million years in age) form the oldest basal complex of Ethiopia, as they do in most of Africa. The Precambrian layer is buried under more recent geologic formations—except in parts of northern, western, and southern Ethiopia, where there are exposed rock layers of granite and schist. Geologic processes of the Mesozoic Era (245 to 66.4 million years ago) contributed sedimentary layers of limestone and sandstone, most of which have been either eroded or covered by volcanic rocks. Younger sedimentary layers are found in northern Ethiopia and on the floors of the Rift Valley. Lava flows from the Tertiary and Quaternary periods (from 66.4 million years ago to the present) have formed basaltic layers that now cover two-thirds of Ethiopia's land surface with a thickness ranging from about 1,000 feet (300 metres) to almost 10,000 feet. The Rift Valley forms a spectacular graven (a massive tectonic trough) running right down the middle of the country from the northern frontier with Eritrea to the southern border with Kenya. Although Ethiopia's complex relief defies easy classification, five topographic features are discernible. These are the Western Highlands, Western Lowlands, Eastern Highlands, Eastern Lowlands, and Rift

Valley. The Western Highlands are the most extensive and rugged topographic component of Ethiopia. The most spectacular portion is the North Central massifs; these form the roof of Ethiopia, with elevations ranging from 15,157 feet (4,620 metres) for Mount Ras Dejen (or Dashen), the highest mountain in Ethiopia, to the Blue Nile and Tekeze river channels 10,000 feet below. The Western Lowlands stretch north-south along the Sudanese border and include the lower valleys of the Blue Nile, Tekeze, and Baro rivers. With elevations of about 3,300 feet, these lowlands become too hot to attract dense settlement. The Rift Valley is part of the larger East African Rift System. Hemmed in by the escarpments of the Western and Eastern Highlands, it has two distinct sections. The first part is in the northeast, where the valley floor widens into a funnel shape as it approaches the Red Sea and the Gulf of Aden. This is a relatively flat area interrupted only by occasional volcanic cones, some of which are active. The Denakil Plain, in which a depression known as the Kobar Sink drops as low as 380 feet below sea level, is found here. High temperatures and lack of moisture make the northeastern Rift Valley unattractive for settlement. The southwest section, on the other hand, is a narrow depression of much higher elevation. It contains Ethiopia's Lakes Region, an internal drainage basin of many small rivers that drain into Lakes Abaya, Abiyata, Awasa, Langano, Shala, Chamo, and Ziway. Together these lakes have more than 1,200 square miles (3,108 square kilometres) of water surface. The upper Rift Valley is one of the most productive and most settled parts of Ethiopia. The Eastern Highlands are much smaller in extent than the Western Highlands, but they offer equally impressive contrast in topography. The highest peaks are Mount Batu, at 14,127 feet, and Mount Chilalo, at 13,575 feet. The Eastern Lowlands resemble the long train of a bridal gown suddenly dipping from the narrow band of the Eastern Highlands and gently rolling for hundreds of miles to the Somalian border. Two important regions here are the Ogaden and the Hawd. The Shebele and Genale rivers cross the lowlands, moderating the desert ecology (Encyclopædia Britannica, 2003).

Himalayan High Lands

The Himalayas 'the measuring rod of earth' is one of the youngest mountain ranges in the world. Its revolution can be traced to the Jurassic Era (80 million years ago) when the world's landmasses were split into two: Laurasia in the Northern hemisphere and Gondwanaland in the southern hemisphere. The landmass, which is now India broke away from Gondwanaland and floated across the earth's surface until it collided with Asia. The hard volcanic rocks of India were thrust against the soft sedimentary crust of Asia, creating the highest mountain range in the world. Its principal mountain range dividing the Indian subcontinent from Naga Parbat in the west, the range stretches for over 2,000-km to the mountains bordering Sikkim and Bhutan in the east (Encyclopædia Britannica, 2003). The west Himalaya is the part of this range that divides Kashmir and Himachal Pradesh from Ladakh. The highest mountains here are Nun and Kun. In Kashmir the subsidiary ridges of the Himalaya include the North Sonarmarg, Kolahoi and Amarnath ranges. Further in the east, the Himalaya extends across to the Baralacha range in Himachal Pradesh before merging with the Parbati range to the east of the Kullu valley. It then extends across Kinnaur Kailash to the swargarohini and Bandarpunch ranges in Uttaranchal. Further it is defined by the snow capped range of the Gangotri glacier and by the huge peaks in the vicinity of Nanda Devi, the highest mountain in the Indian Himalaya. In Western Nepal the range is equally prominent across the Annapurna and Dhaulagiri massifs, while in Eastern Nepal the main ridgeline frequently coincides with the political boundary between Nepal and Tibet.

(a) Pooh: Pooh is a sub-division of Kinnaur district of Himachal Pradesh. This is adjoining area of Spiti valley. It can be divided into two different valleys i.e. Pooh and Hangrang. Both the valleys are marked with cold desert climate and harsh weather with a little rain. Naturally there is no flora, but human settlements and villages having few orchards and crops. The area experiences frequent land slides. Maling land slide in Hangrang valley is known for separating the district into two

parts. At this point approximate 1 Km. area is intercepted by complete washout of road, especially during summer.

(b) Lahul & Spiti: Lahul and Spiti were brought together to form a new district of - of Himachal Pradesh (India) having international boundary with Tibet. It attained the status of a district in the year 1960. Till then it was merely a tehsil of Kullu Sub-division. There are valleys, mountains, glaciers, rivers, forests, pastures, gompas (monasteries) and ancient buildings of the former ruling dynasty. The customs, myths, beliefs and conventions of the simple unsophisticated people are the unique features of this border highland. Every village or a hamlet has a prayer flag fluttering over the Buddhist monastery. These shrines are the centers of the cultural life of the people that have influenced their religious beliefs for centuries and round which their social life revolves. This is a mountainous area that is located between Ladakh and Tibet in the north and the Kullu valley in the south. Lahul begins 51km north of Manali, right after crossing the 3978m (13,127 ft) Rohtang Pass. One can go through this area when one travels north from Manali to Leh. Many of the peaks here are over 6000m, the highest being Mulkila at 6,500m. It is basically a dry barren mountainous area with some green areas. It has some interesting Buddhist gompas and secluded villages. There are some good treks in this area. To reach here from Manali one has to travel over the Rohtang Pass, which is closed a good part of the year because of heavy snow. One can also get to this area coming from Shimla going through the Spiti Valley. It is approached from Zanskar by going over the Shinga La Pass and from Ladakh by going over the Baralacha La Pass (4,870m). About half the people in Lahul are Buddhist and the other half is Hindu. The main local language is Bhoti, which is similar to Tibetan. The capital of the Spiti sub-district is Kaza. The Spiti valley has around 30 monasteries and is often referred to as "little Tibet." Founded in the sixteenth century, the Kee Gompa is the largest and the oldest monastery in the Spiti Valley, supporting a thriving community of lamas. It is located at a height of about 4116 metres above sea level. The highest settlement of the world 'Village-Kibber' (4205 m from mean

sea level) lies in Spiti valley. Following are passes and heights by which the Lahul and Spiti is bounded.

(1) Rohtang (3978m)

(2) Baralacha La (4830m)

(3) Kunzam (4551m) (Photograph 1.2)

(4) Pin Parvati (5319m)

(5) Ghunsarng (5600m)

(6) Monirang (5335m)

(7) Sara Umga (5019m)

(8) Hamta (4268m)

(9) Kugti (5040m)

(10) Kalicho (4803m)

(11) Tarsalamu (5358m)

(c) Everest, K2 and Kanchenjunga: Everest is a Mountain on the crest of the Great Himalayas in Asia, lying on the border between Nepal and China (Tibet), at 27° 59′ N, 86° 56′ E. It is the highest point on Earth. Three barren ridges—the Southeast, Northeast, and West—culminate in two summits at 29,035 feet (8,850 metres; Everest) and 28,700 feet (8,748 metres; South Peak).The mountain can be seen directly from its north-eastern side, where it rises about 12,000 feet (3,600 metres) above the Plateau of Tibet. The peak of Changtse (24,803 feet [7,560 metres]) rises to the north. Khumbutse (northwest; 21,867 feet [6,665 metres]), Nuptse (southwest; 25,791 feet [7,861 metres]), and Lhotse (south; 27,923 feet [8,511 metres]), which also rise around Everest's base, hide the peak from view on the Nepalese side. The summit of Everest reaches two-thirds of the way through the air of the Earth's atmosphere, to where oxygen levels are low. Lack of oxygen, powerful winds, and extremely cold temperatures preclude the development of any plant or animal life on the upper slopes. Precipitation falls as snow during the summer monsoon (May–September). The flanks of the mountain are separated from each other by the main ridges; ice sheets on them cover the slopes to the mountain's base. The summit itself consists of rock-hard snow surmounted by

a layer of snow that fluctuates annually by some 5–20 feet (1.5–6 metres); it is highest in September and lowest in May after depletion by the strong north-westerly winter winds. Individual glaciers flanking Mount Everest are the Kangshung Glacier (east); the East, Central, and West Rongbuk glaciers (north and northwest); the Pumori Glacier (northwest); the Khumbu Glacier (west and south); and the West Cwm, an enclosed valley of ice between Everest and the Lhotse-Nuptse Ridge. The mountain's drainage pattern radiates to the southwest, north and east. The Khumbu Glacier melts into the Lobujya (Lobuche) River of Nepal, which flows southward as the Imja River to its confluence with the Dudh Kosi River. In Tibet the Rong River originates from the Pumori and Rongbuk glaciers, and the Karma River from the Kangshung Glacier. The Rong and Dudh Kosi river valleys form, respectively, the northern and southern access routes to the summit. Like other high peaks in the region, Mount Everest has long been revered by local peoples; its most common Tibetan name, Chomolungma, means "Goddess Mother of the World," or "Goddess of the Valley." (The Sanskrit name Sagarmatha means literally "Ocean Mother.") Its identity as the highest point on the Earth's surface was not recognized, however, until 1852, when the governmental Survey of India established that fact. In 1865 the mountain—previously referred to as Peak XV—was renamed for Sir George Everest, British surveyor general of India from 1830 to 1843. Controversy over the exact elevation of the summit developed because of variations in snow level, gravity deviation, and light refraction. The figure 29,028 feet (plus or minus a fraction)was established by the Survey of India between 1952 and 1954 and became widely accepted. The currently reported figure—29,035 feet (8,850 metres) (plus or minus 6.5 feet [2 metres]) was calculated by an American team in 1999 (Encyclopædia Britannica, 2003).

K_2 also called Mount Godwin Austen, called locally Dapsang, or Chogori the world's second highest peak (28,251 feet [8,611 m]), second only to Mount Everest. K2 forms part of the Karakorum Range (Himalayas) and lies partly in China and partly on the western side of the Indian-Pakistani line of control in Jammu and Kashmir; it is presently under Pakistani administration. The glacier- and snow-covered mountain rises from its base at about 15,000 feet on the Godwin Austen Glacier, a tributary of the Baltoro Glacier. The mountain was discovered and measured in 1856 by Colonel T.G. Montgomerie of the Survey of India, and it was given the symbol K2 because it was the second peak measured in the Karakorum Range. The name Godwin Austen is for the peak's first surveyor, Colonel H.H. Godwin Austen, a 19th-century English geographer (Encyclopædia Britannica, 2003).

(d) Tibet: Tibetan highlands of Himalayas are often called "the roof of the world." Tibet is formed by the Himalayan mass; the highest peak is Mount Everest, which rises to 29,035 feet (8,850 metres) on the Tibet–Nepal border. North of Ma-fa-mu Lake (Mapam Lake; conventional Manasarowar) and stretching eastward is the Kailas (Kang-ti-ssu) Range, with clusters of peaks, several exceeding 20,000 feet. This range is separated from the Himalayas by the Brahmaputra River, which flows across southern Tibet and cuts south through the mountains to India. It occupies about 471,700 square miles (1,221,600 square kilometres) of the plateaus and mountains of Central Asia, including Mount Everest (Chu-mu-lang-ma Feng). It is bordered by the Chinese provinces of Tsinghai to the northeast, Szechwan to the east, and Yunnan to the southeast; Myanmar (Burma), India, Bhutan, and Nepal to the south; the disputed territory of Jammu and Kashmir to the west; and the Uighur Autonomous Region of Sinkiang to the northwest. Lhasa is the capital city. The name Tibet is derived from the Mongolian Thubet, the Chinese Tufan, the Tai Thibet, and the Arabic Tubbat. Before the 1950s Tibet was a unique entity that sought isolation from the rest of the world (Encyclopædia Britannica, 2003). It constituted a cultural and religious whole, marked by the Tibetan language and Tibetan Buddhism. Little effort was made to facilitate communication with other countries, and economic development was minimal. After its incorporation into China, fitful efforts at development took place in Tibet, disrupted by ethnic tension between the

Han (Chinese) and Tibetans and Tibetan resistance to the imposition of Marxist values. Official policy since the early 1980s has been somewhat more conciliatory, resulting in slightly better Han-Tibetan relations and greater opportunities for economic development and tourism.

The Tibetan peoples in China number about 4.6 million, though only about 2 million live in the Tibet Autonomous Region. Tibetans are the descendants of tribal peoples from the Tibetan-Qinghai plateau (Plateau of Tibet) with some mixtures of neighbouring Mongol, Chinese, Indian, and Turkic peoples from Central Asia. Despite efforts to modernize the country and to discourage the power and influence of Tibetan Buddhism, religion remains a powerful and pervasive force. The main beliefs of ancient worship of nature and magic were combined with more formal aspects of traditional Buddhism, and highly ritualized ceremonies employed prayer flags, prayer wheels, and elaborate forms of praying. Before the Communists took power, as many as a quarter of all Tibetans belonged to religious orders. The traditional society was composed of a small group of noble families and a large and poor peasantry. Among these peasants were both nomadic herding peoples and those who practiced a form of subsistence farming. Religious officials and leaders were typically drawn from the noble families.

(e) Karakoram: Karakoram the great mountain system extending some 300 miles (500 kilometres) from the easternmost extension of Afghanistan in a south-easterly direction along the watershed between Central and South Asia. Found there are the greatest concentrations of high mountains in the world and the longest glaciers outside the high latitudes. The borders of Tajikistan, China, Pakistan, Afghanistan, and India all converge within the Karakorum system, giving this remote region great geopolitical significance. The name "Kurra-koorrum," a rendering of the Turkic term for "Black Rock" or "Black Mountain," appeared in early 19th-century English writings. The population of the Karakorum Range is concentrated in three towns—Gilgit and Skardu in Pakistan and Leh in the Ladakh region of India—and in small villages

throughout the region perched on rocky slopes or besides raging torrents (Encyclopædia Britannica, 2003).

(f) Kunlun: The Kunluns of Himalayas extend east to west some 1,250 miles (2,000 kilometres) from the Pamirs in Tajikistan on the west to the Kunlun Pass and the adjacent Sino-Tibetan ranges—Pu-erh-han-pu-ta (Burhan Budai), P'a-yen-k'a-la (Bayan Hara), and A-ni-ma-ch'ing (Amne Machin)—on the east. The width of the Kunluns varies considerably but rarely exceeds 125 miles. In the western margins they form an Inner Asian rampart between the Plateau of Tibet and the Tarim (T'a-li-mu) Basin in western China. A northern fork of the A-erh-chin (Altyn Tagh) Mountains continues this alignment. The southern face of the Kunlun Mountains rises no more than 5,000 feet (1,500 metres) above the Plateau of Tibet, which itself averages some 15,000 feet in altitude (Encyclopædia Britannica, 2003). From the perspective of the oases at the southern edge of the Takla Makan Desert to the north of the mountains, however, the Kunluns form a massive rampart blocking access to the icy barren expanses of the westernmost reaches of Tibet. Despite the extreme climatic and topographic conditions, the Kunluns and adjacent areas support permanent and migratory populations. On the northern slopes are found Uighur, up from the oases, and occasional Mongols; and, south to the northern areas of Tibet, Tibetan pastoral nomads have commandeered large expanses of formerly abandoned steppe grazing lands. Mountain Tajik and Kyrgyz remnants occupy the few settlements in the deep valleys of the western mountains adjacent to the Karakorum and Pamir ranges. Chinese (Han) are omnipresent, with concentrations along the extensive and well-maintained network of gravel roads that has been constructed since 1949.

(g) Pamir: Pamir is the highland of Himalaya region of Central Asia. The mountain area centres on the nodal orogenic uplift known as the Pamir Knot, from which several south-central Asian mountain ranges radiate; these include the Hindu Kush, the Karakorum Range, the Kunlun Mountains, and the Tien Shan. Most of the Pamirs lie within Tajikistan, but the fringes penetrate Afghanistan, Pakistan, China, and

Kyrgyzstan. The core is situated in the highlands of Tajikistan with the highest mountains in the Gorno-Badakhshan autonomous oblast (province). The word Pamir in the local Turkic language denotes the high undulating grasslands that are a feature of the eastern portion of the mountains, especially where they abut Afghanistan and China. In the portion of the Pamirs in the Gorno-Badakhshan autonomous region of Tajikistan, nine-tenths of the population lives above 5,000 feet, and no settlement is located below 11,500 feet in the Kyrgyz sector. Of those residing in the eastern area, three-fifths migrate in the course of their annual pastoral tasks. At high altitude, the Kyrgyz exhibit much greater longevity and lower infant mortality than the Tajik. Substantial population movement has occurred since 1940, when the majority of the residents of the western Pamirs were forcibly removed to the irrigated cotton communes established on the broad river plains in Tajikistan. Agro-pastoral activities, often associated with communal farms, occupy the remaining inhabitants of the Pamirs. Population pressure in Tajikistan—which has a high birth rate and a large proportion of its population living in poverty—has made it necessary to establish new settlements and farms in the western Pamir valleys. This resettlement of formerly depopulated valleys is most evident in the Surkhob and Obikhingou valleys upstream from the huge hydroelectric dams at Norak and Rogun (Ragoon) on the Vakhsh River.

(h) Leh and Ladakh: Leh and Ladakh is Himalayan highland lies in eastern Kashmir are part of Jammu and Kashmir State, in the northern part of the Indian subcontinent. It contains the western Himalayan Ladakh Range. Ladakh covers about 45,000 square miles (117,000 square km) and includes the Karakorum Range and the upper Indus River valley. Ladakh is one of the most elevated regions of the world. Its natural features consist mainly of high plains and deep valleys. The high plain predominates in the east, diminishing gradually westward. In the southeast of Ladakh lies Rupshu, an area of large, brackish lakes which has a uniform height of about 13,500 feet (4,100 m). To the northwest of Rupshu lies Zaskar, a bleak, inaccessible region where the people and the cattle remain

indoors for much of the year because of the cold. Zaskar is drained by the Zaskar River, which, flowing northward, joins the Indus River below Leh. In Ladakh proper, farther to the north, cultivation by means of manuring and irrigation ranges from 9,000 to 15,000 feet (2,750 to 4,550 m). The people are divided into shepherds, who populate the upland valleys too high for cultivation, and the Ladakhis, who till the land around the valley villages. Leh, the most accessible town of Ladakh proper, is an important trade centre and lies 160 miles (260 km) east of Srinagar. The climate of Ladakh is cold and dry. Average annual precipitation is 3 1/3 inches (84 mm); fine, dry, flaked snow is frequent, and sometimes the fall is heavy. Vegetation is confined to valleys and sheltered spots, where a stunted growth of tamarisk, furze, and other plants supply much-needed firewood. The principal products are wheat, barley, millet, buckwheat, peas, beans, and turnips. The only manufacture is woolen cloth. Ladakh was contested by both India and Pakistan; after the cease-fire agreement of 1949, its southern portion went to India and the remainder to Pakistan. In the early 1960s Chinese forces gained control of the northeastern part of the Indian-held portion of Ladakh.

POPULATION CHARACTERISTICS AND ITS DETERMINANTS: A REVIEW

The history of population studies goes back to middle of seventieth century (1662) when John Graunt's pamphlet "Natural and Political Observations Made upon the Bills of Mortality" was published in London (Bhende and Kanitkar, 2001). This "bills of mortality" was based on weekly current reports on burials and christenings in a population of nearly half a million persons in London and its environs. These reports were compiled and maintained from 1603 by Paris clerks (Durand, 1962). Sir William Petty (1623-1687) who was Graunt's contemporary called this newly founded discipline as "Political Arithmetic". Another important contribution to the advancement of population studies was made in London about thirty years after the publication of Graunt's observation by Edmund Halley (1665-1742). In 1693, Halley constructed the first empirical life table, based on the data of births and deaths. He coined the word "expectation of life". Gregory King (1648-1712) contributed to the discipline by estimating the population of England and Wales. This was the first estimation of the population size of the England and Wales, after that first census of England and Wales was held in 1801. In 1761-62, Johann Peter Sussmilch had written a book on population, consisting of 1200 pages and an appendix of 68 tables. He tried to construct mortality tables of universal applicability (Lorimer, 1959). Sussmilch tried to estimate the population of the world in the third edition of his treatise, *The Devine Order*, published in 1765. He also studied the factors influencing fertility, such as age at marriage, disruption of marriage by death, prolonged nursing of infants, effects of various diseases etc.

Most of the research on population during eighteenth and the nineteenth centuries were carried out in the field of mortality and rarely in the field of population dynamics. Some scholars of eighteenth century observed the relationship between the potentiality of population growth and available resources. The Chinese writer Hung Liang-Chi noted that an increase in the means of subsistence was not in direct proportion to that of the population. Thomas Robert Malthus (1766-1834) was a milestone in the field of population studies. For many years, all views on population were classified as pre-Malthusian, Malthusian, anti-Malthusian and neo-Malthusian. In 1798 he published an essay entitled, "An Essay on the Principles of Population. The central theme of essay was that **while man could increase his subsistence only in arithmetical progression, his number tended to increase in geometrical progression.** Three important developments in population studies took place in Europe and the United States in the nineteenth and twentieth centuries: the development of probability theory in statistics, the beginning of census operations and the establishment of the system of civil registration. William Farr who was in General Register Office in England contributed to the methodology of population analysis in many ways, notably by the construction of life tables and the study of occupational mortality. Human fertility sought the attention of scholars only in the twentieth century. The birth rate in England had started declining since the late nineteenth century; and in order to investigate its causes, a Royal Commission was set up in 1943 Britain to enquire the reasons for the falling birth rate. The report of this commission submitted in 1949, made a considerable contribution to the development of population studies. In the United state of America, considerable work on population studies started coming up in early 20th century and by 1937 the Population Association of America was established.

After the Second World War, there has been a splendid progress in the field of population studies. A noteworthy feature of this development was the interest in the study of population of developing countries like India, Pakistan, Philippines, Srilanka, etc. The emancipation of several Afro-Asian countries raised aspiration and hopes for removal of poverty, raising the standard of living of the people and thus ensuring for them a better quality of life. Hence a new era of planning and development dawned in these countries. The planners of these countries were taking keen interest into population characteristics and dynamics. Since the Second World War several international organizations were established for the population studies (Bhende and Kanitkar, 2001).

Among the pioneering organizations, United Nations sponsored several World Population Conferences. The reports of all the conferences sponsored by the United Nations on population issues are being published regularly along with the key papers.

In 1956, the Demographic Training and Research Centre (Now known as the International Institute for population Sciences) was established in Bombay under the joint sponsorship of the Government of India and the United Nations. Since the establishment of this centre, five other regional centres have been set up by United Nations one each at Santiago in Chile, Cario in Egypt, Accra in Ghana, Yaounde in Cameroon and Bucharest in Romania.

As there was much concern over excessive growth of population in developing countries, several research studies were undertaken to cover the problems of growth, family planning and urbanization in those countries. Important among these were the cost-benefit studies of the family planning programme in India and other developing countries, research in the dual reporting system of births and deaths, etc. The deep concern among the Americans in the late 1960s and the early 1970s about rate of growth of their own population.

Some of the valuable contribution in the field of population study was "The Population Bomb" of Ehrlich (1968); documentation of Thomas Robert Malthus's Essay on the Principle of Population by Appleman (1976); Demography the study of Human Population by Yaukey (1985); on the other hand Menard and Mathiot (1987) dealt with Population Perspectives and its Concepts and Issues. Hartman (1987) focused on Reproductive Rights and Wrongs and with the associated Global Politics of Population Control and Contraceptive Choices. Human fertility also seeks attention of scholars like Lutz (1989) he focused on Distributional aspect of Human fertility in Global context. Lancaster (1990) paid attention on Expectation of life, Demography, Statistics and History of World Mortality. Ehrlich and Ehrlich (1990) worked out on Population Explosion. Brig (1995) focused attention on World Population Projections for the Twenty-first Century and its Theoretical Interpretations and Quantitative Simulations. Furthermore demographic transition, concept and issues of population were not lacking interest of demographers, so Jones (1997) edited a volume on Continuing Demographic Transition; whereas Weeks (1999) focused on Population and related concepts and issues. Encyclopedia of Global Population and Demographics by Ness (1999) is a mirror of human numbers on this planet. O'Neil and Balk (2001) comprehensively dealt with world population projection alongwith the limitations of associated factors. Read and Le Blanc (2003) presented the standard model of population growth and regulation, and concluded that the multitrajectory model underscores the complexity of the relationship between population growth and societal change.

In India the history of population studies goes back to (323-300 B.C.) Kautilya, the Prime Minister of Chandragupta Morya, who had written a treatise named *Arthashatra* on policy, In this treatise he described the ways of conducting a population, economic and agricultural census. The *Ain-I-Akabari* compiled by Abul Fazal (1542-1605) contains a comprehensive data on population characteristics, population industry and wealth. After these historic efforts there were long gaps in the field of population enumeration and population numeric were revived with the establishment of the system of decennial census in 1872. Wattal (1958) is pioneer in this field; he started seeking attention of Population Problem in India. A significant development in this discipline took place in 1938, when the Indian National Congress set up a sub-committee of the National Planning Committee to study the problems of food supply, nutrition, social reform, unemployment and social welfare. Beside decennial census, National Sample Survey (NSS) was established in 1949 to produce reliable data on birth and death rates and rates of natural increase. Zachariah (1968) focused on Historical Study of Internal Migration in the Indian Sub-continent 1901-1931. Besides that there are several micro level studies highlighting different components of population dynamics among various Indian Populations (Ghosh, 1970; Barua, 1976; Murty and Ramesh, 1978; Chengal Reddy and Laksmanudu, 1979; Basu, 1986; Rao and Murty, 1984; Basu, Kshatriya and Jindal, 1988; Jain and Visaria, 1988; Basu and Kshatriya, 1990; Kshatriya and Basu; 1993; Kshatriya, Singh and Basu, 1993 & 1997; Kshatriya, 1999a & 1999b; Ranjan, 1999 etc.) Furthermore, Anthropological survey of India has made a great stride in population studies in India. The people of India-Project were devoted to study the Indian populations, and the compilation has since published in various volumes (Singh, 1994, 1994 &1996 etc.).

The NFHS I and II (National Family Health Survey) and RCH (Reproductive Child Health) Survey are yet other monuments, which are prepared across various states providing various features of population characteristics.

There are number of studies in India and its implications in solving population problem. It would be worth mentioning here that various micro level studies on different ethinic groups (small or large) would provide baseline information about population of a particular region as every group and region has its own problems. In this context Himalayas in south-east Asia provides a unique situation with its great diversity in different spheres. High altitude region and its populations are different from lowland; they are mysterious, risky, fascinated and challenging in almost all the aspect, these areas are in general secluded since centuries, unapproachable for others who do not belongs the region. There are limited means of communication and transportation; and with many deep and furious rivers and rivulets it is difficult to cross these waterways in spite of these problems, approximately 20-25 million people reside above 3000 m from mean sea level (De Jong, 1968). These people are distributed in Himalayas, Karakoram, Tien Shan, Pamir Caucasas, Alps, Andes and Rocky Mountains etc. (Clegg et. al., 1970). According to Weiner (1964) 12 percent of total world's population are residing in mountains. Many researches have under taken on different socio-economic, demographic and physiological aspects of these populations. The available studies are mainly confined to the high altitude stress on human fertility and mortality in the Andean region, and sporadically in Himalayan region and Ethiopia.

Monge (1948) noted that Spanish settlers of the sixteenth century believed that altitude reduced their fertility. Weihe (1964), Miller (1974), Baker and Little (1976), Baker (1978), Heath and Williams (1981), Goldstein et.al. (1983), Basu et.al. (1984), Gupta et.al. (1987) discussed the human biology and population dynamics of high altitude.

A number of studies have reported the adverse effects of high altitude stresses (mainly hypoxia) on fecundity and fertility in the Andean region (James, 1966; Heer, 1967; Hoff, 1968; Baker and Dutt, 1972; Abelson et. al., 1974; Hoff and Abelson, 1976). The studies of Bangham and Sacherer (1980), Gupta (1980), Weitz et. al. (1981) reported similar findings in

Himalayan region. Frisancho and Baker (1970), Lang & Lang (1971), and Frisancho (1981) reported that the high altitude physical environmental stresses delay menarcheal age in human female in Andean region. Similar findings were reported by Pawson (1976), Miklashevskaya (1979), Bangham and Sacherer (1980), and Beall (1983) for the Himalayan region. But the investigation of Kashiwazaki et. al. (1988) on the Bolivian Japanese did not observe such adverse effect of high altitude, which may be due to their being non native in the high altitude La Paz in Bolivia.

In a detailed analysis in Bolivia, Dutt (1980) did not find any significant altitude related difference in the mean numbers of total pregnancies and live births, but noticed a significant reduction in number of living children, as a result of significantly increased childhood mortality rates at high altitude. He stated that differences in neonatal and early childhood mortalities might have biased or complicated the study impact of altitude on fertility. Beside that there is a contradictory finding too on altitude infant and child mortality and altitude-prenatal mortality (Cruz-Coke, 1967; Buck et.al., 1968; Hoff, 1968; Clegg et.al. 1970; Gupta et.al. 1987; Lebedeva and Musuraliev, 1987; Kashiwazaki et.al. 1988).

Many scholars e.g. Stycos (1963 & 1965), Heer (1964), Heer and Turner (1965), Whitehead (1968), Bradshaw (1969), De Jung (1970), Goldstein (1981), Goldstein et. al. (1983), Gupta (1985) had focused their attention on fertility and factors responsible for low fertility at high altitude. These studies pointed out that apart from the genetic factor, various demographic, economic, socio-cultural, and other physical environmental factors viz. migration of males to low land, relatively high age at first birth and average pregnancy gap, higher proportion of women in labour force, least acculturation, differences in marriage practices and exposure to the risk of conception, rural-urban differences, health differences, under enumeration of children, under reporting of births etc. are responsible for low fertility at high altitude.

Kashiwazaki et. al. (1988) observed that higher age at marriage and age at menarche are the major factors explaining fertility performance, while altitude (hypoxic stress) explains only less than 3 percent of the variance in the same.

Abelson et.al. (1974) mentioned that the differences in marital patterns and socio-economic status, as well as migration itself did not appear to account for the differences in fertility between the studies populations.

Goldstein et. al. (1983) investigated the relationship between high altitude hypoxia and fecundity among Ladakhis of Himalayas, India. They found contradictions and problems between the Himalayas and the Andes. Contrary to previous researches this Himalayan population had high fertility. The article compares high and low altitude populations in the Himalayas, and concludes that there is little support for a difference in fertility. The stress is given to socio-cultural and other factors affecting reduced fertility.

Basu et. al. (1984) have explained the low fertility in Lachen than in Lachung in the Sikkim Himalayas in terms of differentials transhumance pattern- a socio-economic attribute, which seems to have led to differential exposure to the high altitude stresses, thereby affecting fecundity/fertility.

Wiley (1998) investigated that long inter-birth intervals, driven primarily by the lactational amenorrhoea associated with breast feeding were the important determinants of low natural fertility in several populations. In Ladakh low rate of marriage among women might be attributed to the practice of polyandry, as also to the primary and secondary sterility, resulting in low completed pairs of reproductive age. The age specific fertility rates were also unexpectedly low. The most likely explanations for low marital fertility include sterility from STDs, high rates of fetal loss and possibly nutritional constraints on ovarian hormone status.

Kshatriya et.al. (1997) investigated anthropo-demographic features and health care practices among the Jaunsaris of Jaunsar-Bawar, Dehradun, and Uttar Pradesh; and found moderately high TFR (Total Fertility Rate) and CBR (Crude Birth Rate) of 3.84 and 32 respectively.

Bhasin and Nag (2002) discussed the fertility pattern of various population groups of the state of Jammu and Kashmir and found strong relationship between fertility behaviour and gender inequality. Furthermore they also utilized regression statistics to understand relationship between various social, cultural and economic variables and fertility. They found various interrelated factors accounting for the fertility and other related demographic factors in Ladhakh.

Population Size

The size of population is usually first demographic fact which is obtained by different agencies to pursuance of various activities. The concept of 'population size' or 'total population' is not so simple. There are two simple ideal types of total population counts, the *de facto* and the *de jure*. The former comprises all the people actually present in a given area at a given time. The latter is more ambiguous. It comprises all the people who "belong" to a given area at a given time by virtue of legal or residence, caste, creed, religion or some similar criterion. In obtaining the size of population, census is adopted as powerful method. The earliest censuses were often a mere headcount, but the purpose of census in modern time is to produce statistical data on various aspect of any population. There are many other agencies, which estimates and projects the size of population for a particular region, country as well as for the world as a whole. Population Reference Bureau (PRB), Economic and Social Commission for Asia and Pacific (ESCAP), UNICEF, UNFPA, and Census of India are among such agencies. The size of population varies according to area, altitude, and climate. There is a lot of factors determine the size of population in a given area in a particular time. In the year 2000, world's population size was estimated to be more than 6 billion, whereas India's population size as per census 2001 was 1.027 billion. Himachal Pradesh is one of the hilly states of Indian Himalayas, its population is 60,77,900, furthermore for one of the district (viz. Kinnaur) of this state the size of total population was enumerated 78344. India's population is diverse in nature as there is tribals (84.32 million) scheduled castes (166.63 million) as well as people of different religious background. According to Cohen and Small (1998) in 1994, 33.5% (or 1.88×10^9) of the world's total population was living within 100 vertical metres of sea level. The study of population composition is most fundamental aspect of population characteristics. Population composition is the internal structure of a population group, with respect to one or more demographic traits, such as age, sex, marital status, economic status, educational characteristics, ethnic composition at a specified point of time e.g. Census of India 1991 enumerated 8.08 percent scheduled tribe and 16.48 percent scheduled caste population in the country.

Age Composition

Age is an important measurement of life span of an organism. The age composition of a population is of major importance in demographic analysis, since it is potential source to study the characteristics of population growth. It also indicates the relative level of development of an area. In developed region, the proportions of persons tend to be higher in the older than in the younger age groups (old population structure) while the reverse is discernible in developing regions (young population structure). To comprehend the overall population composition, a population pyramid is also generally constructed. The shape of pyramid depends on the past vectors of fertility, mortality migration, and nuptiality operating in an area/population. Age structure of a population within a community is considerably affected by the relative numbers at each age. Many types of planning, particularly planning of community institutions and services, require data on age composition. Age is an important variable in measuring potential population, the potential voting population, potential manpower, etc. Age data are required for preparing current population estimates and projections; projections of households, school enrolment, labour force, etc; and projections of requirements for schools, teachers, health services, food and housing. Age is the most important variable in the study of fertility, mortality, nuptiality, and certain other areas of demographic analysis. Despite of censuses and large scale surveys there are many micro level studies on different population focused on age composition. Basu, Gupta et.al. (1989); Patra (2001); Bhasin and Nag (2002); Kotal and Baruah (2004) are some of the authors who described age-composition among different Himalayan Population.

Sex Composition

The sex composition of a population plays a vital role in the population analysis, since it affects the incidence of births, deaths, and marriage. The migration rates and almost all population characteristics, including socio-economic characteristics, community life are influenced by sex composition of population of that area (Jain, 1975). By the point of sex the total of human population of the world is divided into two halves- male and female. Almost every programme at National level requires separate population data for males and females.

Mostly sex ratio is expressed in the form of sex ratio. Census of India (2001) observed the highest and lowest sex ratios; 1058 for Kerala and 709 for Daman and Diu, respectively. On the whole major northern states like Haryana (861), Punjab (874), Uttar Pradesh (898) have much more lower sex ratios than major southern states of Kerala (1058), Pondicherry (1001), Tamil Nadu (986), Andhra Pradesh (978), Karnataka (964), chiefly due to gender inequality and differences in status of women; which seems to be better in the southern than in the north/ north western states of India. Kshatriya (2000) reported sex ratio among different tribal population of India which varies from 744 among Sherpa of Sikkim (Eastern Himalaya) to 1098 among Dudh Kharia of Orissa.

Dependency Ratio

The variations in the proportions of children, aged persons, diseased persons and persons of "working age" are taken account of jointly in the so-called dependency ratio. Which is an important statistic derived from the age distribution of population in an area is the dependency ratio, which measures the impact of age composition on the livelihood activity of a population. The dependency ratio is based on the fact that every member of the society is a consumer and only some members are producer (Thompson and Lewis, 1965). The dependency ratio also reflects the level of development of a region. In other words, it attempts to describe the burden of dependency load that is supported by potentially economically active population.

Young Age Dependency Ratio (YADR)

This is a ratio of children under 15 to persons 15 to 64. The over all young age dependency ratio varies widely among different population it was reported 63.09 among Bodhs, 73.04 for Brokpas and 50.09 among Arghuns of Jammu and Kashmir (Bhasin and Nag, 2002), 49.01 among Marcha Bhotia, 56.53 among Juhar Bhotia of Uttaranchal (Chachra and Bhasin,1998). Maheo (1999) found 64.52 YADR among Mao of Manipur. Furthermore Bhasin and Bhasin (1993) reported YADR of 70.82 in Brahmans and 69.5 among Rajputs of Western Himalayas of Himachal Pradesh. Among Indian states, on the basis of Census of India (2001) the highest young age dependency ratio was found in Bihar (78.28) whereas lowest was estimated for Goa (35.25), though national average is 58.33.

Old Age Dependency Ratio (OADR)

Old Age Dependency Ratio is a ratio of persons of age of 65 and over to persons of 15-64 years of age. Alike young age dependency ratio the old age dependency also varies widely among different population across the country as well as in other parts of the world. Among Indian states it varies from 3.72 to 10.86 respectively in Dadar and Nagar Haveli and Kerala, whereas national average is 8.33.

Total Dependency Ratio

The ratio of children below 15 years of age and aged persons of 65 + of age is called Total Dependency Ratio. This is sum of young age dependency ratio and old age dependency ratio. For population of Ladakh (J & K state), it is estimated at 75 (Bhasin and Nag, 2002), whereas for India and the state of Jammu and Kashmir it was found rather high at 85 and 89 in

1981 (Census of India, 1981). Further in 1992, the dependency ratio of India seems to have declined to 75 (Ministry of Health and Family Welfare, 1997).

Marital Characteristics

The composition of marital status is essential part of the study of population characteristics; it has demographic, social and religious significance. It is not simply the number of fertile female that influences the level of fertility in a population, but the number of married fertile females. This is because, in most societies, all but a small fraction of childbearing occurs within marriage, which is the socially and legally recognized childbearing institution.

Age at Marriage

The age at marriage of a woman is an important determinant of population characteristics, dynamics and growth, especially among those where fertility control measure are rarely in practice, e.g. in primitive and tribal societies, remote, rural and hilly areas. The institution of marriage represents the socially sanctioned initiation of cohabitation and child bearing/rearing. And, any shift in this age, can prepone, or postpone the beginning of the reproductive span in societies, where marital fertility is encouraged. Malthus (1798) was the pioneer who recognizes that the preventive checks, such as delayed marriage and permanent celibacy affect fertility. Since then a considerable interest has been generated in studying this determinant and its relationship with fertility. It is well established that age at marriage varies across and within countries/regions. It is higher in the developed countries than in the developing ones (Fernando, 1982). In many Asian countries, the age at marriage is remarkably low, and child bearing rarely occurs outside legal unions. In India too, marriage is considered an important institution and is nearly universal because of the stigma attached to unwed mothers. Practically all births in country like India occur within marriage. The age at marriage is relatively low which leads mostly to early cohabitation and childbirth, resulting in undesirable demographic consequences. The mean age at marriage for Indian women in 1981 was 18.3 years (Census of India, 1981), in 1991 it increased to 19.5 years. According to the Child Marriage Restraint Act of 1978, the minimum legal age at marriage in India is 18 years for women and 21 years for men. Whereas median age of marriage for India was recorded 16.4 years, which varies from 14.7 years for Madhya Pradesh to 23.2 years for Goa (National Family Health Survey-2, 1998-99). The age at marriage is influenced by a number of factors such as place of residence, per capita income, degree of modernization and urbanization, status of women and work force participation by women, educational characteristics and opportunities, family structure, religion, caste, certain traditional cultural practices like dowry, primogeniture mode of inheritance etc. (UN, 1961; 1980; Agarwala, 1962; Bumpass, 1969; Dixon, 1971; Srikantan, 1977; Conde, 1978; Mahadevan, 1979; Eberstadt, 1980; Zachariah, 1981; Caldwell et.al. 1983; Chaudhury, 1984; Singh, 1986; Srivastva, 1986; Bhasin and Nag, 2002). There are several studies across the world indicating that the delayed marriage contributed to the decline in fertility (Pearl, 1939; Glass and Grebnik, 1954; Davis 1963; Freedman, 1963; Hanjal, 1965; Busfield, 1972; Ross et.al., 1972; UNECA, 1981; Udry and Cliquet, 1982, Dyson and Moore, 1983). However, in Sweden and some other West European countries no correlation between increasing age at marriage and declining level of fertility have been found (Coale, 1965). Chaudhury (1984) reported that the age at marriage was the most important factor explaining fertility behaviour in Bangladesh. Early marriage and high fertility is common to African continent (Conde, 1981). Nag (1974) revealed that in both the halves of the world developed and less developed, increase in age at marriage of women has been found to be crucial in the reduction of fertility, although the use of contraceptives diminishes its importance. In India, many studies have demonstrated lower fertility for those women who marry late compared to those who marry at younger ages (UN, 1961; Agarwala, 1962; 1966; Driver, 1963; Wyon and Gordon, 1971). According to Chakraborty and Malaker (1980), World

Bank Fertility Survey (1980), Singh (1986) and Mahadevan (1989) the average number of children ever born is negatively related with age at marriage. Bhasin and Nag (2002) also found that high age at marriage of women, particularly beyond 19 years of age, decline the fertility.

The above description shows that the age at marriage influences human fertility to a considerable extent. Since women have a fixed reproductive span unlike the males, the female age at marriage is of utmost importance. This variable is often referred to as beyond family planning measure because it enhances fertility in developing countries through early marriage and depresses fertility in developed countries by late marriage and reduces the length of the reproductive period. This variable changes slowly over time through social change, particular with the impact of modernization, social obligations, migration, occupational mobility, etc. These differences have been observed in numerous studies conducted both at macro and micro-level in several countries (UN, 1961, 1973; Agrawal, 1962; Busfield, 1972; Mahadevan 1979; Caldwell et.al., 1982 and Sen, 1994). In most of the societies the marriage is quite early, though in many instances it is not consummated until after puberty. There are two explanations for early marriage. One explanation is evolutionary or biological in nature and the other is social structural. The evolutionary explanation focuses attention on the survival of species. Compared to most animals, human reproduction is slow and normally one child is born at a time. Human children need parental care for a longer time to become self-sufficient for survival of the species (Sharma et.al., 1993). To view early marriage as an evolutionary adaptation would be an oversimplification as cultural behaviour almost always intervenes the biological forces. It has been noticed by various scholars that the chances of miscarriages, still births and genetically malformed children are very high among pregnancies occurring at very early age i.e. below 20 years and very late age i.e. beyond 35 years (MacMohan and McKeown, 1953; Ashley Montague, 1939; Fedrick, 1970).

Age at Menarche

The age at menarche is a threshold to sexual maturity of human female. Although it is a biological phenomenon; but it also seek considerable social interest and studied widely from different angles. The period between age at first menstruation and last menstruation in human female is known as reproductive life span. Age at first menstrual period is called age at menarche. This is the first outward sign of a woman's attainment of sexual maturity, and the starting point of reproductive span. Menarche exposes a woman to possible childbearing, and assumes significance. Several factors influence the age at menarche and menopause such as Socioeconomic conditions (Belmaker, 1982; Luoto et.al. 1994), nutritional status (Osteria, 1983; Riley, 1994; Simondon et.al. 1997) physical activity (Malina, 1983; Baker, 1985), altitude level (Beall, 1983; Kapoor and Kapoor, 1986; Gonzales and Villena, 1996), seasonality (Boldsen, 1992), general health and life-style (Parazzini et.al. 1992; Brown et.al. 1996), and genetic parameters (Danker-Hopfe and Delibalta, 1990; Kaprio et.al. 1995; Treolar et.al. 1998). An enumeration of average age at menarche of girls of 24 countries gives the range as 10-18 years (Shah, 1958). Mean ages at menarche and at menopause vary substantially between women across different countries or across different ethnic groups (Belitz, 1977; Gray and Doyle, 1983; Hunt and Newcomer, 1984; Danker, 1986; Ulijaszek et.al. 1991; Flint, 1997; Morabia et.al. 1998). Yet, mean age at menarche for the girls of 67 countries is calculated as 13.53 (SD $\pm$ 0.98) years (Thomas, Renaud, Benefice, Meeüs and Guegan, 2001), in the same study in reference to India (Punjab) Singh and Ahuja (1980) were cited with 14.31 years of age at menarche for Indian women.

The average ages at menarche in hot, temperate and cold climate are reported to be 13.0, 14.3 and 15.8 years respectively; and enumeration of the average age at menarche of girls of 24 countries give the range as 10-18 years (Shah, 1958). Montagu (1948, c.f. Sharma and Chaudhury, 1995) opined that the menarche before 12 years of age is abnormal.

In many studies, it is reported that hypoxia seems to delay the onset of menarcheal age in the Andean region (Frisancho and Baker, 1970; Frisancho, 1981), and also in Himalayan region (Lang and Lang, 1971; Pawson, 1976; Miklashevskaya, 1979; Bangham and Sacherer, 1980; Beall, 1983; Lebedeva and Musuraliev, 1987). Many Scholar calculated mean age at menarche for various population groups of different geo climatic set-ups, Bhasin (1990) reported 15.6 years mean age at menarche among Lepchas, Bhutias, and Sherpas of Sikkim Himalayas; Malik and Hauspie (1986) calculated 16.1 years among Bods of Ladakh; Bhalla et.al (1983) measured it among Punjabi Sportswomen as 15.7 years; Piplai (1983) calculated it for Tamang of West Bengal (15.8 years); Adak and Gharami (2002) reported it 13.5 years among Ladiya women of MadhyaPradesh; Pawson (1974) reported 18.1 years for Sherpas of Nepal; Nag (1965) measured the same among Christian and Non-Christian Khasis of Meghalaya as 19 and 18 years respectively. In a review, Gange et.al. (1989) have concluded that the age at menarche ranges from 12.2 to 18.8 years respectively among the developed and developing nations, 12.2 years found for Urban Italian girls (reported by Danker-Hopfe, 1986) and 18.8 years were recorded for poorly nourished New Guinea women (reported by Gray, 1979). Wood et.al. (1985) have reported even later age at menarche among the Gainj of New Guinea (20.4 years). Adak and Gharami (2002) also observed positive relation between better economic condition and age at menarche. Thus it seems many other factors may be having certain bearing on the age at menarche.

Many studies have also discussed the influence on the age at menarche, of such factors as, hygien awareness, type of physical activities, physique, dietary habits, socio-economic status, rural-urban residence, settlement size, and even family size (Sen, 1953; Shah, 1958; Biswas, 1967; Hillman et.al., 1970; Roberts et.al., 1977; Reddy 1984; Talwar et.al., 1987; Sharma, 1990; Chakravarti and Sinha, 1991; and others). In context of population dynamics, the age at menarche is very important; because in many societies it determines the age at marriage (Mandelbaum, 1974). Since marriage leads to child bearing, Freedman et.al. (1981), and Udry and Cliquet (1982) found that women with early onset are more fecund than those with late age at menarche; which leads to early pregnancy and frequent births.

Age at Menopause

Permanent cessation of menstruation in human females is called menopause. Age at menopause means the age at which a woman had experienced her last menstrual period. Alike the first appearance of menstruation or age at menarche the age at menopause also varies individual-to-individual as well as across the region and ethnic groups. The mean age at menopause of most populations for which measurements exist falls between ages 40 and 50, but the age of menopause of individual women ranges from less than 40 to near 60 (Wilson, 1985). However on the worldwide basis, menopause delayed upto 52 years in France (Salat-Baroux, 1980) and is earliest at 43.6 years, in New Guinea women (Gray, 1979). Alike the age at menarche the age at menopause is also affected by genetic parameters, socioeconomic conditions, general health and life-style, nutritional status, seasonality, physical activity and altitude level. Further it has also noticed that in many high fertility societies, child bearing continues until the menopause; it is slowed down, but not stopped totally by the process of ageing (Eaton and Mayer, 1953). Age at menopause plays an important role in regulation of fertility and ultimately affects the population characteristics.

Reproductive Life Span

The period extending from first appearance of menarche to menopause is known as reproductive life span of a woman. Since there is wide variation in age at menarche and menopause the reproductive life span also varies from person to person as well as across the region and ethnic groups. The factors influencing the age at menarche and menopause are directly affecting the reproductive life span of a woman; Although, pregnancy and childbearing are governed by a number of factors.

Fertility

Similar to menarche and menopause, fertility or natality is also concerned with the human female. It refers to the reproductive performance or actual bearing of children or live births (sometimes still birth and miscarriages are also included). This is a major component of population dynamics, ensuring the perpetuation of human being. In spite of being a biological phenomenon, fertility is greatly influenced by a number of demographic, economic, political, socio-cultural, physical, environmental and behavioural factors. The study of human fertility occupies a central position in the study of population for several reasons. Human fertility is responsible for biological replacement and for the maintenance of the human society. The growth of the population of the world depends entirely on human fertility. Any society replenishes itself through the process of human fertility. Thus, in population dynamics, fertility is a positive force of attrition caused by mortality. If this replacement of human numbers is not adequate - that is, if the number of deaths in a particular society continues to be more than that of births, that society would face the danger of becoming extinct. On the other hand, excessive replacement of human numbers can also create several social and political problems for a country.

There are various studies across the world highlighting that human fertility is determined and affected by a number of factors such as *current age of women* (UN, 1961; Heer, 1966; Heer and Smith, 1968; Bogue, 1969; Yankaver, 1970; Harrington, 1971; Chandersekhar, 1972; Ekanem, 1972; Jain, 1974; Heer and Wu, 1975; Agarwala, 1975; Lapham et.al., 1975; Frisancho et.al., 1976; Mitra, 1978; Ketkar, 1979; Tuncer, 1979; Miro and Potter, 1980; Talwalkar, 1980; Chaudhury, 1982; Mahadevan, 1985; Singh, 1986; NFHS-I, 1992-93 and Bhasin & Nag, 2002;), *Economic characteristics* (UN,1961 & 1985; Heer,1964; Namboodiri,1964; Heer and Turner,1965; Davis, 1967; Blake, 1968; Kasarda, 1971; Bhatnagar, 1972; Dixon, 1975; Germain,1975; Bangladesh Fertility Survey,1975; Demery and Renselaar,1979; Eberstadt,1980; Cain,1984 and Kasarda et.al.,1986), *Women employment* (Jaffe, 1959; Collver and

Langois, 1962; Westoff et.al., 1963; Blake, 1965; Collver, 1966; Miro and Martens, 1968; Berelson, 1969; Kasarda, 1971; Rosen and Simmons, 1971; Goldstein, 1972; Birdsall, 1977; Espenshade, 1977; Chaudhury, 1978; Standing , 1978; Oppong, 1983; UN, 1985), *Income or wealth resources* (Grabill et.al., 1958; Freedman, 1959; Becker, 1960; UN, 1961; Weintraub, 1962; Stycos, 1963; Kuroda, 1963; Adelman, 1963; Driver, 1963; Heer, 1966; Spengler, 1966; Agarwala, 1966; Bogue, 1969; Ridker, 1969; Willis, 1973; Bean and Wood, 1974; Schultz, 1974; Jain, 1975; Frisancho et.al., 1976; Chang et.al., 1979; Leibenstein,1979; Basu et.al. ,1980; Mamdani, 1981; and Singh, 1986) *ownership of land* (Bangladesh Fertility Survey, 1975; Driver, 1963; and Flinn, 1986), *educational characteristics and level of educational attainment* (Kiser, 1960; UN, 1961; 1973; 1979; & 1980; Adelman, 1963; Driver, 1963; Coale, 1965; Samuel, 1965; Heer, 1966; Blake, 1967; Stycos, 1968; Miro and Martens, 1968; Bogue, 1969; Minkler, 1970; Agarwala, 1970; Kasarda, 1971; Mitchel, 1971; Tuncer, 1971; Ekanem, 1972; Mandelbaum, 1974; Rele and Kantikar, 1974; Farooq and Tuncer, 1974; Snyder, 1974; Bhatnagar, 1975; Ghosh, 1975; Bangladesh fertility survey, 1975; Berelson, 1976; Leiberman, 1976; Birdsall, 1977; Graff, 1979; Bravo-Casas, 1979; Cladwell, 1980; Mamdani, 1981; Srivastva and Saksena, 1981; Zachariah, 1981; Jain, 1981; Dyson and Moore, 1983; Tonfer, 1984; Caldwell et.al. ,1984; Ahmad, 1985; Singh,1986; Mahadevan, 1989; and Bhasin & Nag, 2002;), *Religion* (Eaton and Mayer, 1953; Lorimer et.al., 1954; Driver, 1960; UN, 1961; & 1971; Rele, 1963; Agarwala, 1966; Kirk, 1966; Westoff and Potvin, 1966; Dandekar, 1967; El-badry, 1967; Mazur, 1967; Srinivasan, 1967; Day, 1968; Nag, 1968; Stoeckel and Chaudhury, 1969; Rao and Mathen, 1970; Aitken and Stoeckel, 1971; Lannoy, 1971; Mandelbaum, 1974; Visaria, 1974; Rele and Kantikar, 1976; Westoff and Ryder, 1977: Sri Lanka Fertility Survey, 1978; Potts and Selman, 1979; Nagi, 1981; Misra, 1982; Mahadevan, 1989; Pick et.al., 1990; and Bhasin & Nag, 2002), *organization and family structure* (Lorimer et.al., 1954; Davis, 1955; Bebarta, 1961; Driver, 1963; Hashmi, 1965; Nag, 1967; Nag,1972; Nag,1975; Pakrasi and Malakar, 1967; Stoeckel and Chaudhury, 1969;

Husain, 1970; Gould, 1972; Hall, 1972; UN, 1973; Datta, 1961; Bebarta,1967; Caldwell, 1981; Chaudhury, 1982; Vlassoff and Vlassoff, 1983; Morgan and Rindfuss, 1984; Singh, 1986; and Bhasin & Nag, 2002); *gender Preference or preference of children of a particular sex* (UN,1961; Davis,1963; Freedman,1963; Kirk,1966; Pathare, 1966; May and Heer, 1968; Minkler, 1970; Coombs,1977; Freedman and Coombs,1974; Arnold et.al., 1975; Heer and Wu, 1975; Stinner and Mader,1975; Mueller, 1976; Cain,1977; Jones, 1977; Wyon and Gordon, 1971; Chaudhury, 1978; Nag et.al., 1978; Park, 1978; Goody et.al., 1981; Miller, 1981; Chaudhury, 1982; Cleland et.al., 1988; Nag, 1985; Arnold and Zhaoxiang, 1986; Das Gupta, 1987; NFHS-2, 1998-99; and Bhasin & Nag, 2002), *notion towards average family size or ideal number of children* (Freedman, 1963; Van Keep, 1971; Inoue, 1978; Raman and Pakrasi, 1980; Goldstein, 1981; Das et.al. 1981; Laurenson et.al. 1985; Kashiwazaki et.al. 1988; and Bhasin & Nag 2002), *place of residence- rural or urban* (Davis, 1951; Taeuber, 1958; Whelpton et.al., 1966; Bogue, 1969; De Jong, 1972; Petersen, 1975; Sri Lanka Fertility Survey, 1975; Cladwell, 1976; BravoCasas, 1979; UN, 1961; 1979; Nag, 1980; Oberai and Singh, 1980; Trovato and Gridstaff, 1980; Bertrand et. al. ,1981; Gaisie, 1981; Cochrane, 1983; Kasarda et.al., 1986; Pick et.al., 1988; NFHS-2, 1998-99; Bhasin and Nag, 2002), *availability or unavailability of medical facilities* (Bhasin & Nag, 2002) etc.

Altitude has considered as one of the physical environmental determinants of population components. This is because such zones are characterized by multiple stress complexes, particularly hypoxia, which is believed to affect fecundity, fertility, mortality, physical maturity, growth and development.

Monge (1948) summarized the anecdotal evidences concerning the effects of altitude on the reproductive physiology of the Spanish settlers of highland Peru and Bolivia. Men taken to high altitude generally showed temporary reduction of sperm count and elevated numbers of abnormal spermatozoa (Donayre, 1966; Sobrevilla 1967, Donayre et.al 1968), although Sobrevilla (1967) reported that sperm production was normal among high altitude natives.

Guerra-Garcia et.al. (1965) showed a temporary fall in the amount of testosterone secreted by sojourners to high altitudes. Exposure to hypoxia damage seminiferous epithelium and also causes changes in libido in man, which however may be temporary.

Monge et.al (1945) observed infertility in couples migrating to high altitudes. Native low altitude women taken to high altitude may suffer disturbances of the menstrual cycle (Llarena and Coyotupa 1976, c.f. Gupta et.al. 1989), dysmenorrhoea, and alterations in the duration and intensity of the menstrual flow, although evidence of an ovulation in women living at high altitude is yet unconfirmed (Harris et.al., 1966; Donayre, 1966; Sobrevilla, 1967; Abelson, 1976), but contrary evidences have been reported by Harrison et.al. (1969) from Ethiopia. Data on sexual maturation in human females indicate that menarche is delayed in Andean high altitudes (Cruz-Coke et. al., 1966; Frisancho and Baker, 1970; Frisnacho, 1981), the Himalayan region (Ward, 1969; Lang and Lang, 1971; Pawson, 1974 and 1977; Beall, 1983) and Kirghizia (Miklashevskaya et.al., 1973; Miklashevskaya et.al., 1979). Valsik et.al. (1963) showed an increase of menarcheal age with altitude in Central Europe. Further in both male and females the development of secondary sexual characteristics is delayed (Mikalashevkaya et.al. 1973, Frisancho 1981) at high altitude in both the Andes and Kirghizia; however no such delay was noticed among the Ethiopian highlanders (Clegg et.al. 1972). Beall (1983) showed that the age at menopause in a Himalayan population was accelerated compared to other populations, thus confirming Flint's (1974) findings. Relatively recent studies on the high altitude effects on fertility suggest a depressing effect (Cruz-Coke et.al., 1966; Donayre, 1966; Hoff, 1968; Baker and Dutt, 1972; Way, 1972; Abelson et.al. 1974; Abelson, 1976; Hoff and Abelson, 1976; Dutt, 1980; Clegg, 1978). In Ethiopia, reproductive performances of both high and low altitude natives are similar (Baker, 1978; Harrison et.al. 1969). In the Tien Shan region, fertility is reduced at high altitude among Tibetans in Chinghai Province. However, there is a lack of consistency with regard to fertility level in the Himalayan region (Lang and Lang, 1971; Weitz et.al., 1978, Bangham and Sacherer, 1980; Beall and Goldstein, 1981; Goldstein 1981a&b, Goldstein et.al. 1983, Ross 1984, Laurenson et.al. 1985).

The effect of altitude on fertility is not universal and straightforward at each of the population/subpopulation levels; it is greater in Himalayan region than in other high altitude regions of the world, particularly Andes, Ethiopia and Tien Shan-Pamir (Gupta, et.al. 1989). Many scholars have reported the adverse effects of high altitude stresses (mainly hypoxia) on fecundity and fertility in the Andean region (James, 1966; Heer, 1967; Hoff, 1968; Baker and Dutt, 1972; Abelson et.al., 1974; Hoff and Abelson, 1976). Similarly, certain studies in the Himalayan region, also generally seem to support the similar observation (Bangham and Sacherer, 1980; Gupta, 1980, Weitz et.al., 1981). But some of these scholars have also pointed out the adverse effect of hypoxia on neonatal and infant mortalities, spontaneous abortions, leading to reduced fertility and lower survival rate of offsprings (James, 1966; Whitehead, 1968; Baker and Dutt, 1972; Abelson et.al., 1974; Hoff and Abelson, 1976). In a detailed analysis in Bolivia, Dutt (1980) did not find any significant altitude related differences in the mean number of total pregnancies and live births, but noticed a significant reduction in numbers of living children, as a result of significantly increased childhood mortality rates at high altitudes. He stated that differences in neonatal and early childhood mortalities might have biased or complicated the study of the impact of altitude on fertility. However, contradictory reports on altitude-infant and child mortality and altitude-prenatal mortality also exist (Cruz-Coke, 1967; Buck et.al., 1968; Hoff, 1968; Clegg et.al., 1985; Gupta et.al., 1987; Lebedeva and Musuraliev, 1987; Kashiwazaki et.al., 1988). However, many studies have doubted the single factor concept of adverse effects of hypoxia on fertility and pointed out that, apart from the genetic factor, various demographic, economic, socio-cultural and other physical environmental factors e.g. migration of males to lowland, relatively high age at first birth and average pregnancy gap, higher proportion of women in the labour force, least acculturation, differences in marriage practices, under enumeration of children, underreporting of births etc. are responsible for the low fertility at high altitudes (Stycos, 1963, 1965; Heer, 1964; Heer and Turner, 1965; Whitehead, 1968; Bradshaw, 1969; De Jong, 1970; Goldstein, 1981; Goldstein et. al., 1983, Gupta, 1985; Laurenson et.al., 1985). Kashiwazaki et.al., (1988), in their study in Bolivia, observed that late age at first pregnancy due to later age at marriage and age at menarche are the major factors explaining fertility performance, while altitude (hypoxic stress) explains only less than 3 per cent of the variance in the same. However, Abelson et.al. (1974) mentioned that the differences in marital patterns and socio-economic status, as well as migration itself did not appear to account for the differences in fertility between the study populations. Basu et. al. (1984) have explained the low fertility in Lachen than in Lanchung in the Sikkim Himalayas in terms differential transhumance pattern– a socio-economic attribute, which seems to have led to differential exposure to the high altitude stresses, thereby affecting fecundity/fertility. Further, contradictory evidence have also been presented. Harrison et.al. (1969) and Baker (1978) had not found any difference in the reproductive capacity of high and low land Ethiopian samples. And, relatively high fertility was reported from Himalayan high lands (Nepal and Ladakh) by Gupta (1980). Goldstein (1981) and Goldstein et.al. (1983); stated that the low fertility in Khumbu Sherpas (Nepal) is not typical of high-altitude Tibetan populations, but rather that the Himalayan (Tibetan) populations generally have moderately high fertility as compared to other Tibetan populations living at moderate altitudes.

In fact, the direct effect of hypoxia in reducing fertility appears rather controversial (Abelson, 1984; Basu and Gupta, 1984; Hoff, 1984), and the relative contributions of hypoxic stress as well as ethnic, demographic, other physical environmental factors in determining the fertility level in high altitudes do not seem to clear yet. Gupta et.al. (1987) have reported that, fertility data of Sherpas particularly mean completed fertility rate, mean number of live births and surviving children and total fertility rate are not affected by altitude only, concomitant socio-cultural factors may also have important, and perhaps even overriding effects of the same. While, Lebedeva and Musuraliev (1987) have reported higher mean fertility rate per women, and mean number of live births at high altitudes of Pamir than at low altitudes of Tien Shah in Kirghizia. Therefore the effect of high-altitude stresses may not have uniform and universal but varied effects on fertility, and that a host of independent determinants other than hypoxic stress are also influencing the same, can be grasped, when the range of completed fertility rates for high altitude populations, reported in the literature is considered. The completed fertility rates seem to vary from the low values of 5.8 in Chilean Aymara (Cruz-Coke et.al., 1966), or 3.2 in Bhotias of Nepal (Laurenson et.al., 1985) to the high values of 8.5 in Chilean Aymara (Cruz-Coke et.al., 1966), or 7.4 in Limi, Tibet (Goldstein, 1981). Bangham and Sacherer (1980) have reported a completed fertility rate of 7.6 for the Sherpas of Helambu of Nepal, situated at 2600m, while Goldstein et.al. (1983) have presented a rate of 7.2 for the same population. In another study, completed fertility rate were estimated by regression equation for Japanese married women living at Bolivian high altitudes (3600m) has been found rather low (2.5) in comparison to their counterparts (3.9) at 350m, (Kashiwazaki et.al., 1988).

It may be noted that the range of completed family sizes (for all women) varying from 5.3 (among rural population of northern China as well as in villages nearby to Bombay) to 9.5 among Hutterites of North America. And, reliable estimates of level of fertility suggest that hunters and gatherers and horticultural populations living in varied physical environment in various parts of the world tend to have values in the lower range of natural fertility of national populations. For example, the completed family sizes (for all women) for Dobe Kung Bushmen of Africa seems to be about 4.7 (Howell, 1979), and for the Gainj of New Guinea, it appears 4.3 (Wood et.al., 1985). However, Early (1985) has questioned the low fertility estimates reported for forager populations, on the basis of data quality and infanticide.

In relation to completed family sizes among most of the high altitude populations seems to be within the range of natural fertility and are not very low. According to another classification of completed fertility rates (Nag, 1968) most of the estimates noticed in high altitude populations seems to lie in the 'high' category (5.51 and above). Baker (1978) has additionally pointed out that, even though all of the reported completed fertilities are somewhat below the maxima, they are providing for rapid population growth and would provide for more than replacement at even the highest of expected mortality rates.

A Comparative study of different mountain regions was also done by Gupta et.al. (1989), and concluded that high altitude Himalayan populations differ from Andean highlanders in respect of their mechanism for combating the environmental stresses, but are similar to Ethiopian highlanders. In another words, the Andean highlanders choose a different adaptive strategy for their survival as compared to Himalayan and Ethiopian highlanders. However, elucidation of the strategies adopted by each, the factors causing adoption of differential strategies, the relative contributions of the various physical environmental, socio-cultural and ethnic factors in different mountain systems and population groups and subgroups within each and the relative degrees of success achieved by different populations under different environments, following different adaptive strategies, using rigorous methodology, is of crucial importance.

Fertility is measured by the birth statistics. These vary with the aspect of fertility that they are describing, their degree of refinement or elaboration, whether they are summary measures or specific measures. Crude birth rate (CBR), General Fertility Rate (GFR), Total Fertility Rate (TFR), Age Specific Fertility Rate (ASFR), Gross Reproductive Rate (GRR) and Marital Fertility Rates are some measures of fertility need to be discussed for better understanding.

Crude Birth Rate (CBR)

This is a crude measurement of fertility that how many children are born in a year per 1000 population. As per Population

Reference Bureau World Population Data Sheet (2003), Crude Birth Rate for World is 22 for developed country it is estimated to be 11, whereas for less developed country it was found to be 24, African countries are leading with CBR 40, Europe having lowest CBR 10, North America (14), Asia (20), Latin America (23), Oceania (32) are in between, for India this estimate is 25. Though as per SRS (2004) the crude birth rate within India varies from 31.6 in Uttar Pradesh to 14 in Kerala. The states having higher CBR than national average are Assam (26.6), Bihar (30.9), Haryana (26.6), Madhya Pradesh (30.4), Rajasthan (30.6), Jharkhand (26.4), Meghalaya (25.8), Dadar and Nagar Haveli (30.4). The state of Himachal Pradesh having CBR slightly less than national average (i.e. 20.7); further within the state lowest CBR was estimated for Kinnaur district (9), which is less than the average of Europe (10); highest CBR 23 was to be estimated for Hamirpur and Kullu. Very few developed countries had achieved the CBR 9 or less, this is remarkable that for Kinnaur district of Himachal Pradesh the estimated CBR is equal to the countries like Bularus, Greece Austria, Italy and Japan. Among tribal population of India CBR was estimated as high as 75 among Soligas of Karnataka State of southern India (Murty, 1987), whereas lowest was recorded among Santhal of West Bengal (Kshatriya, 2000). Among Gaddis a middle altitude tribal population of Himachal Pradesh the CBR was estimated to be 28.4 (Bhasin and Bhasin, 1993).

General Fertility Rate (GFR)

General fertility rate is comparatively refined measure of fertility, to obtain it inspite of whole population, women at risk of child bearing age are considered, in this way, how many children in a year are born from per 1000 of women of child bearing age (15-44 or 15-49) are calculated. The SRS (1999) estimates of GFR (from 15-49 years of women) for Indian states shows that Uttar Pradesh state has highest GFR 146.7 and lowest was estimated for Kerala (61.1), whereas the national average was 103.2, for Himachal Pradesh the GFR was found to be 84.7.

Age Specific Fertility Rate (ASFR)

Age specific fertility rate (ASFR) is more refined measure of fertility as for its estimation the women of reproductive age groups (15-49 years) are further grouped in conventional five-years age groups, from 15-19 years to 45-49 years, which minimize the effects of misreporting of ages by mothers, and distortion produced by variations in the age composition. Then it computed for each of five-years age groups, how many children are born from these women per 1000 in a particular year is calculated, so this gives a detailed panorama of fertility in a population at a specified time/period. As the age of mother is an important factor affecting the fertility level and the rate of child bearing is not uniform throughout all the ages. Despite macro level studies there are many micro level studies as described by Kshatriya (1997); Das & Saikia (1999) and Kotal & Baruah (2004) give emphasis on age specific fertility rate among different tribal population as well as comparison with national population.

Total Fertility Rate (TFR)

The TFR is a summary measure, based on the ASFRs that gives the number of children a women would bear during her reproductive years if she were to experience the ASFRs prevailing at the times of the survey. Mathematically, the TFR is five times the sum of all the ASFRs for the five years age groups. As per Population Reference Bureau World Population Data Sheet (2003), Globally TFR varies from 1.5 for more developed countries to 3.1 among less developed countries. For Africa it was estimated to be 5.2, for North America 2.0, for Asia 2.6, for Europe 1.4, and for Oceania 2.4, whereas for world it was estimated to be 2.8. For Indian states SRS (1999) estimated TFR, according to that 3.2 TFR was estimated for India, though it varies from 1.8 for Kerala state to 4.7 for Uttar Pradesh, for Himachal Pradesh it was found to be 2.4. There are many micro level study e.g. Gupta et.al. (1989); Prakash & Malik (1990); Bhasin & Bhasin (1993); Kapoor (1996); Kshatriya, et.al. (1997); Chachra & Bhasin (1998); Samal, et.al. (2000); Bhasin and Bhasin (2000); Patra (2001); and Pandey (2002) focused on TFR of different tribal populations.

Marital Fertility Rate (MFR)

When general fertility rate (GFR), age specific fertility rate (ASFR) and total fertility rate (TFR) are calculated only for married women of reproductive ages (15-49 years), then these measures are called marital general fertility rate (MGFR), marital age specific fertility rate (MASFR) and marital total fertility rate (MTFR) respectively.

MORTALITY

Literally speaking mortality is the state of being subject to death or loss of life on a large scale or a number of deaths in a given period. As it is apparent that mortality or death is a continuous biological phenomenon and; universal among the creatures born in this world. It is one of the three components of population change; the other two are fertility and migration. Mortality is a recurrent force of attrition, tending to reduce the population size- a major negative control in balancing of vital processes. It is also an excellent indicator of fitness, survival and growth of population and economic, social status and well being of people. Historically, the factor of mortality has played a dominant role in determining the growth of population, the size of which fluctuated in the past mainly is due to variations in mortality. In fact, it was the single most important contribution to demography that the sharp declines in mortality rates, rather than any rise in the fertility rates, have been responsible for bringing about a rapid growth of population. Man's attempt to regulate this component has been relatively successful almost everywhere. Industrialised countries reduced their death rate since 1650, whereas developing countries achieved it in early decades of twentieth century (Dorn, 1972). But due to untamed fertility, population pressure had increased rapidly, particularly in developing countries, created a situation of disequilibrium. In spite that mortality levels are still quite high in many regions of the world, particularly in developing countries; besides, of various preventive efforts and earlier decline. In developing countries too, there is wide variation in mortality levels among different population groups. There is various studies (Ghosh, 1970;

Sharma, 1978; Sirajuddin and Basu, 1984; Murty and Ramesh, 1978; Basu, 1998; Kshatriya, 2000) exhibited that mortality components are high among tribals and furthermore it is affected by economic, social-cultural, attitudinal, physical environmental factors.

Many scholars paid attention on mortality pattern of high altitude populations (Gupta, et.al. 1989). Grahn and Kratchman (1963) demonstrated on the basis of US census data that mortality is positively correlated with altitude and Mazess (1965) showed a similar pattern for neonatal mortality in Peru. Harrison et.al. (1969) showed that mortality was higher in high altitude Ethiopia. The abortion rate was also found to be higher at high than at low altitudes (Harrison et.al. 1969). The Andean studies suggest that altitude related stress tend to increase neonatal mortality (Baker, 1978). Clegg (1978) suggested that altitude related stresses might have caused increased abortion rates in Nepal and Ethiopia, whilst the Andean studies showed a reduction of the abortion rate at high altitude (Baker, 1978).

There are many studies on mortality pattern and fertility and mortality differentials of different Indian Himalayan and non-Himalayan population (Ghos, 1970; Barua, 1976; Murty and Ramesh, 1978; Chengal Reddy and Lakshmanudu, 1979; Rao and Murty, 1984; Basu, Kshatriya and Jindal, 1988; Bhasin and Kshatriya, 1990; Basu and Kshatriya, 1990; Reddy and Chopra, 1990; Wood et.al., 1992, Kapoor et.al. 2003). Kapoor et.al. (2003) seeks special attention as it present critical review of fertility and mortality differentials among 24 population groups of the Himalayas, they found higher relative contribution of fertility component (I_m) to the index of total selection (I_t).

Mortality rates and ratios are being widely used for a number of purposes; employed in explaining trends and differentials in overall mortality, for deciding priorities for health and development programmes and allocation of resources, in designing interventions, and in the assessment and monitoring of public health problems and programmes. Further more it provides clues for epidemiological research (Basu, 1998).

It is established fact that mortality has declined globally due to control over epidemics, famine, war and advancement in medical technology. Though some region and population groups are still experiencing high mortality. In India too, the death rate has shown a progressive decline from 36.3 in 1921-1930 to 10.1 in 1992 (SRS, 1992), currently it is 8.5 in 2000 (SRS, 2002). The efforts to decline mortality have been a greater success than to decline fertility. Interestingly, this rate is not much different from death rates (in 2003) of certain countries of developed world such as Denmark (11) Germany (10), United Kingdom (10), Norway (10) and Sweden (11). On the other hand, in many developing and least developed countries, particularly in Africa and South Asia, the death rates (in 2003) have been noticed higher than the rate in India (Afganistan-18, Mozambique-28, Malawi-22, Mali-20, Niger-20, Ethiopia-15) [Population Reference Bureau, 2003]. However, in India too, large variations are noticed, it varies from 5.1 in Delhi (Union Territory) to 10.5 in Orissa (Bigger state); States like Madhya Pradesh (10.3), Uttar Pradesh (10.3), Assam (9.6), Bihar (8.8), Kerala (6.4), and Maharashtra (7.4) are in between. In Smaller states like Chhatisgarh (9.6) Himachal (7.2), Jammu and Kashmir (6.2), Mizoram (5.2), and Sikkim (5.7) it is moderate (SRS, 2002). According to NFHS-2 (1998-99) it is highest in Orissa (12.9) and lowest in Kerala (6.0). Whereas Himachal and Jammu & Kashmir have registered death rate of 8.3.

An important use of crude death rate is that it provides one of the bases for computing the rate of natural increase in population. In this respect, it may be compared with the crude birth rate. Though this is very useful indicator of the level of mortality in any population, it is not a refined measure, as is evident from its very name, it suffers from several limitations. To come over the inherent limitations of the crude death rate, age specific death rates are used.

According to NFHS-2 (1998-99) the age specific death rates for Indian population during 1997-98 for age group 0-4 was 18.3 while according to SRS (1997) it was 23.1. At the same time for the age group 40-44 it was estimated as 7.7 and 7.5

respectively according to NFHS-2 and SRS. Whereas; for the age group 70 + it was estimated as 104.2 and 83 .5 by these same agencies.

Crude Death Rate (CDR)

Alike crude birth rate, which a crude measure of fertility; crude death rate is a crude measure of mortality in which how many deaths per 1000 population had occurred in a specified year is computed. As per Population Reference Bureau World Population Data Sheet (2003), for world the crude death rate was 9, for more developed countries it was 10, whereas for less developed countries the CDR was found to be 8, in Africa it was 14, for North America it was 8, in Asia it was 7, for Europe it was estimated to be 12.

Age Specific Death Rate (ASDR)

It has been noticed that death does not occur equally in every ages, but it is greatly affected by age. Early ages of life are more crucial and death prone. The probability of death declines with the rising age of individuals. So, computation of age specific death rate gives a refined measure of mortality. It calculated for a particular age. How many deaths per 1000 population of particular age had occurred in the particular year is called age specific death rate.

Infant Mortality and Early Childhood Mortality

Infant and early childhood mortality is a principal vital event of population dynamics. The rates of Infant and early childhood mortality reflect a level of socio-economic development and quality of life and are used for monitoring and evaluating population and health programmes and policies. In India, even though the infant mortality rate has also fallen dramatically from 219 per thousand births during 1916- 1920 to 68 in 2000 (SRS, 2002), the rate of decline seems slower than that noticed in case of the overall death rate. And the present estimate still appears somewhat high, when seen against the rate for developed countries as a whole (8.5 in 2000). The national average also marks wide variations. In 2000, among Indian states, Orissa experiencing highest infant mortality rate (95) while, it is lowest in Kerala (14). The states like Bihar (62), Madhya Pradesh (87), Assam (75), Rajasthan (79), Himachal (60) and Jammu and Kashmir (50) are in between. There is slight difference between the estimations made by NFHS-2 (1998-99) and SRS (2002). The common causes of infant mortality are diarrhoea, vaccine preventable diseases and acute respiratory infections (Sahay, 2001).

Furthermore, the intensity of infant mortality rate vary markedly from very early to the latter part of the first year of life for this reason it is divided into two parts viz. neonatal and post neonatal mortality.

NFHS-2 (1998-99) has returned neo natal mortality of 43.4 for India. It is reported to be highest in Madhya Pradesh ((54.9) followed by Uttar Pradesh (53.6), Meghalaya (50.7), Rajasthan (49.5) and Orissa (48.6). The state of Himachal Pradesh reveal low neo-natal mortality rate (22.1), but the lowest was recorded for Kerala (13.8).

Post-Neonatal Mortality Rate

Where neonatal deaths are caused due to endogenous or antenatal factors, the post neonatal deaths are caused by exogenous or environmental causes. It includes unhygienic and faulty care or neglect of the infant, unhygienic weaning practices, and several others causes viz. economic, educational characteristics of parents etc. Hence, it is more amenable to control by medical, nutritional and childcare improvements and also overall development measures. In fact most of the developed societies, where medical care has achieved the death rates are low, it is post neonatal deaths that have been reduced the most, with the result that a majority of all infant deaths account for most of the infant deaths. In India, and among most of the states within India, as estimated by NFHS-2 (1998-99) the neonatal mortality (43.4) is higher in comparison to the post neonatal mortality (24.2), because exogenous factors account for significant proportion of neonatal deaths as well. In Himachal Pradesh neonatal mortality was 22.1 while post neonatal mortality was 12.3.

Role of Health Facility and Health Providers

Population characteristics are determined by a host of factors, not a single factor can work independently. Role of health facility and health providers in population dynamics is least studied; but it is an important factor affects the population characteristics in a particular region and environment especially secluded and geographically isolated places its important enhanced due to limited human mobility, limited means of communication and transportation; although the health seeking behaviour, knowledge, practice and attitude of people are other factors. Sources of health care for household i.e. sub-center (SC), primary health center (PHC), community health center (CHC), District Hospital; availability of private practiceners, accessibility to the practiceners of other system of medicine such as Ayurvedic, Homeopathic, Unani, Siddha; believe on traditional healer and their presence and readiness. Home visits of health and family welfare workers and its quality; matter discussed during home visit. Knowledge and skill of health providers, their motivation and devotion to the work and community; Facilities such as residence, transport, medicine and other essential equipment provided to the health providers counts a lot in determining the fertility, mortality and migration of people from particular area and ultimately it leads to determining the population characteristics of the region.

SELECTION INTENSITY

Literally, selection intensity means the level of fitness of a population; which is essential for its survival and perpetuation through increase in numbers from generation to generation in a given environment, which ultimately leads towards evolutionary changes. This is maintained by a population through natural selection. Any differential in fertility or mortality is known as natural selection, which helps population in a particular environment. According to Harrison (1990) natural selection is differential viability and/or fertility according to genetic constitution and refers to genetically determined variation in Darwinian fitness. Neel (1958) has pointed out that despite global mortality reduction and diminished constraints, there is a great need for studying selective factors in advanced and primitive societies, to understand the past, present and future trends of human population. The study of such population components is of considerable importance not only in understanding population structure but also in measuring evolutionary dynamics.

Theoretical aspect of natural selection in human population were studied by a host of scholars (Wallace, 1871; Fisher, 1930; Wright, 1938; Coon, 1955); but Crow (1958) has devised an index that facilitates quantitative estimation of selective pressure provided the reproductive pattern of a population is known. This index I refer to the total amount of selection and consists of two components – mortality I_m and fertility (I_f). It measures the proportion by which fitness would increase with specific birth and death rates if they were all selective and the genetic component in differential fertility and mortality is relatively small, due to the interplay of a host of environmental (physical, socio-economic, cultural and behavioural factors (Crow, 1966; Cruz-Coke et.al., 1966; Matsunaga, 1966). Thus, It does not represent total (net) intensity, but only its upper limit (maximum) for the potential action of natural selection intensity, accordingly renamed as- "Total index of opportunity for Natural Selection (Crow, 1966).

Later on, Johnston and Kensinger (1971) modified Crow's (1958) index, by incorporating embryonic mortality. It was further modified by Basu et.al. (1988). Subsequently, a substantial number of studies were undertaken. Spuhlar (1962, 1976) reviewed and compared a large number of studies from all over the world and pointed out that the value of I ranged from 0.23 among Hutterites in the United States and Canada, to 3.69 among Peri in Bismark Archipelago.

In India too, several studies have attempted to measure the total potential of selection in various populations through differential fertility and mortality and study the effects of various factors including economic, socio-cultural, and physical environmental factors, such as altitude etc., on the same (Basu, 1967, 1972; Ghosh, 1970; Talukdar, 1971; Mukherjee, 1972;

Reddy and Mukherjee, 1975; Chaudhuri, 1976; Chakravarty, 1976; Barua, 1976, 1983; Murty and Ramesh, 1978; Reddy and Lakshmanudu, 1979; Gupta, 1980; Rao and Murty 1984; Padmanabha, 1985; Basu et.al. 1988; Bhasin and Kshatriya, 1990; Sarkar et. al., 1994; Patra and Kapoor, 1997; 1998; Sarkar, 1997; Kapoor and Patra, 1998; Sudhakar et.al., 1998; Kapoor and Kshatriya, 2000; Bhasin and Nag, 2002; Gharami et.al. 2003; Kapoor et.al., 2003). Here observations made by Kapoor et.al. (2003) were more remarkable as it was on 24 Himalayan populations which revealed that the contribution of fertility component (I_f) in determining total index of selection (I_t) are stronger than mortality component (I_m), simultaneously they observed that both I_f and I_t are strongly associated with I_t and accounts for 76 per cent and 67 per cent variability in I_t respectively.

Chapter 2

MATERIAL AND METHODS

In this Chapter, we shall make an attempt to give a brief description of the material and method used for present investigation. The material of the study collected from Himalayan highlands of Himachal Pradesh, particularly from district Kinnaur. Beside primary information plenty of secondary data collected from variety of sources including published literature, census, national family health survey (NFHS), rapid household survey (RHS), Britannica encyclopedia, wikipedia and different webpages. The details of materials and methods are being described below:

MATERIAL

Sample Size

A total of 820 households were covered from 27 villages of the selected district (Kinnaur). Firstly, village list of the district Kinnaur were obtained and a total of 30 villages 13 from middle altitude zone (i.e. Kalpa sub-division) and 14 from high altitude area (i.e. Pooh sub-division of the district) were selected on the basis of PPS. In the second phase households were selected randomly, in order to constitute a total sample size of 820 households. Out of these 820 households, 394 households were from Kalpa subdivision (middle altitude zone) and 426 from pooh subdivision (high altitude zone). Incidentally, all the Kinnaura from middle altitude show non-mongoloid ethnic affinities while all the high altitude Kinnaura reveals mongoloid ethnic affinities. The name of villages along with its approximate altitude and household covered are presented in Table 1, followed by profile of selected villages.

Profile of Villages

Middle Altitude

The village covered from middle altitude ranges between 1200 metre to 2500 metre from mean sea level. This region is rich in flora and fauna as compared to high altitude region. The world famous and rare species of *Neoza Pine* (Chilgoja) are found in this region. Despite of Natural forest of *Neoza Pine* abundant apple orchards can be seen in this region; As soon as one goes to beyond 2500 metre the floral coverage decreases in the proportion of the rise of altitude. The middle altitude comprises the areas of Nichar, Kalpa and Sangla tehsils while high altitude region is under Morang and Pooh tehsils. The village profile of the villages studied in Middle Altitude is given below:

1. Brilingi: Village Brilingi is near to district headquarter Reckong Peo. The village has driven its name from a particular species of tree, locally known as Brele tree, which is abundantly found in the village. The village is center of Buddhism in Kalpa valley as having monastery and school for giving religious education to young people. There is one tall statue of Bhagvan Buddha. The village is scattered on the slope of Kalpa valley one has to walk or climb for the village on vertical terrain and narrow passage. There are abundant apple orchards and agricultural fields in the village. These orchards and fields separates houses from each other, hardly two or three families are located in groups, but majority of houses are alone. There is separate Kuhl for irrigation of orchards/fields, and Chasma for drinking water. Most of the people of this village belong to labour class. There is one Anganwadi center and one primary school in the village. For higher education children go Reckong Peo or Kalpa. The villagers found district hospital hardly 5-7 km from their residence. According to an estimate the approximate height of village Brilingi is found to be 2300 metre from mean sea level.

Table 1
Village Wise Distribution of Household Population and Sex Ratio

	Altitude (in metre)	*Household Covered*		
		N	*% from Particular Zone*	*% from Total*
Name of Village		*Middle Altitude*		
Kilba	2000	35	8.9	4.27
Khawangi	2100	32	8.1	3.90
Sudharang	2120	32	8.1	3.90
Telingi	2250	33	8.4	4.02
Kothi	2290	29	7.4	3.54
Brilingi	2300	32	8.1	3.90
Duni	2300	18	4.6	2.20
Kashmir	2300	31	7.9	3.78
Yuwarangi	2300	30	7.6	3.66
Saryo	2320	31	7.9	3.78
Khawanta	2350	21	5.3	2.56
Pangi	2350	32	8.1	3.90
Kalpa	2400	38	9.6	4.63
Total	–	394	100.0	48.05
Average Altitude	2260			
		High Altitude		
Morang	2800	35	8.22	4.27
Akpa	2950	16	3.76	1.95
Kanam	2890	7	1.64	0.85
Thangi	2900	17	3.99	2.07
Dubling	3420	27	6.34	3.29
Pooh	3420	64	15.02	7.80
Giabong	3500	18	4.23	2.20
Leo	3450	36	8.45	4.39
Maling	3560	30	7.04	3.66
Nako	3610	41	9.62	5.00
Hango	3700	10	2.35	1.22
Chango	3600	23	5.40	2.80
Shialkher	3855	65	15.26	7.93
Sumra	3800	37	8.69	4.51
Total	–	426	100	51.95
Average Altitude	3390			
Grand Total (Middle + High Altitude)		820		100.0
Average Altitude of Total Villages		2916		

2. *Duni:* This village is parallel to Kalpa and Saryo villages. It is a scattered village, there is hardly clear-cut passage to move from one to another house as the village is scattered on the slope of Kalpa valley one has to walk or climb for the village on vertical terrain and narrow passage. There are abundant apple orchards and agricultural fields in the vertical terrain of village, the orchards and crops are grown on terrace of vertical valley. There is Kuhl for irrigation of orchards and fields and Chasma for drinking water. The village has one Anganwadi center and one primary school. The orchards and fields separates houses from each other hardly two or three families are located in groups but majority of houses are alone. The approximate height of village is less then to the heig'ıt of Kalpa and greater then Brilingi i.e. 2300 metre from mean sea level.

3. *Kalpa:* Kalpa is one of the oldest villages of the Kinnaur, the village having its historical importance and records. The whole valley is known by the name of this village. During feudal rule or British rule or in pre-independence period it was known by the name of village-Chini, during that period village was one of the tehsil headquarter of district Rampur of Bushair state. The village was district headquarter of the district Kinnaur too. And recently the district quarter is shifted to a lower village Reckong Peo. The village having some old building constructed by Britishers as well as district authorities. Still there are tehsil headquarter as well as headquarters of some other district heads like Executive Engineer (PWD), Banks and other officials. The district hospital of the village is degraded to Community Health Center (CHC) as district hospital is shifted to its new building at Reckong Peo. The village is oldest center of education as missionaries started first school in the area in late of nineteenth century. Today there is schools upto Higher Secondary level. The village is also a center of tourism as it is in the highest altitude in the Kalpa valley, the approximate altitude of the village is estimated to be 2400 metre from mean sea level. There are some good hotels and lodges to accommodate tourists. Tourist also fond of the place due to its location, climate and facing to Kinnar-Kailash. From this village only the Shiva-ling of Kinnar Kailash mountain can

be seen. Kinnar Kailash Mountain is the highest peak in Kinnaur its height is around 7000 metre. The uppermost part of the mountain is covered with glacier, and in lower portion there are some villages like Tangling, Pubari etc.

The village Kalpa is one of the biggest village of the district, which having good marketing center. This is the only compact village in the valley. There are separate temples of Vishnu and Nagin in the center of village. Side by side of these temples there are Stupa of Buddha, which gives a clear idea that the village is inhabited by the follower of Buddhism and so called Hinduism. There is one Kankani too in the entrance of village on old Hindustan-Tibet road. The village is linked with other villages, as well as by National Highway No.22 by a link road. There is bus stop in the center of the village, from where buses are available to Pangi, Rogi, Reckong Peo and other places.

4. *Kashmir:* Because of beauty of village, it got the name of one of the famous Himalayan State of India. This Himalayan State is called heaven on the earth. The village Kashmir possibly given similar look to its first originator who given the name Kashmir. The village is somewhat parallel to village Kalpa and on the side of village Duni but above from Brilingi. The village is thinly populated and widely scattered on the Kalpa valley. There is no temple or monastery in the village as such. But the former pradhan of village has constructed a big satsang bhavan, which is devoted to a new sect known as Radha-swami sect. The houses are constructed near to Chasma a water source. There are three or four Chasmas. There is one primary school at the top of village and near to road head. In the same way there is one Anganwadi center too in the village. The village is covered with apple orchards. The villagers have to walk at least 1 to 3 or 5 km from road head to reach their residence. Village Kalpa and Reckong Peo are almost at same distance, but Kalpa is somewhat nearer than Reckong Peo.

5. *Khawangi:* The village is situated at the lower end of Kalpa valley, below to district headquarter Reckong Peo. It has driven its name from the word Khwang, which means earthen pot. The National Highway No.22 passes below the village. The National-Highway and Reckong Peo, Kalpa, Pangi

link road goes from upper end of the village. The village has mixed kind of settlement compact-cum-scattered. It has compact settlement around the temple, the temple is at the center and as distance increase from temple the village is being scattered. The devta of this village is known as Markaring. In this village Kolies have one separate temple, which is near to the temple of Markaring, but it is not functioning. Alike other villages, this village is also equipped with Kuhl for irrigation and Chasmas for drinking water. There is primary school and Anganwadi in the village. For higher education, good medical facility and marketing people have easy access to district headquarter Reckong Peo. Though they have to walk or climb around 1 to 5 km. As being on road head from three sides, the walking distance reduced upto the road-end and road-end to residence. The approximate estimated altitude of the village is 2100 metre from mean sea level.

6. *Khawanta:* Khawanta and Pangi are twin villages; there is no geographical boundary between the villages. It comes under Pangi Panchayat. Alike other village, this village is also a scattered village on extreme vertical valley. Equipped with Kuhl for irrigation and Chasmas for drinking water. The village having one Anganwadi center. For education children have access to schools of Pangi village. The same is for medical facilities. The village is linked with other villages as well as National Highway No. 22 by a linked road there is regular bus services in morning and evening to Kalpa and Reckong Peo villages. Pangi Nalah a furious vertical fountain is source of Kuhl for this village as well as for many other villages of Kalpa valley, isolates the twin villages from rest of the villages of Kalpa valley. The distance of this village from Kalpa and Reckong Peo is almost same (10-15 km). The approximate height of the village from mean sea level is 2350 metre. The bus stand is at lowermost part of the village. The road ends with bus stop and vertical narrow cemented pedestrian starts to enter in the village. After climbing some distance around 100 metre the cemented pedestrian converts into non-cemented dusty and stony passage further after 50 or 100 metre there is no such passage now people like us starts quadrupedal

locomotion or tracking with very caution because missing of one step or loose grip of hands may roll down. But people of the village are habitual to walk on such a difficult terrain, as it is part of their routine life.

7. Kilba: The village Kilba is in Sangla Tehsil of the district Kinnaur. It is on another bank of river Satluj as on the opposite bank of river, there is National Highway and village Tapri. There are two way to reach the village Kilba one is through road via Karchham and other is by short-cut through rope-way from Tapri. We used both the way first for entering and second for escaping. Both the way was risky. Before some days there were cloud burst on the top of valley. On the flood of this cloud burst the road at a point had cut down and sweep-up in floods. The bus-services to the village were stopped since this calamity. The village is among one of those villages, which has lost its people, animals and agricultural/horticultural fields in a devastating flood in river Satluj in the night intervening 31st July and 1st August, 2000 at 11.00 PM. The flood started its play of the havoc at Khab and ended its play at Chaura village of district Kinnaur. The flood was so devastating that as many as 56 people and 12 Bridges over river Satluj were completely washed away. There is Primary Health Center, Schools and Anganwadi Center in the village. The Bus stop is at the middle height and starting point of village. The village is scattered around the temple of Narayan Devta. The PHC and Schools are at the other end of the village. The village is equipped with good natural sources of water, there are Chasmas generating ice-cold water perpetually and forcefully. The force of stream of one Chasma is so powerful and speedy that it seems that a 5-horse-power or more powerful water pump is running and streaming the water. The area around Chasma is cemented there is open water tank too. People take bath and wash cloths in the stream of Chasma as well as they fetch drinking water too from it. The estimated height of the village is 2000 metre from mean sea level.

8. Kothi: The village has driven its name from old palace of Vanasur. It was believed that there was fort of mythological character–Vanasur. The fort or palace in Hindi is called Kothi.

The village seems to be among old villages of Kalpa valley; and famous for its religious importance. There is temple of Chandika Devi, the deity is considered as supreme deity over other deities of different villages of the district. The deity is like a supreme administrative authority, and it visits to other sub-ordinate deities of other villages. There is one small pond and relics of temple like structure, which are believed to be associated with *Pandvas* of Mahabharat period. The village is equipped with natural resources like Chasmas for perpetual supply of drinking water to the villagers. Kuhls are constructed for irrigation of agricultural and horticultural fields. The village is scattered around the temple. There is no road in the village; the narrow pedestrian is used by villagers to reach the road, which goes through Reckong Peo village. There is primary school and Anganwadi center in the village. For higher education, health services and shopping villagers have access to Reckong Peo. The estimated height of the village is 2290 metre from mean sea level.

9. Pangi: As described earlier, village Pangi is parallel to village Khawanta. There is common bus stop for both the villages. The village Pangi has driven its name from its geographical situation and settlement pattern. Pang (pang= stair like) in Kinnauri dialect denotes its vertical settlement in stair or terrace like geography. The settlement of village is scattered type. The village has a women pradhan. There is Panchayat Ghar, School and Ayurvedic health center (dispensary) in the village. There are some tea stall and refreshment enterprises at bus stop. The melted road ends with bus stop. At bus stop there is some space, which is used as car parking by car owners of the village, there are two or three cars and some motorcycle in the village. The vehicle owners are helpless to leave their vehicle at bus stop, as vehicle cannot reach to their residence. There is a temple of Sheshering devta in the village. Apple orchard and Kuhls are spread all over the village. There is Chasmas as source of drinking water. The approximate height of village from mean sea level is estimated to be 2350 metre from mean sea level.

10. Saryo: Village Saryo is just like an extension of village Kalpa, though it is separate from Kalpa, one Kachha link road connects Kalpa from Saryo. The village is widely scattered among apple orchards and agricultural fields in the slope of Kalpa valley. The name of village is driven from its settlement pattern, geography and patches of cultivable land. As Saryo in Kinnauri dialect denotes to patches of cultivable land. There is no particular, school or health center in the village as villagers have easy access to old district headquarter Kalpa as well as new district headquarter Reckong Peo. There is Kuhls for irrigation purposes and people fetch drinking water from perpetual Chasmas. The estimated average altitude of the village is 2300 metre from mean sea level.

11. Sudharang: Village Sudharang is a scattered village, in the vertical slope of Kalpa valley. It is 1-2 km from district head quarter Reckong Peo, as well as parallel of it. The houses are scattered far and wide in the forest of *Neoza pine* and apple orchards. There is one primary school and Anganwadi center in the village. The village also has timber-depo of forest department and staff quarter for forest guard. Chasma is perpetual source of drinking water and for irrigation purpose Kuhls are developed in proper manner. The average estimated altitude of village is 2120 metre from mean sea level.

12. Telingi: The village Telingi is scattered around the temple of Mahasu. One young Lama is also living in the village, though there is no monastery or Gompa devoted to Buddhism, but near temple one stupa is established for the purpose. The Lama's room is well decorated and gives spiritual look; he used his room as monastery. People come to his room for different religious and magico-religious purposes. There is primary school and Anganwadi center in the village. The villagers have easy access to district headquarter Reckong Peo for various purposes of day-to-day life. Alike other village, the people of this village also fetch drinking water from Chasma or use a PVC pipe from Chasma to their kitchen or bathroom to pull the water easily. The village is situated at an approximate altitude of 2250 metre from mean sea level.

13. Yuwarangi: Yuwarangi is also one of the adjoining village to district headquarter Reckong Peo. It is above to Reckong Peo and below to Kalpa and Saryo as well as opposite to village Brilingi. There is no road in the village, only pebble, stony and narrow pedestrian connects one house to other. The houses are scattered far and wide in the forest, apple orchards and agricultural fields. Chasma is converted into tap, so villagers fetch drinking water from these taps. Though, there is no temple and school in the village, but has one Anganwadi center. The one extreme or corner of village touches the Reckong Peo-Kalpa link road. The approximate height of the village from mean sea level is 2300 metre.

High Altitude

The high altitude region is marked with barren, fragile and vertical high mountains having almost no natural floral coverage. The villages are comparatively compact and in vertical setups. The layer and the colour of the soil is also different from Middle Altitude region. People residing in high altitude have Mongoloid ethnic appearance and practice Buddhism; Survival is more difficult because of more harsh weather, rugged terrain, low oxygen pressure and less natural resources. During summer the greenery is extremely limited to the scanty apple orchards and agiicultural fields near to villages.

1. Chango: This village of Hangrang valley is at the international border of Chinese occupied Tibet and India. The International border is around 30 km from the village. There are villagers who had marital relation beyond the border. They also had marital relation with Bodhs of Spiti valley of Lahul and Spiti district of the state. The village is inhabited on the river deposits of river Spiti and one of its tributaries. Being on the river deposit, the village has got some plain land, which is usually rare in Kinnaur district. The settlement pattern of the village is mixed type? compact as well as scattered. This is first village in my expedition, which has proper defined, jeepable, un-melted road inside the village. Except apple orchards and agricultural fields the whole valley is barren and naked. Rarely any tree can be visible in whole valley. The National Highway No. 22 passes below this village; at bus stop there are one or two shops, one hotel-cum tea stall. There is one hand pump too, at bus stand, which used for fetching drinking water by passengers and shopkeepers of bus stand. The village is equipped with a civil hospital, patwar-khana, rest house, schools Anganwadi center, telephone exchange and timber depo of forest department. The dominant and only religion followed by people of this village is Buddhism, there is one monastery at the top of village. The entrance is marked with Kankani (a village gate), Mane and Stupa. The houses are marked with Chhokten and Thorchok. Kuhl is developed for irrigational purpose. The estimated height of village from mean sea level to be 3700 metre. Though the village is at National Highway but it remains in seclusion during summer as at Maling landslide point around 1 km length of highway is sweep up. In such a condition transshipment is started, after land slide buses remain in those sides where they were before landslide. Transshipment is also not easy as stones falls from vertical landslide area of fragile valley.

2. *Giabong:* The village Giabong is one of the village of Ropa valleys. This is among big villages having CHC, Bank, HDO (Horticulture development officer), schools, Anganwadi, Buddhist monastery, shops and other important offices and enterprises of civil important. The village Giabong and Ropa valley is distant located from National highway; one link road connects the village and valley to National highway at the confluence of one of the tributaries of Sutluj. Initially, this link road is melted but as it proceeds towards inner part of the valley it converts into non-melted road. The condition of road says that the valley is fragile and experiences frequent landslide. Some of the buses run between Reckong Peo and Pooh, enters to Ropa village, which is the last village of the valley passes through Giabong. Two or three buses enter in the valley and passes over Giabong. Though the Ropa valley is deprived of floral coverage but there are some sparse forest pine trees near the rivulet especially at Giabong village, otherwise only grasses are visible at rare places in whole of valley. The settlement pattern of the village is scattered type. Usually the villagers are Buddhist. There is Mane and Stupa at the center or entrance of village. The houses are marked

with Chhokten and Thorchok. As the region is marked with low floral coverage, the apple orchards are also in less proportion of agricultural land. But the quality of apples is better than middle altitude. There is Chasma and hand-pumps in the village, to fetch drinking water. Alike other villages irrigation was done through Kuhls. The estimated height of the village is 3500 metres from mean sea level.

3. Hango: Village Hango is one of the remotest villages in the district. It is around 25-35 km from road head (village-Leo). Recently a jeepable road is under construction, which will link the village from National highway. The primary health sub-center (PHSC) of the village is upgraded to PHC but one health worker alone is running this PHC. There is one school, which is upgraded to middle level. The village is scattered on the steep of the valley. Alike other villages of high altitude region, this village and surroundings steep hills are also deprived of floral coverage. Only few apple orchards are developed nearby the village and water sources. Otherwise coarse grains like barley, *ogla* and *phafda* etc. were produced in agricultural fields. Most of the agricultural fields at upper and middle part of valley are deprived of irrigational facility; hence after harvesting the crop of coarse grains, the fields are barren. People of this village are poorer by economic and natural resources. Their cloths were dirty. Children at school were also not very healthy, as they were seems to be lacking of proper nutrition and hygienic mode of life. The estimated height of village Hango is 3690 m. from mean sea level. The neighbouring village of Hango is Choling. Both villages are known together as Hango Choling.

4. Leo: The village Leo is around 15 to 20 km from tehsil headquarter Yangthang and around 15 km from National highway. One melted link road connects the village with National highway the village is inhabited at the bank of river Spiti. The people of this village usually defecate in riverbank especially during summer, as there is some space in the gorge of river. Though they also had Chhaksa (the locally designed toilet) in their home, which they use in winter. The river at this point is following along opposite site of village Leo and corrosion that wall of gorge, which may possibly; create some more places for village in future. The village having two phases one is old village. Many houses of old villages are damaged in an earthquake though some houses are reconstructed and people are still living in those houses. After earthquake some new houses are built at some distance this is new village and other phase of village Leo. There is school, Anganwadi, sub-center (PHSC), shops, and Stupa in the village. Mane is at the entrance of village as well in the main passage. There is well developed Kuhl. The village is surrounded by apple orchards and barren fragile hills. There is also a nursery of horticulture development department of Himachal Pradesh government. The approximate altitude of village is 3550 metre from mean sea level. To facilitate drinking water among villagers the Chasma is converted into tap water. There are three or four such points in the village, simultaneously villagers also uses Kuhl water for drinking purposes if it is clean and clear, which usually have. The villagers are facilitated by regular bus services, in morning and evening.

5. *Maling:* The village Maling is known alongwith its neighbouring village Nako. These two villages are at the uppermost part of Hangrang valley. There is link road, which connects the village from National highway; villagers are facilitated with regular bus services especially in morning and evening. The road not goes directly to village Maling, but it goes to village Nako and passes from near to village Maling. The village is such an altitude and unique face of valley that in summer too, the place is very cold and requires sweater even during sunny days of summer. The settlement pattern of village is compact and vertical type, houses are scattered in the slope of valley and marked with Thorchok, which gives an idea that village is dominating by Buddhist people. There are perpetual Chasmas for drinking water. The agricultural field is below to the village. There is hardly any orchard near to village. Few apple trees are visible in agricultural field. The village has school, Anganwadi center and PHSC (Sub-center). The estimated average height of village from mean sea level is 3660 metre.

6. *Nako:* Village Nako is developing as one of famous tourist center in Hangrang valley. There is one lake in the village,

which is a cause of attraction of tourist to the village. Usually in such a height lake is rare. The settlement pattern is compact type at one side of lake. The houses are marked with Thorchok, which gives an idea that village is dominating by Buddhist people. There is a temple of Thakur devta on the bank of lake. There is one rest house of irrigation department, which having two room. There is school and Anganwadi center. The village also has shops. One private hotel is also under construction at the bus stop. Some of the villagers have dual residence, during summer they come to village Nako's house and to spend chilled winter they migrate to Ka village, which is at lower altitude below to Nako village. There is perpetual Chasma for drinking water. Most of the agricultural fields are outside the village, together at lower portion of the valley. Few apple trees are also visible in agricultural fields of the village. The average estimated height of village is 3662 metre from mean sea level.

7. Shalkher: Alike village Chango Shalkher village of Hangrang valley is also at International border, the village people had marital relation beyond the border as well as in neighbouring district Lahul and Spiti, as the village also touches the border of this district. Tabo village of Lahul and Spiti is feasible center for villagers for different purposes, as they were cut off from the main area of their own district Kinnaur, because of Maling land slide point. Originally Shalkher village is away and at some height from National highway No. 22. The village has also extended along the road, which seems to be new and recent settlement. There are sub center (PHSC) at road head, tea stall cum momo noodles stall and one or two shops of general goods are also along the road. The settlement along the road fetch drinking water from hand pumps and Chasma both, where as the people of main village or old settlement uses tap water for drinking purposes, the water supplied through tap, is basically Chasma water. The school, Anganwadi, Panchayat Building, Monastery and Stupa as well as Mane are in old and main village. The agricultural/horticultural fields and human settlement are separate. Some lands are near to old settlement and some along the road at the bank of river Spiti. The average estimated height of the village is 3860 metre from mean sea level. The distance of district headquarter from village is around 130 km. The tehsil headquarter Yangthang to be 20-25 km and the sub-divisional headquarter is more than 60 km away from the village. The nearest village to Shalkher's people is Chango, from where they receive health and educational facilities as well as other available civil amenities.

8. *Sumra:* Sumra is last village of Hangrang valley as well as the district Kinnaur on the National Highway No. 22. Recently the village is adopted by ITBP (Indo-Tibet Border Police) for its proper development. This is a small village with approximately 35-45 households. The settlement of village is compact type. The village was in complete isolation, though it is not far away from highway, but it is on the opposite bank of river Spiti. One small tributary of Spiti also isolate the village. There is a hanging bridge over spiti to reach the village, but there is no bridge on another Khad (small rivulet). A wooden structure is used to cross the furious Khad. To cross the Khad is also not easy because of its deep up and down. Each step in steep is breath breaking. There is Mane and Stupa at the entrance of village. As one enters in the village he feels peculiar sting of animal dung, spread here and there inside the village, possibly Chhaksas (local toilet) also adding sting in the village air. There is school, Ayurvedic health center and Anganwadi in the village. One Medical Officer is posted in the Ayurvedic health center. Chasma is converted into tap water to facilitate drinking water facility to the villagers. The estimated height of village is 3900 metre from mean sea level. There is no natural flora in or around the villages it is surrounded by barren dusty hills which are dull pinkish in colour.

9. *Pooh:* Pooh is sub divisional headquarter, tehsil headquarter and block developments headquarter. There are other important offices of different departments like PWD, irrigation, ICPD, health (BMO), Horticulture, solar energy, desert development and treasury etc. in the village. The village also have military cantonment. The village is 68 km away from

district headquarter, there are many land slide point on the way which frequently intercepts communication, but still there is no college neither in this village in the whole high altitude region. The village has school, upto higher secondary level only. The village has rest house, telephone exchange, STD booth, Xeroxing facility, private practiceners, shopping centers and market equipped with many essential civil amenities. There is Mane, Stupa and Gompa or Monastery in the village. The houses are marked with Chhokten and Thorchok. The settlement pattern of village is mixed type compact and scattered. There is rare natural floral coverage; the surrounding valleys are completely naked rocks or soils or dull pinkish colour. The opposite bank of river Satluj, towards the Rishi-dongri glacier, there are some sparse and thin forest in very limited area. The international border is not very far from the village; it would be around 60 km. The neighbouring villages are village Dubling and Dubling. The village experience scarcity of drinking water especially during summer, so army personnel and water tanker were deployed to facilitate drinking water to the villagers. There is one fountain near to village known as *Tinku Nalah*; the army tankers brought drinking water from that Nalah, in morning and evening. The orchards and agricultural fields also deprived of irrigational water. Beside Kinnaura, the tribe, the village is also inhabited by government officials of different places of state and country. The estimated height of village varies between 2837 and 3420 metre from mean sea level.

10. Morang: Though Morang is a group of villages as per official record there are village like Graming, Sheiling, Thawaring etc. But for convenience of this study this is considered as one village. This is small administrative center with some important offices, community health center (CHC), rest house, school, shops and other important centers of civil amenities. The village is on the opposite bank of river Satluj and slope of valleys. There is hanging bridge over Satluj to cross the river. One melted road connects the village to the National highway. The link road further extends to village Thangi, from Thangi onward the road converts into a mule track and goes to village Kuno and Charang. There is one rivulet in between the village; it divides the hill in two parts. Both of the banks of rivulet forms steep, the village is scattered in both the side of rivulet among apple orchards and sparse forest. The surrounding hills of Morang are also thinly covered with forest of pine trees. There is Kankani in the entrance of village at old passage; one Gompa is also at the top of village. Villagers fetch drinking water from Chasma. There is well developed Kuhl for irrigation. Estimated height of village is 2800 metre from mean sea level.

11. Thangi: The village Thangi is scattered on extreme vertical valley. There are School, Anganwadi and Ayurvedic health center (Dispensary) in the village. There is also a Rest house of irrigation department and a private hotel, which seems to be not functioning. At bus stop there is one ITBP camp. The bus stop is dead end for buses. A number of tourist and trackers reach to village by bus. From this village a number of trekking starts which ultimately end at Chitkul. The trekkers reach Chitkul village of Sangla valley via Kuno and Charang village. There is a temple of Urmig Devta. The Lama had good hold in the village; he resides in a newly constructed house cum monastery. There are Chasmas in the village. Villagers are using piped water for drinking and other purposes, the pipes carrying water from perpetual water source Chasma. The approximate height of village is 2900 metre from mean sea level. There is abundant apple orchard in the village.

METHODOLOGY

Selection of Study Area

For present investigation Kinnaur district of Himachal Pradesh was selected keeping in view the uniqueness of its area and people. The district is located in the greater Himalayan region. The whole greater Himalayan region was in complete seclusion for many years and recently developed its link to the outer world. Kinnaura of this area are polyandrous and patriarchal; the mode of property inheritance among them is primogeniture.

Remote areas of Himalayas, like district Kinnaur has hardly been explored scientifically for its population characteristics.

The district is divided in two ecological zones: 1. Middle Altitude and 2. High Altitude. The villages settled at below 3000 m height of mean sea level is considered as Middle Altitude Zone, Kalpa and Nichar sub-division fall under this ecological zone, whereas Pooh sub-division fall under second zone (i.e. High Altitude zone), which is 3000 m above mean sea level.

Study Techniques

A number of tools and techniques were employed for collection and analysis of data in accordance with the objectives of the present study.

A. Quantitative Data Collection

The quantitative data was designed to generate requisite information with the help of a set of schedules developed on the basis of pilot survey.

(i) Pilot Survey and Development of Schedules: Before the commencement of indepth fieldwork, a pilot survey was conducted in order to plan and determine the techniques of data collection as well as to provide significant insight into various aspects involved i.e. with respect to area, population group, settlement pattern, life events, planned and unplanned changes in the group and region, impact of different development programmes etc. The pilot survey was carried out between April and May 2001 for a period of two weeks in Reckong Peo village of Kalpa Sub-division and Pooh village of the Pooh sub-division of Kinnaur and in some surrounding of Reckong Peo as well. The purpose of survey was to demarcate geographic area of the population proposed to be studied, its structure, distribution and the feasibility of study.

(ii) Development of Household Schedules: On the basis of the pilot survey and the secondary sources information, sets of detailed interview schedule were developed consisting of closed, open and multiple responses questions. The main schedule to be administered to each household consisted of

two parts viz. household schedule which dealt with social, economic, demographic and health seeking behaviour of tribal households, schedule for currently married women, which dealt in detail with the antenatal and postnatal care and questions related to gender bias. Separate schedules were developed for health providers viz. government practitioners, private practitioners, health workers (male and female), supervisors, programme officers and trained birth attendants (TBA). The schedules were prepared and modified before final data collection.

B. Qualitative Studies

Greater emphasis was laid on qualitative study to create free flow of information on various components of population characteristics. The following qualitative techniques were used.

(i) Focus Group Discussion (FGD): To collect qualitative information, at least one FGD in each village were conducted according to guidelines developed well in advance corresponding to the objectives of the study and experience gained from pilot survey. FGD was conducted with the group which was homogenous in respect of age, sex, education, occupation, caste and creed. All the participants of the FGD were provided with equal opportunity to express his/her viewpoints on the issues. The listeners were provoked to speak. The overall situation was kept harmonious and incase where the discussion was deviating from the objective, the harmony was established through jokes and examples of routine life. The age range of the member of Focus Group Discussions were 35 to 44 years. Following issues were covered in FGD's:

(1) Awareness of Health Facilities

(2) Awareness of Family Planning Programme

(3) Family size

(4) Age at marriage

(5) Opinion about health and treatment

(6) Utilization of health services available at health centers

(7) Tradition of gender difference

(8) Socio-cultural practices related to pregnancy and child birth, etc.

(ii) Case Studies: Case study is a detailed history and records of happenings. It is also a chain of incidence of problems and successes happening in the life of people and the details of measures adopted to tackle the situations and combat the problems. It starts with the gestation of a problem and continues to the current status of the problem. Another technique adopted for collection of qualitative information was case studies. Despite of collecting data in structured schedule, information were gathered through case studies taken from pregnant women, lactating women, sterile couples, spouses adopted family planning techniques, failure cases of family planning, patients of some specific diseases, patients at home, people attending clinics, traditional healers (Lama), priest of village temples, community leaders etc.

Testing of the Tools

In the last week of May 2001 the second visit was conducted to test the preliminary schedule (research tool) and modified in view of its shortcomings. Then, final data collection was completed in three phases from June to October 2001, July to August 2002 and July to September 2003, from 12 villages of Middle Altitude and 11 villages of High Altitude.

Main Field Work for Primary Data Collection

Keeping in view the climatic condition and stress due to high altitude, it was decided to complete the fieldwork and data collection in three phases. The summer season in Himalayan highlands is the best season to visit the place; hence, it was executed in summers of the year 2001, 2002 and 2003. The first phase was of 5 months from June to October of 2001. The second phase was of 2 months from July to August of 2002 and the third phase was of 2 and half months from July to September 2003.

As already mentioned the data was collected using different tools and techniques. A set of semi-structured interview schedule containing both open and close-ended questions was developed to collect information from individual respondents, households and village. To probe the information provided by the respondent participant, semi-participant and non-participant observation techniques were adopted. It was always remembered that for the full and complete expression of the respondent, it was ensured that respondent was at ease during interview. Hence, informal discussions are encouraged during interview. To keep ethical issue in mind the consent of *panchayat pradhan* (also known as *sarpanch*) was obtained in advance before entering in the village. Before conducting interview the people were taken in confidence. The purpose of data collection was explained to the respondents and consent was taken before gathering information. During entire process of data collection accommodation was obtained within the village either in pradhan's house or at the residence of any staff (i.e. school teacher, civil engineer, telephone operator, medical or paramedical staff) or in guest house.

Detailed data regarding age, sex, marital status, current measures of economic and educational characteristics, fertility, mortality, causes of deaths etc. were collected for all the members of the households to obtain the general demographic profile. Comprehensive information of individual respondent related to ages at various stages of life pregnancy/birth history; particulars of each conception etc. were collected for exploratory fertility, child (offspring) mortality etc. Beside information on health seeking behaviour and role of health functionaries were obtained. In case of pregnant women or lactating mother the information were gathered in the second part of the schedule, containing the questions related to maternal and child health care, immunization and family planning. The last section of the schedule was about the gender bias. All these information were crosschecked from either the spouses of the respondents or senior members of the households.

There was a great variation in the spoken dialect in different blocks and in villages in Kinnaur. Though they use to speak Hindi but in remote villages people were fluent alongwith their own dialect. To over come the language barrier during data collection, some common words of their respective dialect were learned before starting data collection. Young educated chap of village or the people who frequently move out of the district were of great help in teaching the local dialect and as mediator, health workers, anganwadi workers, School teachers, other officers also served as a mediators during the interview, case studies and FGDs.

Secondary Data Collection

Demographic/population studies on high altitude populations have shown interesting results. There are a number of contradictory findings associated with the relationship of cultural ecology of high altitude with fertility. Secondary data were collected in the present study, which comprised of research articles, documentation and articles on social, economical, biological and other environmental factors affecting the population and other high altitude groups National and area specific statistics related with population of the Himalayan regions were also obtained from various documentation centers, chief of these published materials are census, statistical hand book, national family health survey (NFHS), rapid household survey (RHS), Britannica encyclopedia, wikipedia and different webpages etc; beside of published materials a number of unpublished materials viz. reports, doctoral thesis and dissertations were also consulted and used.

Processing and Analysis of Data

After editing and coding the schedules a structure for data entry was developed in MS-Excel worksheet. Three different sheets were used for three different parts of schedules. First sheet consisted of (a) identification particulars, (b) fertility pattern, (c) mortality pattern, (d) socio-economic profile of the household, and (e) occupation and income. Second sheet consisted of (a) identification particulars, (b) fertility history, (c) natal details, (d) immunization status of child, (e) knowledge and practice of family planning, and (f) gender differences. Third sheet consisted of household census. To avoid wrong entry and for the convenience of data entry every cell of the sheet was validated. Finally in addition to MS EXCEL, SPSS and epi-enfo softwares were also used for the analysis of data.

DEMOGRAPHIC ANALYSES

The demographic analysis includes various measures, applied on data to study the demographic profile of the population under study.

Measures of Population Composition

There are different measures of analyses of population composition. The measures used for analyses of composition in the present study are being described below:

A. Age and Sex Composition

In this, the population under investigation was sub-divided into conventional age groups (i.e. 0-14, 15-49, 15-59, 60+ years) and sex. This was followed by the construction of population pyramids.

(i) Dependency Ratio: Three dependency ratios were estimated in the present study.

1. Young Age Dependency Ratio

$$\text{Young Age Dependency Ratio} = \frac{\text{Population aged 0-14 years}}{\text{Population aged 15-59 years}} \times 100$$

2. Old Age Dependency Ratio

$$\text{Old Age Dependency Ratio} = \frac{\text{Population aged 60+ years}}{\text{Population aged 15-59 years}} \times 100$$

3. Total Dependency Ratio

Total Dependency Ratio = Young Age Dependency Ratio + Old age Dependency Ratio

(ii) Index of Aging

$$\text{Index of Aging} = \frac{\text{Population aged 60+ years}}{\text{Population aged 0-14 years}} \times 100$$

B. Sex Composition

Sex ratio and masculinity proportion were estimated as under:

1. Sex Ratio

$$\text{Sex Ratio} = \frac{\text{Population of Female}}{\text{Population of Male}} \times 1000$$

2. Masculinity Proportion

$$\text{Masculinity Proportion} = \frac{\text{Population of Males}}{\text{Total Population}} \times 100$$

Measures of Educational Characteristics

Educational Characteristics of a population is measured by age-specific literacy rate as the level of educational attainment, were estimated as under:

1. Literacy Rate

$$\text{Literacy Rate} = \frac{\text{Number of Literates in a population}}{\text{Total population}} \times 100$$

2. Age Specific Literacy Rate

$$\text{Age Specific Literacy Rate} = \frac{\text{No. of Literates in an age group in a population}}{\text{Total population in that particular age group}} \times 100$$

3. Level of Educational Attainments

Percent distribution of literate in a population by their educational level, age and sex.

Measures of Marital Characteristics

Marital characteristics of study population were analyzed as percent distribution of population classified by marital status, age and sex; Percent distribution of different type of marriages per household; central values, deviation, and chi-square test were applied to investigate the differences between the sexes and among the groups.

Measures of Biological Characteristics

Different biological characters viz. age at menarche and menopause, fertility, mortality and morbidity etc. of study population were analyzed. Central value, range, variation, deviation etc. were calculated for age at menarche and menopause; linear regression and scattered plot diagram were also used to see the difference and pattern.

A. Measures of Fertility

Various measures of fertility were estimated as described below:

1. Crude Birth Rate

Crude Birth Rate (CRB) was estimated as under:

$$\text{Crude Birth Rate} = \frac{\text{Number of live birth in a population in a specified year}}{\text{Mid-year Total Population}} \times 1000$$

2. General Fertility Rate

General Fertility Rate (GFR) was estimated as under:

$$\text{General Fertility Rate} = \frac{\text{Number of live birth in a population in a specified year}}{\text{Population of women of Reproductive age group in that population in that specified period}} \times 1000$$

3. Age-Specific Fertility Rate (ASFR)

Age Specific Fertility Rate (ASFR) was estimated as under:

$$\text{Age Specific Fertility Rate} = \frac{\text{Number of live births to the women of specified age group in a population in a specified year}}{\text{Total number of women of that particular age group in that population in that specified period}} \times 1000$$

4. Total Fertility Rate (TFR)

Total Fertility Rate (TFR) was estimated as under:

$$\text{Total Fertility Rate} = \frac{\Sigma \text{ASFR} \times 5}{1000}$$

5. Gross Reproduction Rate (GRR)

Gross Reproduction Rate (GRR) was estimated as under:

$$\text{Gross Reproduction Rate} = \frac{\Sigma\text{ASFR} \times 5}{1000} \times 0.49 \text{ OR TFR} \times 0.49$$

6. Mean Age at Childbearing

$$\text{Mean Age of Childbearing} = \sum_{15}^{49} \frac{\text{X} \times \text{ASFR}}{\text{ASFR}}$$

7. General Marital Fertility Rate

General Marital Fertility Rate or GMFR was estimated as under:

$$\text{Fertility Rate} = \frac{\text{Number of live birth in a population in a specified year to the married women in the reproductive age group (or 15-49 years of age)}}{\text{Total number of married women of reproductive age group (or 15-49 years of age) in that specified population}} \times 1000$$

8. Age-specific Marital Fertility Rate (ASMFR)

Age-specific Marital Fertility Rate or ASMFR was estimated as under:

$$\text{Age-specific Marital Fertility Rate} = \frac{\text{Number of live births in a specified year from the married women of a particular age group in a population}}{\text{Total number of married women in that particular age group (15-49 years of age) in that population in that specified age group}} \times 1000$$

9. Total Marital Fertility Rate

Total Marital Fertility Rate or TMFR was estimated as under:

$$\text{Total Fertility Rate} = \frac{\Sigma\text{ASMFR} \times 5}{1000}$$

10. Child Women Ratio

In the present study child women ratio or general fertility ratio is computed from children under the age of five years and women of 15-50 years of age.

$$\text{Child Women Ratio} = \frac{\text{Population of children under 5 years of age}}{\text{Population of women aged 15-49 years}} \times 1000$$

B. Measures of Mortality

1. Crude Death Rate (CDR)

Crude Death Rate or CDR was estimated as under:

$$\text{Crude Death Rate} = \frac{\text{Number of deaths in a population in a specified year}}{\text{Mid-year Total population in the same year}} \times 1000$$

2. Age Specific Death Rate (ASDR)

Age Specific Death Rate or ASDR was estimated as under:

$$\text{Age Specific Death Rate} = \frac{\text{Number of deaths in a specified age group in a population in a specified year}}{\text{Mid-year Total population that particular age group in the same year}} \times 1000$$

3. Under 5-Mortality Rate

Under 5-Mortality Rate was estimated as under:

$$\text{Under 5-Mortality Rate} = \frac{\text{Number of child deaths under 5 years of age group in a population during a specified year}}{\text{Mid-year Total population of children below 5 years of age}} \times 1000$$

4. Infant Mortality Rate (IMR)

Infant Mortality Rate or IMR was estimated as under:

$$\text{Infant Mortality Rate} = \frac{\text{Number of infant deaths of under one year of age in a population during a specified year}}{\text{Number of live births in that population during the specified year.}} \times 1000$$

5. Neonatal Mortality Rate

Neonatal Mortality Rate was estimated as under:

$$\text{Neonatal Mortality Rate} = \frac{\text{Number of infants deaths of 1-28 days of age in a population in a specified year}}{\text{Number of live birth during that specified year}} \times 1000$$

6. Post-Neonatal Mortality Rate

Post-Neonatal Mortality was estimated as under:

$$\text{Post-Neonatal Mortality Rate} = \frac{\text{Number of infants deaths between 28-365 days of age in a population during a specified year}}{\text{Number of live birth during that specified year}} \times 1000$$

Exploratory Analyses

Exploratory Analyses of fertility and mortality were done on the basis of different dependent and independent variables. The list of variables is presented in Table 2. Three dependent variables (2—fertility related variables and 1—child mortality related variable) have been considered for finding out the most ideal relationship with the independent variables in the present investigation (Table 2).

Selection Intensity

The index of opportunity for selection has been computed following Crow (1958), Johnston and Kensinger (1971) and Basu et.al. (1988). According to Basu et.al. (1988) the relative contribution of deaths in the age group 0-5 years (child mortality) and from 5 years to reproductive age (juvenile mortality) is significantly high. In order to elucidate the specific contribution of these components, the post-natal mortality index in Johnston and Kensinger's (1971) methodology has been fragmented and computed. The reproductive histories of respondents (aged 45 years and over) who have completed their reproductive life span have been considered for these computations.

Table 2
List of Dependent and Independent Variables Used for Different Kind of Analysis

S.No.	*Variables*
A.	*Dependent variables*
1.	Mean Number of Children Ever Born (per women)
2.	Mean Number of Children Surviving (per women)
3.	Child loss ratio (per women)
B.	*Independent Variables*
1.	Mothers' Age
2.	Age at Marriage of Mother
3.	Mothers' Education
4.	Marriage Distance (in Km)
5.	Family Structure
6.	Type of Marriage Practiced
7.	After Marriage When Couple Start Living together?
8	Age At Marriage of Father
9.	Number of Live Birth Male Child
10.	Number of Live Birth Female Child
11.	Number of Surviving Male Child
12.	Number of Surviving Female Child
13.	Number of Child Deaths
14.	Abortion Occurred
15.	Still Birth Occurred
16.	Premature Delivery Occurred
17.	Number of Pregnancy Experienced by Mothers
18.	Source of Drinking Water
19.	Type of House
20.	Source of Lighting
21.	Fuel Used
22.	Toilet Used
23.	Living Standard
24.	Owing Agricultural Land

1. *Crow's Index of Natural Selection*

The index of opportunity for Natural Selection (I) following Crow (1958) has been calculated as:

$$I_t = I_m + \left(\frac{1}{P_{sl}}\right) I_f$$

Where $I_m = \frac{P_d}{P_{sl}}$ and $I_f = \frac{V_f}{(x)^2}$

Here,

I_m = Index of opportunity for Natural Selection due to pre-reproductive mortality (mortality from birth to reproductive age – below 15 years);

I_f = Index of opportunity for Natural Selection due to Fertility.

$\bar{x}$ = Average number of live births per women aged 45 years and above who have completed their reproductive life span;

V_f = Variance (average deviation from mean) of number of live births;

P_d = Proportion of pre-reproductive deaths;

P_{s1} = Proportion of survivors from birth to reproductive ages

Proportion of pre-reproductive deaths (P_d) is calculated from children ever born from mothers of age of 45 years and above (who have completed their fertility) and pre-reproductive deaths, as cited below:

$$\text{Proportion of pre-reproductive deaths (Pd)} = \frac{\text{Children ever born from mothers of age of 45 years and above (with completed fertility)}}{\text{Children died before attaining reproductive age (under 15 years) born from these mothers}}$$

Proportion of survivors were calculated from subtracting P_d from 1, as given below:

$$P_{s1} = 1 - P_d$$

2. *Johnston and Kensinger's Index of Natural Selection*

The index of opportunity for Natural Selection (I_2) following Johnston and Kensinger (1971) has been calculated as:

$$I_2 = I_{me} + \left(\frac{1}{P_b}\right) I_{mc} + \left(\frac{1}{P_b\, P_{s1}}\right) I_f$$

Where $I_{me} = 1 - \frac{P_d}{P_b}$, $I_{mc} = \frac{P_d}{P_s}$, $I_f = \frac{V_f}{(\bar{x})^2}$ and $P_b = 1 - P_d$

$$P_d = \frac{\text{Total Prenatal deaths experienced by the mothers of age of 45 years and above (with completed fertility)}}{\text{Number of pregnancies experienced by the same mothers of age of 45 years and above (with completed fertility)}}$$

Here,

I_{me} = Index of opportunity for Natural Selection due to embryonic mortality

I_{mc} = Index of opportunity for Natural Selection due to pre-reproductive mortality (mortality from birth to reproductive age – below 15 years);

I_f = Index of opportunity for Natural Selection due to Fertility.

x = Average number of live births per women aged 45 years and above who have completed their reproductive life span;

V_f = Variance (average deviation from mean) of number of live births;

P_b = Proportion of survivors to birth

P_d = Proportion of pre-reproductive deaths;

P_s = Proportion of survivors from birth to reproductive ages.

Chapter 3

AREA AND PEOPLE

This chapter is devoted to the vivid details of the land and people. The present study was conducted in the district Kinnaur of Himachal Pradesh state of the Republic of India, which is also called Bharat or Bharatavarsha in its National language Hindi. It is the second largest country in the world with more than one billion population, it is an independent republic since 15th August 1948, the region and its people had passed through the historic past of various cruel accessions of invaders including British colonialism. It occupies the greater part of South Asia and situated between 20^0 latitude of north Equator and 80^0 east of Prime Meridian. There are 28 states, each with a substantial degree of control over its own affairs, and 7 less fully empowered union territories. Much of its territory lies within a large peninsula, surrounded by the Arabian Sea on the west and the Bay of Bengal on the east; Cape Comorin, the southernmost point of the Indian mainland, marks the dividing line between these two bodies of water. Off the extreme southeastern coast, the Gulf of Mannar and the Palk Strait separate India from the island nation of Sri Lanka.

It is boon of nature to the country that the land is full of natural resources and bio-diversity. Where it is surrounded by ocean in south, the north is bounded by Himalayas; rivers originated from mountain system of Himalayas, Satpura, Vindhya, Aravallis and others irrigate the plains.

It is known from archaeological evidence that a highly sophisticated, urbanized culture—the Indus Civilization—dominated the northwestern part of the subcontinent from about 2600 to 2000 BC. From that period on, India functioned as a virtually self-contained political and cultural arena, which gave rise to a distinctive tradition that was associated primarily with Hinduism, the roots of which can largely be traced to the Indus Civilization. Other religions, notably Buddhism and Jainism, also originated in ancient India, but their presence in India are now quite small. It is one of the most ethnically diverse countries in the world. Apart from its many religions and sects, India is home to innumerable castes and tribes, as well as to more than a dozen major and hundreds of minor linguistic groups from several totally different language families.

Economically and socially, India has made great strides since independence. It has a well-developed infrastructure and a highly diversified industrial base, its pool of scientific and engineering personnel is reputedly the third largest in the world, and the pace of its agricultural expansion has more than kept up with the growth in its population. Social legislation in India has done much to alleviate the disabilities previously suffered by formerly "untouchable" castes, tribal populations, women, and other disadvantaged segments of society. But still, tribal populations of the country are at different stages of development and seeks attention of governments, researchers, academicians, non-governmental organizations (NGOs). They had unique set-ups socially, culturally, linguistically, economical and geo-ecologically. The present study population is unique among the tribals too, from different angles— as they practice polyandry and inhabit in middle and high altitude of greater Himalayan region.

THE HIMALAYAS: ORIGIN AND GEOLOGICAL DETAILS

The Himalayas are known to be young fold mountains. Young, because these have been formed relatively recently in the earth's history, compared to older mountain ranges like the

Aravallis in India, and the Appalachian in the USA. They are known as fold mountains because the mountains extend for 2500 km in length in a series of parallel ridges or folds. About 250 million years ago. During this time, all the earth's land was a single super continent called Pangea, which was surrounded by a large ocean (Encyclopaedia Britannica 2003).

Around 200 million years ago (also known as the Middle Permian Period), an extensive sea stretched along the latitudinal area presently occupied by the Himalayas. This sea was named the Tethys. Around this period, the super continent Pangea began to gradually split into different land masses and move apart in different directions. As a result, rivers from both the northern Eurasian land mass (called Angara) and the southern Indian land mass (called Gondwana) started depositing large amounts of sediments into the shallow sea that was the Tethys. There were marine animals called

The continents, 180 Million Years Ago.

The continents, 65 Million Years Ago.

The Continents, Today.

Figure 1: Origin of Himalayas on the Planet

ammonites living in the sea at the time. The two land masses, the Eurasian and the Indian sub-continent, moved closer and closer. Indian plate was moving north about at the rate of about 15 cm per year (6 inches per year). The initial mountain building process started about seventy million years ago (or the Upper Cretaceous period) when the two landmasses (or plates) began to collide with each other. As a result, the already shallow seabed rapidly folded and was raised into longitudinal ridges and valleys (Encyclopaedia Britannica 2003).

Soon afterwards, about 65 million years ago (Upper Eocene Period), came the second phase of mountain building. The bed of the Tethys started rising again. The sea retreated, and the seabed was elevated into high mountain ranges (Encyclopaedia Britannica 2003).

Later, about 25 million years ago (Middle Miocene Period) came another mountain building period, which led to the formation of the low Shivalik ranges. After this, periodic mountain building phases occurred as the Indian plate pushed against the Eurasian plates, which led to the Himalayan ranges rising further. The last major phase occurred 600,000 years ago. Only within this period during the Pleistocene Epoch (1.6 million to 10,000 years ago), the Himalayas become the highest mountains on Earth.

Although the phase of major upheaval of the Himalayas has passed, the Himalayas are still rising, albeit at a much slower rate. The Indian plate is continuously moving north at the rate of about 2 centimeter (cms) every year. Because of this reason the Himalayas are rising at the rate of about 5 millimeter per year. This means that the Himalayas are still geologically active and structurally unstable. For this reason, earthquakes are a frequent occurrence in the entire Himalayan region. It has to be understood that it is impossible to detect the movement of the plates and uplifting of the Himalayas by casual observation. However, a modern technology called Global Positioning System (GPS) has made it possible to measure even such a slow movement of the plates. The Alps in Europe are another example of a mountain chain that formed due to the collision of tectonic plates.

INDIAN HIMALAYAS: MAJOR INDIAN HIMALAYAN REGION

Himalayan range covers the entire northern part of India, nestling 11 states of the country within it, five of these states are major states. The ancient Indian pilgrims who have travelled in these mountains since time immemorial coined a Sanskrit word for the Himalayas meaning "Abode of Snow".

Some of the reasons why people have been so fascinated by the Indian Himalayas is because of the Hindu pilgrim routes, the low valleys that abruptly rise up in high mountain ranges, the lovely trekking hikes, densely forested areas lying just a mountain range away from barren cold deserts, and the lovely people of the mountains with their unique hospitable lifestyles.

Jammu and Kashmir

Jammu and Kashmir are really three regions: the foothill plains of Jammu; the lakes and blue valleys of Kashmir rising to alpine passes, the high altitude plains and starkly beautiful mountains of Ladakh, which lies beyond those passes. It's enough to move one to poetry. Sri Nagar is Kashmir's summer capital and Jammu, the winter capital. Among the most attractive part that this Indian state has is the adventure opportunities that can be segregated into trekking, mountaineering and Trans Himalayan Jeep Safari.

What can make a mountaineering expedition, an adventure one could never forget? If its done on the glaciers that are still craving to be explored. The Himalayan range offers some of the most rigorous mountaineering challenges one can ever come across. The glaciers of Ladakh and Kashmir regions can test one's survival to the fittest and most testing of them all is the Siachen glacier, known as the largest glacier outside the Polar Regions.

Uttaranchal

Lying in the north of the vast and bountiful expanse of India and cradled in the awesome beauty and calm serenity of the stately Himalayas, Uttaranchal - the "Devbhumi" that has attracted tourists and pilgrims from world over since time immemorial. Comprising of eight hill districts and an area and population that equals the state of Himachal Pardesh, Uttaranchal is an expression of divinity, austerity, meditation, penance and attainment.

Uttaranchal is a paradise for adventure sports. The sheer variety ranging from Mountaineering, Trekking, Skiing, Skating, Water Sports to Aero Sports like Hang Gliding, Paragliding make Uttaranchal one of the most attractive destinations for adventure sports not only in India but the world over.

Sikkim

A former kingdom Sikkim is now one of the States of India. It is rooted to the Himalayan Massif like a scale on the neck of a Dragon. One of the smallest states of India, it is bounded by Nepal to the west and Bhutan to the east, by the Tibet

Map 1: Different Himalayan Divisions Under Indian Republic

Autonomous Region of China to the north and northeast and by West Bengal to the south. Shrouded in heavy mist, the guardian deity Kanchenjunga both protects and terrifies the inhabitants of the magical kingdom of Sikkim. An awe-inspiring mass of rock clothed in dazzling white snow, this Himalayan giant in the world's third highest peak at 8,590m (28,199ft). The name itself means 'house of five treasures' represented by its five soaring summits.

The North-Eastern States-Seven Sisters

The reason has so much to see, so much to experience and so much to write about that it would take volumes. The region of northeastern India will whet the appetite of the traveller, the tourist, the anthropologist, the observer. It is impossible to describe the nuances that make this area unique, challenging and interesting. Get to any one place and the result will be that you will return for more. The seven sisters comprise of Assam, Arunachal Pradesh, Nagaland, Manipur, Tripura, Meghalaya and Mizoram. While the seven sisters are unique in their own way, the major Himalayan destination over here is Arunachal Pradesh. The state provides abundant scope for angling, boating, rafting, trekking and hiking. Besides, there are a number of wild life sanctuaries and national parks where rare animals, birds and plants will fascinate the visitor.

HIMACHAL PRADESH

The State Himachal Pradesh is a land of eternal snow peaks and enchanting mountains with altitudes ranging from 350 metres to 6975 metres above mean sea level. It is located between Latitude 30⁰ 22′ 40" N to 33⁰ 12′ 40" and Longitude 75⁰ 45′ 55" E to 79⁰ 04′ 20" E (Economic and Statistics Department, Himachal Pradesh, 2001). It has a deeply dissected topography, complex geological structure and a rich temperate flora in the sub tropical latitude. Blessed with furious rivers, ravines, lakes, flowers, ancient shrines and beautiful people, is one of the great attractive place of tourists. The combination of snow covered peaks and fountains of warm water are unique boon of the nature to the land and people. The earliest known inhabitants of this region were tribals called Dasas, who entered the hills from the Gangetic plains. Around 2000 BC Aryans entered in these regions, resulting a number of tribal republics called Janpadas, Began to emerge in geographically separate regions of the state. After Independence, 30 princely states of the area were united and Himachal Pradesh come into existence on April 15th, 1948 as a centrally administered territory. At that time the state had four districts viz. Chamba, Mahasu, Mandi and Sirmaur. The total area of the state during its emergence was 25,839 sq. kms. Later in 1951, it became a part 'C' state under a governor with a 36 member legislative assembly and three-member cabinet. In 1954, Bilaspur, another part 'C' state was merged with Himachal Pradesh thereby adding one more district with an area of 1168 sq. km. and the strength of its assembly was raised to 41. On November 1, 1956, it again becomes a union territory the Lieutenant Governor designated as chief; and the assembly was abolished. In 1960, a new border district was carved out from Mahasu district; this new district is called Kinnaur. On 1st November, 1966, it was enlarged by merging the districts of Kangra, Shimla, Kullu, Lahul-Spiti, the Nalagarh Tehsil of Ambala district, some parts of Una Tehsil of Hamirpur district and Dalhousie of Gurudaspur district of the then Punjab state. With this merger the total area of Himachal Pradesh increased to 55,673 sq. kms and its population to 28,12,463 (Census 1961). On 25th , January, 1971, Himachal Pradesh attained statehood having 10 districts viz. Bilashpur, Chamba, Kangra, Kinnaur, Kullu, Lahul-Spiti, Mahasu, Mandi, Shimla and Sirmour.

Reorganization of the districts took place on September 1st, 1972; as a consequence two more new districts namely Una and Hamirpur were created from Kangra. Another new district viz. Solan come into existence from the reorganization of district boundaries of existing districts- Mahasu and Shimla.At present, the State is divided into 3 zones, 12 districts, 51 sub-divisions, 72 blocks, 2922 Gram Panchayats having 16779 villages.

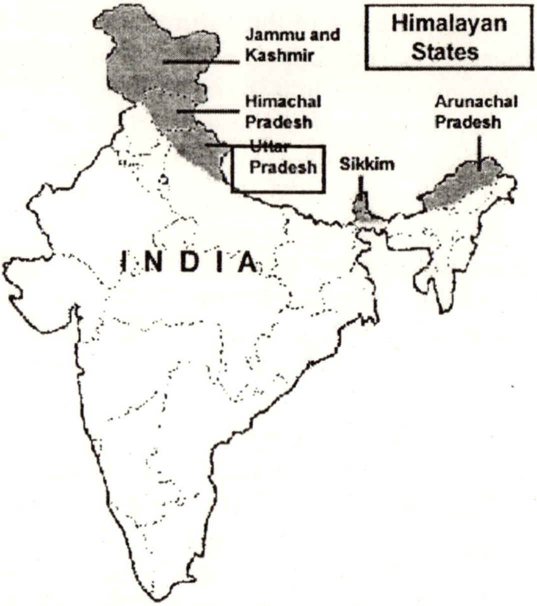

Map 2: Location of Different Indian Himalayan States

Historical Background

Himalaya is cradle land of Human civilization as oldest fossils of Ramapithecus and Shivapithecus were collected from Indian Himalayas. The historical records of Himachal Pradesh state can be traced around 2000 BC, when Aryans entered in these regions, resulting a number of tribal republics called Janpadas, Began to emerge in geographically separate regions of the state. After Independence, 30 princely states of the area were united and Himachal Pradesh come into existence on April 15th, 1948 as a centrally administered territory. At that time the state had four districts viz. Chamba, Mahasu, Mandi and Sirmaur. The total area of the state during its emergence was 25,839 sq. kms. Later in 1951, it became a part 'C' state under a governor with a 36 member legislative assembly and three-member cabinet. In 1954, Bilaspur, another part 'C' state was merged with Himachal Pradesh thereby adding one more district with an area of 1168 sq. km. and the strength of its assembly was raised to 41. On November 1, 1956, it again become a union territory the Lieutenant Governor designated as chief; and the assembly was abolished. In 1960, a new border district was carved out from Mahasu district; this new district is called Kinnaur. On 1st November, 1966, it was enlarged by merging the districts of Kangra, Shimla, Kullu, Lahul-Spiti, the Nalagarh Tehsil of Ambala district, some parts of Una Tehsil of Hamirpur district and Dalhousie of Gurudaspur district of the then Punjab state. With this merger the total area of Himachal Pradesh increased to 55,673 sq. kms and its population to 28,12,463 (Census 1961). On 25th, January, 1971, Himachal Pradesh attained statehood having 10 districts viz. Bilashpur, Chamba, Kangra, Kinnaur, Kullu, Lahul-Spiti, Mahasu, Mandi, Shimla and Sirmour.

Reorganization of the districts took place on September 1st, 1972; as a consequence two more new districts namely Una and Hamirpur were created from Kangra. Another new district viz. Solan come into existence from the reorganization of district boundaries of existing districts- Mahasu and Shimla.

The State is divided into 3 zones, 12 districts, 51 sub-divisions, 72 blocks, 2922 Gram Panchayats having 16779 villages. Presently, the strength of the Legislative Assembly of Himachal Pradesh is 68. The state is represented by 4 Member of Parliament and 3 member of Rajya Sabha to the union legislature. There is one High Court, one Public Service Commission and three Universities in the state.

Geo-Climatic Details of the State

There is wide variation in topography of the state. The altitudes ranging from 350 metres to 6975 metres and simultaneously deeply dissected topography and complex geological structure supports climatic difference resulting into variation of flora and fauna. Physiographycally the state can be divided into five zones – viz.

(i) **Wet Sub Temperate Zone:** it comprises Palampur and Dharamshala of Kangra district, Joginder Nagar area of Mandi district and Dalhousie area of Chamba district.

(ii) **Humid Sub-Temperate Zone**: it includes Kullu and Shimla districts and parts of Mandi, Solan, Chamba, Kangra and Sirmaur districts.

(iii) **Dry Temperate-Alpine High Lands:** consist of major parts of Lahul and Spiti, Kinnaur and Pangi valley of Chamba districts.

(iv) **Humid Sub Tropical Zone**: contains Bilaspur district, Major parts of district Mandi, Nahan area of district Sirmour, Bhattiyat valley of district Chamba, Nalagarh area of district Solan, Dehragopipur and Nupur areas of District Kangra

(v) **Sub-Humid Sub-Tropical Zone:** it comprises district of Una, Paonta-sahb area of District Sirmaur, and Indora area of district Kangra.

Climate and Seasons

The State can be divided into two regions: the southern part, which is almost as hot as the plains and the northern region having a temperate summer and a winter with extreme cold and heavy snowfall. The rainfall is around 180 cms.

The climate of the state is widely varies according to the elevation. It gets colder as the elevation increases and gets rains as the elevation drops. As a result the temperature and climatic changes flora and fauna also changes. All of a sudden there can be occurrences of monsoons, floods, high winds, snowstorms and other types of precipitation, which makes the climate over here, quiet an unpredictable and dangerous.

There are two major seasons i.e. winter and summer. During the winter the state receives the maximum snow with very icy temperatures. Summer is quiet mild over here, making the places overt and quiet good for summer holiday hideouts. Usually the Alpine Himalayan region receives snow throughout the year.

The regions such as Pooh sub-division of Kinnaur district, the district of Lahul and Spiti are deprived of monsoon. Humidity is always low in these regions, and receives only a few centimeters of rainfall during whole year. These regions also experience some of the coldest temperatures anywhere in the world, and it doesn't get any warmer till the spring season in late April or early May. These areas are also known as cold desert zone of the state, Where in June, daytime temperatures frequently rise to 20⁰C, the snow on the passes melts and most of the treks can be undertaken from then on until the middle of October. Rainstorms can occasionally be experienced in July and August. By September the conditions are ideal, and they normally remain so until late October even though night temperatures may fall below freezing point. By November, the early winter snows fall on the passes closest the area.

After October the daytime temperatures drop, but the weather is generally settled until the middle of November when the first of the heavy winter snows fall on the high mountain passes. Winter months from December to March are often miserable. April and May are characterized by heavy precipitation, which falls as snow in the mountains, restricting trekking over the passes until the spring snows melt in June.

Most of the areas of Kangra, Chamba, Kullu, Shimla, Solan, Una, Sirmour. Bialspur and Mandi districts of the state come under the influence of the Indian monsoon that sweeps up from the Bay of Bengal, bringing heavy rainfall from early June until the end of September. The post-monsoon months of October and November provide settled conditions, with clear views of the mountains, although temperatures during night above 3,500m frequently fall below freezing point.

Socio-Demographic Profile

Population

The State has a population of 60,77,248 (2001 census) Average density of population is 109 persons per sq. km and ranges from 2 in district Lahul & Spiti and 369 in district Hamirpur (Table 1).

The decennial growth rate between 1991 and 2001 was + 17.53 per cent despite of + 20.79 per cent of 1981 and 1991. District Solan (+30.64 per cent) has recorded highest rate followed by Kullu (+25.60 per cent), Sirmaur (+20.72 per cent), Una (+18.43 Per cent), Kinnaur (+17.79 per cent) and Chamba (+17.09 per cent). The growth has been lower than the State average in the remaining districts. Further according to census

(1991). The majority of population is rural (91.3 per cent). Most of the villages are small dwellings having total population less than 500 (81.5per cent), Only five villages having population more than 5000.

Tribal Population

Himachal Pradesh has a large area under tribal belt, which covers two districts of Lahul & Spiti, Kinnaur and Chamba district. Geographically about half the area of the State is covered under tribal belt whereas the population tribal population is just 2.2 lakhs i.e. 4.2 per cent of the total population of the State (1991).

Sex Ratio

The sex ratio of the state is 970 females per 1000 males as per 2001 census. This is the second highest in the country after Kerala. NFHS-2 has estimated the sex ratio for the State at 1013 in 1998-99. In contrast to the country, the sex ratio has been steadily increasing in the State. There are five districts out of twelve, having sex ratio >1000 as is evident from Table 1.

Demographic Transition: Past, Present and Future

Population of the State, which was 2.8 million in 1961 had grown to 5.1 million at the time of last census (1991), current estimate is 6.07+ million (census, 2001). It has increased more than 2 folds during last 40 years. Though the achievement of the State in controlling population has been commendable in terms of decrease in CBR, TFR and increase in CPR as compared to many other states, yet rural CBR (22.9) and TFR (2.18) are still high and it is a matter of concern, especially when rural population constitutes approximately 91 percent of the total population.

With the current annual growth rate at 1.48 percent, it is estimated that the population would double in about 50 years i.e. by 2050 the population would be approximately 13 million. However, by 2020 it would be about 9.4 million. With such a high population increase, the State would require additional resources to meet health care, education, employment and

Table 1
Population Distribution, Percentage Decadal Growth Rate, and Sex Ratio and Population Density in Himachal Pradesh, India (1981-2001)

	Population 2001			*Decadal Growth Rate (per cent)*		*Sex Ratio*		*Pop. Density / sq. km.*	
State/District	*Person*	*Male*	*Female*	*1981-91*	*1991-01*	*1991*	*2001*	*1991*	*2001*
Himachal Pradesh	6077248	3085256	2991992	20.79	17.53*	976	970*	93	109*
Chamba	460499	234812	225687	26.40	17.09	949	961	60	71
Kangra	1338536	660224	678312	18.50	14.01	1024	1027	205	233
Lahul Spiti	33224	18413	14811	-2.51	-6.17	817	804	2	2
Kullu	379865	197035	182830	26.68	25.60	920	928	55	69
Mandi	900987	447271	453716	20.40	16.05	1013	1014	197	228
Hamirpur	412009	195971	216038	16.17	11.62	1105	1102	330	369
Una	447967	224299	223668	19.17	18.43	1017	997	246	291
Bilaspur	340735	171074	169661	19.41	15.35	1002	992	253	292
Solan	499380	269451	229929	26.02	30.64	909	853	197	258
Sirmaur	458351	241109	217242	23.72	20.72	897	901	134	162
Shimla	721745	380244	341501	20.84	16.90	894	898	120	141
Kinnaur	77007	40878	36129	19.69	9.93	856	884	11	12

Source: Census of India
*On the basis of projection

other needs of the people. As for Family Planning, unmet needs, which were assessed at 9 percent during NFHS-2, 1998-99, shall have to be met, with a particular emphasis on spacing methods, especially among low parity couples.

Literacy

As per 2001 census, the estimated percentage of literates in Himachal Pradesh is 77.13 Per cent (excluded Kinnaur District). National Sample Survey Organization (NSSO) also estimated almost same for 1997, according to which there were 77 Per cent literacy, (87 Per cent males and 70 Per cent females).

Economy

Due to the large rural population and hostile geographic and weather conditions, the State is still backward and poor in terms of economy. Households survey for poverty (1998-99) shows that of the total 10,36,996 households in the rural areas of the State, 2,86,112 are below poverty line, which is 27.59 Per cent of the total households.

Agriculture and Horticulture

Agriculture is the main occupation of the people, contributing 35.87 Per cent towards the State Gross Domestic Product. Apple cultivation is of special significance for the economic emancipation of the people living in the higher hills of the State. With stone and citrus fruits growing in sub-tropical and sub-humid areas, the State is now known as Fruit Bowl of India.

Crops like wheat, maize and pulses are grown here. Agriculture production is 16 lakh tons per year and horticultural production is 4.36 lakh tons.

Water supply in Rural Areas

Out of total 45,367 habitations, 26,730 are fully covered, and 14,047 are partly covered with piped drinking water supply. 4590 habitations are yet to be covered. The position of rural water supply has further improved with the installation of a large number of hand-pumps, but only in villages situated on the road heads.

Electrification

It is claimed that 100 percent electrification of villages has been achieved. Though some villages in tribal areas are not electrified. However, 98 Per cent households in the State are electrified.

Rural Roads and Communication System

Out of 16997 villages in the State, only 7522 (44.5per cent) are directly linked with the all weather roads. Total motorable road in the State is 20,270 kms out of which 7394 kms. is metalled. About 9000 villages have connectivity. Road length, in absolute terms, is 34 kms per 100 sq. kms. Rail communication is restricted to a few kilometers only. The telecommunication system in the State is good and has eased the problem of communication to a large extent.

Health Infrastructure

Public Sector

Modern System of Medicine: The State has a fairly extensive network of health institutions. The position as on 31st March 2000 is reflected hereunder (Table 2).

Table 2
District Wise, Health Institution in Himachal Pradesh.

District	*CHs*	*CHCs*	*PHCs*	*CDs*	*ISM Inst.*	*S/Cs*
Bilaspur	2	5	17	11	67	110
Chamba	4	7	28	11	102	161
Hamirpur	2	5	17	6	72	150
Kangra	8	12	50	34	223	447
Kinnaur	2	3	17	0	44	34
Kullu	1	3	14	5	65	99
Lahul & Spiti	1	3	9	5	24	32
Mandi	6	9	44	13	165	300
Shimla	9	6	47	30	149	241
Sirmaur	5	3	24	14	82	143
Solan	5	3	20	17	78	172
Una	2	3	12	9	73	125
Total	48	65	302	167	1153	2069

In addition to the above, there are two teaching hospitals, two leprosy hospitals, two TB hospitals, two Medical Colleges and three Dental Colleges. Besides there are Civil Dispensaries, which are run by different departments (Police, University), Boards (HPSEB), Projects like NJPC, BSL, Central Government Organizations (Railways, Defence, Cantonment Boards) and semi-government organizations. Total bed capacity in the public sector is 8747.

Indian System of Medicine: The State has shown keen interest in promoting Indian System of Medicines, especially Ayurveda, which is widely popular, acceptable and affordable system for the people of the State. There is a separate department for ISM&H in the State. The ISM institutions as on 1.1.2000 were given in Table 3.

Table 3
ISM Institutions as on 1.1.2000 in Himachal Pradesh

System of Medicine	*Institution*	*No. of Institutions*
Ayurvedic	College	1
Ayurvedic	Hospitals	22
Ayurvedic	Dispensaries	1109
Unani	Dispensaries	3
Homeopathic	Dispensaries	14
Panchkarma	Unit	2
Amchi	Clinic	4
Total		1153

Total Bad Capacity 410.

Private Sector

This is a fast developing sector in the State now. A large number of private clinics, nursing homes have sprung up mainly at Shimla and other district towns. A few private hospitals have been set-up at sub-divisional level. Total bed capacity of private sector in the State is about 500.

NGO and Voluntary Sector: NGO and Voluntary sector is not providing curative services in the State so far. However one free hospital is being set up in District Hamirpur by a charitable organization.

Distance From Nearest Health Facility: According to NFHS - 1 (1992), median distance of a sub-centre and PHC is 3.5 and

6.9 kms respectively. Percent distribution of villages according to distance from the nearest health facility in Himachal Pradesh is shown in the following Table 4.

Table 4
Distance from the Nearest Health Facility

	Health Facility					
Distance	*Sub-Centre*	*PHC*	*PHC or PHSC*	*Hospital*	*Disp/ Clinic*	*Any Health Facility*
Within village	14.9	3.3	17.8	–	14.5	28.8
Less than 5 Kms.	44.5	23.4	51.6	–	51.1	55.7
5-9 Kms.	17.6	35.5	22.0	18.8	21.7	14.2
10 Kms.	13.5	38.6	8.4	63.3	10.6	1.3
Median distance (kms)	3.5	6.9	2.9	15.9	3.5	2.2

Source: NFHS 1-1992

This survey did not take into account Ayurvedic and other institutions, the inclusion of which would have shown the distance more clients friendly with the opening of more health institutions; the situation has further improved after 1992. According to the figures available as on 30 June 2000, maximum radial distance covered by a Sub-Centre, PHC and CHC are 2.93, 7.66 and 16.51 kms respectively.

Buildings: The status of health institutions regarding their location in Government or private or others premises as on 31 March 2000 is shown in the Table 5.

Table 5
Position of Buildings for Health Institutions in the State (as on 31 March 2000)

Health Inst.	*Total*	*In Govt. Building*	*Other Premises*
Sub-Centres	2069	1161	908
PHCs	302	165	137
CHCs	65	54	11
CDs	155	80	75

Source: Department of Health and Family Welfare.

Many sub-centres and PHC are still located in private or donated buildings.

Coverage by Health Institutions: Coverage norms for opening Primary Health Care institutions fixed by Govt. of India, have by and large, been achieved as shown in Table 6.

Table 6
Average Rural Population Covered by Health Institutions as on 30 June 2000

	Norms Set by GOI on Number of Population Per Institution		
Institutions	*For Plain Areas*	*For Hill State*	*Average Rural Population being covered (Current Situation) Per Institution in the State (H.P.)*
SUB-CENTRE	5,000	3,000	2,698
PHC	30,000	20,000	18,485
CHC	120,000	80,000	85,883

Source: Department of Health and Family Welfare.

Staff Position: The position of major categories of staff in health sector of the State is shown in Table 7. It is evident from the Table, that there are still many vacancies with regard to categories like Medical Officers, Staff Nurses, Health Workers, Lab Technicians, and Pharmacists etc.

Table 7
Staff Position (as on 1 January, 2000) in The Department of Health and Family Welfare

	Number of the Posts		
Name of the Post	*Sanctioned*	*In Position*	*Vacant*
Medical Officers	1498	1369	129
Staff Nurses	1427	1107	320
F.H.Workers	2210	1974	236
M.H.Workers	2011	1594	417
Sr.Lab. Technicians	612	457	155
Lab. Asstts.	169	115	54
Pharmacists	857	684	173
Chief Pharmacists	80	73	7
Radiographers	183	143	40
Ophthalmic Asstts.	145	95	50
OTAs	95	77	18
Male Health Supervisors	413	385	28
Female Health Supervisors	350	385	20

Source: Department of Health and Family Welfare.

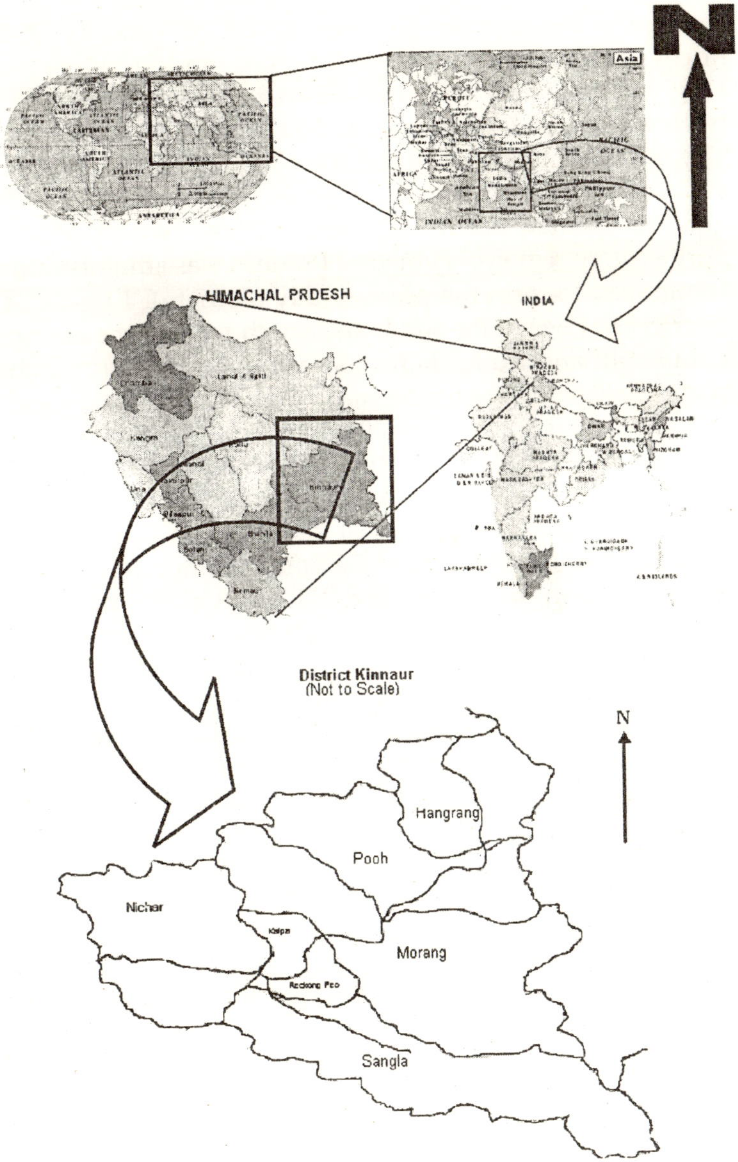

Map 3: Showing the Location of Study Area—District Kinnaur (H.P.)

DISTRICT KINNAUR

Currently, the area lies between 31^0-05′-55″ and 32^0-05-20″ north latitude and between 77^0-45′-0′ and 79^0-0′-50″ east longitude is known as District Kinnaur, it is among one of the twelve districts of Himachal Pradesh state of Indian Republic. The word Kinnaur is derived from the word *Kinnar. Kinnars* are often referred in Hindu religious books. They are neither god nor human but in-between of these two. In 1960 the northeastern region of Himachal Pradesh was administratively recognized to form the present- day district of Kinnaur. The district thus lies to the south and south west of the district of Lahul spiti and Kullu shares its eastern border with Chinese occupied Tibet. It lies on the bank of Sutlej, Spiti, Baspa and its tributaries. It is spread over 80 km in length and about 64 kms in breadth (Bhatt1997). The total area of the district is 6401 sq kms. Which is 11.5 percent of the total area of the state. The district headquarter is located at Reckong Peo. The district is a land of scenic beauty at the same time, it comprises cold desert zone too. Sangla, Kalpa and Nichar valleys are among enchanting valleys with lush green forest, and apple orchards; while Yangthang, Pooh, and Ropa etc. valleys experiences cold desert with no natural flora. Although the district provides extra ordinary scenic beauty, but it is considerably rugged, the road communication network is very poor. National Highway No. 22 is constructed in place of old Hindustan-Tibet road, which goes side by side the river Sutlej, the river it self passes through narrow fissures of extremely vertical mountains. The vertical valleys are blasted towards the river to construct the present National Highway. In many places the road looks like a tunnel, mountain is hanging over the road, and below this road the deep furious rivers is flowing. Many hanging bridges are constructed over rivers to make transportation easy and convenient. But after all these efforts, the road communication network is not very efficient. The conditions of roads are very poor and during monsoon season one can witness frequent land slide at different places in district forcing transshipment and blank communication. Cloud burst, sudden broken glacier and melting of glaciers pour flood and sweep up roads in many places are also among the causes of blank communication and casualties in the district. Where melting of glaciers sweep-up roads during summer, these glaciers come down during winter with huge storage of snow, magnificent rocks and soils and break the communication, for a long gap. During winter whole district experience extreme cold weather, almost all the places are covered with snow only deep rivers are unaffected with winter and this snowfall. Small fountains, waterways and tributaries are also frozen during this kind of harsh weather, and sometimes *Chasma,* the only source of drinking water is also frozen, especially, in the high lands. Human habitation is generally found up to the height of 4500 metres., from mean sea level. However highest peak of the district has been estimated to be 6816 metres above the mean sea level. On the basis of altitude and divergent climate the district can be divided into upper and lower Kinnaur. The dividing line by altitude can be taken as 2500 metres above mean sea level between the upper and lower Kinnaur. Upper Kinnaur is at the high altitude; it is a cold desert zone, with no or very few rainfall. While Lower Kinnaur is full of vegetation and lush green forest of precious *Neoza pine,* which is hardly, found anywhere else in Asia. Abundant apple orchards can be seen within these forests. Desert development project is started to grow vegetation in high altitude, that's why few apple orchard can also be seen in naked, desert valleys of Upper Kinnaur too. Now, apple orchards are essential part of Kinnaur district and a good source of income of its people. After 1962 Chinese occupation on Tibet, the district has special strategic importance and therefore, it has been given especial attention with reference to various developmental schemes. But due to vertical settlement, any developmental activity is a difficult task, inspite of vertical settlement, the house holds are scattered, especially in the Lower Kinnaur, many times there is hardly any clear-cut passage between two houses. It is very difficult to reach majority of houses, almost in all the villages, except few one, those, which are on road heads. Without quadrupedal locomotion it is impossible for outsiders to reach the houses. Settlement pattern in Upper Kinnaur is comparatively compact, but rest of the problems is same as in Lower Kinnaur. The inhabitant of these houses carries every essential item of livelihood from road head, or market, on the head or back load, which is a very difficult task. They also carry their orchard production for trade in the same way, to the road head for its further transportation, to bring down the heavy loaded boxes of apple is a problematic job. To construct a house in such a vertical valleys is not easy, firstly there is problem of fetching land, appropriate by the point of residential house, it must be in the stable portion of the valley, should be near to perennial water sources. After the selection of land, to make it plain to start construction is another problem. And lastly to collect different component of building construction is still more difficult, require labour, time and cash to purchase material as well as to hire labour. Now these people are imitating the low land people and started constructing cemented RCC buildings, and concretizations are started in this greater Himalayan region too.

Origin of Name and Historical Account of the District

It is believed that the district derived its name from its inhabitants who are Known as Kinner, or Kinnaura. According to an Indian traveler— Sanskritayan, the original name of the district was Kimpurus Desh i.e. land of Kimpurusa (Raha &Mahato, 1985).

In the absence of authentic historical record the early history of Kinnaur region is obscure and the reference of the Kinnaura or Kannaura and there land is by the large confined to legends and mythological accounts. It would be worthwhile to look at the region of Kinnaur alongwith general conditions of northern India particularly the hilly regions of Himalayas during the period from 6th century B.C. India was divided in to sixteen great Janpadas and several smaller ones. Among them Gandhara, Kamboja, Kuru, Koshal, Mull, Vajji, Panchal, Sakya were either in the southern Himalayas ranges or had territories extended up to Himalayans ranges. Among the states that were flourishing in the six century B.C. The kingdom of Magdha was the first to make a successful bid for supremacy under Bimbisara. Its emperor belonging to Sunga, Nanda and Maurya dynasties carried their banners upto the inhabited parts of inner Himalayan region. Chandragupta Maurya brought about its political unification under one scepter, negotiated an alliance with Parvataka (Himalayan King) before empire building. With the help of several frontier tribes such as Kiratas, Kambojas, Panasikas and Valhika, he built up the great Mauryan Empire. The empire of Ashoka extended upto natural boundaries of India and beyond that in the west. After the collapse of the Mauryan empire the Kushanas established an extensive empire within and beyond India in the northwest. Emperor Kanishkas hegemony spread over Kashmir and the Central Asian regions of Kashgar, Yarkand and Khotan. His hold extended upto the territory of the Inner Himalayas and Kinnaur must have been the part of this empire. In the meantime northern India was divided into a number of small kingdoms and autonomous tribal states. Under such a divided country the Gupta empire grew. Samundragupta's empire included the territories of Rohilkhand, Kumaon, Garhwal, Nepal and Assam. Its northern boundary was along the high Himalayas. Kinnaur must have been included in it too. Early in the seventh century A.D., Harsha came to power at Thaneshwar in A.D. 606. During the course of four decades he had established a most powerful empire in India. All the existing kingdoms of Kapisa, Kashmir, Kuluta, Satadru, Mon-li-pa-lo (Ladakh) and Suwarnagotra (in the high Himalayas) were incorporated in his empire. After the death of Harsha in A.D. 647 the country was once again divided into old principalities of the sixth century B.C.

It appears that the princes being adventurous owing to territorial greed first went to these high hills and established themselves on varying territories in accordance with their powers. Particularly the area between Sutluj, its tributaries and Baspa upto Mansarover was under the rule of Thakkers from very early times. They were known by the place they had occupied like that of Chini Thakur and Kamru Thakur, under the overall suzerainty of Mauryan and Gupta kings later on. It was the Thakur of Kamru who proved strongest of all the other chiefs of the area and annexed their territories by force sometime after the fall of the Kanauj Empire and laid the foundation of the state of Bushahr, to which the region of Kinnaur belonged till the dissolution of the state very recently.

By the beginning of the fourteenth century the entire area of Kinnaur was divided in seven parts, locally called *sat khund*. There was further splitting up of and the area came to be covered with many small hegemonies, which were constantly warring against, or allying with, each other as conditions required. The neighbouring *Bhots* (people of Lahul and Spiti) also found time to jump into the fray and did not desist from creating trouble. There are various forts like labrang, Morang, and Kamru forts telling the story of that age.

In the medieval period, though some of the hill states such as Kangra, Chamba and Sirmaur were attacked and made tributary to the Mughal emperor at Delhi, Bushahr state could not be reached by any adventurer of that time. The consolidation and addition of territories of the Bushahr state continued during the period also. The *Thakoorais* of *Dulaitoo*, *Kurungoloo* and *Kuaitro* were annexed about *Samwat* 1611 when Raja Chhatar Singh who brought the whole area of the erstwhile Bushahr State under his control. He was considered most virtuous ruler during his reign. There is no particular account about his successor Kalyan Singh. The successor of Kalyan Singh according to genealogy was Raja Kehri Singh. He is the highest skilled warrior of the time. Kehri Singh's successors were not of the same mettle. Besides mention in genealogy of Bushahr State, nothing is known about Vijay Singh and Udai Singh. It is said that one Raja Ram Singh made Rampur his capital in place of Sarahan and Kamru. During his reign a series of contests began with the Raja of Kulu (Kullu) and Bushahr had lost the territory of Seraj. It seems that the territories, which were annexed by Raja Kehri Singh became free during the weak rule of Raja Rudra Singh. But his successor Ugar Singh took them over by force of arms.

According to Punjab states Gazetteer-Shimla hill States from 1803 to 1815 the erstwhile states of Bushahr faced the menace of Gurkhas invasions. Immediate after the death of

Raja Kehri Singh, The Gurkhas made massive attack on Bushahr. The minor ruler and his mother who could not withstand the attack fled away to Namru leaving behind a rich treasury at Sarahan. The Gurkhas looted the treasury and completely destroyed the records of the state. Keeping Gurkhas of Nepal had extended their dominions greatly during the end of the eighteen-century. Amar Singh Thapa, the Gurkha leader went up to Kangra valley. He was drawn from the valley by the superior forces of Ranjit Singh and those of raja Sansar Chand of Kangra. The tract between the Satluj and Jamuna came under British protection by the treaty of 1809 between Ranjit Singh and the British Government Thus the British Government took positive step to expel the Gurkhas and after a long and desperate struggle, completely defeated Amar Singh Thapa on 15th April 1815. On the conclusion of the Gurkha war Raja Mahendra Singh was granted a *sanad* on 6th November 1815. It gave *Khaneti* and *Delath thakurais* to Bushahr and a part of *Rawin*, which was a district of the state, was transferred to Keonthal, Kumharsain was constituted a separate Thakurais.

From the foregoing account it would appear that during the princely days Kinnaur valley acted as a bulwark to the Bushahr state. However with the lapse of dominancy, the Kinnaur then known as Chini tehsil was merged to form a part of then Mahasu district. The Parganas *Atharahs Bish* comprised of village *Nichar, Sungra, Kangos, Ponda, Baro, Bari, Tranda, Chaura* village with patwar circle at Ponda. The *Paragana Bish* consisted of the revenue estates of *Nathpa, Kandhar, Barakamba, Chhotakamba, Garshu* and *Rupi* with patwar circle at *Rupi* were in Rampur tehsil.

In fact then Chini tehsil covered the entire Kinnaur valley beyond Wangtu, which was created in 1891 by the then ruler *Tika Raghunath Singh.* Thus 1891 onwards Chini tehsil continued to be in existence with its vast area beyond Wangtu uptill 1960. Since 1947 it was a tehsil of the then Mahasu district. By 1960 the importance of reorganizing border area was realised and consequently in view of ethnic and cultural considerations the areas, which were partly in Rampur tehsil, were reorganized into a separate District forming the present Kinnaur district.

Climate

By virtue of its location, the district Kinnaur experiences the cold temperate climate, which is characterized by long winters from October to March and short summer from June to September. June is the warmest month in the lower Kinnaur. The upper Kinnaur is a cold desert area, which is an arid tract here the warmest months are July and August. The rainfall in lower Kinnaur upto Wangtu does not vary greatly from rainfall in Shimla, i.e. about 200 cm. Beyond that, the amount of rainfall decreases progressively. The climatic conditions in different valleys of Kinnaur do not vary only with elevation but also with the direction of valley faces, width of valleys, type of soil and rocks. The flora and fauna varies according climatic conditions of the region.

CLIMATIC CONDITIONS

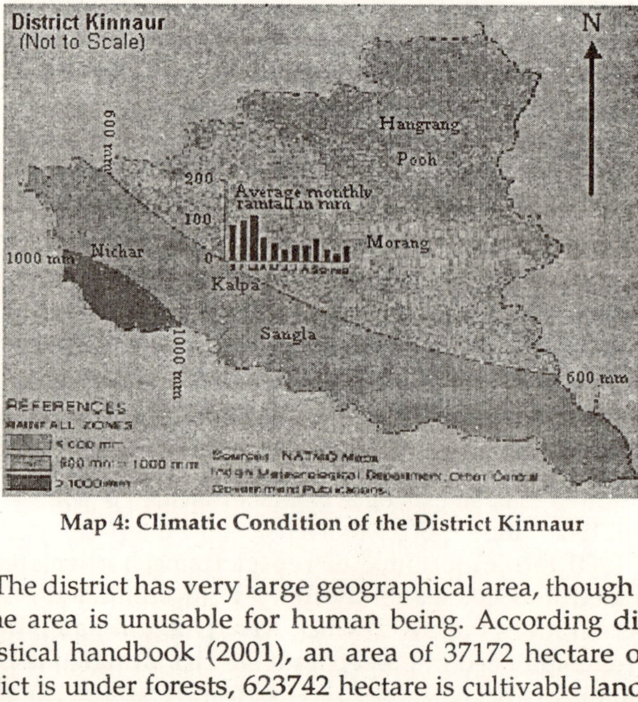

Map 4: Climatic Condition of the District Kinnaur

The district has very large geographical area, though most of the area is unusable for human being. According district statistical handbook (2001), an area of 37172 hectare of the district is under forests, 623742 hectare is cultivable land and 255502 hectare is unusable land (especially for agricultural purposes). The soil in Kinnaur generally consists of sand, sandy loam, clay loam, gravel etc. The types of soil vary according to proportion of these constituents. Type of soil found in different part of the district is also evident from Map.

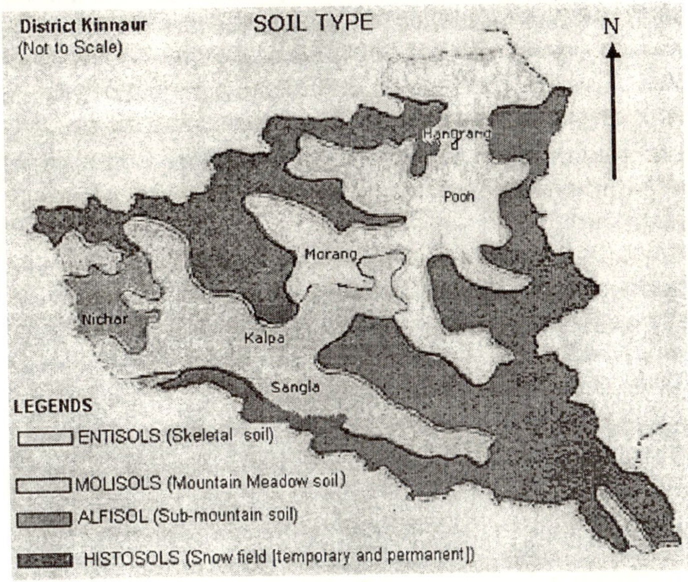

Map 5: Soil Type in Different Region of the District Kinnaur

Minerals

District Kinnaur is rich in mineral deposits. Different minerals, precious stones, rocks and deposits have been observed and reported from various parts of the district. Copper stratums have been noticed near Rangwar, North-West of Ropa valley. China clay deposits have been found between Asrang and Lippa villages. Fluorspar layers of rare occurrence have been noticed at Wangtu. Occurrence of small quantities of gold in almost of the Himalayan Rivers is well known. Mica is found in Tangling *Khad* (rivulet). Gemstone viz. Amethyst and Kaynite have also been noticed at certain places in Kinnaur. Pyrite has been reported in Chargaon (village), Shiasu *Khad* (rivulet) and Purbani (village). Quartz Crystals also occur at some places. Silver deposits are reported to exist near

Chargaon. Talc occurs near Thakthow, a hamlet of Asrang. Deposits of gypsum are reported from Shalkher and Chango villages. Rough slate quartiles are also found in the Sangla valley and these are used for roofing purposes. Further detail of rocks and minerals found in the district is shown in following map.

ROCKS AND MINERALS

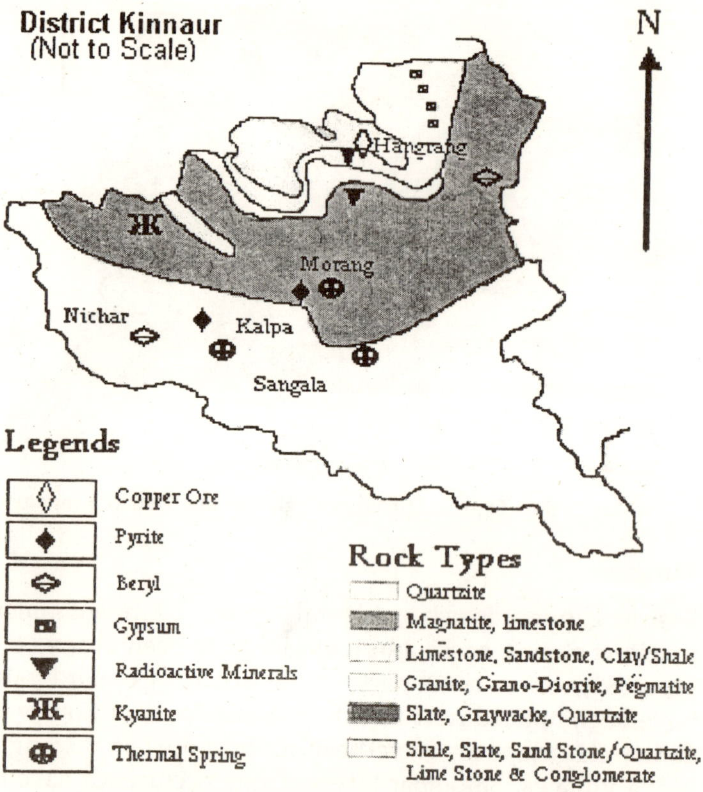

Map 6: Rocks and Minerals in the District Kinnaur

Flora and Fauna

In Kinnaur district, three types of natural vegetation are found:

(1) As the Lower Kinnaur having moist climate it experiences rain and snowfall both, most of this region is under natural as well as agricultural and

horticultural floral coverage, the high lands of this region having glaciers and meadows. The wet zone forests are found on the left side of the Satluj valley where common variety is Kail, Spruce and Fir trees. In the depressed tracts, broad-leaved trees of horse chestnut (*Aesculus)*, hazelnut, maple (family-*Aceraceae*), bird cherry and walnut (*Juglans*) are found.

(2) The dry zone forests from Nichar to Kalpa. Deodar reaches its optimum height and development in this zone. At lower levels, pine trees abound, while in the higher tracts blue pine, spruce and silver fir (*Abies alba*) trees are found. Some of the species are *Neoza pines, Pinus geradiana* (Chilgoza), *Pinus longifolia, Pinus excelsa* (Cheed), *and Pinus smithiana. Neoza pines or Pinus geradiana* (Chilgoza), which produce edible nuts, grow in this zone and are the only forests of Neoza in India.

(3) The parts adjoining Tibetan border contain arid zone forests consisting of rose dog and dwarf bushes. On higher elevations with cool aspects, *Prunus dulcis* (Almond), *Pinus geradiana* (Chilgoza), *Cedrus deodara, Feijoa sellowiana* (Pine apple) *etc.* grows.

Fauna

Alike other parts of Himalayan region, the district Kinnaur was once rich with domestic and wild alpine fauna. But with the growth of population and the new constructions and other development woks, the number of these animals has steadily decreased. Some of these wild animals are blue sheep, brown bear, hill fox, jungle cat, flying fox, Himalayan languor, Himalayan black bear, Himalayan palm civet, Himalayan ibex, leopard, monkey, musk deer, snow leopard, Himalayan wolf etc. Besides these there are numerous species of small insects, reptiles, birds and other kind of animals.

Road Transport System

At present, as a whole the road transport system is not very much satisfactory in the district Kinnaur. Though it has developed unimaginably during last five decades. Earlier, even a few years after independence, the area was secluded. Some mule track and bridle paths actually represented road. The condition was more piteous due to peculiar mountainous situation of the district. In 1948 there were no jeepable or motorable roads. The Hindustan Tibet mule road was link with the outside world. After the formation of Himachal Pradesh an ambitious plan of road development was prepared for this area. In 1959 the first jeep reached to Kalpa through newly constructed National Highway No. 22. Today, as per district statistical hand book (2001) there are a total of 962 km roads (including National Highway) in the district, which comprises of 177 km two way, 408 km one way, 72 km jeepable and 305 km mule tracks. The HPTC (Himachal Pradesh Transport Corporation) providing bus services between the villages of different valleys (or Administrative divisions) as well as it running buses from National capital Delhi (ISBT Kashmiri gate) to district headquarter Reckong Peo, State capital Shimla to Reckong Peo and linking the district to other important places of state and country. The HPTC regional office district Kinnaur is functioning with a convoy of 47 buses, 1 truck and 1 Jeep. Besides these there are 194 big and small (two and four wheeler) registered vehicles in the district, which includes 51 Jeeps, 55 car and vans and 24 mini trucks.

Photograph 1: A View of National Highway No. 22 in the Gorge of Satluj

Photograph 2: A view of Road-block on National Highway No. 22 in the Gorge of Satluj below to Village Akpa

Frequent land slides; natural calamities (earth quake and floods) intercept the road communication. Furthermore, there are still villages (viz. Kuno- Charang, Hango-Choling, Namgiya etc.), which has access through mule track only. Villages like Chango, Shalkher and Sumra were completely secluded during summer, due to sweep-up of approximately 1 km road near to village Maling. The transshipment on this landslide point is also very risky due to continuous stone fall, furious stream and melting valley. Once the road is sweep-up it takes 2-4 months for its reconstruction. The villagers are habitual of such type of intercept and transshipment; accordingly the bus services are being managed to their scheduled time on both the end as per convenience of passengers and for uninterrupted transportation.

The Upper Kinnaur has more piteous condition on the aspect of road transportation, as landslide is more common in the fragile upper valleys. There are many points in the National Highway No.22 where stones rolled down on just a flow of breeze. In many places of the highway, the road is covered by landslide, in such a case the new road is constructed over old one, which is buried 5-25 feet underneath. From Rampur Bushair to Pooh the National Highway (No. 22) is constructed on the wall of gorge of river Satluj. From Pooh and onward, commencing the point of confluence of river Spiti and Satluj, the high way enters on the gorge of river Spiti.

Villages are 500 metre to 50-70 km away from the highway. Some of the villages are connected through link-roads. The link roads too, do not entered into villages but it ends up out side the village or either below the village or above the village. At least 500-1000 metre walk on vertical slope or climb is required to reach the village. The villagers carry all livelihood items on their back from road end to their houses, and vice-versa in case of agricultural and horticultural products.

Post, Telegraph and Wireless Services

The postal department is functioning in the district with 1 head post office at Reckong Peo (district head quarter) assisted by 12 sub post offices, 59 branch post offices and 113 post boxes. It is clear from the number of post offices that this service is not available in every village; one post office is shared by neighboring villages too, the distance of post offices from villages varies from 5 to 10 km. The postal services are being suffered by intercept in road transport and some times it takes long time to reach a letter. After, development of telephonic communication and its network in the district, people are less dependent on postal services for routine communication, Besides that the district headquarter and tehsils headquarters are also equipped with wireless stations. There are 11 wireless stations and 8 Telegram offices in the district.

Telephone Services

For telephone exchange there is one satellite center in the district. Almost every household (>90 per cent) is equipped with independent telephone connection. The problems faced due to vertical settlement and poor road transport services are neutralized by the fascinating services of telephonic network. Though still it needs extension and maintenance, because often the exchanges are found out-of-order. At the same time, one engineer is looking after 4-5 exchanges. During field visit, it was observed that a Junior Engineer posted at Pooh was responsible for Pooh exchange, Yangthang exchange and Chango exchange, at the same time his services is taken outside district too. He visited Kaza and Kibber exchanges of district Lahul and Spiti. The villages, which are in extreme remote, such as Kuno-Charang (approximately, 35 km away from road head), Hango-Choling (approximately, 25 km away from road head) and others are still deprived of electricity and telephone. The facility of telephone and electricity will minimize the remoteness of such villages.

The People

The district Kinnaur is inhabited by Kinnauras, who are designated as Scheduled Tribe. From Anthropological perspective, Kinnaura present a more complex picture in terms of their identity; there are clearly two ethnic groups Rajput or Kanet (ST) and Kolies (SC). Rajput or Kanet presents peculiar situation. Particularly there is no Kanets today even in official records. Everybody identifies himself with Rajpoots. It is observed that there are two clear-cut divisions in terms of habitations. This may be designated as Upper Kinnaur and Lower Kinnaur. The Upper Kinnauras considered themselves ethnically superior than Lower Kinnauras as they inhabiting in highlands, though Lower Kinnauras are economically and politically dominant over Upper Kinnauras. Furthermore, Upper as well as Lower Kinnauras considered themselves as offspring of *Pandvas*, the mythological legendary characters of *Mahabharat* the Hindu epic, though majority of Upper Kinnauras perusing Buddhism and majority of Lower Kinnauras worshipping deities like— Chandika, Sheshering, Markaring, Kashoraj, and others who were considered as offspring of famous devil of Mahabharat period known as *Vanasur*. Upper Kinnaura can be associated with an area above an altitude of 2500 metres and Lower Kinnaura below 2500 metres. Lower Kinnaura is concentrated in Kalpa, Nichar and Sangla valley. They are basically migrants largely from Shimla and Rampur districts. According to Raha & Mahato (1985) and Chadra (1992) too, Kinnauras do not belong to a single ethnic group, but it comprises five different ethnic group of people;

among them Rajput or Kanet are the most important and dominant group, followed by Koli who are weavers, leather worker and agriculturist; The two other groups the Lohar (iron, silver and gold smith) and the Badhi (carpenter and mason), the last group is mentioned as Nanglu, who are basket makers, and found only in lower Kinnaur. During present investigation first three groups were encountered but the last two were not found, may be they were in Nichar Tehsil. Beside these ethnic groups the District Kinnaur is also inhabited by few immigrants, they were from Nepal, Tibet, and other parts of India. In Upper Kinnaur, at International border of Chinese occupied Tibet and adjoining District Lahul & Spiti of the State (H.P.), there are villages like Sumra, Shalkher and Chango, where in many of households, either of the spouses is from Tibet and adjoining district. Inspite that in village Shalkher, there was one household having a spouse (male) from Nepal, in one more family the spouse (male) was from Udhampur District of Uttranchal State of India. In village Leo too, one spouse (male) was found from Kerala State of India. Similarly, in Lower Kinnaur, immigrants of Nepal and other parts of India are in abundant, they also had marital relation with different group of Kinnauras, as well as they migrate seasonally in search of employment and wages.

Rajput of Kalpa practice both Hinduism and Buddhism. Historical facts are centered on Rampur Bushair. There is no vivid account of Kalpa valley or anything beyond that. Reckong Peo is more than 100 km from Bushair and it takes 5 hours by bus. The waves of migrants from low land found Kinnaur as great treasure. During 150 years they not only become affluent but also political and economically dominant. Where people of Upper Kinnaur were always struggling for subsistence due to harsh environment and tough challenging ecological conditions, they hardly had large land holding. So they were rendered economically and politically weak. Further they were not willing to pursue more favourable environment. Moreover with its border with Tibet, Upper Kinnauras had trade link with Tibetans. Due language and cultural similarity with them, they hardly found feasible to come down and settle. They are closer culturally and biologically with the people of Tibet. On the other hand, the economic and political dominant Rajput in Lower Kinnaur seen Kinnaur district to be declared as Scheduled area and got maximum benefit out of this. In this context, it may be stated that population belonging to Upper Kinnaur have mongoloid affinities and population belonging to Lower Kinnaur have non-mongoloid affinities. Upper Kinnauras are Kanets a term, which is obsolete now, and the Lower Kinnauras are Rajput, the term Rajput is used by both Lower as well as Upper Kinnauras. The title Rajput perhaps identify them with mainstream affluent Rajputs. But marriage alliances and structure of clan of Upper Kinnauras are distinct from Lower Kinnauras.

(i) Population: As per projection of Census (2001), there are 83950 person in the District Kinnaur, comprising of 45353 males and 38597 females. The estimated sex ratio of the district is 851, masculinity proportion calculated on the basis of projected population is found to be 54. As the District is spread on an area of 6401 sq km, hence the land people ratio i.e. density per sq km was 13 (Table 8).

(ii) Population Composition (SC/ST/General): Kinnaur district is a Tribal district all of its original residents are designated the status of Scheduled Tribe; even the Scheduled Caste population of the district is Scheduled Tribe. Therefore they enjoy dual status— Scheduled Caste and Tribe together. The fragmentation of Scheduled Caste, Scheduled Tribe and Other Caste population as per last three censuses is depicted in Figure 3.2 and Table 3.9. In 1971, there were 19 per cent Scheduled Caste, 68 per cent Scheduled Tribe and 12 per cent General population. In 1981, the proportion has changed, the population of Scheduled Caste people declined to 11 per cent, whereas population of Scheduled Tribe and Others had reached to 75 per cent and 14 per cent respectively. But as per 1991 census, the population of Scheduled Caste and General Caste had augmented to 27 per cent and 18 per cent respectively, whereas the population of Scheduled Tribe had declined to 56 per cent. Again the census 2001 has recorded an increment on proportion of the population of Scheduled Tribe

Table 8

Population Characteristics of the District Kinnaur (H.P.) as per Decennial Censuses (1901 to 2001)

Census Year	*Population*			*Growth Rate (%)*	*Sex Ratio*	*Masculinity Proportion*	*Density/ Sq. Km*	*Literacy Rate (%)*		
	Male	*Female*	*Total*					*Total*	*Male*	*Female*
1901	14252	12980	27232	–	911	52.3	4	NA	NA	NA
1911	14710	13760	28470	4.55	935	51.7	4	NA	NA	NA
1921	14664	13527	28191	-0.98	922	52.0	4	NA	NA	NA
1931	15685	14760	30445	8.00	941	51.5	5	NA	NA	NA
1941	17400	15838	33238	9.17	910	52.3	5	NA	NA	NA
1951	16654	17821	34475	3.72	1070	48.3	5	5.5	NA	NA
1961	20808	20172	40980	18.87	969	50.8	6	15.35	26.45	3.90
1971	26407	23428	49835	21.61	887	53.0	8	31.96	43.19	20.23
1981	31598	27949	59547	19.49	885	53.1	9	42.48	53.19	31.46
1991	38394	32876	71270	19.69	856	53.9	11	58.36	72.04	42.04
2001	40878	36129	77007	8.05	884	53.8	12	NA	NA	NA

NA=Not Available

to 72 percent, Simultaneously the population of 'Others' (General Caste people) is constant on 1991 estimation but the population of Scheduled Tribe had decreased to 10 per cent of Total population. It is clear from the above discussion that the population proportion of Scheduled Caste and Scheduled Tribes had decreased in the area whereas the population of immigrants (i.e. General Caste people or Others) had increased correspondingly.

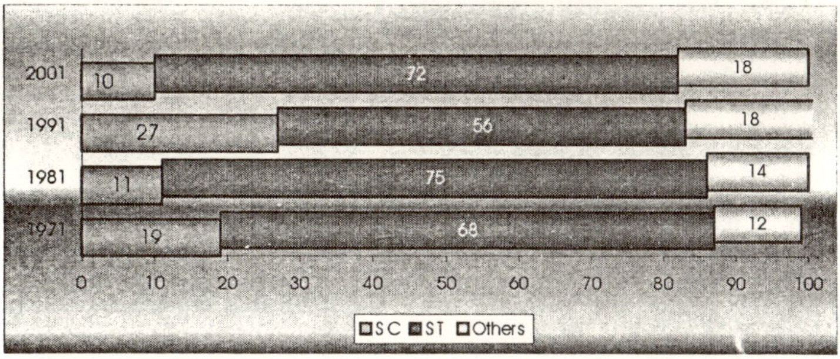

Figure 2: Percentage Distribution of Scheduled Caste, Scheduled Tribe and Other Caste Population during last Three Censuses in Kinnaur District of Himachal Pradesh.

Table 9
Population Distribution of Scheduled Caste (SC) and Tribe (ST) in Different Administrative Divisions (District/Block/Sub-division) of the District Kinnaur During Last Three Censuses.

	1971			*1981*			*1991*		
District/ Sub-Division/Block	*Total*	*SC*	*ST*	*Total*	*SC*	*ST*	*Total*	*SC*	*ST*
Kinnaur	*49835*	*9669*	*34090*	*59547*	*6331*	*44583*	*71270*	*19153*	*39609*
Pooh	16413	1376	13000	18931	1239	13093	23861	7553	11339
Kalpa	19217	4123	12168	21784	2607	15914	26137	7828	13800
Nichar	14205	4170	8922	·18832	2485	15576	21272	3772	14470

Population Growth

During last one century, exponential population growth has been experienced in the District. In 1901 there were 27232 persons in the district, comprising of 14252 males and 12980 females. The next census of 1911 has recorded a growth of 4.55

per cent, but the census of 1921 has reported a decline of –0.98 per cent, after that in every decennial census rapid growth has been noticed in the total population of the district (Figure 3).

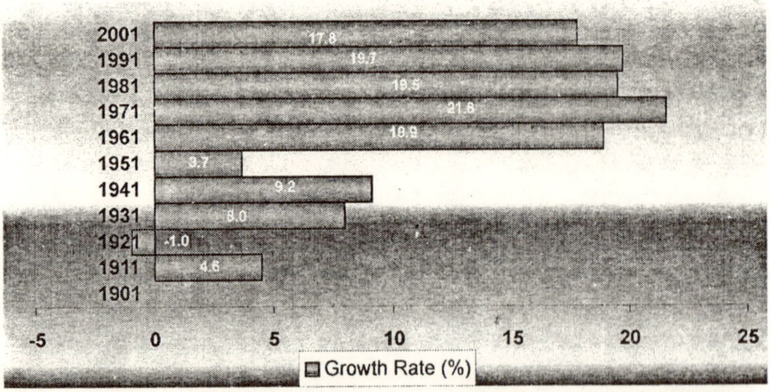

Figure 3: Decennial Growth Rate of Population in Kinnaur District of Himachal Pradesh during Last One Century (1901-2001).

Sex Ratio

The early records reveal that the sex ratio of the district was fleeting around 911 to 941 especially during 1901 to 1941. In 1951 the sex ratio was recorded quite high 1070 women per 1000 male. Similarly in 1961 too, the sex ratio was good, 969 women per 1000 men. But later on sharp decline in sex ratio was noticed, and this trend is continuing, as evident from census 1991 & 2001. Contrary to that as sex ratio declines the masculinity proportion in the area is increasing. Furthermore, sex ratio of Scheduled Caste and Scheduled Tribe people in the district reveals different picture; among first group (SCs) the sex ratio as per 1991 census is 938 female per 1000 of male, which vary from 987 in Sangla Tehsil to 917 in Nichar Tehsil; whereas among later group (Tribe or ST) the sex ratio were found to be 1082, which further vary from 1006 to 1191 women per 1000 of men in different administrative divisions of the district (Table 10).

Density

The district Kinnaur covers 11.7 per cent of the total area of the state, which has a very low density of population. As per

Table 10

Distribution of Population and Number of Villages in Kinnaur District (H.P).

	Total Population		*SC Population*		*ST Population*						
District/Tehsil/ Sub Tehsil	*Male*	*Female*	*Total*	*% of Total Pop.*	*Sex Ratio*	*Male*	*Female*	*Sex Ratio*	*Male*	*Female*	*Sex Ratio*
Kinnaur District	*38,394*	*32,876*	*71,270*	*100*	*856*	*9882*	*9271*	*938*	*19021*	*20588*	*1082*
Pooh sub-division	11119	10153	21,272	30	913	1958	1814	926	6697	7773	1161
Morang Tehsil	5019	4837	9,856	14	964	885	846	956	3071	3659	1191
Pooh Tehsil	3992	3422	7,414	10	857	1010	932	923	1971	2335	1185
Hangrang Tehsil	2108	1894	4,002	6	898	63	36	571	1655	1779	1075
Kalpa sub-division	14108	12029	26,137	37	853	3985	3843	964	6676	7124	1067
Kalpa Tehsil	8493	6904	15,397	22	813	2169	2050	945	3891	3913	1006
Sangla Tehsil	5615	5125	10,740	15	913	1816	1793	987	2785	3211	1153
Nichar Sub-division	13167	10694	23,861	33	812	3939	3614	917	5648	5691	1008
Nichar Tehsil	13167	10694	23,861	33	812	3939	3614	917	5648	5691	1008

estimation, in 1901 the population density was 4 person per sq km which was constant upto 1921. From 1931 and onward upto 1951 the population density increased to 5 person per sq km, further the trend was continued, in 1961 it was 6 person/sq km, in 1971, 1981, 1991 and 2001 there were 8, 9, 11 and 13 person/sq km. Except Lahul and Spiti district (where density of population is 2 person/sq km and it is constant since (1971) records are available) no other district of Himachal Pradesh is so much sparely populated. This is probably because of the difficult topography and unkind climate as well as because of the current domicile policy, according to which none of the outsiders are legally allowed to purchase land or occupy any un-transferable property.

Distribution of Population

As evident from Table 10, most of the population (70 per cent) of the district Kinnaur is concentrated in middle atitude region, in Kalpa and Nichar sub-divisions, while rest 30 per cent is residing in highlands, which fall under Pooh sub-division, furthermore, the highest valley (Hangrang Tehsil) having only

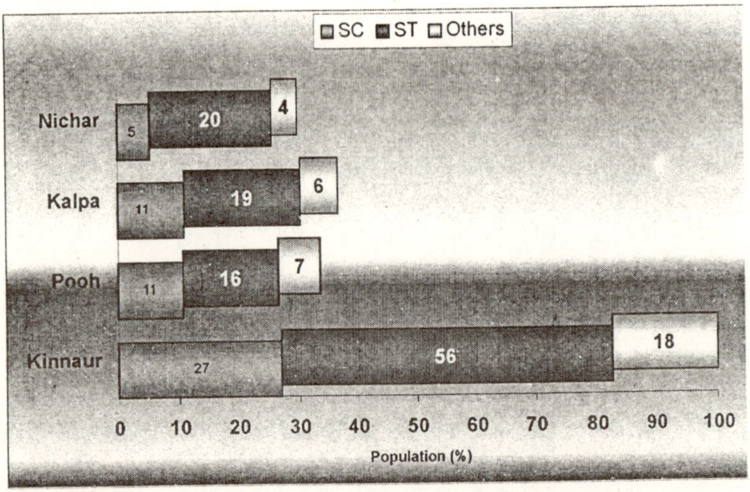

Figure 4: Percentage Distribution of Scheduled Caste, Scheduled Tribe and Other caste Population as per 1991 Census in Different Parts of Kinnaur District of Himachal Pradesh.

6 per cent population of the total. The concentration of Scheduled Caste, Scheduled Tribe and General or Others in different valleys is depicted in Figure 4.

Literacy

The district has achieved tremendous success during last 50 years in the field of literacy; in 1951 there were only 5.5 per cent literate in the district, which gradually increased and every decennial census, has recorded satisfactory growth of literate people. During early days female literacy was meager in comparison to male literacy, but over the time the gap has narrowed. In 1991 the total literacy reached to 58.36 per cent, whereas male literacy was 72.04 per cent and female literacy was 42.04 per cent.

Administrative Setups in the District

Western extreme of the district forms international border with Tibet (China), hence keeping in view the strategic importance of the area, since 1963, single line administration were introduced in the district. Under this system the deputy commissioner (DC) is the pivot, round whom the entire administration revolves in the district. He wields wider administrative and financial powers than any other in the state of Himachal Pradesh. Under this system the Deputy Commissioner writes the annual confidential reports (ACR) of all the officers in the district. In 1965 the Deputy Commissioner was delegated the power of transferring the

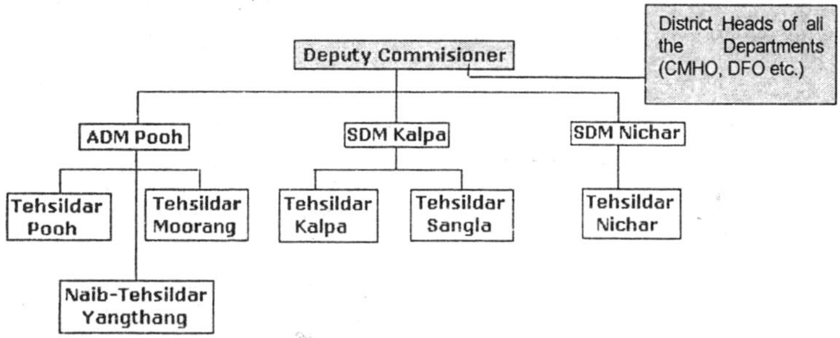

Flow Diagramme of Administrative Setup in the District Kinnaur

subordinate staff (class-III and IV) within the district in consolation with the head of the office concerned. This enabled him to ensure the co-ordination of all departments. He is empowered to sanction casual leave and tour programs of all district level officers (including CMHO). The development schemes of various departments have also to route through the Deputy Commissioner.

Supply and Distribution System

There is great difference in the production and demand of food grains in the district. Simultaneously, being a hilly tract with poor transportation system, the supply of essential items including food grains is not an easy task. To make available the food grains and other essential good there are three kind of distribution system. The first come private retailers in different villages and trading centers of the district. In the second category, we can put the PDS (public distribution system) of the government, its godowns and outlets of different villages. And third-one are canteens of armed forces in different cantonment areas of the district.

There were total 57 outlets of PDS in different village of different valleys of Kinnaur in the year 2001, these outlet had sold 343 metric ton rice, 776 metric ton sugar, 28 metric ton edible oils, 640 metric liter diesel, 166 metric liter petrol and 1867 metric ton coal during 2000-2001 at an optimum price, as fixed by government. Besides that Himachal Pradesh State Corporation had also distributed 1974 metric ton rice in the district to full fill the demand of food grains in the area.

Educational Facilities

In country like India, development of formal educational facilities is recent phenomena, it started with rise of British rule, again during its initial stage it was available for certain group of people not for all. The universalization of Education in India was taken place hardly three to four decade ago. Tribal, hilly and rural areas were further discriminated in the course of development of better educational institutions and facilities. The regions like Kinnaur district, which were secluded due to geographical barriers and remoteness, any developmental activity started belatedly. The same was happened in case with the development of educational facilities in the district.

Before the advent of the modern education, the educational system in Kinnaur was based on traditional system. Usually the kids of the house, particularly the males, were taught reading and writing (in *Tankri*) by the head of the households (male). In villages having monasteries, the Buddhist monks used to teach and preach religious education. But the credit for modern education goes to the foreign missionaries. The Moravian Mission first opened regular school in Kinnaur, one at Pooh and the other at Chini (present Kalpa), as early as 1899, Rev. J.T. Bruske, a missionary of the Moravian Mission, opened a school for the boys at Pooh. And this was the first school in Kinnaur district. But the school was soon closed with departure of Mission. Again in May 1900, Rev. Bruske and his wife took up the ambitious plan and opened a school in a small two roomed house in the village Chini (at present Kalpa). The school was started functioning regularly with 12 students (male). In 1920 the school at Chini was upgraded to lower middle standard. Later on in 1944 it was converted into a middle school, and eight years later it came up as a high school in 1952. The next primary school started functioning in 1914. Later on Raja Padam Singh of Bushair state took keen interest in education and established a good number of school in many villages of Kinnaur. Actually the modern education started in Kinnaur after independence.

There were only 1 high school 3 middle school and 62 primary including pre-primary schools in Kinnaur in 1961, whereas in 2001 the number of schools increased many folds, as per district statistical handbook (2001), there are 37 high schools, 33 middle schools and 189 primary including pre-primary schools. Since 1996, one college is also functioning in the district at district headquarter Reckong Peo. During the period of 2000-2001, the primary (including pre-primary) schools were equipped with 537 teachers and 7887 students, in 33 middle school, there were 161 teachers and 4596 students, in the same way in 37 high/higher secondary schools, the number of teachers were 510, where as in the only college of the district there were 17 teacher for 231 students. Despite these educational institutions and schools, there are ITI (Industrial training institute) too.

Health Facilities

Primarily the people of Kinnaur are dependent on government health institutions, as there are no private practitioners (except 1 or 2 in lower Kinnaur) in the district. NGOs (Non-Governmental Organization) have very poor coverage and restricted to health education and RCH (Reproductive and Child Health) activities. The district has wide spread network of modern system of medicine and ISM (Indian System of Medicine) & Homeopathy. There are 2 hospitals, one is district hospital situated at district headquarter Reckong Peo and other one is civil hospital located at village Chango, 3 CHC (Community health centres),3 TB (Tuberculosis) centres, 3 Leprosy elimination centres, 4 Maternity centres, 5 Dental clinics, 6 X-ray clinic, 17 PHC (Primary health centres) and 34 PHSC (Primary health sub-centres) of modern system of medicine. Simultaneously, ISM (Indian system of medicine) & Homeopathy also has quite expanded network with 1 district hospital at district headquarter Reckong Peo assisted by 40 Ayurvedic Health Centres (also known as Ayurvedic Dispensaries) at periphery level. The health system of the district is equipped with 85 doctors, 44 Dais, 13 staff nurse, 58 health workers and 25 compounders and pharmacists (District Statistical Handbook, 2001). Beside above described health infrastructure, there is a number of traditional healers known as *Lama* they practiced Tibetan system of medicine and herbal medicine as well as they are magico-religious practiceners.

Banking Services

The first bank, in Kinnaur, was established as a branch of Himachal Pradesh State Cooperative Bank, at Kalpa, in 1961. Currently, there are number of cooperative societies in different villages of the district. These cooperative societies are involved in promotion, development and assistance of agricultural, horticultural and small-industrial activities. Besides that there are 18 branches of different banks (viz. United commercial bank, State bank of India, Punjab national bank and Union bank of India) in different regions of the district.

Watermill (*Panchakki*) vs. Hydro-electric Projects

There are tremendous natural resources and appropriate situations to construct hydroelectric power projects, in several rivers and rivulets. In early days people were using this natural power through traditional instruments for various purposes, but not for generating electrical power. There are flourmills in several villages, which were run through swaying the way of furious waterways. The stream coming with force was directed to a fan like wooden structure, which is attached to the long pivot of upper part of a round-shaped big stone-crusher. The stream runs the fan and attached, which revolves the pivot of crusher, as well as crusher itself, because the pivot has permanent and strong attachment with crusher-stone, and in this way grains like wheat, barley, *ogla, phafda* etc. were crushed between revolving upper part and stable lower part of crusher-stone, to obtain flour through such kind of water driven flourmill, which are popularly known as *panchakki.*

Now a day, the district is identified as a paradise to generate electricity through hydroelectric projects. Some of the sites for construction of such projects were already identified, few of them are ready, few are already functioning, but still the search for more sites and process to adopting land and other things continue. The details of identified sites and ongoing project are given below:

Name of Hydroelectric Project	*Capacity*
Nathpa Jhakri Hydroelectric Project	1500
Solding Hydroelectric Project	12
Sanjay Hydroelectric Project	120
Karchham-Wangtu Hydroelectric Project	460
Shongthong-Karchham Hydroelectric Project	225
Rukti Hydroelectric Project	NA
Thopan-Powari Hydroelectric Project	400
Thangi-Thopan Hydroelectric Project	300
Baspa Hydroelectric Project	300

Desert Development Project

An ambitious project to convert deserts of high lands into lands of greenery, orchards and fields; is being run under the supervision of Deputy Commissioner and in the leadership of ADM Pooh. The project is devoted for conservation of natural resources and development of deserts as agricultural/ horticultural lands or pasturelands, development of *Kuhls* for irrigation and other purposes. Furious streams generating from glaciers are being swayed towards human settlements and agricultural/horticultural fields. The projects provide wages to the high altitude people as well as ensuring the development of the high altitude region.

In this way it can be summarized that the region of Himalayas governed by Indian republic is known as Indian Himalayas. Ten independent states (small and big) of Indian republic has grown-up on this region. Each state is unique in its people their socio-economic status, cultural-linguistic backgrounds as well as divergent from geo-climatic angle. Himachal Pradesh is one of these states, comprising of 12 districts. Kinnaur is one of them, which is 100 percent rural. Being at international border the district has strategic importance too. Its indigenous people are known as Kinnaura, who are distinctive not only in physical features but also culturally and linguistically.

Chapter 4

ETHNOGRAPHIC PROFILE OF KINNAURA

Indian mythology is full of with the stories of Kinner, Nag, Gandharva, Rakshasha, Devta, Rishi etc. Some of the investigators have an opinion that the mythological Kinner and present day Kinnaura of district Kinnaur may be same or descendents of mythological people. In this chapter you will find vivid descriptions of the present day Kinnaura. What is the reality of mythological Kinners would be to described in the also preceding section.

KINNAURA—THE PEOPLE

Origin, Composition and Nomenclature

The people inhabiting, the district Kinnaur of Himachal Pradesh are known as Kinnaura. They are indigenous occupants of the area. Majority of them identify themselves as Rajputs, they suffixe 'Negi' as a common title after their names. Some of the authors (e.g. Raha and Mahato, 1985 and Chandra, 1992) had associated the term Kinnaura with Indian religious mythology. These authors tried to describe the term Kinner, as mentioned in Vedas, puranas, epics and other religious books, which means half-god or godly-people or angle like people. Ethnically, genetically and religiously, Kinnaura are heterogeneous group of people. Earlier researchers and travelers had reported five different ethnic groups viz. Kanet, Koli, Badhi, Lohar and Nangloo in the district Kinnaur. But today Kanet is an obsolete term; Raha and Mahato (1985) opined that it was a derogatory term, indicating to *kunit* and *Kanya-het*. *Kunit* means who is not performing his duties as per norms— a violator, whereas *Kanya-het* means a father who have a lot affection for daughter, *Kanya* is a Hindi word, it is synonym of daughter and *het* means liking or affection or love. According to a hearsay, in the ancient period, there were custom of female feticide or female infanticide among Rajput, the occupants of the region. But, some of these Rajput had violated the norms of killing the newly born daughter; hence they were called Kanet (the term 'Kanet' was possible derived from Hindi words either *Kunit* or *Kanya-het* or both) by the 'daughter killer group of Rajputs' of the area. This hearsay leads to conclude that the region was inhabited by one more group, who were known as Rajput. Most probably these Rajputs, including Koli, Badhi, Lohar and Nangloo were immigrants. Perhaps they migrated from low land of northern India from erstwhile Rampur Bushair, which was ruled by Rajput families. In the post independence era too, the Rajputs were dominant as well as affluent in the region. Simultaneously, keeping in view the strategic importance of the area, the district as a whole is recognized as scheduled area. Furthermore, the economically affluent and politically dominant Rajputs also got the status of scheduled tribe and took maximum benefits of the status of scheduled tribe. As on today, all the inhabitants of district Kinnaur enjoy the status of scheduled tribe. The reason of omission of this term 'Kanet' is that there is no-official use of the term; such as for getting caste certificate or for admission in school/college/government-job or getting any benefit of government's schemes, ethnic identity of a person is not required. At the same time, in post independence era, two major groups of people emerged in the area, scheduled caste and scheduled tribe. Scheduled caste include artisan group of people viz. Koli (basically weaver, tailor and leather worker), Badhi (carpenter or wood worker and mason), Lohar (gold, silver and iron smith) and Nangloo (basket maker); whereas scheduled tribe include Kanets/Rajputs as well as all the scheduled caste people. In this way the scheduled caste people are enjoying the dual status; they are getting benefits of both scheduled tribe as well as scheduled caste. But, at the same time, they are most deprived group of people and lagging behind at all fronts.

It is observed that there are two clear-cut divisions in terms of habitations too. This may be designated as middle and high altitude region. The high altitude can be associated with an area above an altitude of 3000 metres and middle altitude can be associated with altitude ranging between 2000-3000 metres. Kalpa, Nichar and Sangla valley fall in middle altitude zone and its habitant are migrants largely from Shimla and Rampur districts. Whereas Kinnaur of high altitude are always struggling for subsistence due to harsh environment and tough challenging ecological conditions, they hardly had large land holdings. So, they were rendered economically and politically weak. Moreover with its border with Tibet, the high altitude Kinnaura had trade link with Tibetans. Due to language and cultural similarity with them, they hardly found feasible to come down and settle. They are culturally and biologically closer to the people of Tibet. Thus, the high altitude Kinnaura are Kanets a term, which is obsolete now, and the middle altitude Kinnaura are Rajput by and large, but the term Rajput is used by both middle as well as high altitude Kinnaura. Due to assimilation of these two groups marital alliances are also common among them, resulting into infiltration of gene of moderate degree. As for as religion is concerned, Rajput of Kalpa valley shows hybridization of both Hinduism and Buddhism. Hinduism is practiced in a different form, where all the rituals are being conducted by non-Brahmin *Pujaras* or Buddhist monk *Lama.* Infact there is no Brahmin in the region. As an Anthropologist one can view Rajputs as not a single entity but as two conspicuous entities, one belonging to high altitude and other middle altitude former showing mongoloid affinities, while later showing non-mongoloid affinities.

On the basis of genetical analysis, Papiha (1985) had concluded that Tibetan contribution was 76 per cent to Pooh Kanet while its contribution decreased to 51 per cent in Nichar's Kanet. In Kolis, the contribution of Tibetan was only 15 per cent. The historical association of various regional population of Kinnaur also indicates the possible direction of mongoloid gene flow. In the present study however, the middle altitude Kinnaura comprise of the population with non-mongoloid ethnic affinities, while the high altitude Kinnaura comprise Kinnaura with mongoloid ethinic affinities.

Clans or Khandan

There are various clans and khandans among Kinnaura. These Khandan are unilateral descent group, are patrilineal and exogamous in nature. They indicate a person's identity, his family of origin and his social position. According to Raha and Mahato (1985), there are two types of Khandan in Kinnaur villages— firstly, the original Khandan and secondly the immigrant Khandan. The members belonging to the former type are the earliest inhabitants of the village while the members of the latter type either came to this village on migration and settled in the village later on or came to this village as wives or as son-in-law. There is functional difference between these two types of Khandan. The member of the original Khandan can take direct part in the social, economic, political and religious functions of the village while those of the immigrant Khandan cannot. Only the members of the original Khandan can become the functionaries of the temple and the gompas (monasteries). Most of the posts of these religious institutions, such as pujaras, mathus, bhandari etc. can be held by the descendants of the original Khandan. The original Khandan is held in high esteem.

In Kinnaur these Khandan are characterized by their location in particular geographical area. A particular Khandan are found in a particular village. The Khandan of one village is usually different from that of other village.

Village wise details of Khandan found during investigation in different villages of different valleys indicate that most of Khandan in many villages are restricted to single households. Few Khandan like Charus, Bisht, and Mathus etc. are common upto Pooh valley but these Khandan are completely absent from Hangrang valley.

Physical Features

By nature Kinnaura are beautiful in look and gesture. Possibly, the early visitors or travellors of the area found them so beautiful and healthy that they recorded them as godly people% Kinner. According to Hindi mythology the Kinner were dancer and singer in Indra's assembly (Indra was Emperor of Gods). In general they have good physique, healthy and slim body. Majority of Kinnaura have yellow skin colour. They are medium stature with broad nose and have straight hairs. On the basis of physical feature Kinnaura can be divided into four major groups:

1. *Mongoloid people:* High altitude region is mostly inhabited by these people. They have yellowish or slight brown skin colour; black, straight, coarse head hair; scanty body and facial hair; broad flat face with prominent cheekbones; oblique eye with narrow slit-like opening and internal epicanthic eye fold. The nose is mesorrhine or platyrrhine, average stature varies from short to medium. They can be further categorized under Malay Type. Where agricultural/horticultural land is sufficient and productive they are economically better otherwise they are economically backward. Majority of them follow Buddhism. They speak Kinnauri dialects, which have influence of Tibetan dialects and languages. They also speak Hindi, but their pronunciation of Hindi word is different in manner, which gives Tibetan flavor.

Photographs 1: Kinnaura of High Altitude

1. Non-mongoloid people: Middle altitude region, by and large, is inhabited by such kind of people, who show physical similarity with Indo-Aryans. They had sharp and long nose with comparatively narrow aperture. Fair complexion—pinkish to brownish skin colour, eyes have dark colour, they have plentiful body and facial hairs. Their stature varies from medium to tall. Possibly, they are descendent of low land people of northern India or rulers' families of the region. They owing clans like Rajput, Halmandi, Thakur, Bisht, Charus, Bhandari reflects such Indo-Aryan features. They are well off and affluent. They speak different Kinnauri dialects. They can speak Hindi fluently as per standard pronunciation.

Photographs 2: Kinnaura of Middle Altitude

Among non-mongoloid, the other group is known as scheduled caste and they are untouchable for rest of the people; traditionally they were shoemakers, weavers, menial-workers, carpenter, mason and smiths. Socio-economically they are downtrodden. Physically they resembles to Indo-Dravidian people. They had light to dark brownish skin colour; hair is usually black and slightly wavy; head hair is plenty; body and face hair is sparse to medium. Forehead is usually rounded, Nose is mesorrhine—broad to medium in size and it is depressed at the root. Face is narrow and medium of length; there is little or no prognathism; brow ridges are moderately developed. Their stature varies from short to tall. They speak different Kinnauri dialects. They can speak Hindi fluently as per standard pronunciation.

3. *Admixed group:* Another group is emerging with admixture of different elements. There are marital ties between middle and high altitude Kinnaura, with mongoloid and non-mongoloid ethinic affinities. Besides, the land is visited and served by the people of different region, religion and race, one cannot completely denied with the possibility of introduction of such a foreign kind of element among Kinnaura. There are very remote villages like Leo where one family was found, in which male partner was from Kerala State of India. He came to serve the district as government employee of Horticulture department but he fallen in love and married a Kinnauri girl. Now they settled in Leo village with bride's parent. They also had kids. In the same way in one family of Shalkher village the male partner is from Udhampur district of Uttaranchal State of country, they not only had kids but now they are grand-parent. In middle altitude too such marital alliances are not rare. One Bengali doctor is married to a local Kinnauri girl and is settled in Reckong Peo (district headquarter). A person came to serve Indo-Tibetan Border Force as pharmacists; he resigned from the job and got married to a girl of Kilba village of Sangla valley. Now they are settled in Reckong Peo. The woman is employed in state government and the male has a medical store. They also had two kids. These are few example of infiltration of genes among Kinnaura from other sources.

Since Kinnaura had trade link with Tibetans, there were marital alliances with Tibetan too. There are many such couples in Sumra, Shalkher and Chango villages, where one of partner is from Tibet and Nepal. Thus, there is growing amount of admixed taken place among Kinnaura.

Photograph 3: School going children in Village Sudharang

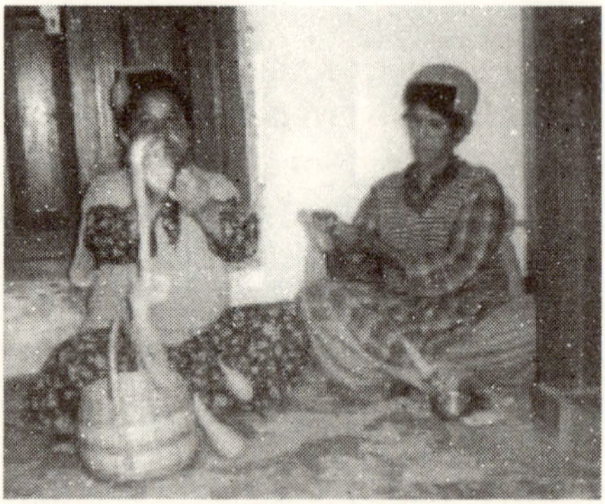

Photograph 4: Koli Weavers of Middle Altitude Region

Dress-Pattern and Attire

Usually dressing pattern and use of garments varies according to age, sex, perception of individuals, socio-economic condition of household, ecology of the region, exposure to outer world including mass media, television, cinema etc. The attire of Kinnaura also influenced and designed according to these very factors.

The district Kinnaur experiences cold temperate climate, which is characterized by long winters from October to March and short summer from June to September. June is the warmest month in the middle altitude region. The high altitude region of Kinnaur is a cold desert area, which is an arid tract; here the warmest months are July and August. So the people of Kinnaur usually wear woolen garments over the year. Their traditional dresses are decorated with beautiful designs.

Men's Dress

The young generation has least gender bias on clothing as young unmarried girl too wear jeans, trouser and shirt, though traditionally there is clear-cut distinction between male and female dresses. The male dress includes Chhuba, Suthan, Chamu Kurti, Kameej and Thepang and Gachhang. Thepang and Gachhang is commonly used by men and women both.

(1) *Chhuba:* It is a long woolen coat upto or even below knee. Now a days, it is being replaced by long coat imported from plains or being prepared locally. The readymade long coat are chief, light and more protective.

(2) *Coat:* Now a days, cotton coat of varied design is common among youngsters as long coat or Chhuba is more useful during snowfall and severe cold of peak of winter.

(3) *Suthan:* It denotes woolen trousers. This is made slightly loose with design in the lower edge. Now a day Jeans and cotton trousers are more in use among youngsters.

(4) *Chamu Kurti:* This is a sleeveless woolen jacket.

(5) *Kameej or shirts:* Traditionally woolen shirts were used. But now cotton and terylene shirts are common.

(6) *Thepang or Cap:* Thepang or cap is common and essential part of Kinnaura' headdress. It is common for either sex. It is made of woolen and velvet cloth. The cost of a cap varies from Rs. 150/- to 300/- It is

symbolic in identification of Kinnaura by green velvet cloth. The use of cap as headdress is multipurpose—one is symbolic; and second is ecological as the region experience cold temperate climate means low temperature where being bare head may lead to headache and other health problems. The woolen cap protects the head of users from severe cold. During short summer this cap protects the head from dusty wind.

(7) *Sweaters:* These are woolen garments, knitted or crocheted to be worn on upper body. These are recent introduction among Kinnaura and being imported from plains as readymade. Raw wools also imported to knit sweaters, locally. Military and para-military canteens also supply a good quality and quantity of sweaters. Usually sweaters are of standard size and colours as used in other parts of the country. These garments are also used by women.

(8) *Jackets and winchiters:* These are modern garments. Youngsters and elite group of Kinnaura are fond of these kinds of garments. As these garments are multipurpose they, provide protection against cold weather, light in weight, good and beautiful in look; and also give a distinctive and modern look. These garments are supplementary to traditional garments as during climax of winter traditional garments or long coat more suites as compared to modern. Usually these garments were used in light and open weather. They are of standard size, shape and colours as used in plains and imported from plains. They are made of by different type of materials such as jeans, terylene and wool. These garments are also used by women.

(9) *Undergarments:* Today use of fancy undergarments is common among youngsters; they use cotton *panty* and *baniyan* as undergarments. *Panty* is small cloth designed to cover the gonads and small portion of waist. *Baniyan* is of two types sleeved and sleeveless. It hangs from neck to cover breast, abdomen, and waist and goes upto thigh.

Women's Dress

(1) *Choli:* It is a sleeved blouse, short or full in size. It is made off by woolen, cotton and velvet.

(2) *Dhoru:* This is an important women garment and usually costly. It is prestigious too. This is a short of woolen sari. Its standard size is 4 ½ % 1 ½ yard.

(3) *Chhamli (Pattu):* This is an indigenous shawl made of woolen. Its two ends are held together near the breast by silver pin known as *digra.*

(4) *Salwar and Kurti:* These are not a traditional dress of Kinnauri women but today it is popular among youngsters as well as aged women. Woolen or cotton made salwar and kurti is worn as per of ecological conditions. This garment is also convenient for easy and quick movement in vertical valleys, that's why it become a popular and essential part of women's day to day attire. These days salwar is worn under *dhoru* in lieu of petty-coat.

(5) *Gachhang:* It is a cotton or woolen strip tied at waist to support the *dhoru*. It is also used by men folk too.

(6) *Undergarments:* Now a days, use of brassiere and panty as under garment is common among young Kinnauri women.

Today, there are many good marketing places and shopping centers in district headquarter Reckong Peo as well as at periphery in sub-divisional head quarters and big-villages, where modern as well as traditional garments are available as per requirement of people. Traditionally, most of the traditional garments were prepared by local weavers (Koli). But now a days, there are weaving and knitting training centers in the district, which trained women of the area in the field of weaving and knitting; and now this job is not restricted to Koli weavers only. Hence a good amount of traditional and modern garments of local use and for exporting purposes are prepared in the district. The modern garments are imported from plains. The canteens of military and para military forces in different places of district are also a good source of availability of modern kind of garments.

Ornaments and Personal Adornment

The variety of Jewellery used by Kinnaura is an evidence of their consciousness towards beautification and personal adornment. Silver, gold and pearl ornaments were traditionally used by Kinnauri women, but now a day ornaments of different metals with silver and gold enamel is becoming popular as they these ornaments are chief and affordable to everybody. Gold is less in use, as it is costly and unaffordable and its loss causes a big financial damage. Almost all the traditional ornaments are made of by local goldsmith. The metal is imported from plains. Some ornaments are also purchased from market of Rampur, Shimla and Solan. Besides that there are general merchants in marketing and shopping centers of the district, they work as retailers outlet. A good number of traditional and modern ornaments are also available with these retailer outlets. The ornaments used by Kinnauri women can broadly be categorized into head ornaments, ear ornaments, nose ornaments, neck ornaments, hand ornaments and toe ornaments.

Ornaments of Head

Chak: It is worn by ever-married women. Widows do not wear it. The ornament has round disc with decorative *meenakari* of blue, yellow green and red over it. Its average weight is 30-40 grams.

Shatab: A silver band worn on the head. The weight varies between 100 and 120 grams.

Zuthi: It is a silver flower hung at the end of hair.

Ornament of Ear

Kantai: In upper lobe of each ear 6 to 8 such earrings are worn. Usually these rings are made of silver and in rare cases gold rings can also be seen.

Khul Kantai: This ornament to be worn in the ears in place of *Kantai* rings. This is a ring, which is systematically fixed, in a piece of embroidered cloth.

Jhumku: This is a common type of ear ornament, which is used all over India. This is made of silver, gold and other metals with look of silver or gold. In different part of country it is known by different names. In Kinnaur, traditionally it is a type of silver top with silver chain of which one end remains tied to the cap.

Mool-u: This is a bunch of silver flowers hanging from the hair over the ears.

Ornaments of Nose

Khundoch: It is made gold made small ring hangs between the nostrils.

Laung: Alike Jhumku it is made of silver, gold and other metals; and it is a common ornament worn by Indian women. It is a rod like, dumbbell shaped structure, designed to wear on nose-wings, the outer or upper part of the rod is artistically designed, a coloured or transparent stone or pearls set on top of rod.

Balu: It is a gold made large ring.

Bulak: Now, it is old fashioned and can be seen among aged women, youngsters hardly wear it. It is a comparatively bigger nose ring, which is worn through the hole made in the cartilage partitioning the nostril.

Ornaments of Neck

Kanth Malang: This is silver necklace with 1 to 5 gold beads.

Chandra Malang: This ornament is hardly worn by young women. This is a silver chain made of garland containing beads *pheroza, moonga* and old silver coins of four annas, sometimes one rupee silver coins were used in place of four anna coins.

Trimani: This is a necklace having 3 large gold beads.

Shatungma: This is necklace with a big square, hexagon or pentagon silver box like structure with a lid. Its frontal side is of silver and is engraved while the backside is made of copper. *Tawiz* (talisman) is often kept in this ornament. This ornament is also not very common.

Patkachang or Kachaong: It is a silver ornament, round shaped rod, worn close round the neck.

Shulickcha: Necklace of moonga and some other precious stones.

Ornaments of Hand

Kagun: These are silver or gold rings having blue or red glass or moonga or pheroza fixed on it. Sometimes, gents also wear in their finger. Finger rings are also worn in other parts of country by both men and women.

Dhaglo: These are silver bangles. There are two types of *dhaglo* single and double are in use. The single *dhaglo* are used by unmarried girls whereas double and triple bangles are worn by the married women.

Ornament for Toes

Polrij: This is flat silver ring worn on the toes of left and right legs by the women.

Dress Ornament

Digra: This is a decorative silver sari-clip cum sari-pin used by the females to hold the two ends of *dhoru* or *chhamli* (shawl).

Tamuch or Pechu: This is also used for holding the two ends of the *dhoru* or shawl near the shoulder. It is made of silver.

Personal Hygiene and Sanitation

Now a days personal hygiene and sanitation is considered important by Kinnaura, as they are exposed to outer world through mass media and television etc. They are aware of different hygienic practices, which were earlier not in their custom and traditional accomplishments. The harsh weather, cold climate and ice-cold water are still restricting their personal hygiene practices. The other barrier in personal hygiene is lack of knowledge regarding alternatives of water such as toilet paper, and hygienic dry-cleaning techniques.

The defecation practices and post-defecations personal-cleanliness practices among Kinnaura are not hygienic, particularly among inhabitants of high as well as middle altitude region in general. In high altitude almost every household had locally designed toilet called *Chhaksa*. During chilled winter, they do not go outside for defecation and make use of *Chhaksa;* after defecation they rub the excretory organ by powderous animal dung, thereby avoiding the use of ice-cold water for cleaning the excretory organ. They are also not aware about use of toilet paper; moreover even if they are aware, it is not available easily. It was observed that in some of the household, old newspapers were being used in place of animal dung for cleaning the excretory organs after defecation. The use of *Chhaksa* and related practices are common during summer season too; even if they defecate in open they tend to avoid the use of water and just rub excretory organs with soil, dust, snow or stone pieces. Some people wash their hands with soap, after defecation. In only few houses, sanitary latrines were seen.

Usually, the inhabitants of middle altitude region defecate in open and some of the households have sanitary latrine, too. They also use water for cleaning the excretory organs but during winter they avoid use of water for the purpose and rub excretory organ by snow, dust or stone. The practice of avoiding the use of water for post-defecation cleaning is more common among older people.

Usually they clean their mouth and teeth daily and for this purpose they use twig of some specific green plant known as *Chulli* etc., which is available in their premises. A small, thin and mature twig is chewed properly at one end, which develops in one form of brush. Teeth and gums are smoothly rubbed by this brush, almost 1 to 5 minute. The twig is then torn into two vertical pieces; these pieces are used to clean the tongue. Now a day, however, a variety of toothpastes, toothpowders and brushes are available with them, and they make use of them.

During long winter they hardly take regular bath; usually once or twice in a month. Similarly they don't change their cloths and undergarments frequently. In the same manner, woolen cloths worn by them are cleaned once or twice in a season thus, the cloths they wear are dirty. Precisely for these reason they are more susceptible to various fungal and bacterial infections.

Use of Cosmetics and Make-up

Kinnaura have started using a variety of cosmetic products like creams, talc, sprays, perfumes, lipsticks, blushers deodorants, eye shadows, nail polish etc. Most of these items are imported and are available in the market.

Hairstyle

Most of the Kinnaura usually wear short hair with parting either on the right or left of the head. They are skilled in shaping, trimming and cutting the hair, the scissors; a foreign implement is commonly used for the purpose. Men prefer short hair, with or without parting. Men also visit hair saloons, which were run by immigrant barbers of different district of Himachal and Punjab.

Usually, women keep long hairs. The young women are more particular about hair care. The hair style of the old women is striking. They knit many thin pleats, which are bond together at the end, and decorated with traditional hair band. This style is common in Pooh and Hangrang valley.

Dietary Habits

Kinnaura consume locally produced food grains, vegetables, fruits, oils, pulses meats and imported items of plains. Food grains include barley, maize, ogla, phafda, wheat, pea, *razma*, millets, pulses etc.; green vegetables include viz. potato, cabbage, chilly, mustard, *palak* and reddish There is a abundant production of variety of fruits and nuts like apple, pine apple, apricot, pear, grape, peach, almond, walnut, peanut, hazelnut, pistachidnut, plum, prune, berries, cherries, nuts, etc. Banana and mangoes are available though they are not indigenous products.

Dishes of Kinnaura include breads from flour of ogla, phafda, maize, wheat and barley; however rice is staple food. Among vegetables they make preparations of green leaf of mustard, green pea seed, potato, and razma in high altitude, besides these items they also give preference to *thugpa*, *momo*, noodles and other dishes of Tibetan taste. Kinnaura also consume butter, ghee and oils. Non-vegetarian items, consumed on availability, they consume meat of goat, sheep and yak. Occasionally they also consume the meat of wild animals.

The preparation of vegetarian or non-vegetarian dishes is very simple. Pulses, vegetables or non-vegetable items are boiled; very less amount of spices like turmeric, ginger, garlic, onion, salt and chilly powder are added for flavor. Appropriate amount of oil or ghee is also used. But the preparation of *momo, chomin* and other dishes of Tibetan taste are somewhat tricky and require special utensils and training. The Kinnaura of middle altitude are least skilled in such kind of dishes but in high altitude these dishes are very common.

Momo: Momo are dumplings made from flour and filled with additives spices and vegetables like onions, ginger, garlic, cilantro, cabbage, reddish, tofu and mushrooms. The mushrooms are used in hotels and cafeterias, in domestic preparation it is replaced by reddish and cabbage. For preparation of non-vegetarian momo cabbage and reddish are replaced with meat of got, sheep or yak.

Chomin: Chomin are noodles or noodle soup.

Thugpa: Thugpa is made from the roasted seed flour of barley. The barley seeds are roasted before making its flour. This flour is kneaded with ingredients like sugar, ghee, water etc. the kneaded dough is called thugpa.

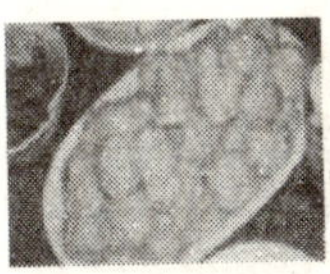

Dumplings (momo)

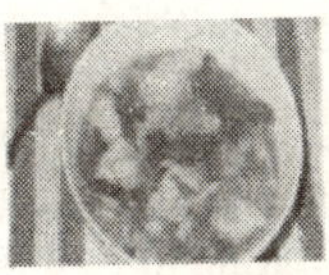

Noodle Soup

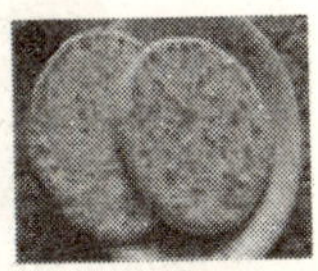

Bread

Full momo

Half moon momo

Thugpa

A Lama eating thugpa

Photograph 5: Dishes (General and Special) of Kinnaura

Smoking and Drinking Practices

Hukka is traditional smoking device, used all over the Kinnaur. It is a hollow cylinder or pipe, which is purely wooden or metal or mixed; having one end broader and other end narrower. Tobacco is filled at the broader end of *Hukka* and lit the fire or kept a burning coal on it, the other end is narrower and used to suck from mouth. Earlier it was very common, but now a day, the tradition of *Hukka* smoking is limited to older people, in limited households. Everybody do not smoke, but majority of Kinnaura are found smoking. During winter, there is restricted outdoor activity, so the frequency of *Hukka* smoking increased. Only adult and old people are allowed to smoke. Adult children avoid to smoke in front of parents and other senior members, and they smoke with their peer group. Besides, *Hukka* they smoke country cigarette (Bidi) or cigarette of different brands. Women also smoke, however their proportion is less than the men.

Photograph 6: A View of Distillation of Country Liquor

Kinnaura are fond of alcoholic drinks. They extracts *arc* (a country liquor) from chulli (fruits of berry like plant). They also extract country liquor from grapes. Extract of these are concentrate and can't be taken without mixing water. Men and women both take alcoholic drinks. Kinnaura are very good hosts, and if someone known or unknown having visit, they accord extraordinary hospitality to any visitor.

Material Culture

Every human group essentially posses a variety of goods, technological and ornamental inventories according to their ecological, biological and geo-climatic set-ups; availability, affordability, socio-economic conditions, knowledge and skill inherited or acquired; Material culture is the sum of these inventories including those elements related to subsistence activities as well as those which are produced for artistic or ritual purposes. The material culture of Kinnaura like land, ornaments and economic pursuits is described separately, here attention have been paid to describe their house, utensil and furniture, implements used for agriculture, horticulture, hunting and fishing purposes, recreational implements, domestic animals, luxurious goods and miscellaneous items like looms possessed by Kinnaura. Recently this tribal group has been exposed to a variety of outside cultural influences; so their material culture is not from self contained and closed system, but it is determined by the circumstances, environment, availability, affordability and exposure to mass media and outer world.

House

Traditionally, construction of houses among Kinnaura was eco-friendly. They construct the houses in a way, which protect them from severe cold and harsh climate. Construction of

Photograph 7: A House Type and Materials used in Construction of House in Middle Altitude (Kalpa Valley)

houses depend on the availability of material in the particular geographical area in Kinnaur. In middle altitude wood is abundantly used for walls, roof and floor, as it is available in plenty. Whereas little wood is used in high altitude due to its scarce availability and high cost. Wood is usually replaced by slate in High Altitude.

Photograph 8: Other Type of Houses in Middle Altitude (Kalpa Valley)

Photograph 9 : House Type and Construction of House in Village Shalkher (High Altitude)

Photograph 10 : A Typical House-type in High Altitude

Rectangular houses are constructed throughout Kinnaur. In high altitude, single and double story houses are built, whereas in middle altitude two and three storyed houses are raised, as the wood is available in plenty. Walls are elevated to a height of about 7 feet or so in all the regions. Further in middle altitude, wooden beams are very much in use for the construction of walls. The walls are made of stones and wooden beams. These horizontal beams act as a sort of frame and hider, because no mortar is used. In some areas, mud is used as mortar; the rest of thing is same. In high altitude, walls are constructed from stone chips and mud. If ground floor is used for living purposes it is made of clay, but in middle altitude, the ground floor is made of wooden plank. Mixture of cow dung and mud is used for plastering the walls from inside.

Moreover the entire region is situated in heavy snowfall area, but its houses have flat roof. Possibly because the flat roof is used for various purpose, such as drying the food grains, vegetables and other items. During winter the inhabitants can clear the snow easily as it accumulates on the flat roof. In middle altitude, houses are being made with steep high-sloped roof of slate, wood or iron sheets.

Earlier, each story had one or two rooms, but these days, they are constructing three to four rooms on each floor, alongwith provision for guest-cum-drawing room. The main living room serves the purpose of kitchen (*Khanalani Kim)* so as to keep the room warm. In the center of room there is specially designed iron hearth with a smoke pipe, which carries smoke outside the house and works as chimney. In this way all the members including the guest can be easily accommodated in this room without the suffocation of smoke generated by firewood, especially during winter. The iron hearth is installed in a small raised platform. The platform is made of mud, in case of wooden plank floor, the platform saves floor from fire and heat of hearth. While the iron hearth emits heat, keeping the room warm, it also serves the purposes for cooking food. Previously there was no provision for bathroom. But these days Kinnaura keeps a small space for this purpose in the newly constructed houses. The family god *Kimshoo* is kept in a corner of main room in every house. Every household has at least one bedroom (*Yakim*). But some houses have two to four bedrooms. Throughout the Kinnaur, inner apartment of the ground floor is used to live especially during winter as it protects against piercing fast winds. As soon as summer approaches, the 1st or 2nd floor and the open rooms are used to live. In front of rooms there is porch (or *baranda*), which is quite spacious, airy and sunny. To make the porch and rooms airy and sunny, windows are constructed with glass and wooden or iron frame. Porch act as common gallery and provide entrance to each of the rooms.

Now a days, changes in the construction of the houses are eminent among Kinnaura. They now construct cemented houses of concrete, bricks and iron-rod supported by pillars, initating the practices of plains and urban areas. Though, concrete houses are less in number and can be counted on fingertips. Such houses are multistoried, can be raised upto 4-5 floors.

Photograph 11: A View of Open Animal Shed

Usually animal shed is on the ground floor of the same residential unit or in the adjoining premises. During summer, big animals viz. *choru, yak, breme*, mules, donkeys and horses are kept in open premises, whereas during winter, these animals are kept in closed rooms usually on the ground floor.

Utensils and Furniture

Utensils and furniture of Kinnaura are especially designed to support the user in combating the adverse ecological circumstances. These things help them in the way of acclimatization. Now a days, they are using plastic, steel, iron, bronze, wooden and copper utensils for different purposes. They import these items from plains. The wooden utensils are locally made. Alike utensils, furniture used by Kinnaura are of varied design and are mostly wooden.

Kinnaura have a good number and type of utensils, and furniture as compared to other major tribal groups of any part of the country, though this is not true for whole Kinnaura. A majority of high altitude inhabitants of Kinnaur living in remote and secluded region have comparatively less of utensils and furniture in their houses. During last two decades, the ownership and use of utensils and furniture among Kinnaura have enriched. Previously, furnitures were rare in Kinnaura households and they used to sleep on wooden floor. Khera or *kherach* (mat of goat's hair) and *pakpa* were used as mats. In some well to do families carpets and *duries* were kept. These days, different types of cots, chairs, tables, almirah have come into use.

Steel or wooden almirah, boxes and trunks are used for keeping cloths and garments. Some other items found in the houses comprise of *kote* (wooden chests) for keeping grains and apricot wooden lamp, stone mortar and pestle etc. Grinding is generally done in *garat* (water-mill), and occasionally in *hasgo-tang* (hand-mill).

The introduction of military and paramilitary forces and installation of their cantonment in various villages of the district has brought forth a varied kind of utensils and furniture. These days, utensils of metals, fiber and plastic are common in Kinnaura households. With the rapid changes in household items it would be worth mentioning here that most of the household has also secured LPG cylinder for cooking purposes.

Some of the kitchenware commonly found with Kinnaura households is as cited below:

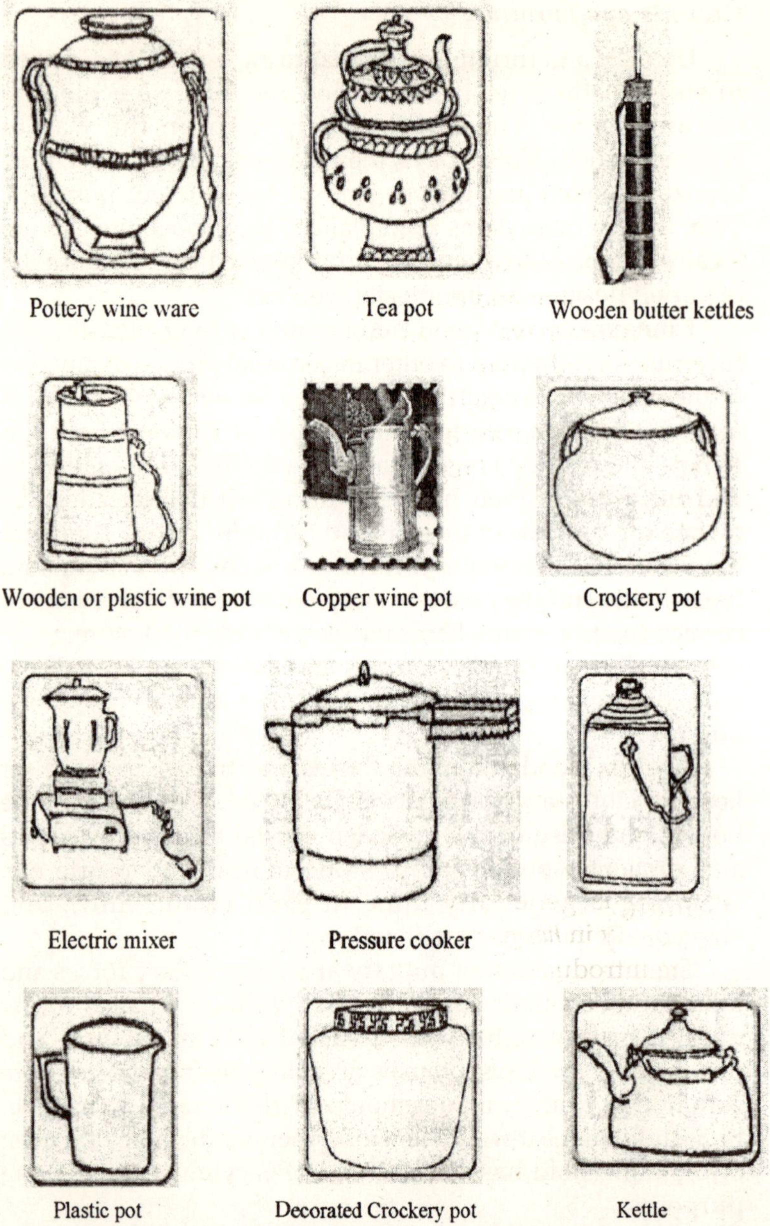

Sketches of Some Common Kitchenware used by Kinnaura

Name of Utensils		
Hindi Name	*In Kinnauri*	*English Name*
Cup (metal or crockery)	Kargyul	Cup
Jug (plastic, metal or glass)	Musarbo	Jug
Ghara (wooden vessel for bringing water)	Zom	Vessel
Karchhi (wooden or steel)	Dogang	Pot
Parat (metal)	Parat	
Tava (metal)	Ron pann	Oven
Chimta (metal)	Chimto	
Patila (metal)	Dig	Pot
Thali (metal)	Nang	Plate
Plate (plastic or metal)	Plate	Plate
Katori (metal or plastic)	Nangach	Bowl
Lota (metal or plastic)	Lotri	Pot
Chamach (metal or fibre)	Khyot	Spoon
Glass (metal, plastic or glass)	Glass	Tumbler
Gagar (metal or plastic)	Gagri	Pot
Dhakkan (metal or plastic)	Dhakona	Covering plate
Tasla (metal)	Chakthalu	
Balti (metal and fibre)	Balti	Bucket
Cane (plastic)	Cane	Cane
Cooker	Cooker	Pressure cooker

Agricultural/Horticultural Implements

The agricultural or horticultural implements found in Kinnaura households include hoe, plough-stall, yoke, sickle, scraper, kilta-koting and hoe-goling etc. Besides these traditional instruments some modern instruments and chemicals also finding place among agricultural and horticultural instruments. These are sprayer, insecticides, sprinklers, plastic pipes etc.

Domestic Animals

The economy of the Kinnaura is based on agriculture, horticulture and animal husbandry; therefore the region is rich in livestock. Animal husbandry is a traditional occupation of Kinnaura and perhaps it is primordial than agriculture/ horticulture and trading. Bajpai (1981) mentioned Kinnaura were nomads earlier, whose main source of life were animals. Probably since 7th A.D. they have settled and started soil cultivation. But till now they have not given up animal breeding. Flocks of sheep, goats and cows, yaks and horses are safety investments for highlanders. Animal breeding, therefore, remains in their tradition. It is worth mentioning that biogeographical diversity of environment also supports animal husbandry in Kinnaur. For the villagers the animals still remained the surest protection in changing mountain conditions. Some mixed breeds of yak, cow and oxen are kept as domestic animal for agriculture/horticultural purposes at high altitude. Beside these a large number of sheep and goats are also domesticated for getting wool, butter and meat, which are essential items for protection from the cold. Horses, mules, donkey and ponies are their load-carrying animals.

Now a days, Kinnaura commonly domesticate goat, sheep, choru and breme. But in high altitude, they domesticate yak, donkey, horses, ponies and mule.

Recreational Implements

Kinnaura spend their leisure time in different ways. Earlier there were no electricity, television and radio. People used to pass their time gossiping with each other, group smoking and drinking. Now almost every household has either colour or black and white television. Those who do not own television, posses radio, tape recorder etc. Games like volleyball, football, badminton and cricket are popular with them and the most popular of all games is carom board.

Many women weave and knit in their leisure time. Previously this was restricted to Koli but these days many of Rajputs (Tribals) also weave shawls and *dhoru*, in their home itself for their own use.

During different celebrations, festivals, ceremonies and procession of devta they enjoy the group amusement in traditional fashion. Different musical instruments and drums are played. People sings and dance. Every temple has some musical instruments and drums, especially for these purposes.

Luxurious Goods

For more than 90 per cent of the households of Kinnaura, telephone is now an essential item which facilitate communication in this exceedingly difficult remote area. Heaters and geezers are also common, though geezers are limited to affluent. Television is common in a majority of the households.

LANGUAGE

Kinnaurese dialect varies from village to village, and from valley to valley. Their first language is Kinnauri and second is Hindi.

According to Grierson (1908), Kanawari dialect comes under the western sub-group of Tibeto-Himalayan group which belong to Tibeto-Burman family of languages. Gerard (1841) had mentioned five different dialects spoken in Koonawar, these are:

(i) The Milchan or common Koonawaree

(ii) The Theburskud, spoken in Soongum

(iii) The dialect used in Lubrung and Kanum

(iv) That spoken in Leedang

(v) The Bhoteea or Tartar.

Mamgain (1971) found that there are more dialects in Kinnaur as mentioned in earlier studies. He categorized the linguistic diversity of Kinnaur as cited below:

(i) Standard Kinnauri dialect spoken in Kalpa Tehsil, Nichar Tehsil and Sangla Tehsil (except Raksham and Chitkul) and Rarang, Ribba, Akpa, Rispa, Thangi, Giabong and other villages of Ropa valley.

(ii) Standard Harijan Kinnauri dialect spoken in Kalpa and nearby villages.

(iii) Kinnauri sub-dialect spoken in Chitkul and Raksham villages.

(iv) Kinnauri sub-dialect spoken in Kuno and Charang villages.

(v) Kinnauri sub-dialect spoken in Nesang.

(vi) Kinnauri sub-dialect spoken in Lippa, Asrang and Jangi villages.

(vii) Kinnauri sub-dialect spoken in Spillo, Labrang, Kanam and Siaso.

(viii) Kinnauri sub-dialect spoken in Sangnam village.

(ix) Kinnauri sub-dialect spoken in Pooh, Debling, Dubling, Khabo, Namgia and villages of Hangrang valley.

Kapoor (1971) on the basis of published material, mentioned five different dialects in Kinnauri language.

(i) *Lower Kinnauri*— Spoken in the north of Sutlej between 92 and 104 miles of Hindustan Tibet Road.

(ii) *Standard Kinnauri*—Spoken on the southern side of the river sutlej, from 92 to 162 miles.

(iii) *Chhitkuli*— The people of Chhitkul and Raksham villages speaks entirely different dialect, which is named as Chhitkuli.

(iv) *Theborskad*— Spoken in the villages like Lippa, Asrang, Sunnam and Shiaso.

(v) *Sumchu*— This dialect is spoken in Kanam. Labrang and Spillo villages.

In the Buddhist dominant area (high altitude), Tibetan dialects are used for religious preaching. The Buddhist hymns are written in Tibetan script and Tibetan languages. The religious books of Buddhism, known as *pothi* is also found in Tibetan script and language only. After independence Hindi became an official language, and is a medium of school education. Thus most of the people are fluent in Hindi. However old people stick to Kinnauri language as they hardly can speak Hindi.

LIFE CYCLE (RITUALS)

Pregnancy and Childbirth

Childbirth is a cheerful occasion in Kinnaura life, but pregnancy is a secrete thing. The pregnancy is never disclosed before 3rd or 4th months. However, from the sixth month onward this remains no more concealed fact. These days,

Health workers, Dais, Anganwadi workers are always in touch with eligible and newly married couples, for early registration of pregnancy, immunization and antenatal care. People are also motivated and they understand the importance of early registration for antenatal care, Hence pregnancies are being disclosed earlier in comparison to older days. Heavy work and load carrying is avoided during last phase of pregnancy, but the geographical condition is such diverse that a pregnant women can't spare herself from doing heavy work like carrying drinking water, firewood collection etc. upto last month of pregnancy. In case of polyandrous family, if required, the woman confirms the fatherhood on the basis of cessation of menstruation. During the advance stage of pregnancy husbands do take care and attend most of the household works and show concern for most of the routine work done by the women. Usually, no ceremony is conducted in connection with first pregnancy.

There are some taboos for a pregnant women during pregnancy she is supposed not to see eclipse, not to visit temples or monastery, not to see dead body or visit the house of deceased during death pollution, not to visit cremation ground as there is a belief that doing such a thing may lead a pregnant woman to give birth to a deformed child.

No particular ceremony is observed at childbirth. In most of the cases delivery is conducted at home. Earlier with the beginning of labour pain the expectant mother was brought to ground floor in the cattle shed (*Khaddu or Khudang*). Some grass leaves were used as bedding. However, this practice is gradually being discontinued. Now, they are aware regarding cleanliness and prefer to conduct delivery in neat and clean room. Old and experienced women of the village serve as TBA (Traditional Birth Attendant). But sometimes, expectant mother alone or with the help of husband also deliver child. Usually blade and scissors are used to cut the umbilical cord; the cord stumped is treated differently in different eco-geographical zones. In middle altitude, usually nothing is applied on umbilical cord. But in some villages the stump is tied by mother's hair or woolen thread. The waste material including rest of umbilical cord is buried in a pit near the house. This is done with the purpose to protect it from any harm of any animal or evils. Newly born child is given bath with warm water. Men folk usually keep away during the childbirth.

After childbirth, pollution is observed upto 5 or 7 days, which depends on mother's health, and during this period all the household members are considered to be polluted. They do not partake in temple functions and other social events. People other than their own clan do not accept food from the house when childbirth occurs. The first ceremony in life cycle of Kinnaura is conducted after a week and is known as *Chhangshiming* or *Shuddhi* or ceremony of cleanliness. The house and cloths are cleaned. Mother and child are given bath. Relatives bring cloths, jewels, cash, ghee, food grains etc as gifts. Worship is organized in the house. Lama generally called as priest to conduct the worship. He reads out *pothi* (the Buddhist religious book), beat drums and plays other musical instruments. A feast is given to relatives who come to grace the occasion.

Slight variation can be observed in birth related rituals and practices in middle and high altitude. The middle altitude Kinnaura are more educated and have better accessibility to health centers; Hence ANC and birth practices of Kinnaura of middle altitude differ from high altitude inhabitants. Rituals of *Suddhi* and worshipping are almost same in middle as well as high altitude inhabitants.

Name Giving Ceremony

To give a name to new born is always a matter of discussion among parents and kin-group. Among Kinnaura the name is given by *Lama*. As a new born attains the age of 3 months or more, a senior member of household or one of the parents of newborn baby visits to *Lama* with the purpose to find out a suitable name to new born. *Lama* do not provide his services free of cost. This is a social, economical and religious interdependence, and parents or grandparents of newborn offer some gift (cash or kind) to *Lama* for securing the name of the newborn. The *Lama* consults his *pothi*, asks day, date and time of birth, and gives a very name to the newborn. It is Buddhist name or Tibetan as per pronunciation and lingual structure. The Buddhist or Tibetan name is common in high altitude. But by the structure, nature and lingual apprehension three kinds of names can be easily observed— 1. Purely Hindi names such as Anil, Ankit, Fagun, Bhism, Bhakti, Budhiram, Arti etc. 2. Purely Tibetan or Buddhist names e.g. Sonam, Dolam, Chering, Chhodup, Angmo, Angzin etc. 3. Mixed kind of names, these names reflect dual nature, these are composition of Hindi as well as Tibetan words. For example Deva Jungmo, Urgyan Singh, Deo Dolma etc. Sometimes a person has two names, one in Tibetan and the other one in Hindi.

The first haircut or head shaving is prevalent in middle altitude. The ceremony is performed when the child attains the age of five years. Child's mother's brother shaves the head of child. In the absence of any such relatives or one whose parents are alive can perform the ceremony. A feast is accorded to the people who come on the occasion. The child gets new clothes and ornaments from the relatives. This ceremony is known as **Jadan.**

Marriage

There are hardly negotiable marriages among Kinnaura. Moreover it is a complex process for Kinnaurese. In case of fraternal polyandry, all the brothers in a household are married together to one woman. Parents are hardly worried about the marriage of their son or daughter. Thus, marriage is by and large elopement.

Many times it happens that after elopement bride dose not grant her consent for marriage, or negotiation between parents of the party dose not reach to any conclusion. In such a cases the eloped bride is returned to her parents. Moreover, elopement has been observed as essential part of marriage rituals, even it has been noticed among well off and quite educated group of Kinnaura, such as Doctors, Engineers etc.

Traditionally Kinnaura were polyandrous. But now-a-day polyandry is on decline. Three main kinds of marriages—

monogamy, polyandry and polygyny are being practiced among Kinnaura.

In some cases monogamy transform into polyandry with severe consequences. In one of the case studies, it was fond that there were two brothers in a household. The elder one was engineer by profession, while the younger one was Law-graduate. The younger brother developed affair with a woman. As per tradition, all the brothers are grooms in a marriage therefore both the brothers were compelled to get married together as per the norms and wishes of their parents. This led to sharing of wife between brothers much against the wishes of younger brother. The union had resulted in 3 children. During the second visit, it was found that the younger brother had committed suicide.

There is another side of coin too. Many times the male partners of fraternal polyandry union depart from the union and get married separately and establish a monogamous union. There are many such cases in which a brother of fraternal polyandry union was not satisfied, he could not adjust with brothers, or the affected brother got married separately and established independent monogamous union had been living far away from the rest of polyandrous union.

Marriage Ceremony

Marriage is solemnized in two phases. The first phase is called *Chhoti Shadi* (*Chhoti* means initial and *Shadi* means marriage) and second is called *Badi Shadi* (where *Badi* means final). After elopement, the pair is brought back to bridegroom's home. Where bride's parents and relatives visit and seek the consent of the girl, if the bride replies in affirmative then her parent start negotiation, being usually a piece of land and a house is secured by bridegroom's parents for newly married couple, and some amount of bride price is given to bride's father.

Functioning and Relevance of Polyandrous Union

Current practice of polyandry among Kinnaura is not considered as primitive characteristic, it is also not considered as progressive feature. Hence, it was not considered as

Photograph 12: Kinnauri Bride in Traditional Wedding Apparel

backwardness of people. Though some activist discouraging practices of polyandry. Thus there are those who favour polyandry and there are also those who are against it.

Those who favour polyandry, opined that polyandry was the way to keep the brothers united, it protected property division among brothers, it protected women from developing illegitimate sexual relationships in the long absence of one husband. Further, it provides perpetual married life to a woman and protected from the curse of widowhood. In monogamous union, in case of death of husband in younger age, the women becomes widow in her peak of life and she had to live with the curse of widowhood. If a widow remarried with a man of other family there are chances of loss of family property as her property will go to remarried union. But in polyandrous union the women had an advantage of not being widowed soon. In case of the death of one husband the other take care of the woman and provide all security.

Polyandry is also a natural method of family planning, i.e. if four brothers practice polyandry, there would be one prime-genitor (mother) in place of four. Moreover it also restricts the division of property.

In a polyandrous union, usually the women stay alternately with every male partner, especially during night. Whole one night she has to spend with a chosen alternate partner. The rest of male partner and other family member stay separate in other rooms as per convenience and availability of rooms. Among male partners, the preference has been given to such a partner, who has returned from a visit or task or duty like sheep or animal rearing or from a long journey of trade or from his posting place (in case any partner is in job and posted outside). The women herself decide who will remain with her. The success of a polyandrous union also depends of intelligence of the women. She has to satisfy every male partner. If a woman has such a caliber to how to satisfy all the male partners, there might not be any conflict among male partners, in connection with less or high privilege by women to any of them.

ECONOMIC PURSUIT

Kinnaura are primarily agro-pastoral tribe. Sheep, goat, ponies and horses have always played an appreciable role in the Kinnaura's economy. The economic structure is primarily agrarian and essentially rural. The size of the land holding is exceedingly small and the methods of cultivation are by and large crude as well as primitive.

Agriculture

These days, agriculture is a primary occupation and principal source of earnings of Kinnaura. Agriculture and animal husbandry is complimentary to each other also. The size of the land holding is exceedingly small and the methods of cultivation are by and large crude as well as primitive. Being a hilly terrain, the agricultural fields are mainly small terraces of slopes of valleys and very few river deposits. In such small terrace cultivation use of modern agricultural instruments are hardly possible. All the agricultural work— ploughing the field, sowing, weeding, irrigation, harvesting, threshing, plucking etc. had done manually or by the help of animals. Moreover, the use of animals are also restricted to ploughing, threshing and load carrying only, the rest of work like weeding, irrigation, harvesting, plucking etc. had to done by men only.

The modern instruments are used only for spraying the insecticides or fertilizers.

Photographs 13: Views of Harvesting

Photograph 14: A View of Threshing Barley by the help of Horses and Donkeys in the Village Hango

GENERAL LAND USE AND CROPPING PATTERN

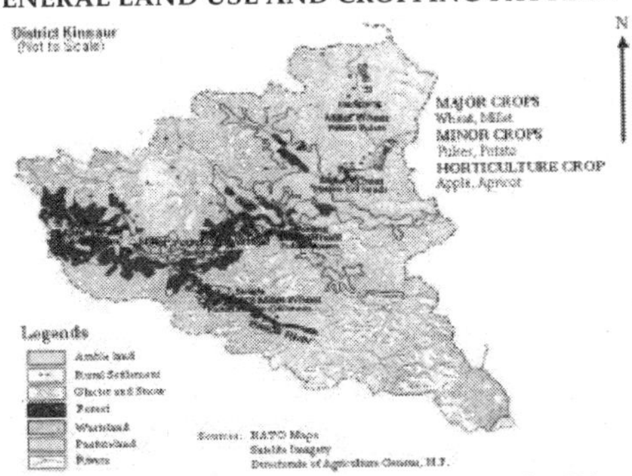

Map 1: General Land Use and Cropping Pattern in the District Kinnaur

Tremendous changes had been noticed in traditional agricultural practices, especially during last five decades. Earlier, horticulture were not so popular, people were also not aware of horticultural practices. In those days, coarse grains were their main agricultural products. These coarse grains are *ogla, phafda, barley and maize*. But, now a days, these grains are not so popular. In very little lands, these are being produced by few households. The other crops being produced in those days were *Razma*, wheat, pea, potato, mustard etc.

As middle altitude region receives monsoon rain and high altitude resemble arid zone, the cropping pattern and kind of crops reaped also differs according to geo-climatic situation of valleys. In high altitude *ogla, phafda*, wheat, barley, pea and potato still remain as the principal agricultural products. Simultaneously, there are fewer orchards in high altitude zone as compared to middle altitude, where horticulture is dominating over agriculture. In middle altitude, the field of *ogla, phafda* is exceptional, now it is an entity of old days for middle altitude Kinnaura; but at the same time, one can witness, the field as well as practice of cultivation of these ancient food grains in Morang, Ropa, Pooh and Hangrang valleys (high altitude zone). In the arid zone of high altitude comparatively more irrigation is required for better yielding of agricultural and horticultural crops.

Table 6
Sowing and Harvesting Months of Different Agricultural Crops in the District Kinnaur

	Months of	
Name of Crops	*Planting*	*Harvesting*
Maize	May-June	October
Wheat	October/April	June/September/October
Barley	October/November/May	June/July/September/October
Mas (pulse)	June	October
Potato	April-June	October
Mustard	October/November	May/June
Pea	April/June	August/October
Razma	May/June	September/October

The cropping season also differ according to elevation of valleys, as the high lands are snow-covered for greater proportion of the year. Usually, agricultural pursuits start in the month of March and wind-up in November. During the months of December, January and February, weather is unkind, the fields are covered with snow and outdoor activity of people is very much restricted.

Horticulture

Today, the economy of Kinnaura is revolving around horticulture. In horticulture too, it is centered on apple. There are abundant apple orchards in middle altitude as well as in high altitude (Photographs 15). The state government also encourages the practice of growing apple orchard, attractive schemes were launched to support the farmers and promote apple production in the area. Quality wise, Kinnaur's apple is better in comparison to the apples of any other region of the country. Its demand is very high in the country as well as abroad. So, this is exported too, and brings good revenue in the district, as well as foreign currency, for the country. Beside apple other horticultural crops of Kinnaur are apricot, pear, grape, peach, almond, walnut, peanut, hazelnut, pistachidnut, plum, prune, berries, cherries, nuts, etc.

Photographs 15: Glimpses from Apple Orchard

According to an estimate of Horticulture Department, during 2000-2001, a total of 7991 hectare land have been brought under horticulture, out of which 6376 were under apple orchards. A total of 21047 metric ton apple were plucked from, and the same quantity were exported in this year.

The poor transportation system has adverse effect on revenue generation. Another drawback affecting the economy of the people is unavailability of good marketing centers for apple. Therefore Kinnaura are dependent on mediators or *adtiyas*. They exploit the people and the real cost of the product do not reach the farmers. Sometimes their apples go waste too, due to natural obstacles in transport.

Fisheries

There are a number of rivers and rivulets in the district; these waterways are tumultuous in nature and carrying ice-cold water from glaciers, where ordinary fish can't survive. Therefore, fishing is rarely practiced in the district and the Kinnaurese are hardly aware about it. Despite this, an exotic species of fish, the brown trout, was introduced in the River-Baspa at Sangla, in 1961-62 by the Fishery Department of Himachal Pradesh Government. Since then fishes are found in middle altitude. Though the fishing has not yet got much economic value to the Kinnaurese, as a result rarely a fishing implement or trap is found in the Kinnaurese households.

Indo-China Border Trade

Indo-China border Trade was in full swing during pre-independence era. After Chinese accession on Tibet it was banned, but later on in 1994 again, the trade was permitted to start. Now a days it is not so in practice, only 15 items can be imported or exported, through barter system.

Government and Private Jobs

A number of Kinnaura are now employed in government jobs. They are employed as class-IV employees, clerks, teachers, police personel, army personnel, bank employees, doctors, engineers and administrators (class-I officers of Indian administrative services (IAS) and Indian forest services) Government job are not restricted to male folk only, but women are also employed in various state and central government jobs. Besides, some private firms and government of India undertakings within and outside the district, also employ Kinnaura in different positions.

Tourism and Hotels

Being a hilly area in inner deep Himalayas, Kinnaur is paradise for tourists, adventurers, researchers and trackers. A good number of tourists from plains of India and different foreign countries visit Kinnaur during summer. There are many hotel, restaurants and lodges, especially in Nichar, Kalpa, Sangla, Pooh and Hangrang valleys.

RELIGION

Three kind of religious persuasion has been noticed among Kinnaura—1.Hinduism 2. Buddhism and 3. Dual Religion (Hinduism + Buddhism together). The high altitude Kinnaura are Buddhist, whereas the middle altitude Kinnaura are so called Hindu by and large as well as they practice Buddhism too. The Hinduism and Dual religious persuasion found in Kinnaur is still a debatable issue because of its eccentricity. The classical Indian Hinduism is driven by Brahmins, who are at the top of caste hierarchy. But here in Kinnaur, they are totally absent. The religious practice of middle altitude Kinnaura, which resemble to Hindus, seems to be indigenous religion, but not Hinduism. Though there are temple and shrines in the region, but most of these temples are of non-Hindu deities, as these deities are to be considered as progeny of a devil known as *Vanasur*. Furthermore, these deities are accepting and demanding sacrifice. Perhaps the early visitors or travellors of the region (like Rahul Sanskrityayana) were Hindu, they found similarity between Kinnaura's religion and Hinduism and started identifying Kinnaura as Hindu. Mostly tribals were secluded from mainstream, they were living in isolation with their own customs, traditions, beliefs, mores, taboos and unique religion. It was neither Hinduism, nor

Buddhism, nor Christianity or Islam or any other religion of contemporary world. Their religious practices developed in its own way, with the mixing up of shamanism, animism and magico-religious practices. Almost all these thing can be observed among Kinnaura religion. As the contemporary religion of the current world came into existence, gradually they started assimilation of tribals. The Kinnaura of high altitude were assimilated by Buddhist of Tibet or they are descendants of Tibet origin who were adopted Buddhism in immemorial past with the spread of preaching of Buddha or after Buddha. But the middle altitude Kinnaura were practicing their indigenous religion; neither Buddhist monk tried to assimilate them with Buddhism nor Hindu Brahmins reached the area and tried to assimilate these people in Hinduism. One or two Christian missionaries who reached them in late Nineteenth century failed to convert the Kinnaura. The Hindu rulers of the area were also not cared to these peoples religion as they were considered as Hindu due to some resemblance. Later on in pre and post independence era the census enumerators of the area misunderstood the religion of the people of the area and counted them as Hindus, as usually happen with the tribal people of other parts of the country.

Hinduism

Hinduism is predominant in middle altitude, especially in Nichar and Kalpa sub-divisions. A different form of Hinduism has been observed among Kinnaura, where all the rituals of day to day life and worship of God and goddesses, control of temple is in the hands of non-Brahmins. Every ancient villages having a Temple in the center of the village, most of these temples are of offspring (sons and daughters) of a devil known as *Vanasur*. As per Indian mythology and great epic *Mahabharat* the Vanasur was contemporary and rival of Krishna and Pandvas. The Temple of Chandika of Kothi village is recognized as oldest one, the deity is considered as superior than other Gods of Kinnaur, as she was eldest daughter of Vanasur. The details of some of the villages having temples, and god or goddess of these temples are as given below:

Name of Village	*God and Goddesses in the Temple of the Village*
Nichar valley	
Mehbar, Chagaon, Sungra, Bhabha	Maheshwar
Maheshwar	Maheshwar
Kalpa Valley	
Kothi	Chandika, Durga
Pangi	Sheshering, Nag
Kalpa	Narayan, Nagin, Vishnu
Telingi	Narayan
Khawangi	Markaring
Barang	Nag, Nagin
Pubari	Parka
Purvani	Shakti Narayan
Sangla Valley	
Batseri	Badrinath
Sangla	Beringnath
Chhitkul	Matadevi
Raksham	Shamser
Kilba	Narayan
Kamru	Badrinarayan
Pooh Sub-division	
Spillo	Khormo
Ribba	Kansraj
Kanam	Dabla
Pooh	Dabla
Morang	Urmig
Thangi	Rapak Shankras

The temples are being run by non-Brahmin priests known *pujaras, mali and bhandari. Pujaras* is the main priest, *mali* is cleaner, he cleans temple, baths the god and cloths the god. *Pujaras* role is ritualistic; he chants mantra, worships and conduct prayers. *Bhandari* is storekeeper-cum-accountant of the temple. In the absence of one and other priest the next one take over his duties.

Religion has intact relation with day-to-day activity of people. All the important work of households as well as initiation of new kind of activity is started with the proper consent of *Devta* (God or Goddess). It is believed that *Mali* is possessed by *Devta*, and during possession, whatever is said by *Mali* is God's word. And people strictly follow it. For matters such as, sowing the field, first or consequent school admission of child, visit to city or town and taking an ill person to doctor people go to their supernatural Devta for consent. If God denies to taking treatment from qualified doctors, the patient is not taken to the doctor.

Belief in Supernatural

The people of Kinnaur have a strong belief in supernatural elements. According to their beliefs, gods, goddesses, deities are benevolent supernatural powers, protect people from miseries of any kind. If these supernatural elements were ignored or not worshipped, the other kind of supernatural power viz. ghosts; spirits and other malevolent supernatural elements become active and bring different melancholy to the people. To keep away the malevolent spirit *Lama* (the Buddhist monk) performs *pooja* or worship, even in Hindu households, Lamas are found performing such kind of rituals.

Photographs 16: A *Lama* Worshiping in a Hindu Household in Kalpa Village (Middle Altitude)

Jurisdiction and Hierarchy of Deities

Deities of Kinnaur are ruling deities, just like Raja of feudal system. According to believe and practice of Kinnaura, every village deity has certain jurisdiction as per the hierarchy of deity. Chandika of Kothi is eldest among all the deities of Kinnaur (Hindu Area or Middle altitude), hence her jurisdiction is entire middle altitude, and she takes care of all the devotees of her jurisdiction. For better and smooth administration in religious and socio-economic life of people, the Chandika of Kothi is assisted by her three brothers who are known by the name of Maheshwar and one sister named Usha.

The *devis* and *devtas* controls beside the religious life of Kinnaura, their social, economic and even political life as well. In every walk of life these deities have powers to decide the duty, fate and punishment etc. Even for the welfare and betterment of its people and area these *devtas* corresponds and converse with the commoners—the human beings— to seek the their help in this matter.

Beside village god there are household deity too, in every Kinnaura house or Rajput houses, which is known as *Ghar ka Devta- Kimshoo*. Almost all the *Kimshoo* are same in power and nature with no fixed morphism.

Morphism of Deities

By the form and structure all the village gods are alike. The whole structure of body of *Devta* is like palanquin. The main structure is made of wooden poles and beams or planks. On a wooden structure having four legs, rests the main body covered with expensive cloths giving the shape to a cylindrical body. On the upper portion of the body some masks or faces made of silver and gold are arranged in a circular fashion. These masks have long thick hair made of wool. This whole body is balanced on two horizontal poles which are fixed with another hollow bamboo pole so as to give it a to and fro motion like a pendulum when it is given some winging motion. The size of deity, its ornamentation and use of gold and silver vary according to superiority of deity.

Inter-god Relationship

The deities of Kinnaur had close relation with each other. The superior deity visits to junior one and this system is known as *Bonning*. Like a senior administrator, the deity planned her tour, as per schedule, she visits almost once a year to each village and is hosted by that village god and the people. The functionaries of temple— *pujaras, mathus,* few *kardars,* some *bajantries* (musicians) and other paraphernalia assemble in the main temple. On deity's order whole team start journey for destined village. The deity is carried on shoulders of four persons, who are *kardars*. On arrival at destined village, whole party is welcomed by the host deity and people of that village. The deity stays one or two days, during this period the deity converses to each other, people sings and dance, country liquor *ghanti* or *arc* is offered to the deities and functionaries. A number of goats and sheep are sacrificed in honour of the deity. Such visits of deities are planned on invitation or on her own accord at regular intervals. Usually Chandika of Kothi village visits her subordinate deities.

This visit of the deity has its own significance as it provides opportunity of assembling the people of different villages at a common platform and exchange views, customs and renews the mutual relation and affords circumstances to develop better understanding.

Buddhism

Buddhism in Kinnaur is more intact than Hinduism. The reason behind it is absent of Brahmins in the region. In middle altitude too, where Hinduism is a dominant religious faith, Buddhist gompas, monasteries, shrines are very common, side by side the Hindu temple. Though it doesn't apply for some of the villages of Nichar sub-division. There is one school too, in the village Brelingi, which is being run by Buddhist monastery, where youngsters were trained in Buddhism or for *Lamaism*. Though Buddhism is being practiced in middle altitude (southern part) too, but it is dominant in high altitude northeastern part of the district, in the area, which lies adjacent to Tibet. It is important to mention that now a days, Buddhism has a great bearing and roots in Tibet. The area under discussion (Kinnaur district) had close contact with Tibet mainly through trade; and adjacent boundaries were freely allowed to share the custom and practices of Tibet. In the pre-independence era, especially before Chinese accession on Tibet, there were marital alliances too of the people of this region to the people of Chinese occupied Tibet. Still there are spouses in Chango, Sumra, Shalkher, Maling, Leo and Nako villages, whose parents were from Chinese occupied Tibet. This area was also ruled by Buddhist Kings, though later on it came under Hindu rulers. Because of these strong factors influence of Tibetan Buddhism on the Buddhism practiced in this part of Kinnaur is apparent. In fact Buddhist Kinnaura looked for spiritual guidance from Tibet (Now a day, Tibet itself resides in India alongwith Dalai *Lama*, in Dharamshala district of Himachal Pradesh) for its religious superiority and physical proximity. Key Gompa and Tabo Gompa of Spiti valley are also the famous monasteries and big centers of Buddhism, These days, waves of Buddhism in Kinnaur is tuned from these centers too. It is quite interesting to reveal that the form of Kinnaur's Buddhism is derived from the Tibetan Buddhism which itself has been very greatly influenced by the classic Indian and Chinese Buddhism.

Sects

According to Raha and Mahato (1985), in Kinnaur, the practice of Buddhism belong to mainly two sects, Nyingmapa and Dukpa, but at the same time, in some village a third sect known as Gelukpa are found. All these Tibetan Buddhism fall under the major faith of Mahayana. Now a days, former two sects also merg with later one and the *Lamas* of former sects too, go to Dharamshala in Himachal Pradesh, the seat of Dalai *Lama* who is patron of the latter sect. So, a particular form of Buddhism is prevalent in Kinnaur. The center of this religion is various monasteries.

Lamaism

The Tibetan Buddhism is also known as *Lamaism* owing to the fact that *Lama* plays pivotal role in the preaching and perpetuation of Buddhism. The Tibetan *Lamaism*, which has its stronghold in Kinnaur Buddhism is based on *tantric* rituals and practices. The *Lama* is not only a Buddhist monk or wanderer like *Bhikshu*. He is not only a preacher but is also a magico-religious practicener. He claims that he can command over the yoga and Shakti and with the help of which he is able to deal with the corpses, demons, ghosts, and such other spirits. He is also an herbal or Tibetan medicine practiceners.

Chandra (1992) had mentioned 7 types of course being run by monasteries for *Lamaism*. These courses are as below:

(1) Twenty-one days course honoring the title of *Chhabchin*.

(2) Four months course honors the title of *Wando*

(3) Eight months course imparting the title of *Landup*.

(4) Fourteen months course imparting the title of *Yidunn*.

(5) Twenty months course imparting the title of *Chhotuk*.

(6) Twenty-seven months course leading to the title of *Tandel*.

(7) Thirty-five months course yields the title of *Ron Yum*.

Jomoism

Female mendicant (*Bhikshuni*) or nuns are known as *Jomo*. They are female *Lama*. The presence of Jomo is not an unique phenomenon in the Kinnaur's Buddhism. The perception about Jomo is that a *Jomo* is Buddhist devotee who renounces the world, sometimes enters the phase of homelessness, stays in monasteries, and does not marry at all. The Kinnauri *Jomos* are usually from high altitude; most of them are from Rajput/ Kanet families. Generally during their early teens they intend to become *Jomo*, either by will or by compulsion go for initiation to renounce the world. Option for *Jomoism* is often encouraged by parents on seeing little prospects for marriage or sometimes even on inquisitiveness of the daughter. At the time of initiation the consent of her parents or elders is rather a must for initiating the girl for *Jomoism*; her head is shaven and clothes are replaced by robe as prescribed in the sect to which she intends to join. Then the girl should leave her home to live in the monastery under the guardianship of some elderly *Jomo* who in some of the cases is her father's sister. But sometimes a *Jomo* is too young in age, may stay with her parents as well as in separate dwelling constructed for her. During the early stage of initiation, a *Jomo* devotes her time mainly in reading the religious literature. As the doctrine provides no marriage but renouncement of the world, a *Jomo* cannot marry and at the same time should not have any liaison with the opposite sex. But this condition is sometimes breached. In such a case they are expelled from monasteries. Sometimes the Jomos become the victims of rape by their colleague *Lamas* or villagers too.

Monastery: Gompa

Monastery is locally called Gompa, which denotes for solitary place. The monastery provides the monastic communal life, which is different from that of village life. In Kinnaur Buddhism monastery plays dual role — one as a common place for *Lamas* and the other as temple to offer worship. The monastery is house-cum temple in which live several persons related through the same pursuit. The structure or architecture of a typical Kinnauri monastery resembles to any typical Kinnauri house of high altitude, with the exception that the central room is quite big and often has a pagoda type roof. This central room serves the purpose of temple. While rest of the rooms serves the purpose of *Lamas* residence, but one room usually provided for *Jomo*. Kitchen, store and the granary are situated within the boundary wall of the monastery. At the doors, there is a small prayer wheel fixed in the niche. A small courtyard serves the purposes of a small garden. Generally monasteries are constructed at some height, above monastery no residential houses or buildings like schools, hospital/PHSC (Primary health sub-center) are constructed.

Chhokten

The pronunciation of the term differs from place to place as *Chhokten, Chhorten or Chhosten,* which refers to one and same religious structure. It stands for the place of worship. Almost in every residential house there is a room or separate dwelling where, *pothi* (the religious literature) were kept as well as there are idol or photograph of Buddha or Dalai Lama, sometimes there is small prayer wheel too in case of wealthier household, this is known as *Chhokten*. In Kinnaur's Buddhism, this *Chhokten* has great importance as its multi-functional role and perception about it, increased its importance. This is not merely a worshipping place, it is believed that it contains the relics of

Buddha, it also has some tantric and magical implications to keep all the evil spirits of malevolent nature away from causing ill effect on either people of their households. *Chhokten* were also erected at all four directions at village boundary to keep evil spirits away from the village but these *Chhokten* are different as compared to *Chhokten* within residential houses. Though in residential houses too the *Chhokten* were erected at all four corners of the house.

Photograph 17: A View of *Chhokten* Placed in side the Home.

Thorchok

Thorchok are flags and banners on which religious messages and doctrine are printed in Tibetan language. These are made of cloths of white, yellow, reddish and green in colors with the inscriptions of black colour. It is usual with monasteries to host Thorchok. Now a days it is common to every household that Thorchok is hosted at the roof of households (Photograph 4.18). The purpose of these flags and banners is to spread the ideals of Buddha coupled with the preaching of various *Lamas* of different sect to a greater extent; at the same time one can easily locate the monastery even from distance, so these flags and banners also works as indicators for travellors, laymen and devotees. Simultaneously it is believed that hosting Thorchok at residential houses will protect the belongings from evil spirits.

Photograph 18: Coloured Thorchok Hosting at the Roof of a House

Kankani

Kankani is gate like structure erected on the pathway entering the village and thus serving the purpose of doorway to the village. Two walls were erected, at the both side of way or road, the height of wall may differ according to requirement, then a pagoda shaped top or roof were constructed to cover the walls as well as way. Some times the wall is provided with some niche. The ceiling is usually painted with murals. In many villages of the region, the entrance is marked by *Kankani* or the village gate (Photograph 19). As one crosses the village gate and enters inside the village, he finds *mane.*

Photograph 19: Kankani and Temple of Village Kalpa

Mane

A *mane* is a high platform or tomb made of loose stones (slates or pebbles) of various shapes and sizes. These stones are inscribed with a hymn *'Om mane padme hum'*. This is a prayer of God sitting on the lotus flower. This hymn carries significant meaning.

OM is the God and is white
MA is the Titans and is blue
NI is men and is yellow
PAD are the beasts and is green
ME is the ghosts and is red
HUM is hell and is black

It is the custom that one passes by the *mane;* he always keeps it on the right hand side.

Photograph 20: A View of Mane and Stupa

Prayer Wheel

The unique feature of Kinnaur as well as Tibetan Buddhism is prayer wheel. At the district headquarter Reckong Peo and at the lower bus stop just in front of D.C.'s office (collectorate), a prayer wheel is exected. This shows the commonness of this religious instrument, faith of people in religion and spread of Buddhism in the area. The prayer wheel is a mechanical devise the use of which is equivalent to the recitation of mantras (sacred syllable or verse). The prayer wheel consists of a hollow metal cylinder, often beautifully embossed, mounted on a rod handle and contain a consecrated written mantra. Each turning of the wheel by hand is equivalent in efficacy to the prayers. Usually, the prayer wheels are found in monasteries only.

Religious Pluralism

The religious pluralism or the practice of following two or more religions at a time is not a unique phenomenon in Indian continent. Mostly the religious pluralism found in other parts of country is a worshipping of two or more gods, following the path shown by two or more religious leader of different sects but of same religious faith; inspite that other kind of religious pluralism also seen such as— worshipping the God, Goddesses and Saints as well as visiting the religious places (temple, mosque, church, monasteries etc.) of different religion concurrently. Generally, it has observed that at the time of religious pluralism, the main religion of an individual remains constant and after practicing the secondary or tertiary religion, the person come back to his principal religion. But, in case of present investigation, it was observed that there is a segment of Kinnaura especially in middle altitude; who practice not only Hinduism, but also practice Buddhism, at the same time.

As the history goes, the people migrated from low land of northern India, and settled in Kinnaur were predominantly Hindus. They were Rajputs and were accompanied by their artisan viz. Koli, Badhi, Lohar and Nangloo (scheduled castes). Whereas, the ancient inhabitant of the area were follower of Buddhism as they had trade link and marital ties with Tibetan people. The Rajput who brought artisans in the area was unable to bring the Brahmins. The area, which was full of challenges and adventure, was also not suitable to the traditionally luxurious life-styled Brahmins. Hence, the Rajputs and their artisans immigrated in the area practised their traditional religious practices, without Brahmins. As a result they started practicing, their traditional religion without Brahmins, or with the help of Buddhist priest *Lama*. The limited numbers of indegenous people of the region came into close proximity of these immigrants, resulting into marital alliances as well as cultural exchange and genetic admixture. Some of them adopted Buddhism, which was practiced by other indegenous people of the area. In this way, the practice of following dual religion developed among the people of the area.

Chapter 5

SOCIO-ECONOMIC CHARACTERISTICS

Hilly people have to struggle with extreme climatic condition, toughest geography, low oxygen pressure, high radiation, least substance and variety of ecologically adverse circumstances. They evolved unique culture to reduce the harshness of the nature, their culture works as cushion between nature and man reflects partially in their socio-economic characteristics which will help in understanding how they adjusting with the nature, how is mode of life in the high altitude region, what are the source of drinking water, do they have electricity or not, which type of house and toilet they construct, what kind of fuel available to them, where they employed, what are their sources of earning, literacy and schooling among them etc. will be discussed in this chapter.

The Asian continent is passing through many dramatic political, economic and demographic changes. The high lands of the continent are not exception of these changes. The population dynamics and its characteristics are widely influenced by the interplay of physical, environmental, biological, economical, political and socio-cultural factors and components like family size and structures, therefore this chapter is devoted to the socio-economic characteristics of the studied population.

BACKGROUND CHARACTERISTICS

Family Type

Family is a universal institution, it is omnipresent either in one or another form. After mother's womb family takes place the care and development of every human being, naturally it affects several aspects of our life, as well as the society and universe. Broadly, family can be described as-Nuclear, Joint and Extended type. The distribution of Kinnaura households according family type is shown in Table 1. Out of 820 households 57.6 per cent belongs to nuclear family types, 23 per cent having joint family system and rest 19.4 per cent were practicing extended family type. Nuclear and extended types of family were slightly higher (60.1 per cent and 20 per cent) in high altitude as compared to middle altitude (54.8 per cent and 18.8 per cent), while joint family is higher (26.4 per cent) in middle altitude as compared to high altitude (20 per cent).

Table 1
Distribution of Households according to Family Type among Middle and High Altitude Kinnaura of Kinnaur District, Himachal Pradesh

			Types of Family							
	Households Studied		*Nuclear*		*Joint*		*Extended*		*Total*	
Region	*N*	*%*	*N*	*%*	*N*	*%*	*N*	*%*	*N*	*%*
Middle Altitude	394	48.04	216	54.8	104	26.4	74	18.8	394	100
High Altitude	426	51.95	256	60.1	85	20.0	85	20.0	426	100
Kinnaur	820	100	472	57.6	189	23.0	159	19.4	820	100

Household Characteristics and Amenities Available

Facilities available in a place affects the demographic variables and determines the population structure of the place, hence it is an important aspect of population studies. Table 2 describing the amenities available to the Kinnaura of Kinnaur district Himachal Pradesh, simultaneously the difference exists among resident of middle and high altitude respectively is highlighted throughout the description.

Sources of Drinking Water

Perpetual sources of drinking water are always essential for survival and existence of human being in any place. Glaciers provide drinking water to many people in different form. The people of Kinnaur are very near to these glaciers, which are the only source of drinking water to these people, in many places it takes the form of small fountain which is called Chasma or Nagasti, which provides chilled water in summer and lukewarm during freezing winter. During summer water is directly taken from Chasma or Kuhl (canal) inspite of stored one because the fresh water is ice-cold. This is one major reason of human settlements near Chasma or Nagasti. The difference between Kuhl and Chasma is that the Kuhl originate directly from glacier, whereas Chasma originate from hilly slope having no direct connection with glacier, but the ultimate source is glacier only. The melted water of glacier is also supplied directly through pipe in the form of tap water.

As stated in Table 2, in Kinnaur almost half (51.1 per cent) of the population shared tap water nearby their residence, though it is not true in case of high altitude Kinnaura. Slightly, more than one fourth (26 per cent) have their own tap and 22.9 per cent use natural perpetual fountain Chasma or Kuhl as source of drinking water. There is hardly any difference in the quality of natural fountain's water and tapped water, especially from the point of view of its purification, because tap water is no different from natural fountain except that it is being carried through a pipe to the household.

The source of drinking water in middle and high altitude is almost same but in high altitude its availability to households is entirely different and difficult. There are villages in which scarcity of drinking water can be seen during summer, government agencies and army people supply drinking water through tankers in such villages. There are 30.3 per cent households in high altitude fetching drinking water directly from Chasma or Kuhl or taking from tankers (supplied by either government agency or army, the water in these tankers is carried from any far located source-furious fountain coming from glaciers) while in middle altitude such scarcity of drinking

Table 2
General Household Characteristics and Amenities Available to the Kinnaura

	Altitude			
Household Characteristics	*Middle*	*High*	*Total*	
	%		N	%
Sources of Drinking water				
Chasma (Natural fountain)	15.0	30.3	188	22.9
Tap shared	49.5	52.6	419	51.1
Tap owned	35.5	17.1	213	26.0
Total	100.0	100.0	820	100.0
Location of Drinking Water				
Outside home	72.1	83.6	640	78.0
Within home	27.9	16.4	180	22.0
Total	100.0	100.0	820	100.0
Types of House				
Kachha	29.9	46.5	316	38.5
Semi-pucca	46.4	42.0	362	44.1
Pucca	23.6	11.5	142	17.3
Total	100.0	100.0	820	100.0
Ownership of House				
Rented	4.1	0.7	19	2.3
Own	95.9	99.3	801	97.7
Total	100.0	100.0	820	100.0
Sources of Light				
Kerosene/other lamp	1.3	1.4	11	1.3
Electricity	98.7	98.6	809	98.7
Total	100.0	100.0	820	100.0
Fuel used				
Firewood/cow dung	4.8	1.2	24	2.9
Kerosene	3.0	1.4	18	2.2
LPG	91.6	97.4	776	94.6
Electricity	0.5	0.0	2	0.2
Total	100.0	100.0	820	100.0
Toilet Used				
No Latrine	49.5	39.7	364	44.4
Own pit (Chhaksa)	18.0	42.7	253	30.9
Own flush	32.5	17.6	203	24.8
Total	100.0	100.0	820	100.0
Disposal of Waste Water				
No drainage	39.3	69.7	452	55.1
Open drainage	60.7	30.3	368	44.9
Total	100.0	100.0	820	100.0
Luxurious Item Owned				
None	7.6	10.6	75	9.1
Radio/stereo/Bicycle	5.8	21.1	113	13.8
Sewing machine	1.5	6.1	32	3.9
TV/VCR/VCP/Refrigerator	41.4	14.1	223	27.2
Motor cycle	33.5	41.8	310	37.8
Car/Jeep/Truck/Tractor	10.2	6.3	67	8.2
Total	100.0	100.0	820	100.0

water is not observed and contrary to high altitude their proportion is just half, 15 per cent fetch drinking water directly from natural sources, almost similar proportion in both low (49.5 per cent) and high altitude (52.6 per cent) access drinking water from shared tap. Again the proportion of the household owing tap within premise is more than double in middle altitude (35.3 per cent) as compared to high altitude where only 17.1 per cent have access to owing tap within residential campus.

Location of the Sources of Drinking Water

In majority of cases (78 per cent) the source of drinking water is away from home, only 22 per cent households are fortunate having the source of drinking water within their premise. As described in above para in respect of middle and high altitude Kinnaura, the proportion of households in both the region, owing tap means the location of drinking water is within home elsewhere it is outside the home and required manual fetching. In high altitude 83.6 per cent households having no access of drinking water within their residential campus, while this proportion is slight less (72.1 per cent) in middle altitude (Table 2).

Types of House

Earlier, the Kinnaura used to construct the house from locally available materials- stone, wood and mud, this type of house are identified as *Kachha,* but recently they are importing bricks, cement, iron rods, tiles from low land to construct a beautiful concretized building which are called as *Pucca,* while Semi-pucca houses are mixture of former two *Kachha* and *Pucca.* In Kinnaur 38.5 percent houses are *Kachha,* 44.1 per cent are *Semi-pucca* and rest 17.3 per cent are *Pucca.*

In respect to middle and high altitude Kinnaura the *Kachha* house are common in high altitude (46.5 per cent) followed by *Semi-pucca* (42 per cent) and *Pucca* (11.5 per cent), contrary to that *Semi-pucca* houses are common in middle altitude (46.4 per cent) followed by *Kachha* (29.9 per cent) and *Pucca* (23.6 per cent).

Ownership of House

Majority of Kinnaura (97.7 per cent) have their own houses, only 2.3 per cent are living in rented houses. In middle and high altitude the ownership of house is slightly different, around 99 per cent of high altitude Kinnaura have their own house, whereas in middle altitude this proportion fall down around 95 per cent, rest less than 5 per cent live in rented house (Table 2).

Source of Lighting: Electrification

As the state of Himachal Pradesh is premier in power generation, it is also leading in electrification, by the experience of such a remote and difficult, tribal area, one can easily guess about the position of state in electric production and consumption. It is easy to produce electricity in Himalayas but it is equally difficult to ensure complete electrification and its supply. Almost 99 per cent of Kinnaura households are electrified, both in middle and high altitude (Table 2). This is big achievement of government and we must appreciate it.

Fuel Used

As stated in Table 2 approximately 95 per cent of Kinnaura use Liquid Petroleum Gas (LPG) as fuel for cooking and other purposes, side by side they also use other traditional fuels e.g. firewood, almost cent per cent households having smokeless *chulha,* one kind of specially designed hearth, during chilled winter this hearth or smokeless *chulha* is used to keep warm their residence, and when temperature fall down below 0^0 C, this hearth keep them alive and all the activities of all the members of household is performed around this hearth, then this room becomes common room and even outsiders are given place in the room nearby the hearth. Around 5 per cent of households have no access to LPG, they are completely dependent on firewood (2.9 per cent) and kerosene (2.2 per cent), only 0.2 per cent people uses electricity as complementary to LPG or Firewood or Kerosene. It is clear that in high altitude the use of LPG is slight more (98.6 per cent) in comparisons to middle altitude Kinnaura (91.6 per cent). Unavailability of firewood in high altitude leads towards the use of alternative fuel and LPG is best alternative for these people. Again state should be appreciated for such a mass use of LPG as fuel.

Defecation Practices and Toilet Used

Three type of defecation practice were observed among Kinnaura, according to defecation practice they use different kinds of toilet, and the unique toilet of Kinnaura is known as *Chhaksa*. This is very common among middle-income group. Generally the houses are double storied, the ground floor is used as store rooms and animal house, the upper floor is used as kitchen, bed-room, drawing room, etc. one room of a corner of house is being used as *Chhaksa*, the same room of ground floor is used as dry septic-tank, those people who use *Chhaksa* they do not use water to clean their excretory organ, inspite of water they use ordinary paper, dust or powder of animal dung to just rub and dry cleaning of excretory organs. As shown in Table 2 one third of Kinnaura used *Chhaksa*, 44.4 per cent used to defecate in open, and 24.8 per cent have access to own flush. The people who have own flush slightly differ from *Chhaksa* using people in defecating practices, they have two options to clean excretory organs- one is water, the use of which depends on the temperature and the second option is to use paper instead of water. The people of third category who have no latrine, used to defecate in open they also have two option for cleaning excretory organs- one is water, this may carry on pot or bottles for the purpose, it is also available from *Kuhl* (canal) which is ice cold glacier water, diverted from furious fountain to utilize mainly for irrigation purposes; the second option is stone or soil dust or snow. In middle altitude the use of *Chhaksa* is less (18.0 per cent) in comparison to high altitude (42.7 per cent), while the use of own flush is just near to double in middle altitude (32.5 per cent) as compare to high altitude (17.6 per cent), contrary to that the own pit (*Chhaksa*) is common in high altitude, it is available to more than double 42.7 per cent of households as compared to middle altitude where only 18 per cent households having this facility.

Disposal of Wastewater

Being in hilly area, there is benefit of natural sanitation; the settlement need not required drainage system like plains. Automatically the wastewater flows down through natural passage, households maintain open drainage from their kitchen, bathroom and toilet, and leave it out side to their premise to flow naturally. Even some households are in such a unique slope they need not to maintain open drainage too. Among Kinnaura only 44.9 per cent of the households maintaining open drainage, rest 55.1 per cent didn't required it. In middle altitude the practice to maintaining open drainage for disposals of wastewater is just double (60.7 per cent) as compared to high altitude where open drainage is seen only in 30.3 per cent of households.

Luxurious Items Owned by Households

In a multiple response it was found that 9.1 per cent of Kinnaura households had not owned the luxurious items as listed- radio, stereo/ cassette player, bicycle, sewing machine, TV/VCR/VCP, refrigerator, motorcycle, car/jeep, tractor, truck. 13.8 per cent owned either radio or stereo/ cassette player or bicycle or any two of three, or all the three items, or any other luxurious item having the same value. Only 3.9 per cent of households owned sewing machine, 27.2 per cent owned television set or video cassette recorder or video cassette player or refrigerators or any two or all of these items, 37.8 per cent of household owning motorcycle and 8.2 per cent owing heavy motor vehicle like car, jeep, truck or tractor.

Kinnaura of middle altitude are rich by the view of owing the luxurious items as compared to high altitude Kinnaura. In middle altitude 7.6 per cent had no access to any luxurious as listed above, while proportion of such household increased 10.6 per cent in high altitude. Furthermore in middle altitude 5.8 per cent owing radio/ stereo/bicycle 1.5 per cent possessing sewing machine, 41.4 per cent having television set, 33.5 per cent have access to motorcycle and 10.2 per cent possessing heavy motor vehicle, contrary to that in high altitude 21.1 per cent have radio/stereo player/bicycle, 6.1 per cent have sewing machine, only 15.1 per cent have access to television set, 41.8 per cent owing motorcycle and 6.3 per cent have access to heavy motor vehicle (Table 2).

ECONOMIC CHARACTERISTICS

Occupational profile of individuals, Income received by the families and proportion of a population engaged in any productive and gainful economic activity is a basic economic characteristic of a population. All the demographic process and economic characteristics are interlinked and influence to each other directly or indirectly; it is also closely linked with development and well being of a population.

Occupation

Economic characteristics of a population are determined by the occupational profile, job opportunities, type of employment and its duration. The occupational profile of Kinnaura of middle and high altitude is evident from Table 3, 4 and 5. It is clear from Table 3 that 36.2 per cent of the total studied population is daily wage earner, they got job in agriculture/horticulture sector, in different developmental projects and construction sites (e.g. roads, buildings, hydraulic power project etc.), 22.2 per cent of the population is employed in agricultural sector, 7.6 per cent are in government jobs, 0.5 per cent employed by private sector, 1.8 per cent engaged in Business, 28.8 per cent are students and 1.8 per cent are Lamas (Buddhist monk). The main labour force (people of 15-59 years of age group), which is actively engaged in gainful economic activity are mainly labour, agriculturist and government employees. Males are in better kind of occupation and variety of jobs as compared to females. In higher age group (60 and over) too, people are engaged in daily wage earning and agricultural sector. The situation is almost same in middle and high altitude with very minute difference as reflecting from Table 3 and 4.

Income

The income profile of the households studied is given in Table 6 followed by Figure 1. It is evident from the table and diagram that more than 95 per cent households having annual income in the range of Rs.12,000/- (Rs. twelve thousands) to Rs.1,000,000/- (Rs. ten lakh or one million), 3.5 per cent families having very low income less than Rs.12000/- (Rs. twelve thousands) and 3 families (0.6 per cent) are found to have annual income more than Rs. 1,000,000/- (Rs. ten lakh or one million). Majority of the population (41.7 per cent) having better economic condition with annual income rupees 1 lakh to 10 lakh, nearly one third (31.1 per cent) of the population having limited economic resources, their annual income ranges between Rs.12,000/- to 50,000/-, while 22.9 per cent families having moderate annual income Rs.50,000/- to 100,000/- (Rs. fifty thousands to hundred thousands). Furthermore in middle altitude, nearly half of the population having annual income in the range of 1-10 lakh, whereas in high altitude more than 65 per cent of the families having annual income less than 1 lakh.

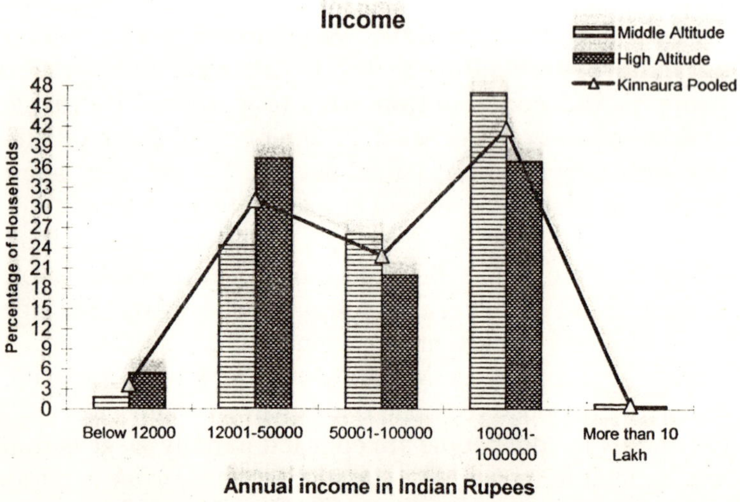

Figure 1: Line-bar Diagram Showing Distribution of Households according to Annual Income

Table 3
Population Distribution of Kinnaura (Pooled) according to Age and Occupation.

Age	Labour		Private Service		Agri/ Horticulture		Govt. Service		Business		Retired Person		Students		Contractor		Lama		Total	
	N	%	N	%	N	%	N	%	N	%	N	%	N	%	N	%	N	%	N	%
0-4	0	0	0	0	0	0	0	0	0	0	0	0	437 (Infants & Toddlers)	100.0	0	0	0	0	437	100
5-9	0	0	0	0	0	0	0	0	0	0	0	0	479	99.8	0	0	1	0.2	480	100
10-14	0	0	0	0	2	0.4	0	0	1	0.2	0	0	516	99.2	0	0	1	0.2	520	100
15-19	488	95.3	1	0.2	13	2.5	3	0.6	2	0.4	0	0	0	0	0	0	5	1.0	512	100
20-24	364	74.4	5	1.0	88	18.0	19	3.9	1	0.2	0	0	0	0	1	0.2	11	2.2	489	100
25-29	228	45.1	8	1.6	167	33.1	60	11.9	25	5.0	1	0.2	0	0	3	0.6	13	2.6	505	100
30-34	132	32.9	4	1.0	152	37.9	78	19.5	21	5.2	0	0	0	0	4	1.0	10	2.5	401	100
35-39	125	33.9	4	1.1	148	40.1	61	16.5	17	4.6	1	0.3	0	0	3	0.8	10	2.7	369	100
40-44	97	35.8	0	0	97	35.8	60	22.1	5	1.8	4	1.5	0	0	0	0	8	3.0	271	100
45-49	81	35.2	1	0.4	85	37.0	48	20.9	4	1.7	6	2.6	0	0	0	0	5	2.2	230	100
50-54	79	40.5	2	1.0	79	40.5	25	12.8	5	2.6	3	1.5	0	0	0	0	2	1.0	195	100
55-59	49	35.5	0	0	64	46.4	17	12.3	4	2.9	2	1.4	0	0	0	0	2	1.4	138	100
60-64	57	37.3	0	0	76	49.7	2	1.3	3	2.0	11	7.2	0	0	1	0.7	3	2.0	153	100
65-69	33	34.0	0	0	52	53.6	1	1.0	1	1.0	2	2.1	0	0	1	1.0	7	7.2	97	100
70-74	24	32.9	0	0	38	52.1	1	1.4	0		4	5.5	0	0	1	1.4	5	6.8	73	100
75-79	21	47.7	0	0	17	38.6	1	2.3	0		3	6.8	0	0	0	0	2	4.5	44	100
80+	23	41.8	0	0	26	47.3	0		0		3	5.5	0	0	0	0	3	5.5	55	100
Total	1801	36.2	25	0.5	1104	22.2	376	7.6	89	1.8	40	0.8	1432	28.8	14	0.3	88	1.8	4969	100

All columns from Labour to Lama are grouped under the heading "Occupation".

Table 4
Population Distribution of Kinnaura of Middle Altitudes according to Age and Occupation.

Age	Labour		Private Service		Agri/ Horticulture		Govt. Service		Business		Retired Person		Students		Contractor		Lama		Total	
	N	%	N	%	N	%	N	%	N	%	N	%	N	%	N	%	N	%	N	%
0-4	0	0.0	0	0.0	0	0.0	0	0.0	0	0.0	0	0.0	211 (Infants & Toddlers)	100	0	0.0	0	0.0	211	100
5-9	0	0.0	0	0.0	0	0.0	0	0.0	0	0.0	0	0.0	241	100	0	0.0	0	0.0	241	100
10-14	0	0.0	0	0.0	0	0.0	0	0.0	1	0.4	0	0.0	255	99.6	0	0.0	0	0.0	256	100
15-19	239	96.0	0	0.0	5	2.0	2	0.8	1	0.4	0	0.0	0	0.0	0	0.0	2	0.8	249	100
20-24	178	75.1	0	0.0	42	17.7	14	5.9	0	0.0	0	0.0	0	0.0	1	0.4	2	0.8	237	100
25-29	110	42.3	3	1.2	87	33.5	32	12.3	20	7.7	1	0.4	0	0.0	3	1.2	4	1.5	260	100
30-34	66	32.0	3	1.5	76	36.9	37	18.0	15	7.3	0	0.0	0	0.0	4	1.9	5	2.4	206	100
35-39	50	30.9	3	1.9	57	35.2	36	22.2	9	5.6	1	0.6	0	0.0	2	1.2	4	2.5	162	100
40-44	51	39.5	0	0.0	37	28.7	31	24.0	5	3.9	2	1.6	0	0.0	0	0.0	3	2.3	129	100
45-49	40	34.5	0	0.0	41	35.3	27	23.3	2	1.7	3	2.6	0	0.0	0	0.0	3	2.6	116	100
50-54	39	45.9	0	0.0	28	32.9	10	11.8	3	3.5	3	3.5	0	0.0	0	0.0	2	2.4	85	100
55-59	25	33.3	0	0.0	32	42.7	13	17.3	2	2.7	1	1.3	0	0.0	0	0.0	2	2.7	75	100
60-64	28	35.9	0	0.0	37	47.4	1	1.3	2	2.6	7	9.0	0	0.0	1	1.3	2	2.6	78	100
65-69	17	32.1	0	0.0	25	47.2	0	0.0	1	1.9	2	3.8	0	0.0	1	1.9	7	13.2	53	100
70-74	13	30.2	0	0.0	22	51.2	0	0.0	0	0.0	3	7.0	0	0.0	1	2.3	4	9.3	43	100
75-79	12	42.9	0	0.0	14	50.0	0	0.0	0	0.0	1	3.6	0	0.0	0	0.0	1	3.6	28	100
80+	15	44.1	0	0.0	14	41.2	0	0.0	0	0.0	3	8.8	0	0.0	0	0.0	2	5.9	34	100
Total	883	35.9	9	0.4	517	21.0	203	8.2	61	2.5	27	1.1	707	28.7	13	0.5	43	1.7	2463	100

Occupation columns: Labour through Lama.

Table 5

Population Distribution of Kinnaura of High Altitudes According to Age and Occupation.

Age	Occupation																			
	Labour		*Private Service*		*Agri/ Horticulture*		*Govt. Service*		*Business*		*Retired Person*		*Students*		*Contractor*		*Lama*		*Total*	
	N	%	N	%	N	%	N	%	N	%	N	%	N	%	N	%	N	%	N	%
0-4	0	0.0	0	0.0	0	0.0	0	0.0	0	0.0	0	0.0	226	100	0	0.0	0	0.0	226	100
5-9	0	0.0	0	0.0	0	0.0	0	0.0	0	0.0	0	0.0	238	99.6	0	0.0	1	0.4	239	100
10-14	0	0.0	0	0.0	2	0.8	0	0.0	0	0.0	0	0.0	261	98.9	0	0.0	1	0.4	264	100
15-19	249	94.7	1	0.4	8	3.0	1	0.4	1	0.4	0	0.0	0	0.0	0	0.0	3	1.1	263	100
20-24	186	73.8	5	2.0	46	18.3	5	2.0	1	0.4	0	0.0	0	0.0	0	0.0	9	3.6	252	100
25-29	118	48.2	5	2.0	80	32.7	28	11.4	5	2.0	0	0.0	0	0.0	0	0.0	9	3.7	245	100
30-34	66	33.8	1	0.5	76	39.0	41	21.0	6	3.1	0	0.0	0	0.0	0	0.0	5	2.6	195	100
35-39	75	36.2	1	0.5	91	44.0	25	12.1	8	3.9	0	0.0	0	0.0	1	.5	6	2.9	207	100
40-44	46	32.4	0	0.0	60	42.3	29	20.4	0	0.0	2	1.4	0	0.0	0	0.0	5	3.5	142	100
45-49	41	36.0	1	0.9	44	38.6	21	18.4	2	1.8	3	2.6	0	0.0	0	0.0	2	1.8	114	100
50-54	40	36.4	2	1.8	51	46.4	15	13.6	2	1.8	0	0.0	0	0.0	0	0.0	0	0.0	110	100
55-59	24	38.1	0	0.0	32	50.8	4	6.3	2	3.2	1	1.6	0	0.0	0	0.0	0	0.0	63	100
60-64	29	38.7	0	0.0	39	52.0	1	1.3	1	1.3	4	5.3	0	0.0	0	0.0	1	1.3	75	100
65-69	16	36.4	0	0.0	27	61.4	1	2.3	0	0.0	0	0.0	0	0.0	0	0.0	0	0.0	44	100
70-74	11	36.7	0	0.0	16	53.3	1	3.3	0	0.0	1	3.3	0	0.0	0	0.0	1	3.3	30	100
75-79	9	56.3	0	0.0	3	18.8	1	6.3	0	0.0	2	12.5	0	0.0	0	0.0	1	6.3	16	100
80+	8	38.1	0	0.0	12	57.1	0	0.0	0	0.0	0	0.0	0	0.0	0	0.0	1	4.8	21	100
Total	918	36.6	16	0.6	587	23.4	173	6.9	28	1.1	13	.5	725	28.9	1	.0.0	45	1.8	2506	100

Table 6
Distribution of Kinnaura Households of Middle and High Altitude according to Annual Income (Kinnaur, Himachal Pradesh)

	Middle Altitude		*High Altitude*		*Kinnaura (Pooled)*	
Annual Income	*N*	*%*	*N*	*%*	*N*	*%*
Below 12000	7	1.8	23	5.4	30	3.7
12001-50000	96	24.4	159	37.3	255	31.1
50001-100000	103	26.1	85	20.0	188	22.9
100001-1000000	185	47.0	157	36.9	342	41.7
More than 10 Lakh	3	0.8	2	0.5	5	0.6
Total	394	100	426	100	820	100

EDUCATIONAL CHARACTERISTICS

Education is a process of refinement in human knowledge, behaviour and practice; its institutionalisation is very recent (hardly 500 years ago) phenomena in the way of human evolution. In country like India it started with rise of British rule, again it was available for certain group of people not for all. The universalization of Education in India was taken place hardly three to four decade ago. Further, educational attainment of tribals and other weaker section of country is limited to higher secondary level very meagre proportion of this section attain higher level of education as they were in the last of the queue. Education is an integral part of demographic analysis; hence it is an indicator of development too.

Educational Attainment

Education is an indicator of development; the human behaviour and practices are greatly influenced by educational attainment, though the educational attainment of a population itself is influenced by development of the region, availability of educational institution, its affordability, efficient transport system, employment opportunities etc. To measure the rate of literacy or educational attainment of a population is an integral part of population studies, as it affects the reproductive behaviour, use of contraceptives, health seeking behaviour, hygiene practices, and occupational profile and status of women.

Table 7
Distribution of Kinnaura (Pooled) according to Age-Specific Educational Attainment.

	Level of Education																	
	Illiterate		*Literate*		*Primary*		*Middle*		*High School*		*Higher Secondary*		*Graduate and Above*		*Professional and Technically Qualify*		*Total*	
Age	*N*	%	*N*	%	*N*	%	*N*	%	*N*	%	*N*	%	*N*	%	*N*	%	*N*	%
0-4	0	0.0	0	0.0	7	100	0	0.0	0	0.0	0	0.0	0	0.0	0	0.0	7	100
5-9	5	1.2	32	7.7	379	91.1	0	0.0	0	0.0	0	0.0	0	0.0	0	0.0	416	100
10-14	3	0.6	3	0.6	198	38.2	278	53.6	35	6.7	1	0.2	1	0.2	0	0.0	519	100
15-19	5	1.0	3	0.6	13	2.5	128	24.8	230	44.5	88	17.0	47	9.1	3	0.6	517	100
20-24	11	2.2	1	0.2	23	4.7	95	19.3	111	22.6	98	20.0	147	29.9	5	1.0	491	100
25-29	40	7.8	9	1.8	62	12.2	108	21.2	120	23.5	64	12.5	101	19.8	6	1.2	510	100
30-34	54	13.5	15	3.7	57	14.2	97	24.2	91	22.7	36	9.0	48	12.0	3	0.7	401	100
35-39	93	25.2	23	6.2	71	19.2	68	18.4	65	17.6	20	5.4	27	7.3	2	0.5	369	100
40-44	84	30.9	29	10.7	46	16.9	43	15.8	35	12.9	4	1.5	27	9.9	4	1.5	272	100
45-49	72	31.3	25	10.9	52	22.6	40	17.4	17	7.4	3	1.3	18	7.8	3	1.3	230	100
50-54	103	52.8	18	9.2	28	14.4	27	13.8	9	4.6	3	1.5	5	2.6	2	1.0	195	100
55-59	71	51.4	14	10.1	30	21.7	11	8.0	5	3.6	2	1.4	3	2.2	2	1.4	138	100
60-64	101	66.0	16	10.5	20	13.1	7	4.6	3	2.0	2	1.3	2	1.3	2	1.3	153	100
65-69	75	76.5	8	8.2	12	12.2	2	2.0	0	0.0	0	0.0	0	0.0	1	1.0	98	100
70-74	64	84.2	1	1.3	3	3.9	4	5.3	2	2.6	1	1.3	1	1.3	0	0.0	76	100
75-79	40	87.0	4	8.7	1	2.2	1	2.2	0	0.0	0	0.0	0	0.0	0	0.0	46	100
80+	49	84.5	3	5.2	3	5.2	2	3.4	1	1.7	0	0.0	0	0.0	0	0.0	58	100
Total	870	19.4	204	4.5	1005	22.4	911	20.3	724	16.1	322	7.2	427	9.5	33	0.7	4496	100

Age and sex wise educational attainment of study population is given in Table 7, 8, 9 and Figure 2. It is apparent from Figure 2 that males have better educational attainment as compared to females. According to pooled data (Table 7) among the peoples of age groups 5-24 the educational attainment is approximately 99 per cent, but as age increases the percentage of illiterates raised proportionately. This is also applicable for middle and high altitude Kinnaura as evident from Table 8 and 9, but in higher age groups (25 years and onwards) the percentage of illiterates are greater in proportion in high altitude as compared to middle altitude. It is very natural because 20 years ago there were hardly proper educational facilities, hence educational attainment were also poor among older people. The other important factor of poor educational attainment among older peoples were undeveloped transport system, no means of communication, least exposure to outer world as there were no communication media like radio and television. The development of the area is considered only after Chinese aggression on Tibet in seventies. Further in Kinnaur 19.4 per cent population is illiterate, 4.5 per cent are just literate, 22.4 per cent attained education upto primary or within primary (class 1-5), 20.3 per cent are middle (class 6-8), 16.1 per cent are high school, 7.2 per cent are higher secondary, 9.5 are graduate and above and only 0.7 per cent were technically/professionally (B.Ed, MBBS, Engineering etc.) qualified. Whereas in high altitude illiterate are more as compared to middle altitude, same in case of with the proportion of people attained education at the level of primary and middle, but in case of higher educational attainment (high school and onward) the proportion of middle altitude Kinnaura is greater (Figure 3). The age wise variation in educational attainment clearly indicates that the trend of attaining higher education is increasing recently.

Literacy Rate

Literacy rates are also known as crude Literacy rates, denote the number of literate, i.e. persons who are able to read and write with some understanding in a population at a specific

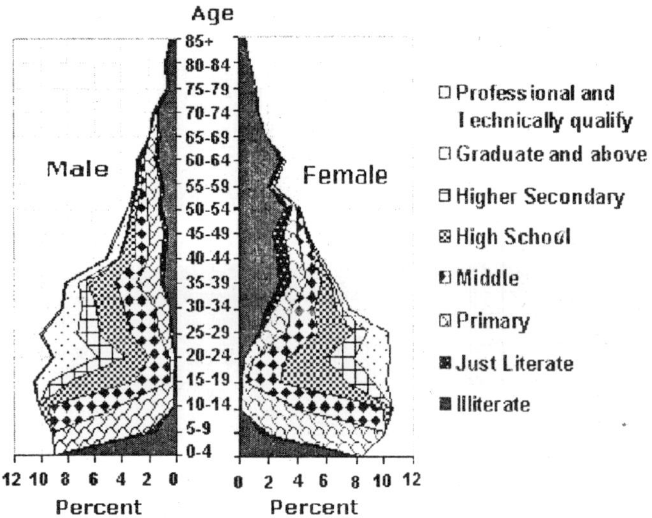

Figure 2: Educational Attainment of the Population by Age and Sex

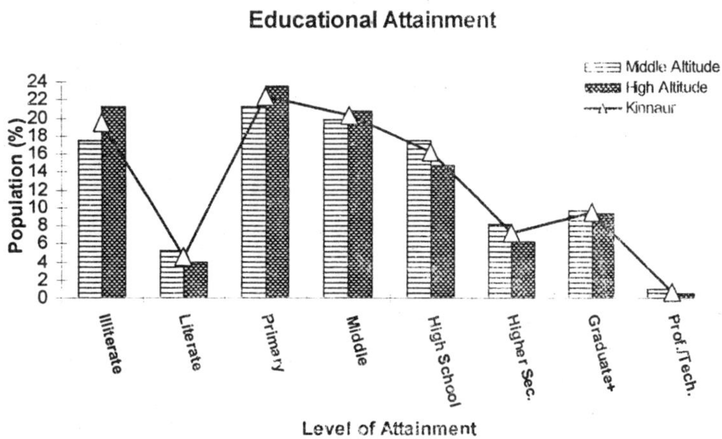

Figure 3: Educational Attainment of the Kinnaura of Middle and High Altitude

time. In the present study, literacy rates both as percentage of total population, and as percentages of population aged 5 years and over have also been estimated. These measures have also been calculated for either sex to assess the gender difference, which is substantial in many developing countries, including

Table 8
Distribution of Middle Altitude Kinnaura according to Age and Level of Education

	Level of Education																	
	Illiterate		*Literate*		*Primary*		*Middle*		*High School*		*Higher Secondary*		*Graduate and Above*		*Professional and Technically Qualify*		*Total*	
Age	N	%	N	%	N	%	N	%	N	%	N	%	N	%	N	%	N	%
0-4	0	0.0	0	0.0	6	46.2	0	0.0	0	0.0	0	0.0	0		0		6	100
5-9	3	1.4	17	8.0	193	90.6	0	0.0	0	0.0	0	0.0	0		0		213	100
10-14	1	0.4	2	0.8	92	36.1	143	56.1	16	6.3	0	0.0	1	.4	0		255	100
15-19	4	1.6	1	0.4	4	1.6	57	22.6	109	43.3	48	19.0	27	10.7	2	.8	252	100
20-24	5	2.1	0	0.0	5	2.1	33	13.9	65	27.3	53	22.3	74	31.1	3	1.3	238	100
25-29	17	6.4	4	1.5	30	11.3	57	21.5	67	25.3	39	14.7	48	18.1	3	1.1	265	100
30-34	23	11.2	11	5.3	26	12.6	45	21.8	52	25.2	21	10.2	26	12.6	2	1.0	206	100
35-39	25	15.4	13	8.0	25	15.4	32	19.8	39	24.1	12	7.4	15	9.3	1	.6	162	100
40-44	35	27.1	13	10.1	18	14.0	28	21.7	17	13.2	2	1.6	14	10.9	2	1.6	129	100
45-49	37	31.9	10	8.6	29	25.0	18	15.5	10	8.6	3	2.6	7	6.0	2	1.7	116	100
50-54	38	44.7	12	14.1	10	11.8	13	15.3	7	8.2	1	1.2	3	3.5	1	1.2	85	100
55-59	34	45.3	9	12.0	16	21.3	6	8.0	5	6.7	2	2.7	1	1.3	2	2.7	75	100
60-64	48	61.5	10	12.8	10	12.8	5	6.4	3	3.8	0	0.0	0		2	2.6	78	100
65-69	37	68.5	7	13.0	7	13.0	2	3.7	0	0.0	0	0.0	0		1	1.9	54	100
70-74	35	77.8	1	2.2	2	4.4	3	6.7	2	4.4	1	2.2	1	2.2	0		45	100
75-79	24	80.0	4	13.3	1	3.3	1	3.3	0	0.0	0	0.0	0		0		30	100
80+	27	75.0	3	8.3	3	8.3	2	5.6	1	2.8	0	0.0	0		0		36	100
Total	393	17.5	117	5.2	477	21.2	445	19.8	393	17.5	182	8.1	217	9.6	21	[illegible]	2245	100

Table 9
Distribution of High Altitude Kinnaura according to Age and Level of Education

	Level of Education																	
	Illiterate		*Literate*		*Primary*		*Middle*		*High School*		*Higher Secondary*		*Graduate and Above*		*Professional and Technically Qualify*		*Total*	
Age	N	%	N	%	N	%	N	%	N	%	N	%	N	%	N	%	N	%
0-4	0	0.0	0	0.0	1	100	0	0.0	0	0.0	0	0.0	0	0.0	0	0.0	1	100
5-9	2	1.0	15	7.4	186	91.6	0	0.0	0	0.0	0	0.0	0	0.0	0	0.0	203	100
10-14	2	0.8	1	0.4	106	40.2	135	51.1	19	7.2	1	0.4	0	0.0	0	0.0	264	100
15-19	1	0.4	2	0.8	9	3.4	71	26.8	121	45.7	40	15.1	20	7.5	1	0.4	265	100
20-24	6	2.4	1	0.4	18	7.1	62	24.5	46	18.2	45	17.8	73	28.9	2	0.8	253	100
25-29	23	9.4	5	2.0	32	13.1	51	20.8	53	21.6	25	10.2	53	21.6	3	1.2	245	100
30-34	31	15.9	4	2.1	31	15.9	52	26.7	39	20.0	15	7.7	22	11.3	1	0.5	195	100
35-39	68	32.9	10	4.8	46	22.2	36	17.4	26	12.6	8	3.9	12	5.8	1	0.5	207	100
40-44	49	34.3	16	11.2	28	19.6	15	10.5	18	12.6	2	1.4	13	9.1	2	1.4	143	100
45-49	35	30.7	15	13.2	23	20.2	22	19.3	7	6.1	0	0.0	11	9.6	1	0.9	114	100
50-54	65	59.1	6	5.5	18	16.4	14	12.7	2	1.8	2	1.8	2	1.8	1	0.9	110	100
55-59	37	58.7	5	7.9	14	22.2	5	7.9	0	0.0	0	0.0	2	3.2	0	0.0	63	100
60-64	53	70.7	6	8.0	10	13.3	2	2.7	0	0.0	2	2.7	2	2.7	0	0.0	75	100
65-69	38	86.4	1	2.3	5	11.4	0	0.0	0	0.0	0	0.0	0	0.0	0	0.0	44	100
70-74	29	93.5	0	0.0	1	3.2	1	3.2	0	0.0	0	0.0	0	0.0	0	0.0	31	100
75-79	16	100	0	0.0	0	0.0	0	0.0	0	0.0	0	0.0	0	0.0	0	0.0	16	100
80+	22	100	0	0.0	0	0.0	0	0.0	0	0.0	0	0.0	0	0.0	0	0.0	22	100
Total	477	21.2	87	3.9	528	23.5	466	20.7	331	14.7	140	6.2	210	9.3	12	0.5	2251	100

India. In 1991, the national literacy rate has been estimated 52.2 percent for the population aged 7 years onwards, for 2001 this estimation is 65.5 per cent (Census of India, 1991 and 2001). As compared to this, the literacy rate for Kinnaura is quite higher 80.47 per cent (for the population of age 5 years onwards). Further, it is slightly higher from the estimation literacy rate (for the population of age 7 years onwards) of census (2001) for Himachal Pradesh state (77.13 per cent) and Kinnaur district (79.68 per cent) but less than the Kerala state (90.9 per cent) of the country (Census, 2001). If comparison made for estimation of literacy rates of census 1991 and 2001 for Kinnaur district, which is 58.36 per cent and 79.68 per cent respectively, there is approximately three-fold increment in one decade only. Further, this difference is more predominant between sexes, among males this increment is less, from 72.04 per cent in 1991 to 87.72 percent in 2001 (around 20 per cent only), while among females this increment is approximately (75 per cent) three-fourth from 42.04 per cent of 1991 to 70.68 per cent in 2001. when the literacy rates for males and females (as percentage of population aged 5 years and above) in the total study population were compared with estimation of census 2001, for Kinnaur district almost similar pattern of differentials as elaborated above have been observed (Table 10). This is a good indication for this tribal population of the study area. This positive change taken place because of continuous efforts for improving literacy, encouragement for enrolling children for school education, opening of schools in remotest villages, provisions for free education and scholarship for tribal people, enhancement in transportation system, women empowerment, implication of Panchayati Raj system and finally over all development of the region.

Table 10 also showing inter-regional difference in the same population, in middle altitude literacy rate is higher (81.66 per cent) as compared to high altitude (77.60 per cent), again in high altitude the sex differential is greater, only 69.39 per cent females are literate as compared to 85.92 per cent of males, whereas in middle altitude this gap is slightly narrow 74.61 per cent and 88.81 per cent respectively for females and males;

further, population pyramid (Figure 4) making it more explicit as showing age-specific literacy percentages among males and females.

Table 10
Literacy Rates among Middle and High Altitude Kinnaura of Kinnaur District Himachal Pradesh

	Literacy Rate					
	As % of Total Population			*As % of Population Aged 5 Years and Above*		
Regions	*Male*	*Female*	*Person*	*Male*	*Female*	*Person*
Middle Altitude	81.10	68.38	74.71	88.81	74.61	81.66
High Altitude	77.77	63.48	70.62	85.92	69.39	77.60
Kinnaur (Pooled)	79.42	65.92	72.65	88.49	72.59	80.47

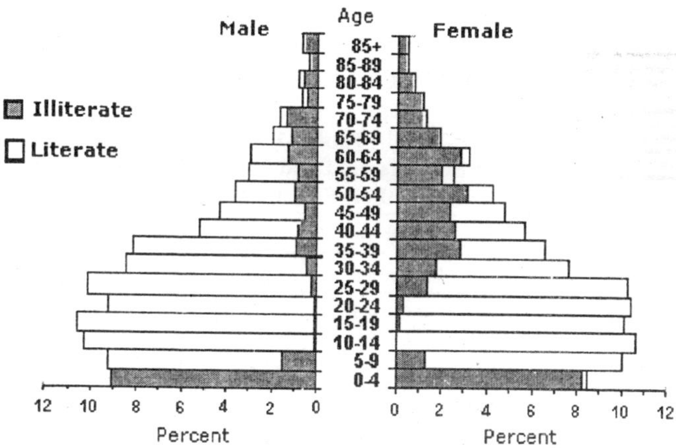

Figure 4: Population Pyramid of Kinnaura Showing Literacy Percentage among Males and Females

MARITAL CHARACTERISTICS

Marriage is a social institution; socially recognized threshold to institutionalized the biological process of reproduction in human being. Marital characteristics of a population is widely affected by biological characteristics such as age, sex, race; socio-economic characteristics viz. custom, mores, taboos, income, occupation, education and environmental features of a place e.g. geography, climate etc. Finally marital status is an important factor in population dynamics as it affects fertility, mortality and migration in various extents, It also affects schooling and labour force participation.

Marital Status

In the present study the distribution of population as per marital status gives an indication (Table 11 and Figure 5) that marriage is almost universal phenomena; the proportion of unmarried (never married) declines with increasing age but not vanishing completely, the proportion of ever married rises in corresponding amount with increasing of current age; widowhood and divorce seem to reduce the married population as age increases, Buddhist monk (religious priests) are not allowed to married, hence the proportion of never married in older age groups included their fraction in both the sexes, children under 14 years of age are never married,

Table 11
Distribution of Ever Married and Never Married Kinnaura according to their Sex and Current Age.

	Males			*Females*		
Current Age	*Married*	*Unmarried*	*Total*	*Married*	*Unmarried*	*Total*
0-4	0.0	9.1	9.1	0.0	8.4	8.4
5-9	0.0	9.2	9.2	0.0	10.0	10.0
10-14	0.0	10.2	10.2	0.0	10.5	10.6
15-19	0.2	10.5	10.6	0.6	9.5	10.1
20-24	1.8	7.4	9.2	4.3	6.2	10.4
25-29	5.5	4.6	10.2	6.8	3.5	10.3
30-34	7.0	1.5	8.5	6.1	1.5	7.6
35-39	6.8	1.4	8.2	5.8	0.8	6.6
40-44	4.8	0.4	5.2	5.0	0.7	5.7
45-49	4.0	0.4	4.5	4.1	0.7	4.8
50-54	3.0	0.6	3.6	3.3	0.9	4.2
55-59	2.7	0.4	3.0	1.8	0.7	2.5
60-64	2.3	0.6	2.9	2.3	0.9	3.2
65-69	1.6	0.4	2.0	1.4	0.5	1.9
70-74	1.4	0.3	1.7	1.0	0.4	1.4
75-79	0.4	0.2	0.6	0.6	0.6	1.2
80-84	0.5	0.3	0.8	0.2	0.5	0.7
85+	0.1	0.2	0.4	0.3	0.2	0.4
Total	42.1	57.9	100.0	43.5	56.5	100.0

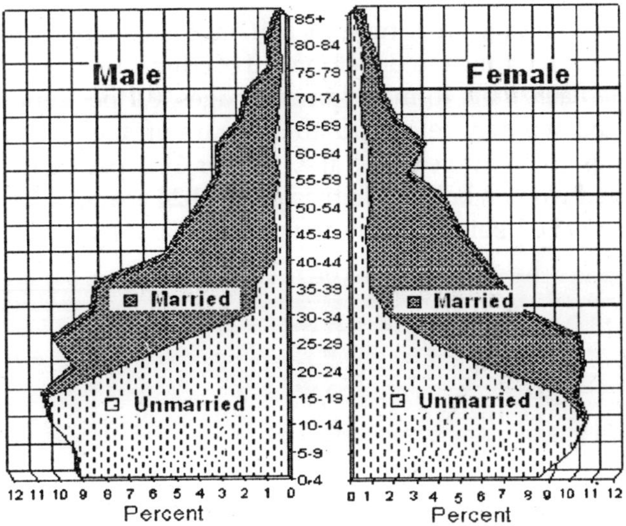

Figure 5: Marital Status among Kinnaura

this is a **transition in age at marriage** and custom and practices of marriage. As already discussed Kinnaura are polyandrous tribal group, earlier all the brothers were married altogether alongwith eldest one, so the youngest get married in early ages, in the present study, the minimum age at marriage was recorded as 10 years, but now-a-days this practice is breaking down and monogamy is being predominant, hence currently nobody of below 14 years of age were found married. Proportion of married males are lower than females in the 15-19, 20-24 and 25-29 years of age groups because of increasing trend of monogamy and lower age at marriage of females. The situation is reverse for age group 30-39 and 55-74 in these age groups males are proportionately more married than females; this is because of polyandry. The age groups 40-44, 45-49, 50-54, and 75 and above are exceptions, though in those days polyandry was predominant practice but the proportion of married females are slightly higher than the males.

Among currently married males, majority of them 57.3 per cent belongs to 25-44 years of age group, only 0.4 per cent belongs to 15-19 years of age group, this shows a great and positive change in Kinnaura marriage, inclination towards regular schooling and development of educational institutions. Still females start to marry in early ages, 0.1 per cent of total married women belong to 10-14 years of age, 1.4 per cent belongs to 15-19 years of age, further 11.3 per cent of total married women belongs to the age of 10-24 years, 54.3 per cent total married belong to the age group of 25-44 years.

Chapter 6

MARRIAGE-POLYANDRY

Marriage is an institution evolved to regulate the sexual relation. It is the basis of human society and family. Without marriage the existence of family and kinship is not possible. It provides a legally and socially sanctioned union between one or more husbands and one or more wives that accords status to their offspring and is regulated by laws, rules, customs, beliefs, and attitudes that prescribe the rights and duties of the partners. The universality of marriage within different societies and cultures is attributed to the many basic social and personal functions for which it provides structure, such as procreation, sexual gratification and regulation, care of children and their education and socialization, regulation of lines of descent, division of labour between the sexes, economic production and consumption, and satisfaction of personal needs for affection, status, and companionship. Predominantly today human being is monogamous but according to classical evolutionist- the marriage is evolved from sexual promiscuity to group marriage than polygynandry, than polyandry/ polygyny and later on monogamy came into existence. Recently homosexual marriages are being recognized and legalized. In 2000 The Netherlands became the first country to legalize homosexual marriages. Several other countries have extended legal rights to homosexual union. The study of marriage, its evolution and transition is very important as its form and structure were changing throughout the human history. In country like India wide variation can be observed with reference to various aspects of marriage. Even form of marriage, way of acquiring spouses, rituals related to it are found varying from one group to other as well as one region to other. Kinnaura is the group, who are still practicing the earliest form of marriage i.e. polyandry in which a female married with two or more males who are generally uterine brothers. In population studies the marriage has special significance as it is the point from where a union is socially permitted for reproduction. In this chapter different aspect of marriage among Kinnaura is discussed in the light of national and regional scenario.

Age at Marriage

Marriage by and large, exposes a person to reproductive activity. Further, it is also determined by various social, economic and biological determinants and varies from place to place and community to community. As evident from Table 1 the mean age at marriage for Kinnaura male was estimated as 22.80 years, while for females 19.58 years. The lowest age at marriage was recorded as 10 years for both males and females; the highest age at marriage for male was 48 years and for females 39 years. The average age at marriage is almost equal in middle and high altitude and more or less same in both the sexes, for males it is 23.5 years and 22.55 years, while for females it is 19.25 and 19.93 years respectively in middle and high altitude area, as also evident from box plot and error bar diagramme (Figure 1 and 2). There is significant difference in age at marriage of males and females. Simultaneously, the high altitude women have significantly higher age at marriage as compared to the women of middle altitude. Further, the independent *t* test applied to find out the differences between mean ages at marriage of sexes of different ecological zones (i.e. middle and high altitude) are displayed in Table 2. It is apparent that significant difference exists in mean age at marriage of sexes as Levene's test is significant with high F value 63.39 and $p<0.0001$, whereas $t=16.8$ with $p<0.0001$. Further the test shows that there is non-significant difference in means of age at marriage of middle and high altitude males and females.

Table 1

Age at Marriage among Middle and High Altitude Kinnaura of Kinnaur District Himachal Pradesh

	Middle Altitude				*High Altitude*				*Kinnaur (Pooled)*			
	Male		*Female*		*Male*		*Female*		*Male*		*Female*	
Age at Marriage	*N*	*%*	*N*	*%*	*N*	*%*	*N*	*%*	*N*	*%*	*N*	*%*
10-15	12	2.2	57	10.3	18	3.5	48	8.9	30	2.8	105	9.6
16-20	180	33.5	343	61.8	184	35.6	297	55.2	364	34.5	640	58.6
21-25	208	38.7	124	22.3	197	38.1	150	27.9	405	38.4	274	25.1
26-30	99	18.4	25	4.5	83	16.1	35	6.5	182	17.3	60	5.5
31+	38	7.1	6	1.1	35	6.8	8	1.5	73	6.9	14	1.3
Total	537	100.0	555	100.0	517	100.0	538	100.0	1054	100.0	1093	100.0
Mean	23.05		19.25		22.55		19.93		22.80		19.58	
S.E. of Mean	±0.204		±0.152		±0.224		±0.168		±0.155		±0.114	
Median	22.00		18.00		22.00		19.00		22.00		19.00	
Mode	20		18		19		19(a)		20		18	
Std. Deviation	±4.712		±3.579		±5.102		±3.888		±4.916		±3.748	
Variance	22.201		12.807		26.035		15.120		24.163		14.049	
Range	31		25		38		29		38		29	
Minimum	10		10		10		10		10		10	
Maximum	41		35		48		39		48		39	

a Multiple modes exist. The smallest value is shown

Chi square test for males x2 =2.69 is insignificant at 9 d.f. (p>.05)

Chi square test for females x2 =8.23 is insignificant value (8.34) at 9 d.f. (p>.05)

Table 2
Showing Levene's Test and Independent *t* Test for Age at Marriage

	Levene's Test		*T-test*				
Variances' Assumptions	*F*	*p-value*	*t*	*df*	*p-value (2-tailed)*	*Mean Difference*	*Std. Error Difference*
Among Sexes							
Equal variances assumed	63.393	0.000	16.918	2135	0.000	3.19	0.189
Equal variances not assumed			16.832	1957.65	0.000	3.19	0.190
Among Males of Middle and High Altitude							
Equal variances assumed	1.811	0.179	1.516	1046	0.130	0.46	0.304
Equal variances not assumed			1.514	1032.20	0.130	0.46	0.304
Among Females of Middle and High Altitude							
Equal variances assumed	1.204	0.273	-3.041	1087	0.002	-0.69	0.227
Equal variances not assumed			-3.037	1073.52	0.002	-0.69	0.227

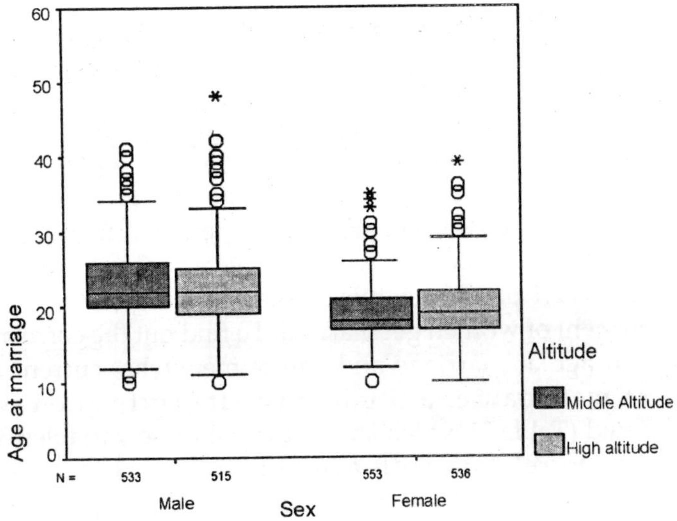

Figure 1: Box Plot of Age at Marriage Showing the Median, Quartiles and Extreme Values among Males and Females of Middle and High Altitude.

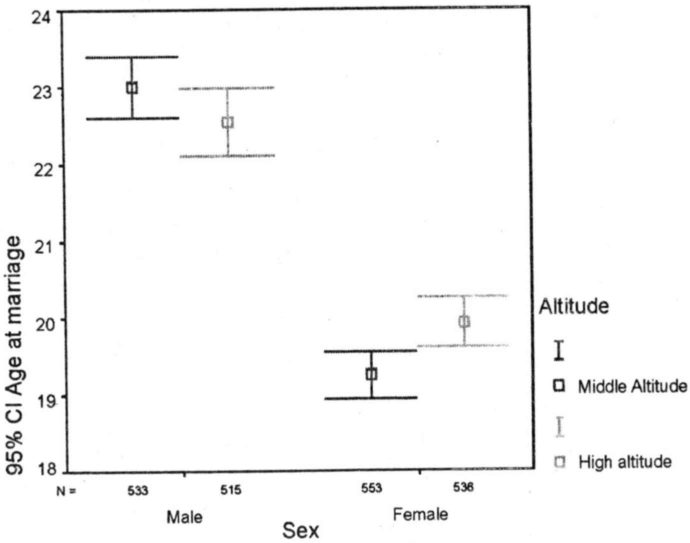

Figure 2: Error Bar Diagramme Showing Standard Error of Mean of Age at Marriage among Males and Females of Middle and High Altitude

Majority of females (68.2 per cent) get married within 20 years of age, early marriages in 10-15 years were recorded only among 9.6 per cent, while late marriage at 31 years onwards were 1.3 per cent. Among males approximately 73 per cent get married at 16-25 years, marriages at early ages 10-15 years is lesser as compared to females, but late marriages at the age of 31 years and onward is greater (6.9 per cent) than females. The females get married within 20 years of age in middle altitude is 72.1 per cent, while at this age in high altitude only 64.1 per cent of women get married. To find out the correlation between age at marriage and age at menarche, current age, age at menopause, altitude bivariate correlation were calculated (Table 3) which shows that all these variables have positive correlation with age at marriage. The multiple regression analysis (Table 4) exhibits that only age at menarche and altitude imposes significant impact on age at marriage of Kinnaura women, whereas current age and age at menopause imposes non-significantly positive impact. Multiple regression coefficient R^2=0.179 is significant at $p<0.001$ with F value 13.16. Still age at marriage of a woman is determined only 17.9 per cent by these predictors rest 82.1 per cent is decided by other predictors.

Table 3
Bivariate Correlation between Age at Marriage, Age at Menarche, Current Age, Age at Menopause and Altitude for Kinnaura Women.

	Age at Marriage	*Age at Menarche*	*Current Age*	*Age at Menopause*	*Altitude*
Age at Marriage	1.000				
Age at Menarche	0.384	1.000			
Current Age	0.086	0.038**	1.000		
Age at Menopause	0.224**	0.261**	0.331**	1.000	
Altitude	0.164*	0.039	0.039	0.291**	1.000

**Correlation is significant at the 0.01 level (2-tailed).
*Correlation is significant at the 0.05 level (2-tailed).

Among males approximately 73 per cent get married between 16 and 25 years of age. Marriages at early ages between 10 and 15 years of age are less frequent (2.8 per cent only) as compared to females; but late marriages at the age of 31 years and onward are greater (6.9 per cent) than females. There is no significant difference in age at marriage of males and females of middle and high altitude Kinnaura ($p > 0.05$), Chi-square test gives a value of $\chi^2 = 2.69$ for males and $\chi^2 = 8.23$ for females at 9 d.f. The females get married within 20 years of age in middle altitude is 72.1 per cent, while at this age in high altitude only 64.1 per cent of women get married.

Table 4
Result of Multiple Regression Analysis (Dependent Variable Age at Marriage) for Kinnaura Women.

Independent Variable	*Zero-order Correlation*	β_1	*SE*	*Standardized Beta*	*t*	*p-value*
Age at Menarche	0.384	0.909	0.154	0.356	5.887	0.000
Age at Menopause	0.224	0.096	0.080	0.081	1.202	0.231
Current Age	0.086	0.014	0.022	0.040	0.653	0.514
Altitude	0.164	0.001	0.000	0.126	2.056	0.041

Multiple Regression Coefficient R = 0.423, $R^2 = 0.179$, SE = 3.418, F = 13.16 and $p<0.0001$.

Table 5
Mean Age at Marriage among Tribal and Non-Tribal Population of Himachal Pradesh and India.

		Mean Age at Marriage			
Country/ State/ Region	*Population Group*	*Male*	*Female*	*Difference*	*Source*
HIMALAYAN REGION					
Eastern Himalaya					
Assam					
	Semsa	22.1	18.4	3.6	Ghosh and Limbu (2002)
	Garo	–	19.6	–	Das and Saikia (1999)
	Total	28.6	25.4	3.2	1998-99 NFHS-2 (2000)
Sikkim					
	Buddhist	23.3	18.4	4.8	Bhasin and Bhasin(2000)
	Hindus	23.6	17.0	6.6	"
	Total	23.2	18.1	5.0	"
	Total	26.2	21.9	4.3	1998-99 NFHS-2 (2000)
Arunachal Pradesh		25.1	21.6	3.5	"

Contd.

Country/ State/ Region	Population Group	Male	Female	Difference	Source
Western Himalaya					
Jammu and Kashmir					
Ladakh (HA)		21.5	17.8	3.7	Bhasin and Nag (2002)
	Bodhs	21.8	18.9	2.9	"
	Baltis	21.8	17.3	4.5	"
	Brokpas	20.8	16.8	4.0	"
	Arghuns	20.2	17.1	3.1	"
	Total	27.1	22.5	4.6	1999 NFHS-2 (2000)
Himachal Pradesh					
Bilaspur		24.9	20.6	4.3	1998-99 RHS (2001)
Chamba		24.6	21.5	3.1	"
Hamirpur		25.5	20.4	5.1	"
Kangra		26.2	21.1	5.1	"
Kinnaur		*24.3*	*20.8*	*3.5*	"
Kullu		24.3	20.4	3.9	"
Lahul & Spiti		25.0	23.0	2.0	"
Mandi		24.6	20.5	4.1	"
Shimla		25.8	21.3	4.5	"
Sirmaur		24.0	20.4	3.6	"
Solan		24.3	20.9	3.4	"
Una		25.9	21.2	4.7	"
H.P.		*25.6*	*21.3*	*4.3*	"
	Total	22.2	15.6	6.6	Census (1961)
	Total	23.5	17.7	5.8	Census (1971)
	Total	24.2	19.1	5.1	Census (1981)
	Total	24.5	20.3	4.2	Census (1991)
	Rural	25.9	21.8	4.1	1992 NFHS-1 (1992)
	Urban	24.9	20.3	4.6	"
	Total	25.0	20.4	4.6	"
	Rural	27.2	23.7	3.4	1999 NFHS-2 (2000)
	Urban	26.6	21.9	4.7	"
	Total	26.7	22.1	4.6	"
Central Himalaya					
Uttaranchal (or erstwhile UP)					
	Johari Bhotia	–	19.5	–	Kapoor (1996)
	Rang Bhotia				"
	Marchha Bhotia				"
	Raji	–	14.96	–	Patra (2001)
	Jaunsaris	–	15.71	–	Kshatriya, et.al. (1997)
	Total (UP)	23.3	19.0	4.3	1998-99 NFHS-2 (2000)

Contd.

Country/ State/ Region	*Population Group*	*Male*	*Female*	*Difference*	*Source*
INDIAN PLAIN					
Madhya Pradesh		23.5	18.9	4.6	1998-99 NFHS-2 (2000)
Patalkot	Bhariya [PTG]	18.1	15.8	2.3	Pandey (2002)
	Bhariya	18.4	15.6	2.8	,,
Raigarh	Birhor [PTG]	17.8	14.7	3.1	,,
	Oraon	18.4	16.0	2.4	,,
Sarguja	Hill Korwa [PTG]	17.0	14.9	2.1	,,
	Pando	17.9	14.8	3.1	
Chhatisgarh				0.0	
Raipur	Kamar	19.6	15.8	3.8	,,
	Gond	19.7	16.0	3.7	,,
Bihar	Total	23.8	18.8	5.0	1998-99 NFHS-2 (2000)
	Santhal	22.4	19.1	3.3	Singh et.al. (1999)
	Sauria	19.6	16.6	3.0	,,
	Mal	20.7	16.4	4.3	,,
	Kumarbhag	20.5	17.7	2.8	,,
INDIA		24.9	19.7	5.2	1998-99 NFHS-2 (2000),,
Delhi		25.8	21.9	3.9	,,
Haryana		24.6	19.8	4.8	,,
Punjab		25.7	22.1	3.6	,,
Rajasthan		22.3	18.3	4.0	,,
Uttar Pradesh		23.3	19.0	4.3	,,
Orissa		26.6	21.2	5.4	,,
West Bengal		26.2	19.6	6.6	,,
Arunachal Pradesh		25.1	21.6	3.5	,,
Manipur		28.6	25.4	3.2	,,
Meghalaya		27.0	23.0	4.0	,,
Mizoram		27.0	24.1	2.9	,,
Nagaland		27.6	23.0	4.6	,,
Sikkim		26.2	21.9	4.3	,,
Goa		30.2	24.8	5.4	,,
Gujarat		24.4	20.2	4.2	,,
Maharashtra		25.3	19.8	5.5	,,
Andhra Pradesh		23.9	18.3	5.6	,,
Karnataka		26.7	20.1	6.6	,,
Kerala		27.9	21.5	6.4	,,
Tamil Nadu		26.6	20.9	5.7	
Kinnaur	*Kinnaura*	*22.8*	*19.5*	*3.3*	*Present study (2006)*
Middle altitude		*,,*	*23.0*	*19.2*	*3.8 ,,*
High Altitude		*,,*	*22.5*	*19.9*	*2.6 ,,*

HA=High Altitude Region
UP=Uttar Pradesh (India)
PTG= Primitive Tribal Group

The comparison of mean age at marriage of Kinnaura males & females with other population groups and states' average is displayed in Table 5, shows that mean age at marriage among Kinnaura (male & female) is higher than Ladakhis (Bodhs, Baltis, Brokpas and Arghuns) but lower than estimations of census of India (1991) and national family health survey (NFHS-1 and NFHS-2) of State of Himachal Pradesh. Simultaneously it was found less than average age at marriage of different Indian state as minimum age at marriage for males was recorded for Rajasthan (22.3 years), but in case of minimum age at marriage for females the lowest was estimated for Andhra Pradesh (18.3 years).

TYPE OF MARRIAGE

Four types of marriages were recorded among Kinnaura, as stated in Table 6, monogamy (83.9 per cent) is predominantly practiced followed by polyandry (13.2 per cent), polygyny (2.6 per cent) and polyandry & polygyny (0.4 per cent). Further, monogamy is slightly greater in proportion (84.3 per cent) in middle altitude than high altitude (83.1 per cent), whereas polyandry is more in high altitude (15.3 per cent) than middle altitude (10.9 per cent).

Table 6
Percentage Distribution of Households according Type of Marriage among Middle and High Altitude Kinnaura of Kinnaur District Himachal Pradesh

Marriage Type	*Middle Altitude (n=394)*	*High Altitude (n=426)*	*Kinnaura (Pooled) (n=820)*
Monogamy	84.8	83.1	83.9
Polyandry	10.9	15.3	13.2
Polygyny	4.1	1.2	2.6
Polyandry & polygyny	0.3	0.5	0.4
Total	100	100	100

Marriage as cultural institution is regularization of sexual relationship, and means of reproduction, to continue existence in the form of progeny. The ancient forms of marriages are currently being practiced by few of indigenous human groups.

Polyandry is one of the ancient forms of marriages and limited to hilly areas of Indian continent. This institution is being extinct rapidly. Earlier it was reported from Toda, Kota, Nayar etc. of southern India. In Himalayan region, Kinnaura, Lahulis, Spitians, Jaunsaris etc. are still practicing polyandry though in varied proportions. Bhatt (1997) reported 48.3 per cent of polyandrous union in Jaunsar Bawar and 30.56 per cent in Rawain Jaunpur. Further the incidence of polyandry and polygyny form of marriages was estimated as 65.7 per cent in Jaunsar Bawar and 44.80 per cent in Rawain-Jaunpur. Raha (1985) reported 48.92 per cent polyandry among Kinnaura. In the present investigation, it has declined to 13.2 per cent with predominant practice of monogamy (83.9 per cent). Further in high altitude the proportion of polyandrous union is more (15.3 per cent) as compared to middle altitude 10.9 (per cent). On the basis of present findings it can be said that among Kinnaura practice of polyandry is being decreased. To better understanding about existence and relevance of polyandry in 21st century let go through a case study being given here:

CASE STUDY

Polyandrous Union

Name	:	K. S. R.
Age	:	47 Years
Sex	:	Male
Education	:	Graduate
Village	:	Thwaring (Morang)
Tehsil	:	Morang
District	:	Kinnaur

This case study is recorded from a polyandrous union of two male partners (fraternal brothers) and one female partner. One of the male partners (younger one) was died few years back; means there were three male partners in the union. The respondent, KSR is a voluntarily retired bank employee; his younger brother is Commandant in Border Security Force posted at Delhi. Right now they have two sons and a daughter. For schooling, children are with his younger brother, who also happens to be the biological father of the children as the union is polyandrous. The mother of respondent is alive, and right now she is widow of two husbands, which means the father of respondent were two brothers. Because this was the season of sowing and harvesting, the wife is at home with the respondent. However, during winter she lives with younger brother at his posting place if he was posted at Urban centers like Delhi. On asking as to why they were practicing polyandry, he replied that it was customary. Parents have the authority to decide whether their children would practice polyandry or monogamy. Polyandry has its own merits and demerits. The root of polyandry lies in the type of the marriage they practice. Even today, marriage by elopement is the only way of marriage in Kinnaur. For elopement, there are two conditions, one is willingness and the other is by force. Now a day, in most of the cases, the prospective spouses know each other. In such cases the prospective bride, elopes at her will. To develop affair is not possible for everyone and therefore, in a family for an example, out of 3 or 4 brothers if two are married by elopement, the other brothers can join them as fraternal partner of polyandry with mutual consent of all. After elopement, the next step is marriage, and it is customary that at the time of marriage all the younger brothers become bridegroom. On the one hand this institution restrict property division, on the other it has demographic implication to check population in area of limited subsistence. Simultaneously, it provides perpetual ever-married status to women. In polyandrous union in case of death of a male partner (husband), the wife does not become widow; she is still ever married upto death of all of male partners (husbands). Thus, polyandry saves a woman from curse of widowhood, and also from the problem of widow-marriage. Further, in case of long absence of any male partner (husband), the wife is never deprived of sexual satisfaction.

The success of polyandrous union depends on intelligence of woman (wife). She has greater role as she is at the center of union. It is her duty that none of the male partner should feel himself deprived. In case, all male partners are at home proper rotation is usually maintained. Simultaneously, it requires very good understanding among brothers (who are husbands or partners of polyandrous union). There are cases of split of polyandrous union. The brother, who is not satisfied in polyandrous union, can marry, but the process of marriage is not so easy.

In this case study it was found (as also told by him) that there was good understanding among brothers. He has taken voluntary retirement after the death of one of the younger brothers who was taking care of mother, wife children and orchard. The life in hills is not easy and a polyandrous union is not merely a union to full-fill biological instinct of sexual desire but it is also a small corporate unit at family level.

The polyandry is relevant only if it have proper function. It can be understood that in hilly tract the land is precious, if the economy is exclusively dependent on agriculture/ horticulture. In such a case only polyandry can avoid the land division. It also works as mechanism of family planning in limiting the family size from generation to generation.

There is example of Toda, who were recently practicing polyandry, but today none of the union is found polyandrous. They are also hill dwellers, but now a day, in the impact of modernization their economic structure is tremendously changed. Similarly, among the Nayar of Kerala the polyandry is the custom of old days, but still there are some families in which visiting husband can be seen. They are still matrilineal.

Finally, it can be concluded that there are deep routed cultural and biological causes behind any cultural institution. They work as extra-somatic mechanism in survival of population in the extreme climatic condition and needs further exploration. There are many explanation of cultural relevance of polyandry in the same way there is need to find out the biological relevance of the institution.

Chapter 7

MENARCHE, MENOPAUSE AND REPRODUCTIVE LIFE SPAN

Biological characteristics are intrinsic properties; these are inherent character, which every organism inherits by birth. There is wide variation among human being, they differ from individual to individual, group to group, and they are categorized in different racial groups, sub-groups and ethnic groups. Each group having some similar kind of biological character, some of these characters are measurable e.g. menarche, menopause, reproductive life span etc. These biological characteristics are very important in the study of population dynamics. In this chapter we will present findings related to menarche, menopause and reproductive life span among Kinnaura. The findings are elaborately discussed in the light of global scenario of these biological characteristics.

MENARCHE

Menarche, the onset of first menstruation, among human female was a matter of interest of varied discipline, this biological phenomena was widely studied for different purposes. The initiation of menstruation depends on various socio-cultural practices, economic status, occupation, nutrition, morbidity, climate, geography inherent genetic constitution and other factors. The first menstruation is a threshold from where a girl enters into her reproductive carrier, the age when first menstruation appears is called age at menarche. Wide variations were noticed in age at menarche of different population groups, it differs from region to region and country to country depending on biological constitution of population, socio-economic, political and environmental conditions etc. The age at menarche is also important from the point of view of human fertility and population characteristics, because it affects the core area of population dynamics.

Age at Menarche

The mean age at menarche among Kinnaura women has been found to be 15.11 (±1.5 SD) years. As evident from Table 1, slight variation has been noticed among middle and high altitude Kinnaura women in respect of age at onset of menarche. In middle altitude the mean age at menarche for Kinnaura women was found to be 15.18 (±1.3 SD), whereas in high altitude the mean age at menarche was 15.03 (±1.6 SD). Further, it is apparent from Box plot and Error bar diagrammes (Figure 1 and 2).

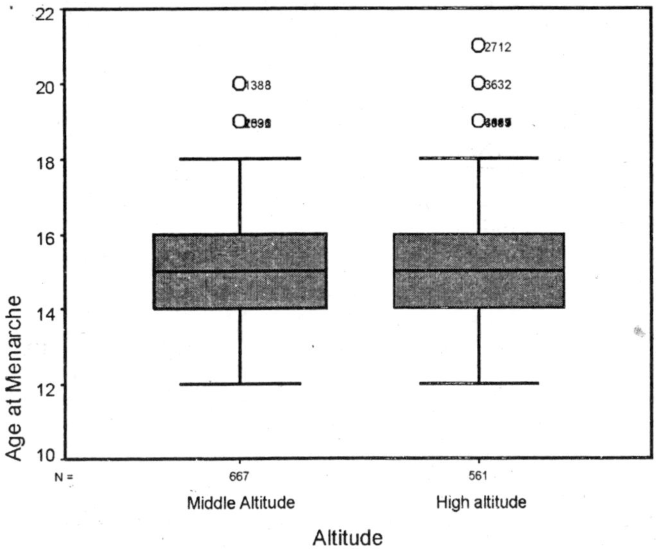

Figure 1: Box Plot of Age at Menarche showing the Median, Quartiles, and Extreme Values among Middle and High Altitude Women.

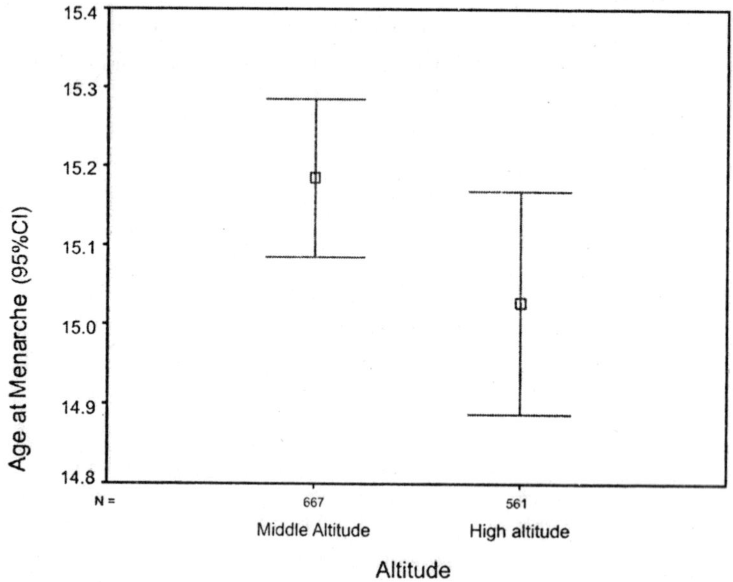

Figure 2: Error Bar Showing Difference of Mean of Age at Menarche Among Middle and High Altitude Women.

Table 1
Mean, Standard Deviation and Standard Error (SE) of Mean for Age at Menarche of Kinnaura Women of Middle and High Altitude

Altitude	*N*	*Mean*	*Std. Deviation*	*SE Mean*
Middle Altitude	667	15.18	1.329	0.051
High altitude	561	15.03	1.685	0.071
Total	1228	15.11	1.503	0.043

Independent *t* test applied to find difference in age at onset of menarche among middle and high altitude women displayed in Table 2 shows that Levene's test for equality of variances is highly significant ($p<0.001$) with F value 29.5 which indicates that variances of age at onset of menarche for middle and high altitude women are significantly different, however the *t* statistics exhibit non-significant difference between means of age at onset of menarche of middle and high altitude women ($t=1.776$ and $p>0.05$) at 1056.2 degree of freedom.

Table 2
Showing Levene's Test and Independent *t* test for Age at Menarche

	Levene's Test		*t-test*				
Variances' Assumptions	*F*	*p-value*	*t*	*df*	*p-value (2-tailed)*	*Mean Difference*	*Std. Error Difference*
Equal variances assumed	29.566	0.000	1.812	1226	0.070	0.16	0.086
Equal variances not assumed			1.776	1056.28	0.076	0.16	0.088

As apparent from Table 3, delayed menarche was occurred among aged women, the women had menarche at the age of 21 years is currently at the age of 60-64, though the women of this age group also had menarche at 12-14 years, 15-17 years and 18-20 years but 59.6 per cent of them had menarche at the age of 18-20 years, In general, the proportion of women had early age at menarche (12-14 years) declines as their current age rises, except the women currently at the age 45-49 and 80 years and above, in other words the age at menarche is declined (secular trend) in this tribal group as 43.4 per cent of 15-19 years of women had age at menarche at 12-14 years, 53.8 per cent of them had menarche at 15-17 years. Simultaneously the women currently at the age 20-24 years 34.9 per cent of them had menarche at 12-14 years, 62.4 per cent of them had menarche at the age of 15-17 years, and 2.8 per cent of them also had menarche at the age of 18-20 years.

Furthermore, majority of women (60.2 per cent) who had menarche at age of 12-14 years belong to the age group of 12-34 years. But the women who had menarche at the age of 18-20 years majority (72.6 per cent) of them are currently at the age of 25-59 years.

In middle altitude 32.2 per cent women had menarche at the age of 12-14 years, 63.3 per cent had at the age of 15-17 years and 4.5 per cent had at 18-20 years of age as compared to 39.1 per cent, 53.0 per cent and 7.7 per cent women of high altitude had age at menarche in these respective ages (Table 3 and 4).

Table 3
Age at Menarche Among Kinnaura Females (Pooled) according to Current Age

	Age at Menarche									
	12-14		15-17		18-20		21		Total	
Current Age	N	%	N	%	N	%	N	%	N	%
12-14	28	100.0	0	0	0	0	0	0	28	100.0
15-19	63	43.4	78	53.8	4	2.8	0	0	145	100.0
20-24	65	34.9	116	62.4	5	2.7	0	0	186	100.0
25-29	60	32.3	117	62.9	9	4.8	0	0	186	100.0
30-34	45	31.7	87	61.3	10	7.0	0	0	142	100.0
35-39	34	30.4	67	59.8	11	9.8	0	0	112	100.0
40-44	32	30.8	66	63.5	6	5.8	0	0	104	100.0
45-49	32	41.0	41	52.6	5	6.4	0	0	78	100.0
50-54	18	28.1	42	65.6	4	6.3	0	0	64	100.0
55-59	12	28.6	22	52.4	8	19.0	0	0	42	100.0
60-64	15	28.8	31	59.6	5	9.6	1	1.9	52	100.0
65-69	11	32.4	22	64.7	1	2.9	0	0	34	100.0
70-74	9	37.5	12	50.0	3	12.5	0	0	24	100.0
75-79	5	27.8	12	66.7	1	5.6	0	0	18	100.0
80+	5	41.7	6	50.0	1	8.3	0	0	12	100.0
Total	434	35.4	719	58.6	73	5.9	1	0.1	1227	100.0
12-14	28	6.5	0		0		0		28	2.3
15-19	63	14.5	78	10.8	4	5.5	0		145	11.8
20-24	65	15.0	116	16.1	5	6.8	0		186	15.2
25-29	60	13.8	117	16.3	9	12.3	0		186	15.2

Contd...

	Age at Menarche									
	12-14		*15-17*		*18-20*		*21*		*Total*	
Current Age	N	%	N	%	N	%	N	%	N	%
30-34	45	10.4	87	12.1	10	13.7	0		142	11.6
35-39	34	7.8	67	9.3	11	15.1	0		112	9.1
40-44	32	7.4	66	9.2	6	8.2	0		104	8.5
45-49	32	7.4	41	5.7	5	6.8	0		78	6.4
50-54	18	4.1	42	5.8	4	5.5	0		64	5.2
55-59	12	2.8	22	3.1	8	11.0	0		42	3.4
60-64	15	3.5	31	4.3	5	6.8	1	100.0	52	4.2
65-69	11	2.5	22	3.1	1	1.4	0		34	2.8
70-74	9	2.1	12	1.7	3	4.1	0		24	2.0
75-79	5	1.2	12	1.7	1	1.4	0		18	1.5
80+	5	1.2	6	.8	1	1.4	0		12	1.0
Total	434	100.0	719	100.0	73	100.0	1	100.0	1227	100.0

Table 4
Age at Menarche among Middle Altitude Kinnaura Females according to Current Age.

	Age at Menarche							
	12-14		*15-17*		*18-20*		*Total*	
Current Age	*N*	*%*	*N*	*%*	*N*	*%*	*N*	*%*
12-14	11	100.0	0	0	0	0	11	100.0
15-19	42	46.2	46	50.5	3	3.3	91	100.0
20-24	35	32.7	70	65.4	2	1.9	107	100.0
25-29	28	26.4	74	69.8	4	3.8	106	100.0
30-34	18	24.7	52	71.2	3	4.1	73	100.0
35-39	15	28.8	33	63.5	4	7.7	52	100.0
40-44	12	22.6	39	73.6	2	3.8	53	100.0
45-49	18	45.0	22	55.0	0	0	40	100.0
50-54	9	27.3	21	63.6	3	9.1	33	100.0
55-59	6	24.0	16	64.0	3	12.0	25	100.0
60-64	6	23.1	18	69.2	2	7.7	26	100.0
65-69	7	38.9	11	61.1	0	–	18	100.0
70-74	3	23.1	8	61.5	2	15.4	13	100.0
75-79	3	25.0	8	66.7	1	8.3	12	100.0
80+	2	28.6	4	57.1	1	14.3	7	100.0
Total	215	32.2	422	63.3	30	4.5	667	100.0
12-14	11	5.1	0	0	0	0	11	1.6
15-19	42	19.5	46	10.9	3	10.0	91	13.6
20-24	35	16.3	70	16.6	2	6.7	107	16.0
25-29	28	13.0	74	17.5	4	13.3	106	15.9
30-34	18	8.4	52	12.3	3	10.0	73	10.9
35-39	15	7.0	33	7.8	4	13.3	52	7.8
40-44	12	5.6	39	9.2	2	6.7	53	7.9
45-49	18	8.4	22	5.2	0	–	40	6.0
50-54	9	4.2	21	5.0	3	10.0	33	4.9
55-59	6	2.8	16	3.8	3	10.0	25	3.7
60-64	6	2.8	18	4.3	2	6.7	26	3.9
65-69	7	3.3	11	2.6	0	0	18	2.7
70-74	3	1.4	8	1.9	2	6.7	13	1.9
75-79	3	1.4	8	1.9	1	3.3	12	1.8
80+	2	0.9	4	0.9	1	3.3	7	1.0
Total	215	100.0	422	100.0	30	100.0	667	100.0

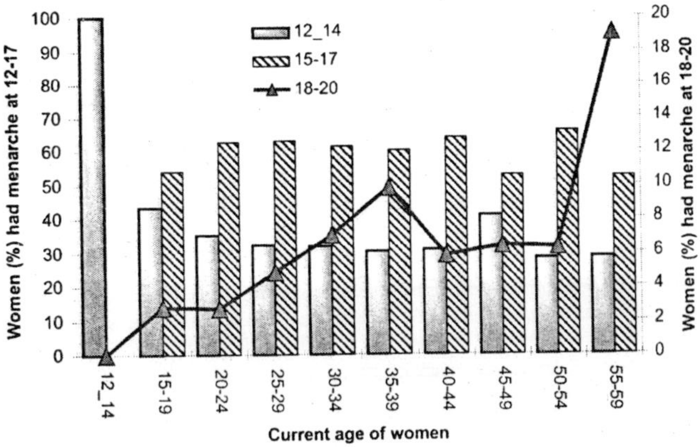

Figure 3: Showing Transition in Age at Menarche among Kinnaura Women.

Trends and Differentials of attaining Puberty among Women

Table 28 showing distribution of Kinnaura women of middle and high altitude of different occupation and varying degree of educational attainment according to their age of attaining puberty.

Occupation and Age at Menarche: Women who are labour by profession, 25.4 per cent of them attain puberty at the age of 12-14 years, 66.8 per cent at the age of 15-17 years, 7.7 per cent at the age of 18-20 years, and 0.1 per cent at the age of 21 years, women employed at private sector had early age at menarche as 20 per cent of them attain puberty at 12-14 years and 80 per cent at the age of 15-17 years. There are women, whose main profession is cultivation in agriculture/horticulture sector most of them (55.9 per cent) attain puberty at 12-14 years of age, rest 43.8 per cent at 15-17 years and very few (0.3 per cent) attain puberty at 18-20 years of age, while women employed in government sector most of them 56.5 per cent had menarche at the age of 15-17 years, slightly less than one third (29.0 per cent) at 12-14 years of age, and 14.5 per cent attain puberty at the age of 18-20 years. 100 per cent of students and housewives had menarche at 12-14 years of age. Most of the Buddhist Nun (68.4 per cent) attains puberty at 15-17 years , 21.1 per cent at the age of 12-14 years and 10.5 per cent at the age of 18-20 years.

Table 5
Age at Menarche among High Altitude Kinnaura Females according to Current Age.

	Age at Menarche									
	12-14		*15-17*		*18-20*		*21*		*Total*	
Current Age	N	%	N	%	N	%	N	%	N	%
12-14	17	100.0	0	0	0	0	0	0	17	100.0
15-19	21	38.9	32	59.3	1	1.9	0	0	54	100.0
20-24	30	38.0	46	58.2	3	3.8	0	0	79	100.0
25-29	32	40.0	43	53.8	5	6.3	0	0	80	100.0
30-34	27	39.1	35	50.7	7	10.1	0	0	69	100.0
35-39	19	31.7	34	56.7	7	11.7	0	0	60	100.0
40-44	20	39.2	27	52.9	4	7.8	0	0	51	100.0
45-49	14	36.8	19	50.0	5	13.2	0	0	38	100.0
50-54	9	29.0	21	67.7	1	3.2	0	0	31	100.0
55-59	6	35.3	6	35.3	5	29.4	0	0	17	100.0
60-64	9	34.6	13	50.0	3	11.5	1	3.8	26	100.0
65-69	4	25.0	11	68.8	1	6.3	0	0	16	100.0
70-74	6	54.5	4	36.4	1	9.1	0	0	11	100.0
75-79	2	33.3	4	66.7	0	0	0	0	6	100.0
80+	3	60.0	2	40.0	0	0	0	0	5	100.0
	219	39.1	297	53.0	43	7.7	1	0.2	560	100.0
12-14	17	7.8	0	0	0	0	0	0	17	3.0
15-19	21	9.6	32	10.8	1	2.3	0	0	54	9.6
20-24	30	13.7	46	15.5	3	7.0	0	0	79	14.1
25-29	32	14.6	43	14.5	5	11.6	0	0	80	14.3

Contd...

	Age at Menarche									
	12-14		15-17		18-20		21		Total	
Current Age	*N*	%	*N*	%	*N*	%	*N*	%	*N*	%
30-34	27	12.3	35	11.8	7	16.3	0	0	69	12.3
35-39	19	8.7	34	11.4	7	16.3	0	0	60	10.7
40-44	20	9.1	27	9.1	4	9.3	0	0	51	9.1
45-49	14	6.4	19	6.4	5	11.6	0	0	38	6.8
50-54	9	4.1	21	7.1	1	2.3	0	0	31	5.5
55-59	6	2.7	6	2.0	5	11.6	0	0	17	3.0
60-64	9	4.1	13	4.4	3	7.0	1	100.0	26	4.6
65-69	4	1.8	11	3.7	1	2.3	0	0	16	2.9
70-74	6	2.7	4	1.3	1	2.3	0	0	11	2.0
75-79	2	.9	4	1.3	0		0	0	6	1.1
80+	3	1.4	2	.7	0		0	0	5	.9
Total	219	100.0	297	100.0	43	100.0	1	100.0	560	100.0

Table 6
Percentage Distribution of Age at Menarche Among Middle and High Altitudes Kinnaura (Females) of Varying Socio-Economic and Biological Background

	Age at Menarche													
	Middle Altitude (n=667)				*High Altitude (n=560)*					*Kinnaur (Pooled) (n=1227)*				
Background	*12-14*	*15-17*	*18-20*	*Total*	*12-14*	*15-17*	*18-20*	*21*	*Total*	*12-14*	*15-17*	*18-20*	*21*	*Total*
Occupation														
Labour	28.5	65.5	5.9	100	21.2	68.4	10.0	0.3	100	25.4	66.8	7.7	0.1	100
Pvt. Service	NA	NA	NA	NA	20.0	80.0	NA	NA	100	20.0	80.0	NA	NA	100
Agr./Hort.	38.6	61.4	NA	100	74.4	25.0	0.6	NA	100	55.9	43.8	0.3	NA	100
Govt. Service	24.1	65.5	10.3	100	33.3	48.5	18.2	NA	100	29.0	56.5	14.5	NA	100
Business	NA	100	NA	100	NA	NA	100	NA	100	NA	66.7	33.3	NA	100
Retired Person	NA	100	NA	100	NA	100	NA	NA	100	NA	100	NA	NA	100
Student/Hw	84.6	15.4	NA	100	100	NA	NA	NA	100	100		NA	NA	100
Contractor	50.0	50.0	NA	100	NA	NA	NA	NA	NA	50.0	50.0	NA	NA	100
Lama	18.2	72.7	9.1	100	25.0	62.5	12.5	NA	100	21.1	68.4	10.5	NA	100
Total	31.7	63.7	4.5	100	39.0	53.1	7.7	0.2	100	35.1	58.8	6.0	0.1	100
Labour	59.5	68.0	86.7	66.2	33.0	78.1	79.1	100	60.6	46.0	72.4	82.2	100	63.7
Pvt. Service	NA	NA	NA	NA	0.5	1.3	NA	NA	.9	0.2	0.6	NA	NA	0.4
Agr./Hort.	30.5	24.2	NA	25.1	53.2	13.1	2.3	NA	27.9	42.1	19.7	1.4	NA	26.4
Govt. Service	3.3	4.5	10.0	4.4	5.0	5.4	14.0	NA	5.9	4.2	4.9	12.3	NA	5.1
Business	NA	0.5	NA	0.3	NA	NA	2.3	NA	0.2	NA	0.3	1.4	NA	0.2
Retired Person	NA	0.2	NA	0.2	NA	0.3	NA	NA	0.2	NA	0.3	NA	NA	0.2
Student/Hw	5.2	0.5	NA	2.0	7.3	NA	NA	NA	2.9	6.3	NA	NA	NA	2.2

Agr./Hort. = Agriculture/Horticulture
Hw = Housewife

Contd...

	Age at Menarche													
	Middle Altitude (n=667)				*High Altitude (n=560)*					*Kinnaur (Pooled) (n=1227)*				
Background	*12-14*	*15-17*	*18-20*	*Total*	*12-14*	*15-17*	*18-20*	*21*	*Total*	*12-14*	*15-17*	*18-20*	*21*	*Total*
Contractor	0.5	0.2	NA	0.3	NA	NA	NA	NA	NA	0.2	0.1	NA	NA	0.2
Lama	1.0	1.9	3.3	1.7	0.9	1.7	2.3	NA	1.4	0.9	1.8	2.7	NA	1.6
Total	100	100	100	100	100	100	100	100	100	100	100	100	100	100
Education														
Illiterate	27.9	28.7	33.3	28.6	30.1	36.0	48.8	100	34.8	29.0	31.7	42.5	100	31.5
Literate	4.7	8.3	16.7	7.5	1.4	8.1	14.0	NA	5.9	3.0	8.2	15.1	NA	6.8
Primary	7.9	12.1	13.3	10.8	11.4	10.8	7.0	NA	10.7	9.7	11.5	9.6	NA	10.8
Middle	20.0	14.5	13.3	16.2	25.1	15.8	9.3	NA	18.9	22.6	15.0	11.0	NA	17.4
High School	21.4	19.0	13.3	19.5	16.9	14.8	14.0	NA	15.5	19.1	17.2	13.7	NA	17.7
Higher Sec.	11.2	9.2	6.7	9.7	5.9	5.7	4.7	NA	5.7	8.5	7.8	5.5	NA	7.9
Graduate +	6.5	8.3	3.3	7.5	9.1	8.4	2.3	NA	8.2	7.8	8.3	2.7	NA	7.8
Prof. & Tech.	0.5	NA	NA	0.1	NA	0.3	NA	NA	0.2	0.2	0.1	NA	NA	0.2
Total	100	100	100	100	100	100	100	100	100	100	100	100	100	100
Illiterate	31.4	63.4	5.2	100	33.8	54.9	10.8	0.5	100	32.6	59.1	8.0	0.3	100
Literate	20.0	70.0	10.0	100	9.1	72.7	18.2	NA	100	15.7	71.1	13.3	NA	100
Primary	23.6	70.8	5.6	100	41.7	53.3	5.0	NA	100	31.8	62.9	5.3	NA	100
Middle	39.8	56.5	3.7	100	51.9	44.3	3.8	NA	100	45.8	50.5	3.7	NA	100
High School	35.4	61.5	3.1	100	42.5	50.6	6.9	NA	100	38.2	57.1	4.6	NA	100
Higher Sec.	36.9	60.0	3.1	100	40.6	53.1	6.3	NA	100	38.1	57.7	4.1	NA	100
Graduate +	28.0	70.0	2.0	100	43.5	54.3	2.2	NA	100	35.4	62.5	2.1	NA	100
Prof. & Tech.	100	NA	NA	100	NA	100	NA	NA	100	50.0	50.0	NA	NA	100
Total	32.2	63.3	4.5	100	39.1	53.0	7.7	0.2	100	35.4	58.6	5.9	0.1	100

NA=Not available

Further, the women had menarche at the age of 12-14 years, 46 per cent of them were labourer, and 42.1 per cent were cultivators; while those who attain puberty at 15-17 years 72.4 per cent of them were labourer; similarly 82.2 per cent of women who had menarche at 18-20 years and 100 per cent had menarche at 21 years were labourer.

In middle altitude the women who are labour by profession they attain puberty early as compared to women of same profession in high altitude; whereas the women who are cultivators and student/housewives, they had early menarche in high altitude despite of middle altitude.

Education and Age at Menarche: The women who had menarche at the age of 12-14 years of age, approximately one third (29 per cent) of them were illiterate, around one fifth (22.6 per cent) had formal education upto middle level, approximately same proportion (19.1 per cent) had education upto high school level, followed by the women having education upto primary level, higher secondary level, graduate and above, just literate and professionally/ technically qualified. More or less same pattern observed among women who attain puberty at the age of 15-17 years of age. But the women who had menarche at the age of 18-20 years most of them (42.5 per cent) were illiterate followed by just literate (15.1 per cent), high school qualified, middle level educated, primary educated and so on. The women who had menarche at 21 year of age, all of them (100 per cent) were illiterate.

Furthermore among illiterates most of them (59.1 per cent) attain puberty at the age of 15-17 years, 32.6 per cent at the age of 12-14 years and rest at 18-20 and 21 years. But the proportion of just literates is highest, 71.1 per cent of them attain puberty at 15-17 years. Among rests 50-62 per cent attain puberty at 15-17 years of ages and more than one third at 12-14 years of age. Those who attain puberty at 18 –20 years most of them were just literate followed by illiterate primary and above.

Table 7
Result of Multiple Regression Analysis (Dependent Variable Age at Menarche) for Kinnaura Women of Middle and High Altitude.

Independent Variable	*Zero-order Correlation*	β	*SE* β	*Beta*	*t*	*p-value*
			Middle Altitude			
Age at marriage	0.382	0.089	0.027	0.258	3.255	0.001
Current Age	0.109	-0.006	0.010	-0.050	-0.593	0.554
Age at Menopause	0.378	0.142	0.036	0.310	3.921	0.001
Altitude	0.114	0.001	0.001	0.069	0.920	0.359
Education Level	0.005	0.032	0.099	0.025	0.318	0.751
Occupation	-0.298	-0.204	0.099	-0.170	-2.048	0.042
Multiple Regression Coefficient $R=0.519$, $R^2=0.269$, $SE=1.110$, $F=8.400$ and $p<0.0001$						
			High Altitude			
Age at marriage	0.378	0.157	0.037	0.340	4.257	0.001
Current Age	-0.065	-0.025	0.015	-0.151	-1.682	0.096
Age at Menopause	0.133	0.080	0.047	0.146	1.710	0.090
Altitude	-0.105	0.000	0.000	-0.026	-0.309	0.758
Education Level	-0.139	-0.243	0.207	-0.103	-1.172	0.244
Occupation	-0.464	-0.608	0.122	-0.417	-4.987	0.001
Multiple Regression Coefficient $R=0.607$, $R^2=0.368$, $SE=1.365$, $F=9.910$ and $p<0.0001$						

To find out the factors affecting age at menarche among Kinnaura women of middle and high altitude, multiple regression analysis was done, which exhibits that different predictors imposes different degree of impact on age at onset of menarche among the women of two different ecological zones. The zero order correlation indicates that among the Kinnaura women of middle altitude except occupation, rest of the predictors like age at marriage, current age, age at menopause, altitude and level of education have positive correlation with age at onset of menarche. The β value indicates that age at marriage and age at menopause imposes significant positive impact whereas occupation imposes inverse significant impact on age at menarche of women; current age also imposes inverse but non-significant impact. The other predictors are altitude and level of education which imposes non-significant but positive impact. Overall the model gives multiple regression coefficient R=0.519, R^2=0.269 with F= 8.4 ($p<0.001$); which indicates that the above cited predictors of age at onset of menarche had only 26.9 per cent role in deciding the age at onset of menarche among the Kinnaura women of middle altitude zone, rest 73.1 percent were decided by other factors.

Zero order correlation for Kinnaura women of high altitude shows negative correlation between age at onset of menarche and current age, altitude, education level & occupation, simultaneously age at marriage and age at menopause only shows positive correlation. The β value indicates that only two predictor viz. age at marriage and occupation had significant impact on age at menarche, respectively positive and negative. Rest two predictors current age and education level imposes negative impact whereas increasing or decreasing altitude in this ecological zone (high altitude) has no impact (β=0), simultaneously, age at menopause had positive impact on age at onset of menarche of Kinnaura women of high altitude (Table 7).

The comparison of mean age at menarche of Kinnaura (15.11 years) with other Indian population were found to be lower than Bodhs (15.43 years) of Jammu and Kashmir, Rang Bhotia (16.00 years), Marchha Bhotia (16.18 years), Dharchula Bhotia of Uttaranchal, Buddhist (15.50 years) of Sikkim, Raji (17.28 years) of Uttaranchal and higher than Garo (12.55 years) of Assam, Gaddi (14.01 years), Brahman (14.21 years), Rajput (13.92 years), Scheduled Castes (14.00 years) of Himachal Pradesh, other tribal and non-tribal groups of Madhya Pradesh, Chhatisgarh, Orissa, Uttar Pradesh, West Bengal, Andhra Pradesh, Rajasthan, Andaman and Maharashtra. Simultaneously the minimum average age at menarche 12.40 years is recorded for Varendra Brahmin of West Bengal, whereas maximum 17.28 years is recorded for Raji tribe of Uttaranchal state and on the basis of available data the average for Indian population is calculated as 13.94 (Table 8).

Furthermore, Thomas, et.al. (2001) concluded on the basis of a large spatial scale that different factors might be responsible for inter-population differences of age variability in menarche in fact, age at menarche seems to be closely related to extrinsic factors such as living conditions and especially, the energy balance allocated to individuals. Hence to correlate the age at menarche with altitude only is not appropriate, this may one of extrinsic factors. It can be clearly seen from the Table 8 that by and large, Himalayan population show delayed age at menarche and can be compared with the population of plain.

Table 8
Mean Age at Menarche, Menopause and Reproductive Life Span among Tribal and Non-Tribal Population Group of India

		Mean Age of			
Country/ State/ Region	*Population Group*	*Menarche*	*Menopause*	*Reproductive Span*	*Source*
INDIAN HIMALAYAS					
Eastern Himalaya					
Assam					
	Garo	12.55	45.85	33.30	Das and Saikia (1999)
	Tai Turung	12.43	–		Barua (1992)
	Ahom	12.96	48.44	35.48	Gogoi (1972)
	Mikirs	12.75			Khatoniar (1972)
	Kalita	12.61			Das & Das (1966)
Arunachal Pradesh					
	Singpho	12.59	43.63	31.04	Kar & Mahanta (1975)
	Adi	14.45			Duarah (1989)
Sikkim					
	Buddhist	15.50	44.35	28.85	Bhasin and Bhasin (2000)
	Hindus	14.62	45.71	31.09	"
	Lepchas	15.55	–		Bhasin and Bhasin (1995)
	Bhutias	15.62	–		"
Western Himalaya					
Jammu and Kashmir					
Ladakh (HA)	14.99	44.67	29.68		Bhasin and Nag (2002)
	Bodhs	15.43	44.49	29.06	"
	Baltis	14.79	44.39	29.60	"
	Brokpas	14.85	44.12	29.27	"
	Arghuns	14.65	45.68	31.03	"
Himachal Pradesh					
	Gaddi	14.01	44.41	30.40	Bhasin and Bhasin (1993)
	Brahman	14.21	44.10	29.89	"
	Rajput	13.92	44.81	30.89	"
	SC	14.00	44.32	30.32	"

Contd...

Country/ State/ Region	Population Group	Mean Age of Menarche	Menopause	Reproductive Span	Source
Central Himalaya					
Uttaranchal (or erstwhile UP)					
	Johari Bhotia	15.10	–	–	Kapoor (1996)
	Rang Bhotia	16.00	–	–	"
	Marchha Bhotia	16.18	–	–	"
	Marchha Bhotia	16.79	–	–	Chachra and Bhasin (1998)
	Dharchula Bhotia	15.36	–	–	"
	Johar Bhotia	16.39	–	–	"
	Bhotia	–	46.27		Singh (1984)
	Rang Bhotia	-	48.00		Kapoor & Kapoor (1986)
	Johari Bhotia	-	46.70		"
	Raji	17.28	-		Samal, et.al. (2000)
	Raji	13.40	45.23	31.83	Patra (2001)
	Jaunsaris	14.59	-		Kshatriya, et.al. (1997)
HIMALAYAN STATES					
	Minimum	12.43	43.63	28.85	
	Maximum	17.28	48.44	35.48	
	Average	14.61	45.29	30.78	
OTHER STATES					
Madhya Pradesh					
Patalkot	Bhariya PTG	13.90	–	–	Pandey (2002)
Raigarh	Birhor PTG	13.90	–	–	"
Sarguja	Hill Korwa PTG	13.60	–	–	"
	Hill Korwas	13.60	–	–	Pandey and Tiwari (1993)
	Gond	12.80	–	–	"
Chhatisgarh					
Raipur	Kamar	13.80	–	–	Pandey (2002)
Orissa					
	Khadia	14.27	–	–	Chaudhury, et.al. (1994)
	Kissan	14.28	–	–	"
	Kondh	13.40	–	–	"
	Oraon	14.07	–	–	"
	Mirdha	13.30	–	–	"
	Gonda	14.32	–	–	"
	Khandayat	13.41			Patnaik (1971)
	Karan	13.28			"
	Brahman	12.94			"
Uttar Pradesh					
	Ranatham	13.26	–	–	Singh and Shukla (1992)
	Jogia Tharu	13.80	–	–	"
	Donguria Tharu	14.00	–	–	"
	Katharia Tharu	13.10	–	–	"
	Panchhimaha Tharu	13.44	–	–	"
West Bengal	Kora	13.76	43.04	29.28	Bhattacharyya et.al. (1995)

Contd...

Country/ State/ Region	Population Group	*Mean Age of* Menarche	Menopause	Reproductive Span	Source
	Bagdi	13.65	–	–	Sarkar and Chowdhury (1967)
	Kayastha	13.30	–	–	Bhattacharyya et.al. (1977)
	Brahman	13.00	–	–	"
	Tili	12.70	47.00	34.3	Talukdar (1977)
	Varendra Kayastha	12.60	46.00	33.4	"
	Dule Bagdi	12.80	46.90	34.1	"
	Varendra Brahman	12.40	47.01	34.61	"
	Jele	12.80	46.40	33.6	"
Andhra Pradesh					
	Kapu	13.79	–	–	Raj J. and Reddy (1977)
	Bagata	13.46	–	–	Annapurna (1972)
	Kummari	13.33	45.89	32.56	Babu and Naidu (1989)
	Mangali	13.13	45.95	32.82	"
	Madiga	13.21	46.07	32.86	"
	Chakali	13.01	44.45	31.44	"
	Koya	13.25	–		Paddaiah (1977)
	Chenchu	14.30	–		Rao & Aruna (1975)
	Muslim	13.14	45.64	32.5	Ramamma & Reddy (1977)
Rajasthan					
	Balija	13.66	–	–	Gunasundaramma & Reddy (1977)
	Bhora	14.88	–	–	Basu & Gupta (1977)
Andaman					
	Oraon	13.47	–	–	Bhattacharyya et.al. (1985)
Maharashtra					
	Mahar	13.98	43.03	29.05	Bhattacharyya et.al. (1991)
	Brahmin	14.34	45.84	31.50	Rakshit (1962)
INDIA (Including Himalayan States)					
	Minimum	12.40	43.03	28.85	
	Maximum	17.28	48.44	35.48	
	Average	13.94	45.43	31.66	
INDIA (Excluding Himalayan States)					
	Minimum	12.40	43.03	29.28	
	Maximum	14.88	47.01	34.61	
	Average	13.50	45.63	32.86	
Himachal Pradesh					
Kinnaur	Kinnaura	15.11	45.45	30.34	Present study (2006)
Middle altitude		15.19	44.58	29.39	"
High Altitude		15.03	46.66	31.63	"

HA=High Altitude Region
UP=Uttar Pradesh (India)
SC= Scheduled Caste
WN=Western Nepal
PTG =Primitive Tribe

MENOPAUSE

Natural cessation of menstruation among human female is called menopause, this is a biological phenomena, the end of reproductive life of a women. Wide variation had been observed among different population groups all over the world on the age at which capacity of reproduction of a woman comes to an end (with varying degree of suddenness). Alike, age at menarche, the age at menopause also being affected by different factors.

Age at Menopause

As evident from Table 9, in the present study the age at menopause among Kinnaura women varying from 35-53 years. The mean age at menopause was estimated as 45.45 years (± 3.18 S.D.). In middle altitude the age at menopause is quite early as compared to high altitude. The mean age at menopause in middle altitude was estimated 44.53 (± 2.89 S.D.) years, whereas in high altitude it is 46.71 (± 3.13 S.D.) as also evident from Box plot and Error bar diagramme (Figure 4 and 5). Because of transition in age at menarche as already discussed, the age at menopause is also in transition.

Data on age at menopause are not abundant, however the available information shows that the mean age at menopause is ranging between 43.03 among Mahar caste of Maharashtra to 48.44 years of age among Ahom of Assam, and the average for Indian population is found to be 45.43 years of age (Table 8).

Table 9
Central Tendency, Deviation and Extreme of Age at Menopause among Kinnaura Women of Different Ecological Zone

	Age at Menopause					
Ecological Zone	*N*	*Min.*	*Max.*	*Mean*	*SE*	*SD*
Middle Altitude	162	35	53	44.53	0.23	2.89
High altitude	126	35	53	46.71	0.28	3.13
Total	288	35	53	45.48	0.19	3.18

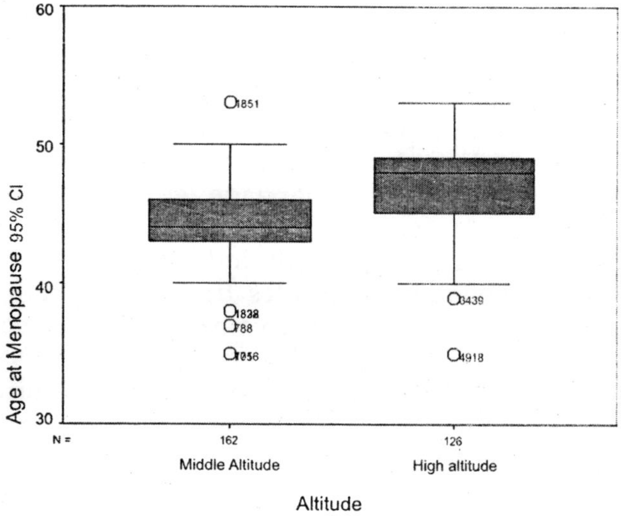

Figure 4: Box Plot Diagramme of age at Menopause Showing the Median, Quartiles, and Extreme Values Among Middle and High Altitude Women

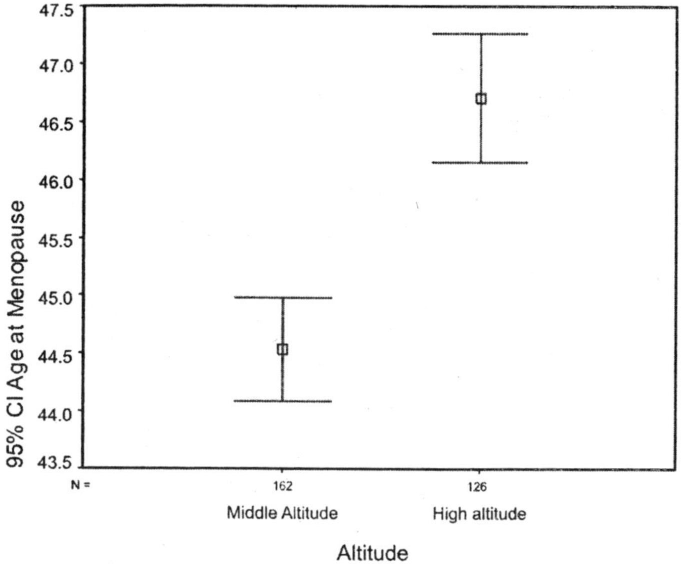

Figure 5: Error Bar Diagramme Showing Distribution of Age at Menopause Among Middle and High Altitude Women

Factors Affecting Age at Menopause

To find out the possible factors affecting the age at menopause of Kinnaura women of different ecological zones (middle and high altitude) multiple regression run keeping the age at menopause as dependent variable and current age, altitude, age at menarche, age at marriage, education level and occupation as independent variables (Table 10). The zero order correlation for middle altitude indicates that among the selected independent variables first four have positive correlation, whereas last two have negative correlation with the age at menopause. Further the β value indicates the same kind of impact, though only age at menarche and current age having significant impact on the age at menopause of Kinnaura women of middle altitude. Overall the model gives multiple regression coefficient R=0.503, R^2=0.253 with F=7.5 ($p<0.001$) exhibits that age at menopause of Kinnaura women of middle altitude is determined only 25.3 per cent by these factors, rest almost 74.7 per cent is decided by other factors.

Table 10
Result of Multiple Regression Analysis (Dependent Variable Age at Menopause) for Kinnaura Women.

Independent Variable	*Zero-order Correlation*	β	*SE* β	*Beta*	*t*	*p-value*
			Middle Altitude			
Current Age	0.319	0.057	0.021	0.225	2.673	0.008
Altitude	0.051	0.001	0.002	0.029	0.374	0.709
Age at Menarche	0.396	0.729	0.180	0.336	4.04	0.000
Age at marriage	0.204	0.027	0.063	0.036	0.432	0.667
Education Level	-0.190	-0.366	0.218	-0.134	-1.678	0.096
Occupation	-0.229	-0.164	0.226	-0.062	-0.724	0.470
Multiple Regression Coefficient R=0.503, R^2=0.253, SE=2.451, F=7.5 and $p<0.001$						
			High Altitude			
Current Age	0.316	0.101	0.03	0.337	3.416	0.001
Altitude	-0.199	-0.001	0.001	-0.128	-1.346	0.181
Age at Menarche	0.124	0.370	0.207	0.203	1.79	0.077
Age at marriage	0.127	0.025	0.084	0.03	0.295	0.768
Education Level	0.051	0.589	0.445	0.134	1.325	0.188
Occupation	0.075	0.388	0.285	0.145	1.363	0.176
Multiple Regression Coefficient R=0.423, R^2=0.179, SE=2.855, F=3.5 and $p<0.001$						

The zero order correlation for Kinnaura women of high altitude indicates that only altitude had negative correlation with the age at menopause, whereas rest of the predictors having positive correlation, further the β value indicates the same kind of impact, though only current age having significant impact on the age at menopause of Kinnaura women of high altitude. Overall the model gives multiple regression coefficient R=0.423, R^2=0.179 with F=3.5 ($p<0.001$) exhibits that age at menopause of Kinnaura women of high altitude is determined only 17.3 per cent by these factors, rest almost 82.7 per cent is decided by other factors.

Finally, these findings are similar to the conclusion of Stanford et.al. (1987), Kirchengast (1992) and Do et.al. (1998) who found significant positive correlation between age at menopause and age at first birth in their respective studies. Thomas, et.al. (2001) concluded on the basis of a large spatial scale that the age at menopause appears to be more sensitive to intrinsic parameters, such as the reproductive history of individuals.

REPRODUCTIVE LIFE SPAN

Reproductive life span of human female is the period between menarche and menopause, in which she is able to bear pregnancy and give births. After the first menstruation, a girl almost becomes biologically active for the process of reproduction, but, in many societies, sexual relationships are initiated only after marriage, and childbearing out of wedlock is socially forbidden. In such societies, childbearing is expected to begin soon after marriage. Biologically the reproductive career of a woman ends with cessation of menstruation. It is reported that from about the age of forty, ovaries become less responsive to estrogen, fertilized eggs give rise to embryos with more chromosomal abnormalities, and menstrual cycles become increasingly irregular, ceasing generally between forty five to fifty years of age. It is well established that an infertile couples can now employ a variety of techniques to conceive. But, at the same time, technology has failed to alter a basic biological limit: the end of a woman's reproductive life span.

Why human menopause happens so early in life as compared to other physiological declines is intriguing. Many biologists have been dissatisfied with the "reproductive senescence" hypothesis and have proposed that menopause might be an evolutionary adaptation. The "risky childbirth" hypothesis points out that pregnancy becomes more hazardous with increasing age and that when a woman dies in childbirth, any young children still dependent on her are also at risk. Thus, middle-aged women might do better to forego the risks of reproduction and enhance their genetic legacy by concentrating their energies on their surviving children and grandchildren. A variant of this theory is that since newborn infants are so demanding, giving birth to additional babies would inevitably lead her to neglect her earlier offspring. Both of these hypotheses view menopause as a gateway to a purposeful new phase in life. In defense of the adaptive hypotheses, anthropologists Kristen Hawkes and Nick Blurton-Jones have noted that the presence of grandmothers in traditional hunter-gatherer societies improves the survival of grandchildren.

Like the reproductive senescence hypothesis, however, the adaptive hypotheses have various shortcomings. First, the risk of dying during childbirth is actually quite low. Even in developing nations, middle-aged women suffer an average risk of only 3 percent. Second, in order to have a chance of becoming a grandmother, a woman must have post-pubescent children. High infant survival rates are largely restricted to the developed nations of the twentieth century. Throughout our evolutionary history, most women would have been lucky to raise any surviving offspring at all, so why should they cease reproduction during middle age? Surely, it would be more plausible for women to have evolved a birth-spacing mechanism that was sensitive to their levels of nutrition and/ or stress, and thus to have prevented further pregnancies only when they were overwhelmed by the demands of their older children. More importantly, most of the women attain natural infertility in pre-industrialized society during middle age. In other words these women complete their family size much before they achieve menopause.

However, older women can potentially leave more descendants by continuing to have their own babies than by looking after their grandchildren. Further, even if postmenopausal women's help does enhance their grandchildren's survival, this would not necessarily account for the origins of menopause, which could have evolved as a side effect of senescence, leaving postmenopausal women with nothing better to do than help care for grandchildren. Over all, these hypotheses of possible causes of end of the reproductive life of the women are not competent to be considered as the best the determinants of the reproductive life span. Naturally it appears to be the by product of multifactorial variables. And there may be many biological and social variables that may determine the reproductive life span of women.

Here is an attempt has been made to find out the possible determinants of reproductive life span among Kinnaura — the polyandrous tribe of Himalayan high lands. The investigation is based on the information collected from 273 postmenopausal women belonging to 25 villages. Out of these 273 women, 155 are from middle altitude and 118 from high altitude.

Here reproductive life span of women is calculated by subtracting the age at menarche from the age at menopause, and the value obtained is considered as the reproductive life span (in years).

The distribution of the reproductive life span of Kinnaura women of middle and high altitude is presented in Table 11, which is further elucidated with help of line graph (Figure 6 and 7). It is evident from Figure 8 that the distribution of the reproductive life span of the women is concentrated between 25 to 35 years. Maximum concentration is recorded for those women who have aggregated 29 years of reproductive life span. The graph is reversed-V shaped, which indicates that the number of women increase rapidly as per increment of reproductive life span as well as their percentage also decline sharply after 29 years of reproductive life span. The cumulative frequency distribution of reproductive life span (Figure 7) shows that 90% of women have less than 35 years of

Table 11
Distribution of Sample as Per Reproductive Life Span.

	Middle Altitude			High Altitude			Kinnaura (Pooled)		
Reproductive Life Span	*N*	*%*	*Cumulative (%)*	*N*	*%*	*Cumulative (%)*	*N*	*%*	*Cumulative (%)*
19	1	0.6	0.6	0	0.0	0.0	1	0.4	0.4
20	0	0.0	0.6	0	0.0	0.0	0	0.0	0.4
21	2	1.3	1.9	0	0.0	0.0	2	0.7	1.1
22	0	0.0	1.9	1	0.8	0.8	1	0.4	1.5
23	1	0.6	2.5	1	0.8	1.6	2	0.7	2.2
24	3	1.9	4.4	0	0.0	1.6	3	1.1	3.3
25	3	1.9	6.3	4	3.4	5.0	7	2.6	5.9
26	7	4.5	10.8	3	2.5	7.5	10	3.7	9.6
27	17	11.0	21.8	4	3.4	10.9	21	7.7	17.3
28	22	14.2	36.0	8	6.8	17.7	30	11.0	28.3
29	35	22.6	58.6	12	10.2	27.9	47	17.2	45.5
30	23	14.8	73.4	12	10.2	38.1	35	12.8	58.3
31	16	10.3	83.7	13	11.0	49.1	29	10.6	68.9
32	13	8.4	92.1	16	13.6	62.7	29	10.6	79.5
33	5	3.2	95.3	9	7.6	70.3	14	5.1	84.6
34	5	3.2	98.5	9	7.6	77.9	14	5.1	89.7
35	2	1.3	100.0	16	13.6	91.5	18	6.6	96.3
36	0	0.0	100.0	6	5.1	96.6	6	2.2	98.5
37	0	0.0	100.0	2	1.7	98.3	2	0.7	99.2
38	0	0.0	100.0	2	1.7	100.0	2	0.7	100.0
Total	155	100		118	100		273	100	

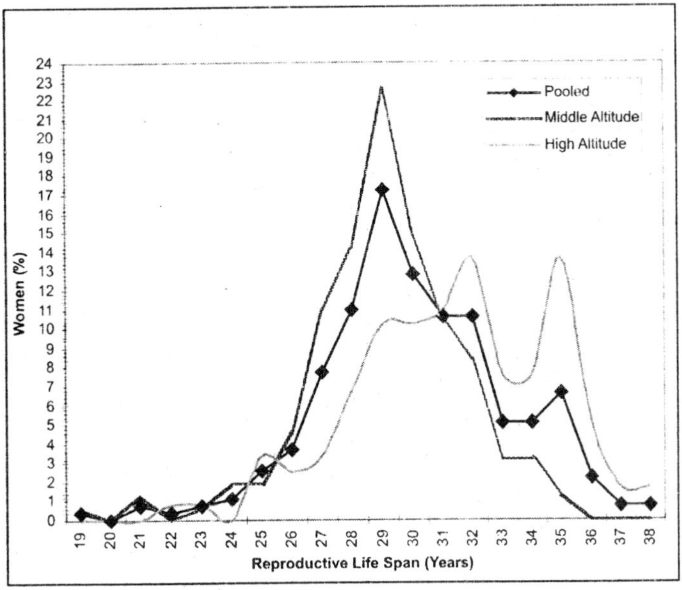

Figure 6: Line Graph showing the Distribution of Kinnaura Women of Middle and High Altitude as Per Reproductive Life Span.

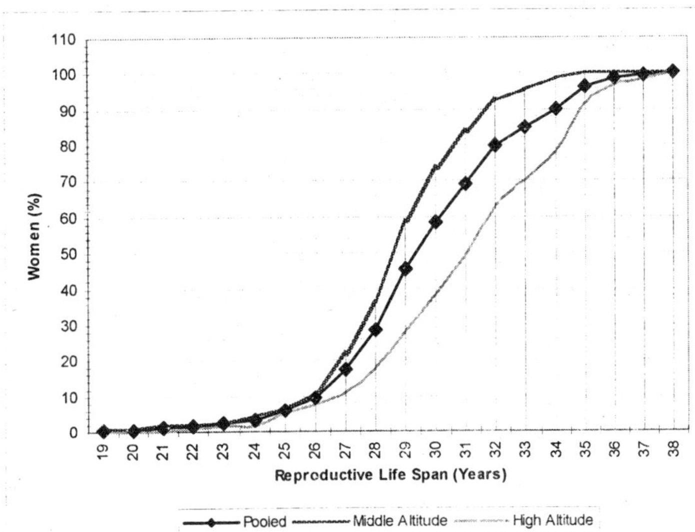

Figure 7: Cumulative Frequency Distribution of Reproductive Life Span among Kinnaura Women of Middle and High Altitude.

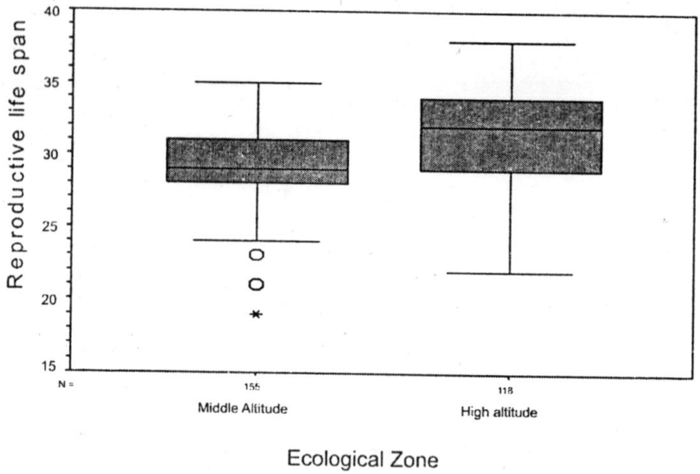

Figure 8: Box Plot Diagramme showing Median Quartile and Extreme Values of Reproductive Life Span among the Kinnaura Women of Middle and High Altitude.

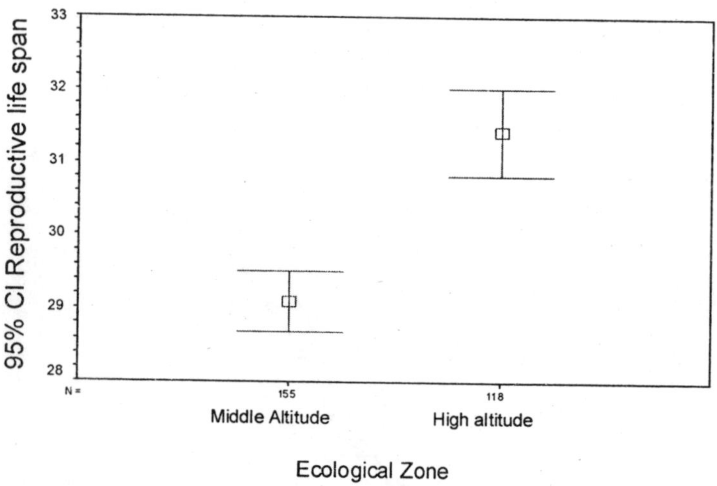

Figure 9: Error Bar Diagramme showing 95% Confidence Interval of Mean Reproductive Life Span Kinnaura Women and Comparison between Middle and High Altitude Women.

reproductive life span, and there is a tendency for extended reproductive life span among high altitude women as compared to middle altitude women.

Table 12
Central Tendencies and Deviations of Reproductive Life Span among Kinnaura Women of Middle and High Altitude.

Central Tendencies and Deviations		*Middle Altitude*	*High Altitude*	*Kinnaura (Pooled)*
Number		155	118	273
Mean		29.10	31.42	30.10
SE of Mean		0.207	0.301	0.188
Median		29.00	32.00	30.0
Mode		29	32(a)	29
SD		2.573	3.267	3.109
Minimum		19	22	19
Maximum		35	38	38
F-Ratio		182.09*	195.69*	437.02*
Percentiles	25	28.00	29.00	28.00
	50	29.00	32.00	30.00
	75	31.00	34.00	32.00

(a) Multiple modes exist. The smallest value is shown.
* Significant at 1% level.

The measures of central tendency and deviation of reproductive life span for the Kinnaura women are shown in Table 12. The mean reproductive life span among Kinnaura women is found to be 30.10 (±3.10) years, and varies from 19 to 38 years. The mean reproductive life span among middle altitude Kinnaura women is found to be 29.10 (±2.57) years, and varies from 19 to 35 years. The mean reproductive life span among high altitude Kinnaura women, however, has been found to be 31.42 (±3.27) years and varies from 22 to 38 years. The facts are further elucidated by the help of box-plot and error bar diagramme (Figure 8 and 9), it is apparent from error bar diagramme (Figure 9) that there are significant difference in the reproductive life span of middle and high altitude women.

For the convenience of the study the reproductive life span can be categorized into short (≤25 years), normal (26-31 years) and extended (≥32 years) and on the basis of this categorization it was found that 63% of Kinnaura women have normal reproductive life span, 31.1% have extended reproductive life span, whereas 5.9% have short reproductive life span. The tendency of extended reproductive life span is greater in high altitude women as 50.8% of high altitude women are found to have extended life span as compared to 16% of middle altitude women (Table 13). The reasons for such a disparity need to be probed further.

Table 13
Distribution of Kinnaura Women as Per Short, Normal and Extended Life Spans.

	Middle Altitude		*High Altitude*		*Total*	
Reproductive Life Span	*N*	*%*	*N*	*%*	*N*	*%*
Short (≤25 Years)	10	6.5	6	5.1	16	5.9
Normal (26-31 Years)	120	77.4	52	44.1	172	63.0
Extended (≥32 Years)	25	16.1	60	50.8	85	31.1
Total	155	100.0	118	100.0	273	100.0

Table 14
Result of Bivariate & Multiple Regression Analysis (Dependent Variable Reproductive Life Span) for Kinnaura Women.

	Coefficients of Regression					*F Statistics*	
Independent Variable	*R*	*r^2*	*β*	*SE*	*t-value*	*F Change*	*p-value*
Continuous Variables							
Age at Menarche	0.240	0.058	-0.500	0.123	-4.075	16.608	0.001
Age at Menopause	0.885	0.783	0.885	0.028	31.228	975.175	0.001
Multiple Regression Coefficient R=1.000, R^2=1.000, SE=0.00, F=2.0145Õ$10^{17}$and p<0.001							
Current Age	0.281	0.079	0.081	0.017	4.823	23.258	0.001
Age at marriage	0.045	0.002	0.037	0.053	0.698	0.487	0.486
Altitude	0.291	0.085	0.002	0.000	5.007	25.074	0.001
Multiple Regression Coefficient R=0.414, R^2=0.172, SE=2.827, F=16.795 and p<0.001							
Categorical Variables							
Education	0.118	0.014	-0.409	0.209	-1.962	3.851	0.051
Occupation	0.093	0.009	0.172	0.112	1.538	2.365	0.125
Marital Status	0.094	0.009	0.996	0.639	1.558	2.427	0.120
Multiple Regression Coefficient R=0.167, R^2=0.028, SE=3.082, F=2.547 and p<0.054							

The regression analysis (Table 14) shows that the reproductive life span is determined mostly by the age at

Table 15

Bivariate Correlation Between Dependent and Independent Variables.

	Y	*X1*	*X2*	*X3*	*X4*	*X5*	*X6*	*X7*	*X8*
Reproductive life span **(Y)**	1.000	-0.240(**)	0.885(**)	0.281(**)	0.045	0.291(**)	-0.118	0.093	0.094
Age at Menarche **(X1)**		1.000	0.240(**)	0.020	0.384(**)	-0.002	-0.048	-.315(**)	-0.018
Age at Menopause **(X2)**			1.000	0.291(**)	0.224(**)	0.290(**)	-0.141(*)	-0.058	0.086
Current Age **(X3)**				1.000	0.086	0.011	-0.302(**)	0.060	0.089
Age at marriage **(X4)**					1.000	0.164(**)	0.026	-0.141(*)	(a)
Altitude **(X5)**						1.000	-0.166(**)	-0.061	-0.100
ducation Level **(X6)**							1.000	-0.03	-0.064
Occupation **(X7)**								1.000	0.121(*)
Mariatal status **(X8)**									1.000

** Correlation is significant at the 0.01 level (2-tailed).

* Correlation is significant at the 0.05 level (2-tailed).

(a) Cannot be computed.

menopause, which accounts for 78.3 % variability whereas the age at menarche accounts for only for 5.8% of variability. Among other determinants, current age of women and altitude are found to have significant correlation with the reproductive life span of the women, However, age at marriage, education, occupation and marital status have non significant correlation with it. It should be noted that the age at menarche and education have negative correlation with the reproductive life span of the Kinnaura women (Table 15).

It can be concluded that the reproductive life span of Kinnaura women is determined by biological factors like menopause and ecological factor like altitude, whereas socio-economic factors like age at marriage, education, occupation and marital status do not play significant role in this event. Of all the determinants considered in the present investigation, age at menopause has been found to have strong positive and

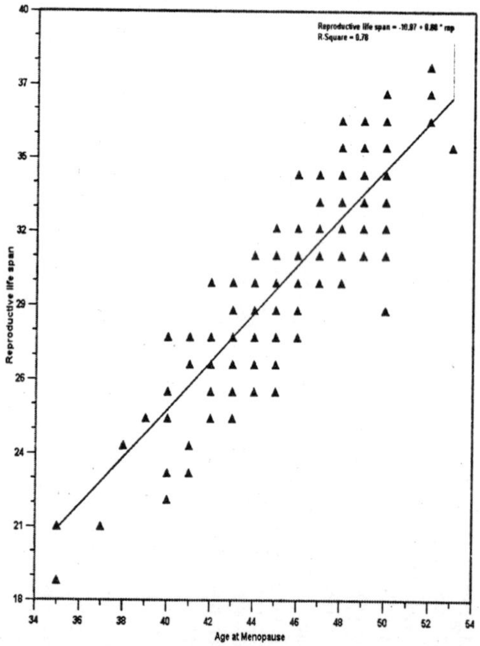

Figure 10: Bivariate Scattered Plot Diagramme showing Positive Correlation between Reproductive Life Span and Age at Menopause

significant correlation with the reproductive life span of women (Figure 10). Thomas et.al. (2000) found the negative correlation between fertility and age at menopause, suggested a possible existence of reproductive costs in humans. It has been recommended that early and high investment into reproduction may result in shorter longevity (Westendrop and Kirkwood, 1998; Thomas et.al. 2000). However, other studies have found a significant relationship betw een fertility and age at menopause (e.g. Walsh, 1978; Kirchengast, 1992; Do et.al. 1998). In the present investigation it was not possible to compute correlation between menopause and fertility, or fertility and reproductive life span. The important finding of the present study is negative correlation between reproductive life span and menarche (Figure 11) and reproductive life span and education. Studies on the different population groups from India on the reproductive life span and its associated variables will shed more light on the dynamics of human fertility.

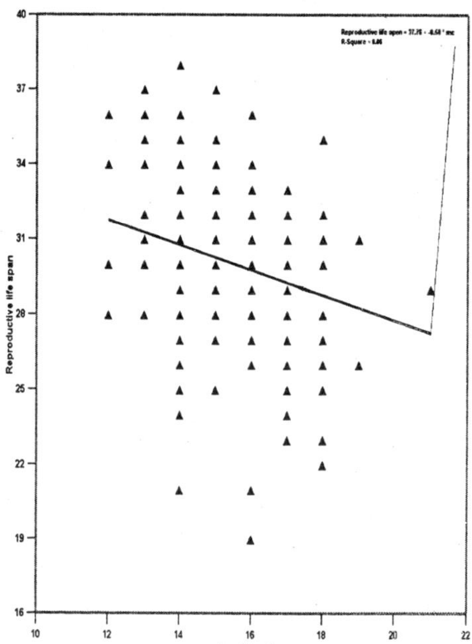

Figure 11: Bivariate Scattered Plot Diagramme Showing Negative Correlation between Reproductive Life Span and Age at Menarche

Chapter 8

POPULATION STRUCTURE AND CHARACTERISTICS

Structure and composition of human population is usually complex in nature. Biological and demographical variation, in human population is apparent from continent to continent and country to country as per geographical and political boundaries. In other words, human population has a unique structure, specific to area, ecology and ethnicity to some extent. The organization of such small and isolated groups can provide important understanding for effective planning and developing alternative strategies.

Capability of human being to survive in adverse circumstances leads to adaptability in the particular environment. The whole phenomena move through cultural changes to biological and genetic changes. The changes come gradually, after many generations. Some changes can be measured directly while some indirectly. Population characteristics of middle and high altitude may reflect differences due to their settlement in different ecological setups. In this chapter an attempt has been made to elucidate the population characteristics of middle (2000-3000 metre) and high altitude (above 3000 metre). Here size, composition (age and sex), dependency ratios and aging index are taken into consideration under this chapter; such analysis of population aims to finding out and measuring the changes taking place and suggest proper strategy to over come the situation.

POPULATION SIZE

Size of population is first demographic fact; total population of an area, community, state or country is required for various planning and administrative purposes; this total population is described as population size, which varies according to time and space.

According to censuses 1901 to 2001, total population of Kinnaur district the State of Himachal Pradesh and India is given in Table 1, and the village-wise population covered under present study is presented in Table 2.

Table 1
Decennial Growth of Population, 1901- 2001, in Kinnaur, Himachal Pradesh, India

	Kinnaur		*Himachal*		*India*	
Census Year	*Pop.*	*Growth Rate*	*Pop. (in 000')*	*Growth Rate*	*Pop. (in 000')*	*Growth Rate*
1901	27,232		1920		238396	
1911	28,470	4.55	1897	-1.22	252093	5.75
1921	28,191	-0.98	1928	1.65	251321	-0.31
1931	30,445	8.00	2029	5.23	278977	11.00
1941	33,268	9.17	2263	11.54	318661	14.22
1951	34,475	3.72	2386	5.42	361088	13.31
1961	40,980	18.87	2812	17.87	439235	21.51
1971	49,835	12.61	3460	23.04	548160	24.80
1981	59,547	19.49	4238	23.71	683329	24.66
1991	71,270	19.69	5170	20.79	846302	23.86
2001	77,007	8.04	6077	17.53	1027015	21.34
Overall growth rate (1901-2001)		114.9		128.0		160.8

Source: Census of India 1991 & 2001.

Village-Wise Distribution of Population

Village-wise households and population distribution of Kinnaura of middle and high altitude is given in Table 2. A total of 13 villages were covered from middle altitude, while 14 villages were covered from high altitude area. The villages of middle altitude are in Kalpa sub-division and the villages of high altitude are in Pooh sub-division of Kinnaur district of Himachal Pradesh state of India. There is no urban area in the district; it is 100 per cent rural. The villages of middle altitude are situated at the height of 2000-3000 metre, while high altitude village are situated at the range of 3000 to 3900 metre from mean sea level. Total 394 households were covered from 13 villages of middle altitude while 426 households were covered from 14 villages of high altitude. The population covered from middle and high altitude is almost equal, 2479 from middle altitude while 2512 from high altitude. As per Table 2, in middle altitude the population covered is distributed in the range of 3.9 to 9.9 per cent in the surveyed villages, while in high altitude it is distributed in the range of 2.3 to 15.2 per cent. Sex ratio is calculated for each village which varies from 780 to 1224 women per 1000 male. Both the highest and lowest sex ratio exists in high altitude villages, if we compare the same for Middle and High Altitude population there is no wider difference, in middle altitude it is slightly higher (1011 women per 1000 male) as compared to high altitude (1002 women per 1000 male). The masculinity proportion clearly indicates the lack of male population in many of village, simultaneously there are some villages in which excess of male population (<50 percent) and such villages are more in number in the high altitude.

Table 2
Village Wise Distribution of Population covered and Sex Ratio

Name of Village	*Sex* *Male*	*Female*	*Total*	*% of Total Population*	*Sex Ratio*	*Masculinity Proportion*
			Middle Altitude			
Kilba	120	116	236	9.5	967	50.85
Khawangi	85	108	193	7.8	1271	44.04
Sudharang	95	106	201	8.1	1116	47.26
Telingi	103	115	218	8.8	1117	47.25
Kothi	125	115	240	9.7	920	52.08
Brilingi	89	93	182	7.3	1045	48.90
Duni	97	106	203	8.2	1093	47.78
Kashmir	47	50	97	3.9	1064	48.45
Yuwarangi	54	62	116	4.7	1148	46.55
Saryo	99	82	181	7.3	828	54.70

Contd...

Name of Village	Sex: Male	Sex: Female	Total	% of Total Population	Sex Ratio	Masculinity Proportion
Middle Altitude						
Khawanta	94	88	182	7.3	936	51.65
Pangi	135	111	246	9.9	822	54.88
Kalpa	90	94	184	7.4	1044	48.91
Total	1233	1246	2479	100	1011	49.74
High Altitude						
Morang	132	123	255	10.2	932	51.76
Akpa	52	50	102	4.1	962	50.98
Kanam	28	28	56	2.2	1000	50.00
Thangi	59	46	105	4.2	780	56.19
Dubling	58	71	129	5.1	1224	44.96
Pooh	190	192	382	15.2	1011	49.74
Giabong	64	75	139	5.5	1172	46.04
Leo	98	88	186	7.4	898	52.69
Maling	83	75	158	6.3	904	52.53
Nako	115	123	238	9.5	1070	48.32
Hango	32	27	59	2.3	844	54.24
Chango	66	72	138	5.5	1091	47.83
Shialkher	118	126	244	9.7	1068	48.36
Sumra	160	161	321	12.8	1006	49.84
Total	1255	1257	2512	100.0	1002	49.96
Grand Total	2488	2503	4991	100.0	1006	49.84

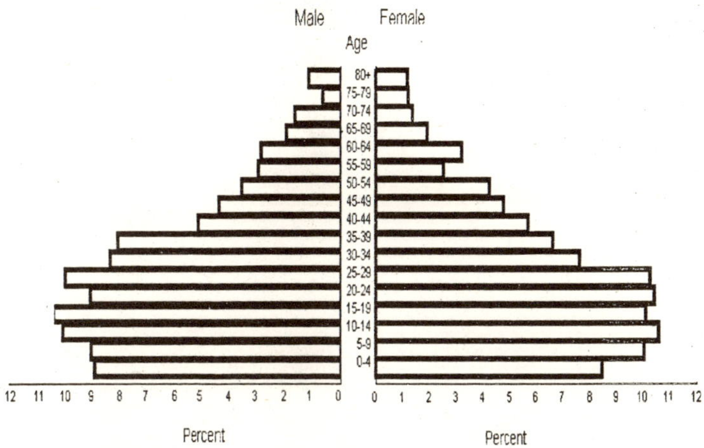

Figure 1: Population Pyramid of Kinnaura (pooled)

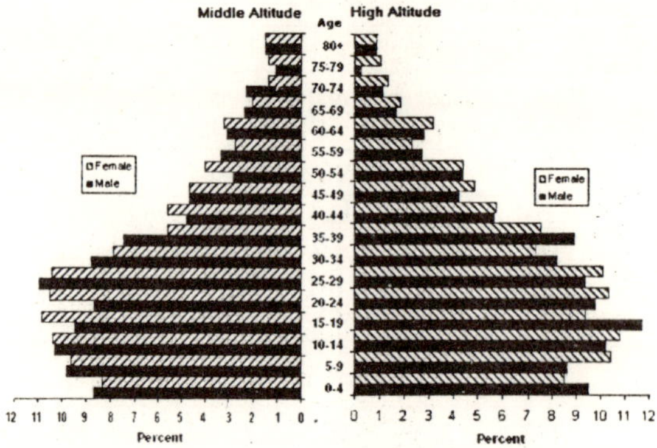

Figure 2: Population Pyramid of Kinnaura of Middle and High Altitude (pooled)

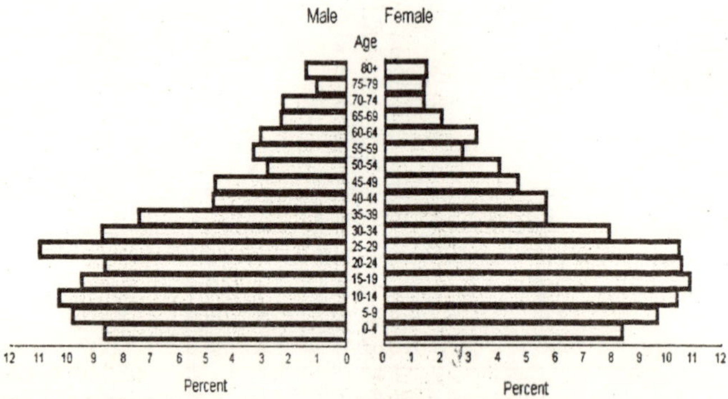

Figure 3: Population Pyramids of Middle Altitude Kinnaura.

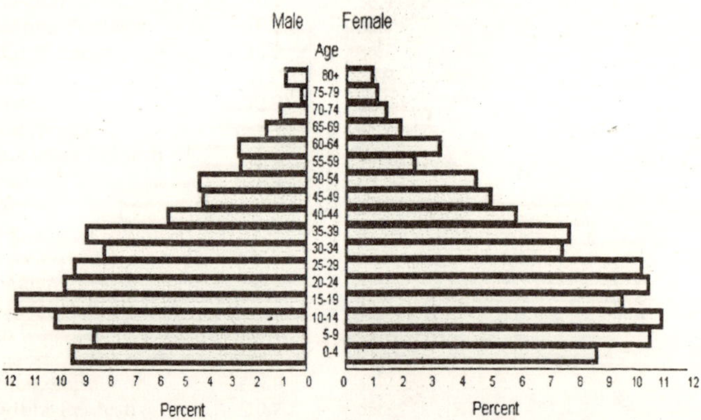

Figure 4: Population Pyramids of High Altitude Kinnaura.

POPULATION COMPOSITION

A population is always amalgamation of people of two sexes and different ages; hence every population has a unique structure, which can be described in terms of its age and sex composition. The structure of a population is closely associated with the number of births, deaths and migrations. In general these events do not occur in the same pattern across all the age groups and both the sexes of all the populations, therefore populations differ from one another with respect to their structure.

The age-sex composition depicts the basic demographic state of a population in a region. It substantially influences the capacity or potential for future population change. Simultaneously, the present structure of population is the result of past changes; i.e. past vector of fertility, mortality, migration, epidemics, natural calamities (flood, earthquake) etc. Therefore, the study of population composition is an essential step towards comprehensive understanding of population characteristics of an area.

Table 3
Age Composition Among Middle and High Altitude Kinnaura

	Middle Altitude		*High Altitude*		*Kinnaur (Pooled)*	
Age Group	N	%	N	%	N	%
0-4	211	8.5	226	9.0	437	8.8
5-9	241	9.7	239	9.5	480	9.6
10-14	256	10.3	264	10.5	520	10.4
15-19	252	10.2	265	10.5	517	10.4
20-24	238	9.6	253	10.1	491	9.8
25-29	265	10.7	245	9.8	510	10.2
30-34	206	8.3	195	7.8	401	8.0
35-39	162	6.5	207	8.2	369	7.4
40-44	129	5.2	143	5.7	272	5.4
45-49	116	4.7	114	4.5	230	4.6
50-54	85	3.4	110	4.4	195	3.9
55-59	75	3.0	63	2.5	138	2.8
60-64	78	3.1	75	3.0	153	3.1
65-69	54	2.2	44	1.8	98	2.0
70-74	45	1.8	31	1.2	76	1.5
75-79	30	1.2	16	0.6	46	.9
80+	36	1.5	22	0.9	58	1.2
Total	2479	100.0	2512	100.0	4991	100.0

Age Composition

The analysis of age composition is a potential source to find out the dynamics of population growth. It also indicates the relative level of development of an area. In a developed region proportion of persons tend to higher in the older than younger age groups, while contrary to that developing region having young population structure. Present data on age is collected in terms of completed years. This (age-data) has been then categorized into five years groups (cohort), instead of single year numbers. Using these standard five years age group, the age composition of presently studied Kinnaura of middle and high altitude area of Kinnaur district Himachal Pradesh is presented in Table 3 and 4. To comprehend the overall age composition in middle and high altitude population pyramids constructed (Figure 1, 2, 3 and 4). On the basis of present data, Kinnaura show a relatively old age structure, with moderate fertility and falling mortality.

The comparison of middle and high altitude shows that the proportion of young and adult are higher in high altitude as compared to middle altitude and proportion of aged (60 +years) is less in high altitude. Out of total population of high altitude 29 per cent are in 0-14 years of age group, 63.5 per cent were in 15-59 years of age group and 7.5 per cent were in 60 + years age group; whereas in middle altitude 28.6 per cent were in 0-14 years of age group, 61.6 per cent were in 15-59 years of age group and 9.8 per cent were in 60+ years age group.

It was estimated that 28.8 per cent of the total population are in the age group of 0-14 years, 62.6 per cent were in the age group of 15-59 and 8.6 per cent were population were aged 60 years and over. In this way among Kinnaura the proportion of broad age group (15-59 years) constitutes 62.6 per cent of the total population, which is higher than that for India (56 per cent) and for Himachal Pradesh, Jammu and Kashmir, Madhya Pradesh, Rajasthan and Gujarat, where this proportion is 57.9 per cent, 55.7 per cent, 52.9 per cent and 52.2 per cent, 59.9 per cent and 56 per cent, respectively (NFHS-2, 2000). Further, person aged 60 years and over according to NFHS-2

(2000) constitute 7.9 per cent in India and 10 per cent in Himachal Pradesh, 8.1 per cent in Madhya Pradesh, 7.5 per cent in the states of J & K, Rajasthan and Gujarat, whereas in present study area the proportion of older people is 8.6 per cent, there is minute difference in this regard in middle altitude (the aged people 60 + years are 9.8 per cent) and high altitude (7.5 per cent). Result of present study indicates that the Kinnaura are passing through the second stage of population transition with growing young workforce and falling proportion of dependents, which is one of the progressive characters of the population.

Sex Composition: Sex Ratio

All the main determinants or factors of population dynamics-births, deaths, migration and marriage is being affected by the sex composition, further these driving forces leads to influence all the population characteristics including socio-economic and community life; hence sex composition of a population has a vital role in population analysis. In addition development of an area also affects the sex compositions of population of that area. Contrary to that the sex composition of a region is being affected by the socio-cultural practices e.g. marriage, family structure; availability of medical facilities and by the environmental factors viz. altitude, temperature, weather etc. of that region. Two basic measures are used here to study the sex composition of the population of Kinnaura— (i) sex ratio and (ii) masculinity proportion.

Table 4
Sex Composition and Sex Ratio (Number of Female Per 1000 Male) among Study Population Kinnaura of Middle and High Altitude.

	Middle Altitude		*High Altitude*		*Kinnaur (Pooled)*	
Sex	N	%	N	%	N	%
Male	1233	49.7	1255	50.0	2488	49.8
Female	1246	50.3	1257	50.0	2503	50.2
Total	2479	100.0	2512	100.0	4991	100.0
Sex Ratio	1011		1002		1006	

The sex composition and sex ratio of present study population has shown in Table 4, 5 and 6. The sex ratio has been found 1006 women per 1000 males, which indicates higher proportion of females than males. This is an important observation. Table 4 indicates a very positive trend for Kinnaura. The comparison between middle and high altitude shows that the estimate is higher for middle altitude (1011) than high altitude (1002). Age-wise sex ratio of Kinnaura of middle and high altitude have shown in Table 5 reveal the low sex ratio for 0-4 years, 15-19 years, 30-34 years, 35-39 years, 55-59 years, 65-69 years and 70-74 years, whereas the rest of the age groups show high sex ratio, variation in middle and high altitude population is also explicit from the Table 5. Overall relatively high sex ratio of the study area indicates high male selective out-migration.

Table 5
Age Group-wise Sex Ratio Among Middle and High Altitude Kinnaura of Kinnaur District Himachal Pradesh

Age Group	*Sex Ratio*		
	Middle Altitude	*High Altitude*	*Kinnaur (Pooled)*
0-4	972	899	934
5-9	992	1213	1096
10-14	1016	1063	1039
15-19	1154	803	958
20-24	1224	1057	1135
25-29	963	1076	1016
30-34	907	893	900
35-39	761	848	809
40-44	1186	1014	1092
45-49	1000	1151	1072
50-54	1429	1000	1167
55-59	829	853	840
60-64	1053	1143	1096
65-69	862	1095	960
70-74	607	1214	810
75-79	1308	4333	1875
80+	1000	1000	1000
Total	1011	1002	1006

Further more the sex ratio in most of the developing countries are disturbed as the proportion of male folk is

Table 6
Age-Sex Composition of Middle and High Altitude Kinnaura of Kinnaur District Himachal Pradesh.

Age	*Middle Altitude*				*High Altitude*				*Kinnaur (Pooled)*				*Total*	
	Male		*Female*		*Male*		*Female*		*Male*		*Female*			
	N	%	N	%	N		%		N	%	N	%	N	%
0-4	107	8.7	104	8.3	119	9.5	107	8.5	226	9.1	211	8.4	437	8.8
5-9	121	9.8	120	9.6	108	8.6	131	10.4	229	9.2	251	10.0	480	9.6
10-14	127	10.3	129	10.4	128	10.2	136	10.8	255	10.2	265	10.6	520	10.4
15-19	117	9.5	135	10.8	147	11.7	118	9.4	264	10.6	253	10.1	517	10.4
20-24	107	8.7	131	10.5	123	9.8	130	10.3	230	9.2	261	10.4	491	9.8
25-29	135	10.9	130	10.4	118	9.4	127	10.1	253	10.2	257	10.3	510	10.2
30-34	108	8.8	98	7.9	103	8.2	92	7.3	211	8.5	190	7.6	401	8.0
35-39	92	7.5	70	5.6	112	8.9	95	7.6	204	8.2	165	6.6	369	7.4
40-44	59	4.8	70	5.6	71	5.7	72	5.7	130	5.2	142	5.7	272	5.4
45-49	58	4.7	58	4.7	53	4.2	61	4.9	111	4.5	119	4.8	230	4.6
50-54	35	2.8	50	4.0	55	4.4	55	4.4	90	3.6	105	4.2	195	3.9
55-59	41	3.3	34	2.7	34	2.7	29	2.3	75	3.0	63	2.5	138	2.8
60-64	38	3.1	40	3.2	35	2.8	40	3.2	73	2.9	80	3.2	153	3.1
65-69	29	2.4	25	2.0	21	1.7	23	1.8	50	2.0	48	1.9	98	2.0
70-74	28	2.3	17	1.4	14	1.1	17	1.4	42	1.7	34	1.4	76	1.5
75-79	13	1.1	17	1.4	3	0.2	13	1.0	16	0.6	30	1.2	46	0.9
80+	18	1.5	18	1.4	11	0.9	11	0.9	29	1.2	29	1.2	58	1.2
Total	1233	100	1246	100	1255	100	1257	100	2488	100	2503	100	4991	100

increasing incomparison to females, unlike the trend observed in the developed ones. For example, while USA (1985), Japan (1984) have returned high sex ratios (showing higher proportion females than males) of 1055, 1033, respectively India (2001) China (1982) Bangladesh (1981), Pakistan (1981), Sri Lanka (1984), Nepal (1985) have shown comparatively low estimates at 933, 941, 905, 962, 946 respectively (UNICEF, 1991; Census of India, 2001).

However within India, the variation in the sex ratios across different regions of India is quite remarkable. As per Census of India (2001) the highest and lowest sex ratios have been observed as 1058 for Kerala and 710 for Daman and Diu, respectively. On the whole major northern states like Haryana (861), Punjab (876), Uttar Pradesh (898) have lower sex ratios than major southern states of Kerala (1058), Pondicherry (1001), Tamil Nadu (987), Andhra Pradesh (978), Karnataka (965), chiefly due to gender inequality and differences in status of women; which seems to be better in the southern than in the north/north western states of India (Table 7, Figure 5).

Table 7
Sex Ratio and Masculinity Proportion among Tribal and Non-Tribal Population of Different Himalayan Region, Himachal Pradesh and India.

Country/ State/ Region	*Population Group*	*Sex Ratio*	*Masculinity Proportion*	*Source*
HIMALAYAN REGION				
Eastern Himalaya				
Assam				
	Semsa	1005	49.88	Ghosh and Limbu (2002)
Sikkim				
	Buddhist	921		Bhasin and Bhasin (2000)
	Hindus	1051		"
	Total	982		"
	Bhutias	996	50.10	Bhasin and Bhasin (1995)
	Lepchas	849	54.09	"
	Sherpas	744	57.35	"
	Tamangs	984	50.41	"
Western Himalaya				
Jammu and Kashmir				

Contd...

Country/ State/ Region	*Population Group*	*Sex Ratio*	*Masculinity Proportion*	*Source*
Ladakh (HA)				Bhasin and Nag (2002)
	Bodhs	956	51.10	"
	Baltis	961	51.00	"
	Brokpas	947	51.40	"
	Arghuns	928	51.90	"
Himachal Pradesh				
	Gaddi	870	53.48	Bhasin and Bhasin (1993)
	Brahman	890	52.91	"
	Rajput	870	53.48	"
	SC	850	54.05	"
Central Himalaya				
Uttaranchal (or erstwhile UP)				
Total (Uttaranchal)	964	50.90		
	Johari Bhotia	1132		Kapoor (1996)
	Rang Bhotia	1209		"
	Marchha Bhotia	1168		"
	Marchha Bhotia	1005		Chachra and Bhasin (1998)
	Dharchula Bhotia	993		"
	Johar Bhotia	960		"
	Raji	818		Samal, et.al. (2000)
	Raji	858		Patra (2001)
	Jaunsaris	889		Kshatriya, et.al. (1997)
INDIA				
Madhya Pradesh				
	Hill Korwas [PTG]	954	–	Pandey and Tiwari (1993)
	Bharias [PTG]	1068	48.35	Pandey (2002)
	Birhor [PTG]	904	52.52	"
	Hill Korwas [PTG]	946	51.40	"
	Bharias	1010	–	"
	Oraon	931	–	"
	Pando	931	–	"
Chhatisgarh				
	Kamar [PTG]	1038	49.07	"
	Gond	895	–	"
India	Total Population	933	52	Census of India, 2001
	ST	978	51	"
Jammu & Kashmir	Total Population	892	53	"
	ST	910	52	"
Himachal Pradesh	Total Population	968	51	"
	ST	996	50	"
Punjab	Total Population	876	53	"
	ST	–	–	"
Chandigarh	Total Population	777	56	"
	ST	–	–	"

Contd...

Country/ State/ Region	Population Group	Sex Ratio	Masculinity Proportion	Source
Uttaranchal	Total Population	962	51	Census of India, 2001
	ST	950	51	"
Haryana	Total Population	861	54	"
	ST	–	–	"
Delhi	Total Population	821	55	"
	ST	–	–	"
Rajasthan	Total Population	921	52	"
	ST	944	51	"
Uttar Pradesh	Total Population	898	53	"
	ST	934	52	"
Bihar	Total Population	919	52	"
	ST	929	52	"
Sikkim	Total Population	875	53	"
	ST	957	51	"
Arunachal Pradesh	Total Population	893	53	"
	ST	1,003	50	"
Nagaland	Total Population	900	53	"
	ST	943	51	"
Manipur	Total Population	978	51	"
(Excl. 3 Sub-Divisions)	ST	980	51	"
Mizoram	Total Population	935	52	"
	ST	984	50	"
Tripura	Total Population	948	51	"
	ST	970	51	"
Meghalaya	Total Population	972	51	"
	ST	1,000	50	"
Assam	Total Population	935	52	"
	ST	972	51	"
West Bengal	Total Population	934	52	"
	ST	982	50	"
Jharkhand	Total Population	941	52	"
	ST	987	50	"
Orissa	Total Population	972	51	"
	ST	1,003	50	"
Chhattisgarh	Total Population	989	50	"
	ST	1,013	50	"
Madhya Pradesh	Total Population	919	52	"
	ST	975	51	"
Gujarat	Total Population	920	52	"
	ST	974	51	"
Daman & Diu	Total Population	710	58	"
	ST	947	51	"
Dadra & Nagar Haveli	Total Population	812	55	"
	ST	1,028	49	"
Maharashtra	Total Population	922	52	"
	ST	973	51	"
Andhra Pradesh	Total Population	978	51	"
	ST	972	51	"

Contd...

Country/ State/ Region	*Population Group*	*Sex Ratio*	*Masculinity Proportion*	*Source*
Karnataka	Total Population	965	51	"
	ST	972	51	"
Goa	Total Population	961	51	"
	ST	893	53	"
Lakshadweep	Total Population	948	51	"
	ST	1,003	50	"
Kerala	Total Population	1,058	49	"
	ST	1,021	49	"
Tamil Nadu	Total Population	987	50	"
	ST	980	50	"
Pondicherry	Total Population	1,001	50	"
	ST	–	–	"
Andaman &	Total Population	846	54	"
Nicobar Islands	ST	948	51	"
Kinnaur	Kinnaura	1006	49.89	Present study (2006)
Middle altitude	"	1011	49.73	"
High Altitude	"	1002	49.96	"

* Projected
SC = Scheduled Caste
ST = Scheduled Tribe
PTG = Primitive Tribal Group.

The sex ratio of Kinnaura has been found 1006 women per 1000 males, which indicates higher proportion of females than males. This is an important observation. As per Census of India (2001) only Hamirpur, Kangra and Mandi districts of Himachal Pradesh having higher sex ratio; Although the same census estimation gives a sex ratio of 851 female per 1000 males, for the district Kinnaur. The sex ratio estimation of the census is for 'total population' and includes "others" which in fact distort the picture. The estimated sex ratio of the tribal group from District Statistical Handbook (2001) comes out to be 1082 females per one thousand males. Moreover, the calculation of sex ratio of studied villages from the ICDS (Integrated Child Development Scheme) records (July, 2001) gives a sex ratio of 1008 females per one thousand males, Similarly the sex ratio was found to be 1003 females per one thousand males for the total population covered in 7 ICDS circle namely Kalpa, Sangla, Akpa, Morang, Spillo, Pooh and Chango. Even the SC population of the district has a sex ratio of 938 females per one thousand males.

The estimation of sex ratio for Total and ST (scheduled tribe) population of Indian states by census of India (2001) shows that the states of north India like Punjab, Haryana, Chandigarh and Delhi, which are economically developed, they are demographically backward, the number of women per 1000 male in such states is less than 900; these states also don't have any tribal population. Only two states of south India viz. Kerala and Pondicherry have more than 1000 women per

Comparative Bar Diagramme of Sex Ratio among Total and Tribal Population in different States of Indian Union (Census of India, 2001) and Kinnaura

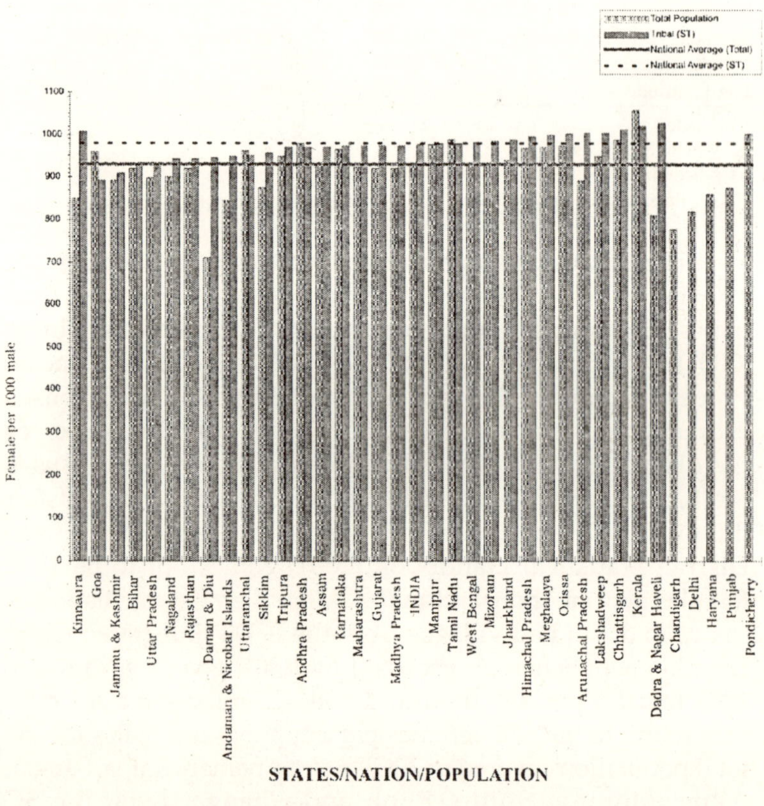

Figure 5: Comparative Bar Diagramme of Sex Ratio among Total and Tribal Population in Different States of Indian Union (Census of India, 2001).

each thousand of males. Out of 35 states of Indian union, 31 having tribal population. The sex ratio of Tribals can be compared with Total population. Except Goa, in none of the state the sex ratio of tribal is less than 900 hundred, further out of 31, in 6 states, the sex ratio of tribals is more than 1000. In this way, it can be concluded that tribals having no sex selection for child resulting into better sex ratio.

DEPENDENCY RATIO

Dependency ratio is based on the presumption that every member of the society is a consumer and only some of them are producer. The ratio of these two types of people is known as dependency ratio. The ratio reflects the level of development of a region, as this ratio declines the level of development enhanced. It is estimated in reference to the proportion of younger (0-14 years) and older (60+ years) people, who are presumed as economically inactive, while the proportion of population at productive ages (15-59 years) is presumed as economically active. The dependency ratio can be estimated in parts as young age dependency ratio (YADR), old age dependency ratio (OADR), and the sum of two- total dependency ratios (TDR). It is an important indicator of population structure and characteristics. It is also an indicator of stage of development as well as the phases of demographic transitions. Today the world population is passing through three kind of demographic transition. The populations, which are in first stage of transition experiencing high mortality, the proportion of young dependents increases, leads to low to moderate economic growth. The example of the second phase of transition is countries like India, such countries experiencing declining fertility, growing young workforce, reducing the number of dependents, these conditions ultimately resulting in increasing productivity. By the third stage, mortality level at each age group is substantially reduced and fertility rates also hit rock bottom leading to considerable increment in the proportion of old age dependents, whereas economic growth is not alike as in second stage. In the present study all the three of dependency ratio have been estimated as evident from Table 8.

Young Age Dependency Ratio

In the present study population the young age dependency ratio has been estimated to be 46.01, for middle altitude this ratio is slightly higher (46.34) as compared to high altitude (45.71). The analyses of sex specific dependency ratio show that female young dependency ratio is slightly higher than for male in both the ecological zones.

To compare the young age dependency ratio of Kinnaura with global scenario an extensive analysis were done based on 2003 world population data sheet (Population Reference Bureau, 2003) of 47 countries of the world as shown in the bivariate scattered plot diagramme (Figure 6) indicates that majority of the countries of world can be categorized in three groups on the basis of YADR and OADR values. The countries having high, moderate, and low young age dependency ratio, fall under circle A, B and C respectively. Some countries are beyond these circles; mainly they are countries of East Asia, except Japan, they forming a separate cluster indicated as D. India is at the top of cluster B with moderate young age dependency ratio. The diagramme is also showing the correlation between young age dependency ratio and old age dependency ratio, the inverse relationship can be noticed between these two indicators, which are strongly associated and accounts for 60 per cent variability (R^2=0.60).

Inter-state Indian scenario is different as it is a big country with 35 (big and small) states, wide cultural, geographical, economical and political diversity, the demographic variation is characterizes in the form of inter-state variation of young age dependency ratio too. The bivariate scattered plot diagramme (Figure 7) plotted with YADR and OADR values of Census (2001) indicates that most of the states fall under four category, they are indicated as circles A, B, C and D. Under the category A, there are states, which were identified as BIMARU states or the states lagging behind in indicators, such states have high young age dependency ratio. In the category B, there are small states with low or moderate young age dependency ratio. Mostly these states are small states and union territories (except 3 north eastern states viz. Manipur,

Table 8
Dependency Ratio and Index of Aging among Middle and High Altitude Kinnaura

		Age Groups									*Dependency Ratio*		
		0-14		*15-59*		*60+*		*Total*					
Region	*Sex*	*N*	*%*	*N*	*%*	*N*	*%*	*N*	*%*	*Aging Index*	*Young Age*	*Old Age*	*Total*
Middle Altitude	M	335	28.8	752	61.0	126	10.2	1233	100	37.61	44.55	16.76	61.30
	F	353	28.3	776	62.3	117	9.4	1246	100	33.14	45.49	15.08	60.57
	Total	708	28.6	1528	61.6	243	9.8	2479	100	34.32	46.34	15.90	62.24
High Altitude	M	355	28.3	816	65.0	84	6.7	1255	100	23.66	43.50	10.29	53.80
	F	374	29.8	779	62.0	104	8.3	1257	100	27.81	48.01	13.35	61.36
	Total	729	29.0	1595	63.5	188	7.5	2512	100	25.79	45.71	11.79	57.49
Kinnaur	M	710	28.5	1568	63.0	210	8.4	2488	100	29.58	45.28	13.39	58.67
	F	727	29.0	1555	62.1	221	8.8	2503	100	30.40	46.75	14.21	60.96
	Total	1437	28.8	3123	62.6	431	8.6	4991	100	29.99	46.01	13.80	59.81

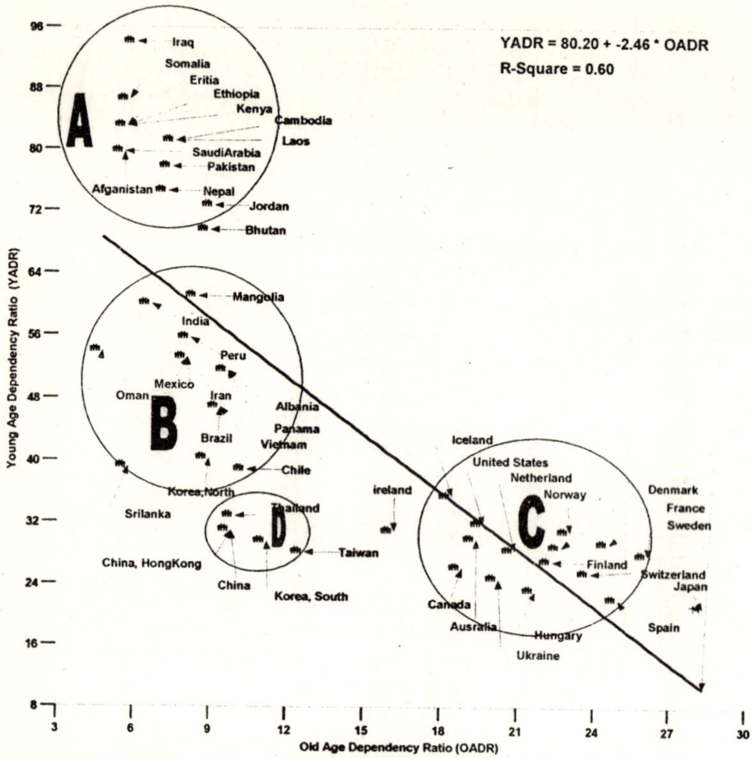

Figure 6: Bivariate Scattered Plot Diagramme of 47 Counties of the World with the Values of Young and Old Age Dependency Ratio (YADR &OADR)

Sikkim and Mizoram), circle C and D is formed with states having moderate to low YADR but increasing old age dependency ratio. Among Indian states too, the correlation between young age dependency ratio and old age dependency ratio is inverse, though the association is poor with negligible variability (R^2=0.00). Further when data for Himalayan states are separately plotted for bivariate scattered diagramme as shown in Figure 8 the correlation between two indicators are strongly associated and accounts for 29 per cent of variability (R^2=0.29).

In the light of above description, it is noticed that the present study population the Kinnaura of Kinnaur District,

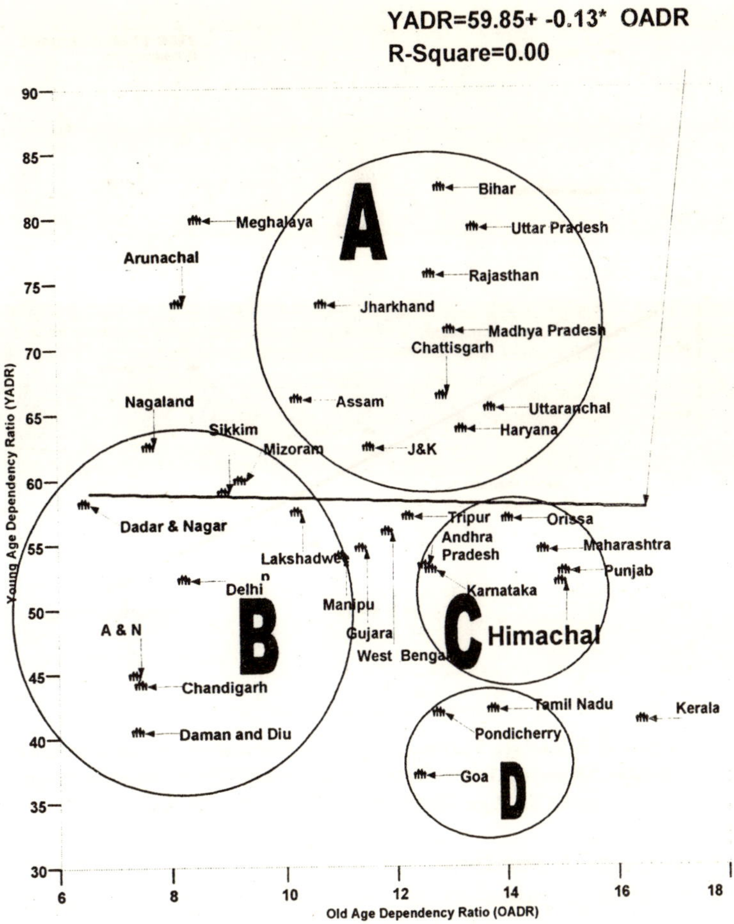

Figure 7: Bivariate Scattered Plot Diagramme of Indian States Showing Inter-State variation and Correlation of Young and Old Age Dependency Ratio (YADR &OADR).

Himachal Pradesh having low young age dependency ratio (46.01). The comparison of middle and high altitude doesn't show any significant difference for middle altitude Kinnaura this ratio is slightly higher (46.34) as compared to high altitude Kinnaura (45.71). Further the comparison of present findings with other studies and various population groups (Table 11) from India and Himalayan Regions portrays that the over all

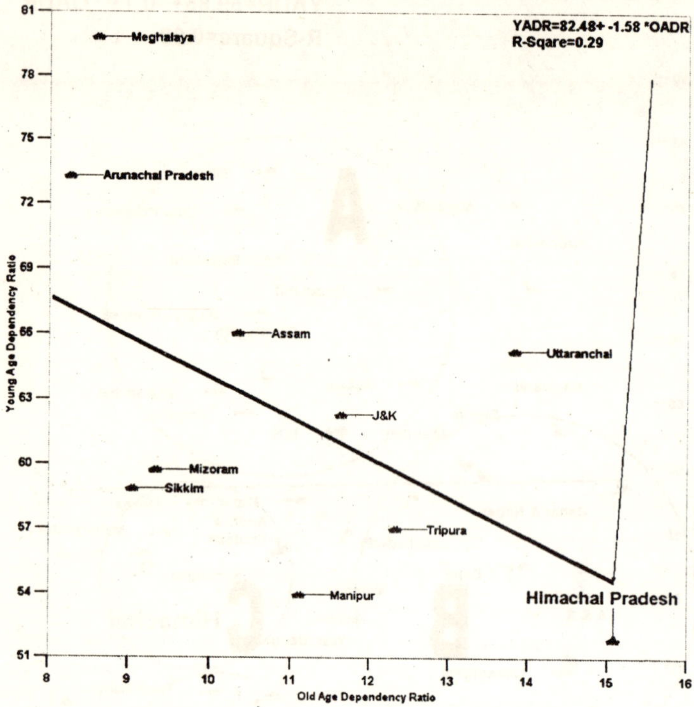

Figure 8: Bivariate Scattered Plot Diagramme of Indian Himalayan States Showing Inter-State Variation and Correlation of Young and Old Age Dependency Ratio (YADR &OADR).

young age dependency ratio among Kinnaura is lower than any other population as also apparent from scattered plot diagramme too (Figure 8). In this way Kinnaura are demographically progressive. They have fewer burdens of growing children resulting into better socio-economic development of region and people.

Old Age Dependency Ratio

The data (Table 8) reveals higher old age dependency ratio of 13.80 for Kinnaura. In middle altitude the old age dependency ratio was higher (15.90) than high altitude (11.79). Among Kinnaura, female old age dependency ratio was slightly higher than male old age dependency ratio, which indicates that the women of 60+ are greater in number in comparison to male folk. Further comparison of two ecological zones indicates that male old age dependency ratio was slightly higher in middle altitude, whereas female old age dependency ratio was higher in high altitude.

As already described the Yong Age Dependency Ratio (YADR) and Old Age Dependency Ratio (OADR) are strongly correlated with inverse relationship. The decline in Young Age Dependency Ratio leads to increase in Old Age Dependency Ratio. The result of present study indicates the same universal phenomena. The fall in Young Age Dependency Ratio of Kinnaura has resulted in the increment of Old Age Dependency Ratio. Therefore the Old Age Dependency Ratio of Kinnaura was estimated to be 13.80, which is higher than average of state (Census of India, 2001) and other tribal and non-tribal population compared (Figure 9 and 12). Though, the comparison of middle and high altitude doesn't show any significant difference in this respect, the ratio is slightly higher for middle altitude Kinnaura (15.90) as compared to high altitude Kinnaura (11.79), simultaneously it indicates that Kinnaura are demographically progressive as compared to other tribal and rural population of the country.

Total Dependency Ratio

The total dependency ratio for Kinnaura were estimated (59.81) was quite low, as compared to any other region of India, for population of Ladakh (J & K state), it is estimated at 75 (Bhasin and Nag, 2002), whereas for India and the state of Jammu and Kashmir it was found rather high at 85 and 89 in 1981 (Census of India, 1981). Further in 1992, the dependency ratio of India seems to have declined to 75 (Ministry of Health and Family Welfare, 1997). As the high dependency ratio implies low per capita production, the relatively low dependency ratio of studied population indicates better level of development of the region, as also observed from household income and standards of living and owing the luxurious goods. Furthermore the total dependency ratio is high (62.24) for middle altitude Kinnaura as compared to high altitude Kinnaura (57.49).

Total Dependency Ratio is the sum of the young and old age dependency ratios. As it is clear from the above discussion these two values have inverse correlation, and vary from population to population, state to state and one country to other, but ultimately, there is equilibrium. The range, mean and standard deviation of YADR, OADR and TDR for world, India, and small Indian Population groups like scheduled tribes and scheduled castes is given in Table 9.

Table 10
Analysis of Correlation and Regression on Total Dependency Ratio (TDR) with Young and Old age Dependency Ratios.

Dependent Variable	*Independent Variable*	*R*	R^2	$\beta1 \pm SE$	*F-Statistics* F-value	*df*	$< p$
				World			
TDR	YADR	0.967	0.935	0.754±0.30	646.997	46	0.001
TDR	OADR	0.591	0.350	-1.459±0.30	24.216	46	0.001
				India			
TDR	YADR	0.977	0.954	0.994±0.38	681.515	34	0.001
TDR	OADR	0.186	0.035	0.866±0.79	1.184	34	0.284
				Small Indian Population			
TDR	YADR	0.961	0.923	0.874±0.05	309.912	27	0.001
TDR	OADR	0.158	0.025	-0.491±0.60	0.661	27	0.423

The contribution of YADR and OADR to TDR in terms of percent is calculated for 47 countries of world, 35 Indian States and 28 different small Indian populations of different regions belonging to Scheduled Tribe and Castes including the present study population (Kinnaura of Middle and High Altitude) is presented in Figure 10, 11 and 12. It is apparent from the figures that the contribution of young age dependency ratio is always greater than old age dependency to the total dependency ratio, except in case of Japan and Spain, where old age dependency ratio is >50%. The regression and correlation analysis (Table 10) indicates that globally the young age dependency ratio accounts for 93.5% variability, and the old age dependency ratio account for 35% variability in the total dependency ratio with strong association and significant correlation. Among the Indian states the young age dependency ratio accounts for comparatively somewhat

Table 9
Range, Mean and Standard Deviation of YADR, OADR and TDR for World, India and Small Indian Population

	World			*India*			*Small Indian pop (Tribal)*		
	Min	*Max.*	*Mean±SD*	*Min*	*Max.*	*Mean±SD*	*Min*	*Max.*	*Mean±SD*
YADR	20.90	94.00	48.78±22.47	36.92	82.16	58.30±11.92	45.71	86.00	66.58±11.64
OADR	04.76	28.36	12.77±07.10	6.59	16.53	11.51±06.59	3.79	15.90	8.22±3.39
TDR	40.85	100	61.55±17.53	47.93	95.12	69.82±12.13	53.75	91.16	74.75±10.58

greater variability (95.4%) in comparison to global level, simultaneously the old age dependency ratio have least role only 3.5%. In the same way, among small Indian population groups, young age dependency ratio accounts for major variability (92.3%) to total dependency ratio as compared to old age dependency ratio (only 2.5%). Neither among Indian states nor among small Indian populations, the old age-dependency-ratio has found any significant correlation with the total dependency ratio (Table 10).

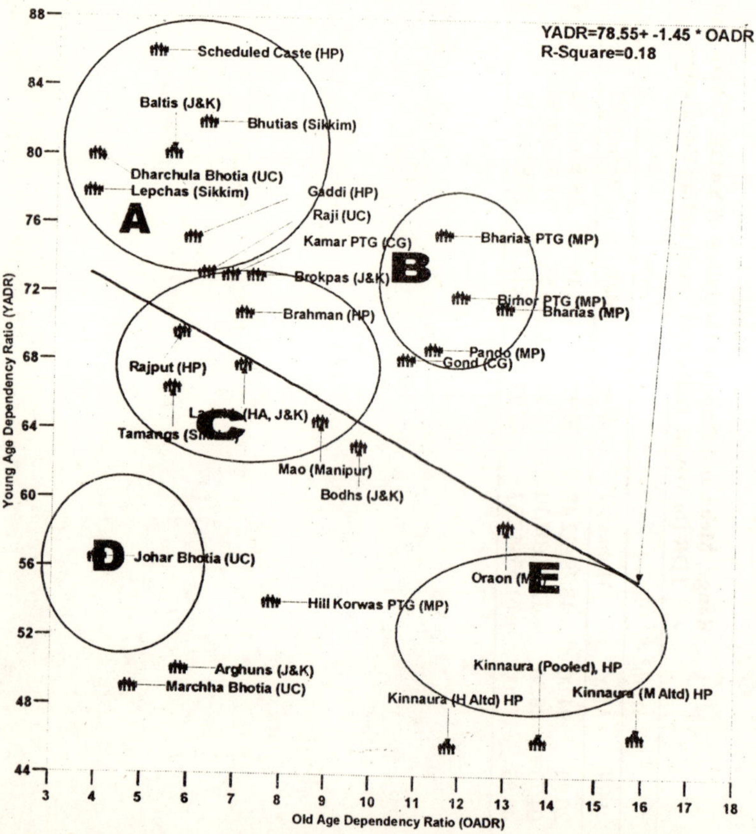

Figure 9: Bivariate Scattered Plot Diagramme of Indian Populations Showing Inter- Population Variation of Young and Old Age Dependency Ratio (YADR & OADR) and Correlation between two Indicators.

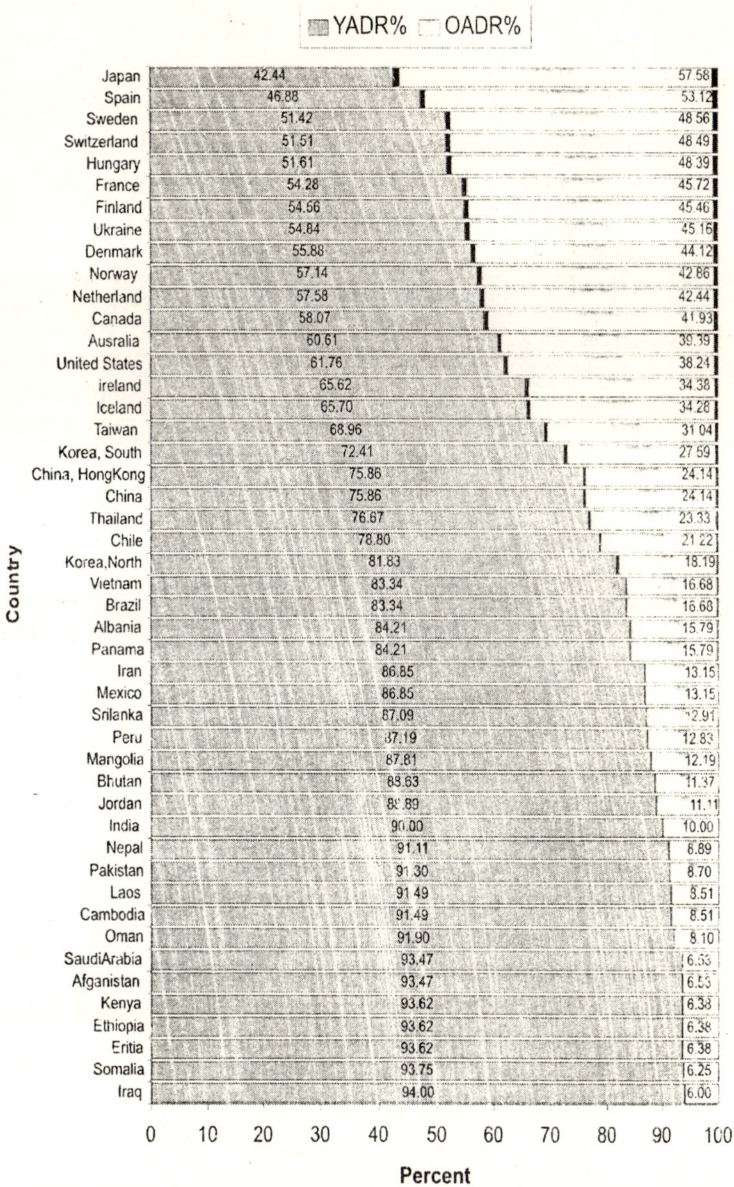

Figure 10: The Global Scenario of the Contribution of Young and Old Age Dependency Ratio to the Total Dependency Ratio (in terms of percentage) among the 47 Countries of the World.

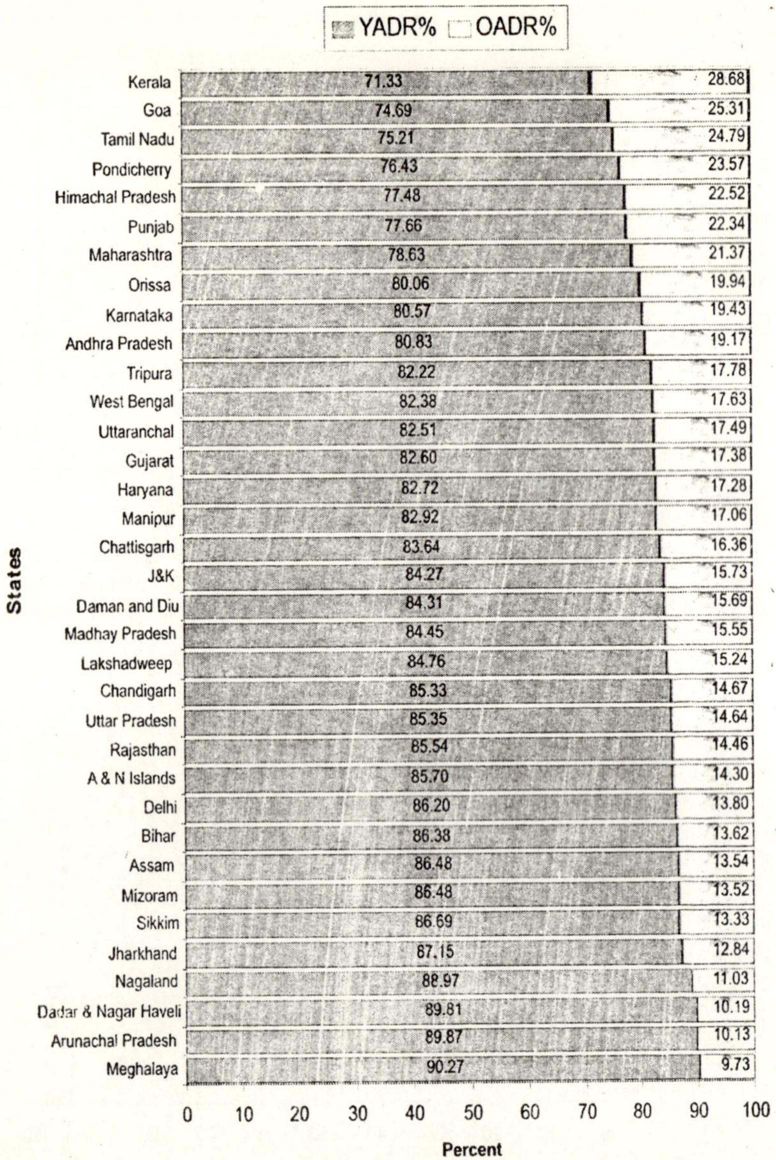

Figure 11: The Indian Scenario of the Contribution of Young and Old Age Dependency Ratio to the Total Dependency Ratio (in terms of percentage) among the 35 states of the country.

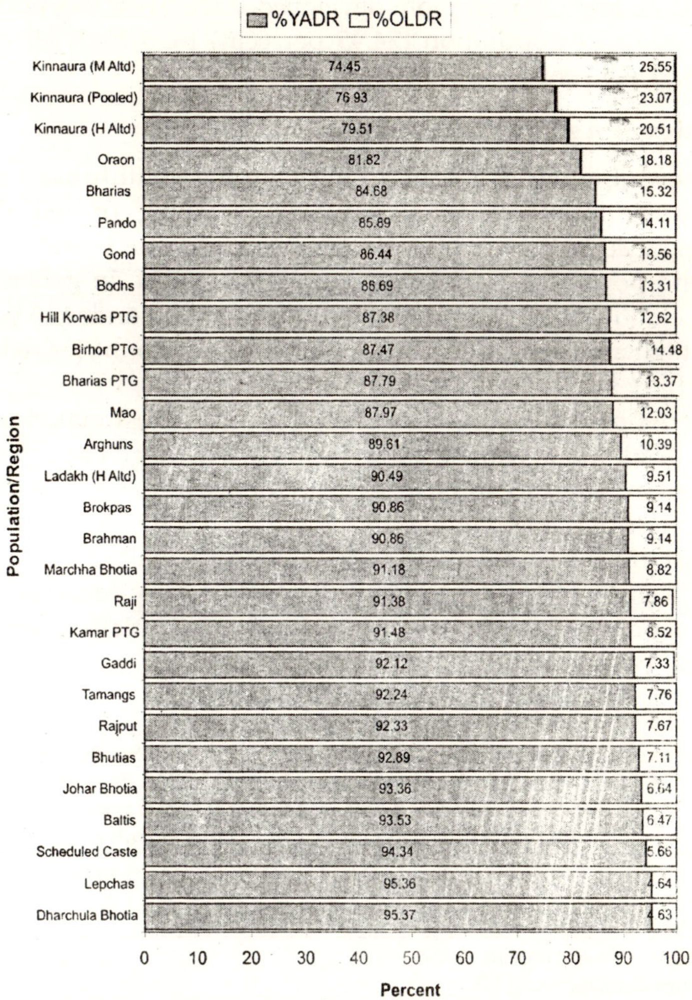

Figure 12: 100% Bar Diagramme showing the contribution of Young and Old Age Dependency Ratio to the Total Dependency Ratio (in terms of percentage) among the 28 small Indian Population.

In the light of above discussion, the findings of present study indicates that among Kinnaura the contribution of young and old age dependency ratios to Total Dependency Ratio are 77 per cent and 23 per cent, respectively (Figure 12); which is an indication of demographically developed stage. Furthermore, middle altitude is in more developed stage, with less burden of younger population (74.45 per cent) than high altitude (79.51 per cent).

Index of Aging

Index of aging is a scale to measure the youthfulness of a population; whether the population is 'young' or 'old'. It is described by the ratio of old persons (aged 60+ years) to the child population (aged 0-14 years). The index, in general is found low, when the proportion of population under 15 years is high and vice-versa. Hence in developing countries, where fertility is high, this index is usually low.

As per census of India 2001, this index is estimated to be 21.07 for India, while it varies from 10.78 in Meghalaya (North Eastern State) to 40.21 in Kerala (Southern State); Himachal Pradesh lies some where in middle with the value 29.06. In 1981, the index was found to be 16 for India, while for the state of Kerala; it was estimated 22. In last two decades, the proportion of senile person increased substantially denoting 'old' population with low fertility rate.

Table 11
Dependency Ratios and Index of Aging among Present Study Population (Kinnaura) and Earlier Studied other Small Indian Populations (Scheduled Tribe/Caste) of Different Himalayan Region, Himachal Pradesh and Plains of India

Country/ State/ Region	*Population Group*	*YADR*	*OADR*	*TDR*	*Index of Aging*	*Source*
INDIAN HIMALAYAN REGION						
Eastern Himalaya						
Manipur						
	Mao	64.52	8.82	73.34		Maheo (1999)
Sikkim						
	Bhutias	81.94	6.27	88.21	7.65	Bhasin and Bhasin (1995)
	Lepchas	77.84	3.79	81.63	4.88	"
	Sherpas	78.95	0.0	78.95	0.0	"
	Tamangs	66.43	5.59	72.02	8.42	"
Western Himalaya						
Jammu and Kashmir						

Contd...

Country/ State/ Region	*Population Group*	*YADR*	*OADR*	*TDR*	*Index of Aging*	*Source*
Ladakh (HA)		67.77	7.12	74.89	10.51	Bhasin and Nag (2002)
	Bodhs	63.09	9.69	72.78	15.36	"
	Baltis	80.09	5.54	85.63	6.91	"
	Brokpas	73.04	7.35	80.39	10.07	"
	Arghuns	50.09	5.81	55.90	11.60	"
Himachal Pradesh						
	Gaddi	75.18	5.98	81.61	7.95	Bhasin and Bhasin (1993)
	Brahman	70.82	7.12	77.94	10.05	"
	Rajput	69.65	5.79	75.44	8.31	"
	SC	86.00	5.16	91.16	6.00	"
Central Himalaya						
Uttaranchal (or erstwhile UP)						
	Marchha Bhotia	49.01	4.74	53.75	9.67	Chachra and Bhasin (1998)
	Dharchula Bhotia	80.00	3.88	83.88	4.86	"
	Johar Bhotia	56.53	4.02	60.55	7.11	"
	Raji	73.10	6.29	80.00	8.53	Patra (2001)
	Jaunsaris	–	–	79.09	–	Chauhan, et.al. (1991)
INDIA PLAIN STATE						
Madhya Pradesh						
	Bharias PTG	75.50	11.50	86.00	15.50	Pandey (2002)
	Birhor PTG	71.90	11.90	82.20	16.60	"
	Hill Korwas PTG	54.00	7.80	61.80	14.40	"
	Bharias	71.30	12.90	84.20	18.20	"
	Oraon	58.50	13.00	71.50	22.20	"
	Pando	68.80	11.30	80.10	16.50	"
Chhatisgarh						
	Kamar PTG	73.00	6.80	79.80	9.30	"
	Gond	68.20	10.70	78.90	15.70	"
INDIAN HIMALAYAN REGION						
Himachal Pradesh (Western Himalayas)						
Kinnaura (Pooled)		46.01	13.80	59.81	29.99	Present study (2006)
Kinnaura (M. Altitude)		46.34	15.90	62.24	34.32	"
Kinnaura (H. Altitude)		45.71	11.79	57.49	25.79	"
Minimum		45.71	3.79	53.75	4.86	
Maximum		86.00	15.90	91.16	34.32	
Average		67.01	8.23	75.04	13.20	
Standard Deviation		11.66	3.40	10.27	7.55	

SC = Scheduled Caste
ST=Scheduled Tribe
PTG=Primitive Tribal Group

In the present study population the index (Table 11) has been estimated to be 29.99 which is quite high denoting 'old' population with low fertility (Figure 12). Further it is higher (34.32) in middle altitude and lower (25.79) in high altitude, though the dependency ratios are higher in middle altitude, but ultimately the difference is insignificant. So the difference may be because of availability of better health care and educational facilities in the middle altitude as compared to high altitude. As evident from Table 11 none of the small population group studied earlier had found such a higher Index of aging in the Indian continent.

Chapter 9

FERTILITY

The process of biological replacement of living creatures and maintenance of its existence is known as fertility. There are three terms which are used as alternatives viz. fertility, natality and birth. Human fertility is responsible for perpetuation of human being on the planet. This is a positive force, through which a population expands, counteracting the force of attrition caused by mortality. If this replacement of human number is not adequate – that is (Birth – Death = less than zero or Death – Birth = greater than zero) the number of deaths in a particular society continues to be more than that of births, that society become extinct after a certain period. On the other hand, excessive replacement of Human numbers can also create several social and political problems for a country. Therefore, the study of human fertility occupies a central position in the study of human population.

Although, there is wide gap between the potential level of fertility (fecundity) and actual performance of the potentiality (fertility), here we discuss about latter. Further, fertility is an event that occurs over time, therefore, knowledge of the current fertility levels; differentials and trends (at a specified time/ period), as well as cumulative fertility/ family size estimates for a population are of vital importance. Additionally, fertility in spite of being biological phenomena, it is significantly influenced by a number of demographic, economic, socio-cultural, environmental, as well as attitude; behavior related to sex preference of children and family size and so on. In this chapter, the current fertility levels, differentials and trends have been studied for Kinnaura. Further this has been followed by exploratory analysis, in which an attempt has been made to study the fertility related variables, viz. number of children ever born, number of children surviving, to explore the possibility of any relationship between these two and a set of independent determinants. All fertility related data have been obtained from complete pregnancy/birth history of respondents (ever married women). Household birth histories have also been checked from elders for inconsistencies.

Crude Birth Rate (CBR)

Crude birth rate is the most commonly used measure of fertility. It indicates the general magnitude of the fertility level of a population/region at a specific time. It is also used to estimate current growth. However it is a crude measure, since the estimation considers the entire population, rather than those exposed to the risk of childbearing. The crude birth rate for the world in 2003 has been estimated as 22 (PRB, 2003). But the variation in the birth rates between the more developed regions (11) and less developed regions (24) appears striking. This difference is also responsible for demographic polarization of the world. The regional summaries show that the birth rates of Europe (10) and North America (14), where most of the developed countries are situated, are quite low. On the other hand, Africa (38), Latin America (23) and Asia (20), where most of the less developed countries located, have high birth rates. However, even within these continents, the birth rate varies substantially. Similarly, it (Birth rate) is not uniform within the country or state it varies from region to region and population to population.

Asia too, shows disparities in birthrates across regions/ countries, East Asia has a low birth rate of 13, and South-Eastern Asia also shows lower birth rates. At the other end, many countries in the South-Western Asia have very high birth rates: Yemen (43), Iraq (35) Palestinian Territory (39). The South Central Asia has a moderately high birth rate of 27. But within

Table 1

Birth Rates, Fertility Rates, Reproduction Rates and Child Women Ratio among Middle and High Altitude Kinnaura (Himachal Pradesh India)

Region/ Population/ State Country	Crude Birth Rate	General Fertility Rate	Total Fertility Rate	Gross Reproduction Rate	Child women Ratio	Total population 0-1 yrs.	Total Population	Number of Women (15-50 yrs)
	$\frac{C^{0-1}}{P} \times 1000$	$\frac{C^{0-1}}{W^{15-50}} \times 1000$	$\frac{\Sigma ASFR \times 5}{1000}$	$TFR \times 0.49$	$\frac{C^{0-5}}{W^{15-50}} \times 1000$			
Present Study								
Kinnaura	21.64	60.81	2.09	1.02	356.60	108	4991	1447
Middle Altitude	19.36	35.09	1.76	0.86	346.26	48	2479	722
High Altitude	23.89	67.95	2.40	1.17	358.62	60	2512	725
NFHS-2								Women 15-49 years
India	24.8	NA	2.85	1.40	NA	11178	486011	89199
Himachal Pradesh	28.2	NA	2.14	1.05	NA	354	16871	3012

NA= Not Available

this region, the birth rate ranges from a low of 15 (in Kazakhstan) to a high of 42 (in Afghanistan), whereas Bangladesh (30), Bhutan (34), Nepal (34) and Pakistan (37) also seems to have high birth rates, India has a moderately high birth rate of 25. Within India too, the diversity in birth rate is evident.

In India, NFHS-2 (2000) estimated crude birthrate for the period of 1998-99, which 24.8 for country, but it varies from 16.6 in Goa to 35.7 in Meghalaya. The major State having birth rate above the national level are Bihar (28.1), Madhya Pradesh (26.7), Meghalaya (35.7), Nagaland (30.4), Rajasthan (29.9) and Uttar Pradesh (31.1), Manipur (25.8) and Mizoram (25.7). Himachal Pradesh has birth rate of 19.9 which is lower than National average.

In the present study, the crude birth rate of total population of Kinnaura is estimated as 21.64, which is less than National average (25), but quite higher than State's crude birth rate (19.9). As evident from Table 1, in middle altitude crude birth rate is quite low (19.36) as compared to high altitude (23.89).

Table 2
Distribution of Crude Birth Rates, General Fertility Rates, Total Fertility Rates, Gross Reproduction Rates and Child-Women Ratio Among Some Tribal and Non-Tribal Population Groups of India and Himalayan Region.

Region/ State/ Country	*Population Group*	*CBR*	*GFR*	*TFR*	*GRR*	*Child Women Ratio*	*Source*
Region and Population Specific Comparative Fertility Measures							
INDIAN HIMALAYAS							
Eastern Himalayas							
Sikkim							
	Buddhist	21.8	92.6	3.1	1.5	553.4	Bhasin and Bhasin (2000)
	Hindus	28.3	108.6	3.2	1.6	516.1	"
	Bhutias	22.2	93.2	3.1	1.5	–	Bhasin and Bhasin (1995)
	Tamangs	24.3	92.3	3.1	1.5	–	"
	Lepchas	20.8	92.1	3.0	1.5	–	"
	Buddhist	21.8	92.5	3.0	1.5	–	"
	Sherpas	19.6	90.9	3.0	1.5	–	"
	Hindus	29.2	108.5	3.1	1.5	–	"
West Bengal							

Contd...

Region/ State/ Country	Population Group	CBR	GFR	TFR	GRR	Child Women Ratio	Source
Kalimpong	Sherpa	–	–	6.6	3.2	–	Gupta et.al. (1989)
"	Lepcha	–	–	5.4	2.6	–	"
Rango	Sherpa	–	–	6.1	3.0	–	"
Echhay	Sherpa	–	–	5.0	2.5	–	"
Munsong	Sherpa	–	–	6.5	3.2	–	"
Lava	Sherpa	–	–	7.1	3.5	–	"
Labbah (Darjeeling)	Sherpa	–	–	5.9	2.9	–	"
Mungpoo (Darjeeling)	Sherpa	–	–	4.4	2.2	–	"
	Total	20.7					SRS (2002)
Manipur							
	Mao	12.0	65.3	4.9	2.4	–	Maheo (1999)
Western Himalayas							
Jammu and Kashmir							
Ladakh[HA]		22.4	88.9	2.7	1.3	563.9	Bhasin and Nag (2002)
	Bodhs	24.4	95.7	2.7	1.7	510.1	"
	Baltis	23.5	98.5	3.1	1.5	689.3	"
	Brokpas	27.1	119.0	3.0	1.5	296.2	"
	Arghuns	14.2	49.8	1.6	0.3	360.1	"
	Total	19.7	–	–	–	–	SRS (2002)
Himachal Pradesh							
	Total	30.8	126.3	3.9	1.9	–	Bhasin and Bhasin (2000)
	Hindu	–	–	2.1	1.0	–	"
	Buddhist	–	–	1.9	0.9	–	"
	Total	28.2	–	2.1	1.0	–	"
	Total	22.1	–	–	–	–	SRS (2002)
High Altitude	Bods	–	–	4.1	2.0	–	Prakash and Malik (1990)
Middle altitude	Bods	–	–	3.6	1.8	–	"
	Gaddis	28.4	110.5	3.5	1.7	–	Bhasin and Bhasin (1993)
	Brahman	25.8	93.3	3.2	1.6	–	"
	Rajput	21.7	83.9	3.2	1.6	–	"
	SC	48.8	201.5	5.9	2.9	–	"
Central Himalaya							
Uttaranchal (or erstwhile UP)							
	Johari Bhotia	48.21	175.2	6.2	3.0	–	Kapoor (1996)
	Rang Bhotia	53.6	186.4	5.8	2.8	–	"
	Marchha Bhotia	35.98	162.4	6.3	3.1	–	"
	Marchha Bhotia	24.1	128.4	4.2	2.1	481.4	Chachra and Bhasin (1998)
	Dharchula Bhotia	15.6	95.2	2.6	1.3	662.6	"
	Johar Bhotia	29.6	56.4	1.9	0.9	325.1	"
	Raji	49.4	198.0	6.5	3.2	–	Samal, et.al. (2000)
	Raji	46.0	213.2	7.4	3.6	–	Patra (2001)
	Jaunsaris	32.0	125.0	3.8	1.9	–	Kshatriya, et.al. (1997)
	Total	20.2	–	–	–	–	SRS (2002)

Contd...

Region/ State/ Country	*Population Group*	*CBR*	*GFR*	*TFR*	*GRR*	*Child Women Ratio*	*Source*
Madhya Pradesh							
	Bharias [PTG]	33.3	–	4.7	2.3	–	Pandey (2002)
	Birhor [PTG]	34.8	–	4.0	2.0	–	"
	Hill Korwas [PTG]	26.6	–	2.9	1.4	–	"
	Gond	43.0	–	–	–	–	Parsuram & Rajan (1990)
	Bhil	43.5	–		–	–	Chaudhary and Kumar (1981)
Chhatisgarh							
	Kamar [PTG]	–	–	3.8	1.9	–	Pandey (2002)
	Total	26.7	–	–	–	–	SRS (2002)
West Bengal							
	Santhal	37.2	168.0	5.5	2.6	–	Basu Sumana (1998)
	Lodha	31.2	133.3	3.3	1.6	–	"
	Kora	41.8		4.2	2.0		Datta (1990)
	Total	20.7	–	–	–	–	SRS (2002)
Orissa							
	Dudh Kharia	38.5	164.0	5.3	2.5	–	Kshatriya and Basu (1993)
	Kutia Konds	–	–	3.6	1.7	–	"
	Total	24.3	–	–	–	–	SRS (2002)
Kerala							
	Total	–	–	3.9	1.9	–	Bhasin and Bhasin (2000)
	Total	17.9	–	–	–	–	SRS (2002)
	State/Country Specific Comparative Fertility Measures						
INDIA		20.9	–	2.85	1.40	–	1998-99 NFHS-2 (2000)
Delhi		20.9	–	2.40	1.18	–	"
Haryana		18.1	–	2.88	1.41	–	"
Himachal Pradesh		15.7	–	2.14	1.05	–	"
Jammu & Kashmir		16.4	–	2.71	1.33	–	"
Punjab		15.4	–	2.21	1.08	–	"
Rajasthan		25.3	–	3.78	1.85	–	"
Madhya Pradesh		22.9	–	3.31	1.62	–	"
Uttar Pradesh		23.5	–	3.99	1.96	–	"
Bihar		22.3	–	3.49	1.71	–	"
Orissa		20.1	–	2.46	1.21	–	"
West Bengal		15.1	–	2.29	1.12	–	"
Arunachal Pradesh		22.3 [SRS]	–	2.52	1.23	–	"
Assam		15.8	–	2.31	1.13	–	"
Manipur		21.4	–	3.04	1.49	–	"
Meghalaya		28.5 [SRS]	–	4.57	2.24	–	"
Mizoram		22.4	–	2.89	1.42	–	"
Nagaland		NA	–	3.77	1.85	–	"
Sikkim		21.8 [SRS]	–	2.75	1.35	–	"
Goa		16.2	–	1.77	0.87	–	"
Gujarat		21.4	–	2.72	1.33	–	"
Maharashtra		21.6	–	2.52	1.23	–	"
Andhra Pradesh		21.4	–	2.25	1.10	–	"

Contd...

Region/ State/ Country	*Population Group*	*CBR*	*GFR*	*TFR*	*GRR*	*Child Women Ratio*	*Source*
Region and Population Specific Comparative Fertility Measures							
Karnataka		18.5	–	2.13	1.04	–	"
Kerala		14.8	–	1.96	0.96	–	"
Tamil Nadu		21.3	–	2.19	1.07	–	"
Indian	*Minimum*	14.8	–	1.77	0.87	–	"
State	*Maximum*	28.5	–	4.57	2.24	–	"
Himachal Pradesh							
Kinnaura (Pooled)		21.6	60.8	2.55	1.25	356.6	Present Study (2006)
Kinnaura (Middle altitude)		19.3	35.0	2.13	1.04	346.2	"
Kinnaura (High Altitude)		23.8	67.9	2.92	1.43	358.6	"

HA= High Altitude
PTG= Primitive Tribal Group
SC= Scheduled Caste
ST=Scheduled Caste
SRS=Sample Registration Survey (2000)
NA= Not Available

Comparisons of Crude Birth Rate of different regions and Indian populations are presented in Table 2 indicates that it varies from minimum 12 in Mao of Manipur (Maheo, 1999) to highest of 75 among Sholiga (c.f. Kshatriya, 2004) and 53.6 among Rang Bhotia (Kapoor, 1996). CBR of Kinnaura is low in comparison to most of Indian population (Table 2), which indicates Kinnaura are progressing well, and demographically forward than other tribal groups of the country.

General Fertility Rate (GFR)

General fertility rate is a refined measure of fertility, as it takes into consideration, the population at risk of childbearing i.e. female at reproductive ages of 15-49 years. However it is also affected by the distribution of females by age in the reproductive span. In the present study general fertility rate for the total population of Kinnaura has been estimated as 60.81, wide regional variation is evident (Table 2) in middle altitude (35.09) and high altitude (67.95) region.

Age Specific Fertility Rate (ASFR)

Age specific fertility rate gives a detailed panorama of fertility in a population at a specified time/-period. It is estimated for conventional five-years age groups, from 15-19 years to 45-49 years, which minimize the effects of misreporting of ages by mothers, and distortion produced by variations in the age composition. As the age of mother is an important factor affecting the fertility level and the rate of child bearing is not uniform throughout all the ages. In fact, fertility is usually concentrated between ages 20-29 years.

Table 3
Age Specific Fertility Rates among Middle and High Altitude Kinnaura.

Age Group	*Middle Altitude*	*High Altitude*	*Kinnaura Pooled*
15-19	0	11.36	5.13
20-24	122.14	138.46	130.27
25-29	84.62	102.36	93.39
30-34	81.63	86.96	84.21
35-39	14.29	63.16	42.42
40-44	14.29	27.78	21.13
45-49	34.48	49.18	42.02

In the present study, age specific fertility rates were estimated for Kinnaura, as evident from Table 3, it reaches in its peak at ages 20-24, with 130 births per 1000 women for total population and it is estimated 122 and 138 births per 1000 women respectively for middle and high altitude. It starts declining as per growing age of mothers as also apparent from the Figure 1. For better understanding of phenomenon and measure the present findings are compared with NFHS-2 (2000) according to which it was estimated 107 for women of 15-19 years of India, though it varies from 21 in Goa to 142 in Madhya Pradesh, for Himachal Pradesh it was 29; the highest age specific fertility rate of 210 per 1000 women was estimated for age group 20-24; which again varies from 89 in Goa to 264 in Rajasthan, in Himachal Pradesh too, the age specific fertility is in peak with 203 birth per 1000 women in the age group 20-24 (Table 4).

Table 4
Distribution of Age-specific Fertility Rates among Different Population Groups of Himachal Pradesh, Jammu & Kashmir, Sikkim and India.

	Age Specific Fertility Rate							
Region/ Population/ State/ Country	*15-19*	*20-24*	*25-29*	*30-34*	*35-39*	*40-44*	*45-49*	*Reference*
INDIA	107	210	143	69	28	8	3	1998-99,* NFHS-2 (2002)
Delhi	36	191	174	59	17	3	0	"
Haryana	92	240	150	62	15	9	7	"
Himachal Pradesh	29	203	130	45	15	6	0	"
Jammu & Kashmir	44	171	181	100	33	10	3	"
Punjab	40	178	158	51	12	3	0	"
Rajasthan	126	264	181	103	48	23	9	"
Madhya Pradesh	142	228	159	81	64	18	6	"
Uttar Pradesh	120	256	208	127	64	18	6	"
Bihar	113	223	180	112	50	18	2	"
Orissa	79	174	138	71	23	6	1	"
West Bengal	107	173	110	47	15	3	4	"
Arunachal Pradesh	66	160	129	68	43	13	–	"
Assam	89	149	116	70	31	7	0	"
Manipur	42	132	173	153	68	26	14	"
Meghalaya	86	211	232	184	105	80	14	"
Mizoram	54	188	167	110	48	9	0	"
Nagaland	56	224	203	162	76	23	12	"
Sikkim	65	171	141	78	53	32	11	"
Goa	21	89	122	90	26	7	0	"
Gujarat	87	230	148	52	18	5	3	"
Maharashtra	129	223	106	34	12	0	0	"
Andhra Pradesh	132	186	87	29	12	3	0	"
Karnataka	112	172	90	37	9	3	1	"
Kerala	39	166	128	40	16	3	0	"
Tamil Nadu	83	189	121	32	10	3	0	"
Minimum	21	89	87	29	9	0	0	
Maximum	142	264	232	184	105	80	14	
Middle altitude	5	130	93	84	42	21	42	Present** study (2006)
High Altitude	–	122	85	82	14	14	34	"
Pooled	11	138	102	87	63	28	49	"

* 1998-99 NFHS-2 (2002)
** Present study (2006)

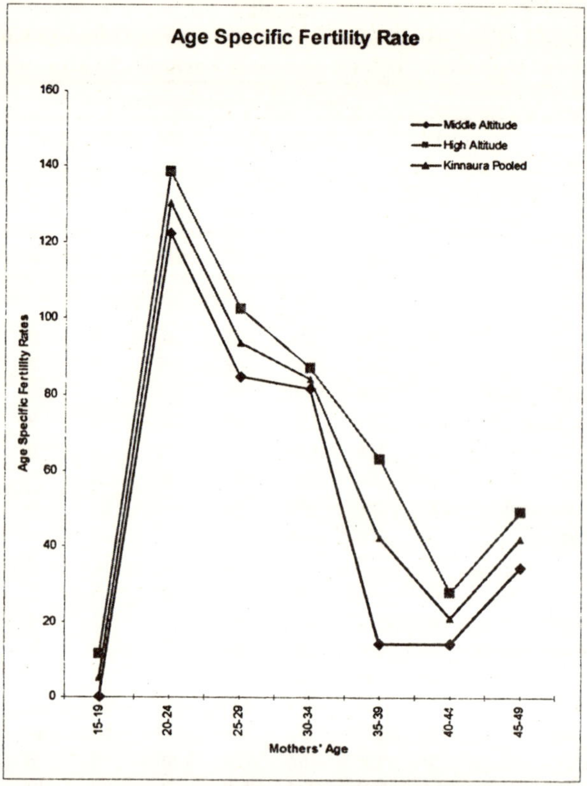

Figure 1: Line Graph Showing Age Specific Fertility Rates among Kinnaura Women

Total Fertility Rate (TFR)

Total fertility rate summarizes the pattern of fertility exhibited by ASFRs and represents a single index of total fertility. It is an estimate of the expected number of children that would be born (ignoring mortality), to a hypothetical cohort of 1000 women in their lifetime, if they all pass through their reproductive years exposed to the schedule of ASFR on which the index is based. In other words TFR expressed per women refers to the number of children a hypothetical average woman would have if, during her lifetime her child-bearing behaviour remain same as that of cross-section of women at the time of observation. In this way, the TFR is a type of standardized rate, as it is not influenced by differences in the age composition.

As evident from Table 1, the TFR for India during 1998-99 was estimated as 2.85, while for Himachal Pradesh it is 2.14. In the present study, total fertility rate for Kinnaura is estimated as 2.09, which seems lower than national and state average. For middle altitude (1.76) this estimation is slightly lower than high altitude (2.40).

Gross Reproduction Rate (GRR)

Gross Reproduction Rate is also considered as replacement Index as it indicates how effectively mothers are replacing themselves with daughters (ignoring mortality), who would bear the next generation. It points towards the average number of female children expected to be born per woman during her entire reproductive span, if there is no mortality, and the fertility schedules represented by the age specific fertility rates continue to remain the same. In the present study, the Kinnaura as a total has registered a gross reproduction rate of 1.02 (Table 1). For middle altitude women the GRR is 0.86, whereas for high altitude, it is 1.18. These findings suggest that in the Kinnaura, a woman would bear on an average about one daughter until the end of the childbearing age (if there were no mortality). The estimation of GRR for Indian States is displayed in Table 2 shows that it varies from 0.87 to 2.24 respectively for Goa and Meghalaya.

MEAN AGE OF CHILD BEARING

Table 5 showing the age specific mean parities among Kinnaura women, the pooled data for Kinnaura shows that mean parities increases alongwith the rise of age, it is highest among older women, except in high altitude, where it is found approximately constant. The estimated fertility rate calculated from $(P_3)^2/P_2$ has been found to be 3.47 for the Kinnaura (pooled data), whereas it varies from 3.47 among middle altitude to 4.76 among the high altitude Kinnaura. It is similar to other tribal groups viz. for Jaunsaris it was found to be 3.81 (Kshatriya et.al., 1997).

MARITAL FERTILITY RATES

Marital fertility rates are more refined measures of fertility as only married women are taken into consideration during estimating these measures. In many societies, only married women are actually exposed to childbearing. The married women of reproductive age (15-49) are really, almost completely, ethically, and legally exposed to child bearing.

General Marital Fertility Rate (GMFR)

General marital fertility rate is a refined measure of fertility, as it takes into consideration, the population who at risk of childbearing i.e. married women at reproductive ages of 15-49 years. However, it is also affected by the distribution of females by age in the reproductive span. As evident from Table.6, in the present study general marital fertility rate for the total population of Kinnaura has been estimated as 60.95, though marital fertility is lower in middle altitude (54.98) as compared to high altitude (131.29).

Here it can be noticed that the general marital fertility rate in the Tibetans of high altitude Limi, Nepal has been reported rather high (274). This could be because of small sample size and short period of the survey (Goldstein, 1981). A comparative detail of GMFR among different population groups is given in Table 7. The minimum of 54.98 is recorded among middle altitude Kinnaura (present study). The maximum GMFR is found to be among scheduled caste population of Himachal Pradesh. Thus the present finding indicates that alike other indicators GMFR is also low to moderate among Kinnaura, which is an indication of demographically a better off state and corroborate the findings related to knowledge and practice of family planning that approximately 70 per cent of respondents are practicing any of available family planning methods or devices.

Age Specific Marital Fertility Rate (ASMFR)

When age specific fertility is computed only for the married women of reproductive age group (15-49 or 15-49+), this is known as age specific marital fertility rate (ASMFR). In the present study, age specific marital fertility rate was computed

Table 5
Estimation of Fertility from Age Specific Average Parities Among Kinnaura of Middle and High Altitude.

	Kinnaura								
	Middle Altitude			*High Altitude*			*Pooled*		
Age Group	*Number of Women*	*Number of Births*	*Mean Parity*	*Number of Women*	*Number of Births*	*Mean Parity*	*Number of Women*	*Number of Births*	*Mean Parity*
16-19	2	2	1.00	4	12	3.00	6	9	1.50
20-24	42	66	1.57	30	103	3.43	72	115	1.60
25-29	74	176	2.38	66	211	3.20	140	330	2.36
30-34	61	182	2.98	67	250	3.73	128	382	2.98
35-39	55	208	3.78	77	298	3.87	132	466	3.53
40-44	51	202	3.96	59	197	3.34	110	422	3.84
45-49	36	151	4.19	43	144	3.35	79	338	4.28
50-55	33	161	4.88	36	113	3.14	69	331	4.80
56+	33	201	6.09	35	118	3.37	68	378	5.56
Total	387	1349	3.49	417	1446	3.47	804	2771	3.45
Estimated Total Fertility or TF= $(P_3)^2/P_2$			=3.47			2.65			4.76

for Kinnaura as shown in Table 6. The pooled data shows that the age specific marital fertility is highest 317.76 among the women of age group of 20-24, followed by women of age group 25-29 years, 30-34 years, 15-19 years, 50-53 years, 45-49 years, 35-39 years and lowest (24.19) is among the women of 40-44 years.

There is wide difference between age specific marital fertility rate and age specific fertility rate (ASMFR - ASFR = Fertility contributed by Unmarried Women), which shows that sufficient number of unmarried women are exposed to child bearing. Such practices of child bearing by unmarried women is more common among the women of high altitude; further, the difference is wide for age group15-19 and 20-24 suggests that premarital sexual relation is remarkably high in this Tribal group. The same findings were recorded during the focus group discussions (FGDs) and case studies. The comparison of middle and high altitude Kinnaura indicates that age specific marital fertility rate is higher for all age groups in high altitude as compared to middle altitude. The comparison of means shows that there is significant difference in middle and high altitude in age specific marital fertility rates. Paired sample *t* - Test run in SPSS gives the values t= -2.874, df=6 and p<0.02 for ASMFR. Whereas the marriage index returns insignificant difference in middle and high altitude t=0.297 at 6 df, p=0.776, indicates that the impact of marriage on fertility is not varied (or equal) in two different ecological zones.

CASE STUDY

Unmarried Mother

The respondent was employed as Female Health Worker at CHC (Community Health Center) Pooh. She fell in love with a doctor posted in the same CHC. The love affair leads to physical relation, which resulted into a son. Now the son is 6 year old and going to school. The doctor is transferred elsewhere. The lady was staying with her father alongwith 6-year-old son. The father of the lady has opinion that it happens in Kinnaur (not too frequently) that young girls develop affair with local people or outsiders. If they conceive, they give birth. Sometimes in such cases, a male member may come forward to accept her but many times such girls suffer and are left to live with their parents. In the present case the respondent has no complaint with the cheater lover. In Pooh (village) only, there are 5 to 10 such women who have given birth to child before marriage and are living with their parents.

Table 6
Marital Fertility and Gross Reproduction Rates among Middle and High Altitude Kinnaura.

Population/ Eco-Zones	*General Marital Fertility Rate*	*Total Marital Fertility Rate*	*Marital Gross Reproduction Rate*
Kinnaur	60.95	3.79	1.85
Middle Altitude	54.98	2.80	1.37
High Altitude	131.29	4.63	2.26

Table 7
Distribution of Marital Fertility Rates and Reproduction Rates among some Tribals and Non-Tribal Population Groups of India and Himalayan Region.

Region/ State/ Country	*Population Group*	*GMFR*	*TMFR*	*MGRR*	*Source*
INDIAN HIMALAYAN					
Eastern Himalayas					
Sikkim					
	Buddhist	148.5	–	–	Bhasin and Bhasin (2000)
	Hindus	178.7	–	–	"
	Bhutias	154.9	–	–	Bhasin and Bhasin (1995)
	Tamangs	157.8	–	–	"
	Lepchas	141.3	–	–	"
	Buddhist	148.5	–	–	"
	Hindus	178.6	–	–	"
Western Himalayas					
Jammu and Kashmir					
Ladakh[HA]					Bhasin and Nag (2002)
	Bodhs	144.3	5.2	2.5	"
	Baltis	137.2	3.4	1.6	"
	Brokpas	153.8	6.0	2.9	"
	Arghuns	75.5	2.9	1.4	"
Himachal Pradesh					
	Gaddis	145.1	–	–	Bhasin and Bhasin (1993)
	Brahman	122.2	–	–	"
	Rajput	115.0	–	–	"
	SC	236.8	–	–	"
Central Himalaya					
Uttaranchal (or erstwhile UP)					
	Johar Bhotia	90.9	4.1	2.0	Chachra and Bhasin (1998)
	Marchha Bhotia	194.4	5.6	2.7	"
	Dharchula Bhotia	135.5	2.8	1.3	"
	Raji	226.0	7.5	3.6	Samal, et.al. (2000)
	Raji	227.6	7.3	3.5	Patra (2001)
Himachal Pradesh					
Kinnaur		60.95	2.55	1.25	Present study (2006)
Middle altitude		54.98	2.13	1.04	"
High Altitude		131.29	2.92	1.43	"

[HA]= High Altitude [PTG]= Primitive Tribal Group SC= Scheduled Caste ST=Scheduled Caste

Table 8
Age Specific Marital Fertility Rates and Index of Marriage (ASFR/ ASMFR) among Middle and High Altitude Kinnaura.

	Middle Altitude		High Altitude		Kinnaura (Pooled)	
Age Group	ASMFR	Index of Marriage, C_m	ASMFR	Index of Marriage, C_m	ASMFR	Index of Marriage, C_m
15-19	0.0	0.000	100.00	0.114	71.43	0.072
20-24	262.30	0.466	391.30	0.354	317.76	0.410
25-29	118.28	0.715	168.83	0.606	141.18	0.661
30-34	106.67	0.765	103.90	0.837	105.26	0.800
35-39	15.63	0.914	74.07	0.853	48.28	0.879
40-44	16.39	0.872	31.75	0.875	24.19	0.874
45-49	40.82	0.845	56.60	0.869	49.02	0.857

Paired Sample t Test

	t	df	p-value
ASMFR	-2.874	6	0.028
Index of Marriage	0.297	6	0.776

Total Marital Fertility Rate (TMFR)

Total marital fertility rate is refined measure of total fertility rate (TFR); it is cumulative value of age specific marital fertility rates at the end of the reproductive period. It indicates the average number of children expected to be born per married woman during the entire span of the reproductive period, if the age specific marital fertility rates (on which the rate is based) continue to be the same and there is no mortality. In the present study, total marital fertility rate is calculated for middle and high altitude Kinnaura. As evident from Table 8, the total marital fertility rate (TMFR) among Kinnaura is 3.79, whereas it varies from 2.80 in middle altitude to 4.63 in high altitude.

Marital Gross Reproduction Rate (MGRR)

As already described Gross reproduction rate (GRR) is a replacement index, the marital gross reproduction rate (MGRR) is a refined measure of this index, as such in earlier one all the women of reproductive age group are taken into consideration, here the index is developed on the basis of married women of reproductive age. Table 6 clearly showing that marital gross reproduction rate is 1.85 for pooled data whereas for middle altitude this estimation is lower (1.37) as compared to high altitude (2.26). This finding broadly suggests that five women would bear on 9 daughters until the end of the childbearing age.

CHILD WOMAN RATIO

Child woman ratio is also referred as 'general fertility ratio'. This is very useful indicator of fertility. This is computed by dividing the number of children of under 5 years old in the population by the number of women 15-49 years old. The childbearing ages in the denominator are approximated by the ages 20 to 49 or 15 to 44 or 15 to 50. This depends on the lowest and highest age of women at which they are exposed to the risk of child bearing. It must be noted that the children under 5 years of age may have borne up to 5 years prior to the census date (or date of investigation) when women were up to 5 years younger. Although some mothers are left out they have contributed so few of the children under 5 that the inclusion of younger or older ages would include mostly women who are not exposed to risk.

In the present study Child-woman ratio were computed from the number of children under 5 years of age and number of women at the age of 15-50 years. As evident from Table 1 the child-woman ratio among Kinnaura is 356.60, in middle altitude the ratio is lower (346.26) as compared to high altitude (358.62). It means that the number of children per women is higher in high altitude, in other word the burden of children of under 5 years of age is greater on high altitude as compared to middle altitude.

FERTILITY PERFORMANCE

Fertility performance of Kinnaura women and extent of its dispersion (Figure 2, 3, 4 and 5) is evident from Table 9 and 10, Out of 820 household, there were 803 mothers in different age groups, they wore a total of 3045 number of pregnancies, out of these pregnancies 93.7 per cent (2854) were successful outcome, in the form of live births, in other word foetal wastage

Table 9

Number of Mothers, Pregnancies Experienced by them, Total Number of Children Ever Born and Children Surviving among Kinnaura of Middle and High Altitude

Region/ Population	*Number of Mothers*	*Number of Pregnancy*	*Mean Pregnancies*	*Children Ever Born (Live Births)*	*Children Surviving*	*Foetal Loss*		*Mean Number of Live Births*	*Variance of Live Births*
						N	%		
Kinnaura	803	3045	3.7	2854	2453	191	6.3	3.48	3.588
Middle Altitude	386	1510	3.9	1379	1186	131	8.7	3.50	3.869
High Altitude	417	1535	3.6	1475	1267	60	3.9	3.46	3.343

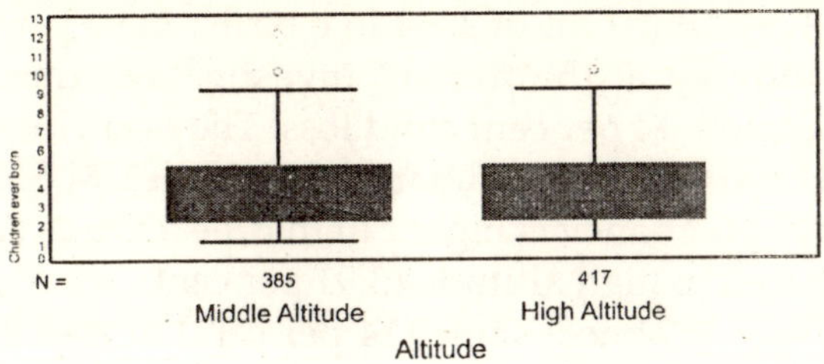

Figure 2: Box Plot Showing Median and Dispersion of Number of Children Ever Born in Middle and High Altitude

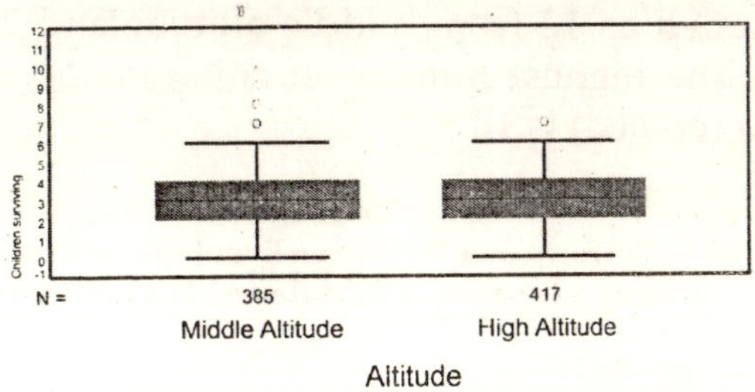

Figure 3: Box Plot Showing Median and Dispersion of Children Surviving in Middle and High Altitude

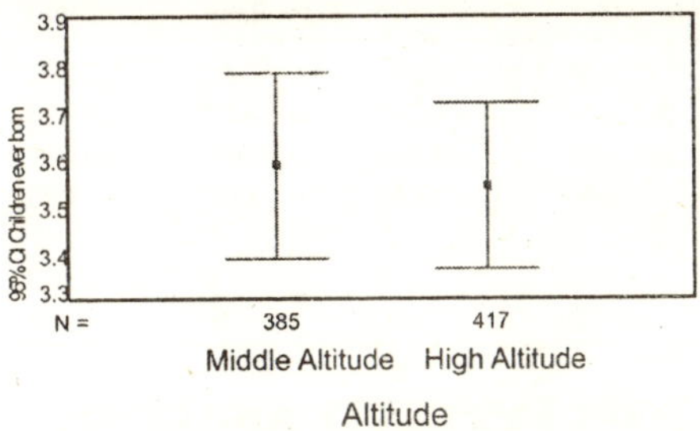

Figure 4: Error Bar Showing difference of Children Ever Born in Middle and High Altitude

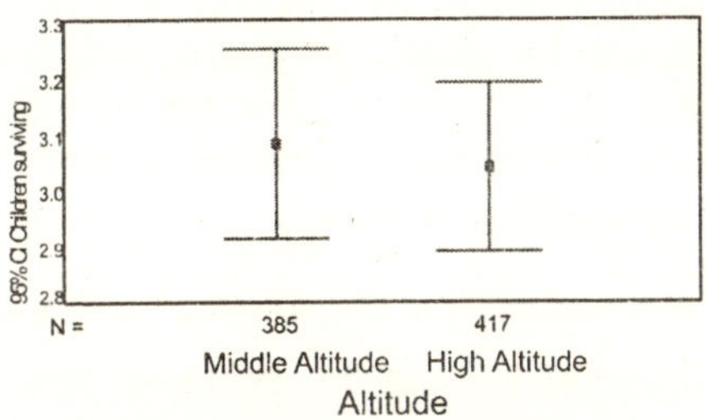

Figure 5: Error Bar Showing difference of Children Surviving in Middle and High Altitude

were 6.3 per cent. Out of 2854 live births 85.94 per cent (2453) were surviving at the time of investigation; means there is approximately 14 per cent child loss. The mean number of live birth per women was estimated as 3.48. (±1.94 S.D.) Further, the loss of pregnancy is higher in middle altitude (12 per cent) as compared to high altitude (3.91 per cent), whereas the ratio of child loss is almost same (14 per cent) in middle and high altitude respectively.

The highest number of children ever born from one woman was recorded as 12 from middle altitude and 10 from high altitude. The highest number of children surviving among Kinnaura (pooled) is 10.

Table 10
Fertility Performance (Children Ever Born and Surviving) among Kinnaura of Middle and High Altitude

	Kinnaura					
	Middle Altitude		*High Altitude*		*Pooled*	
Statistics	*Children Ever Born*	*Children Surviving*	*Children Ever Born*	*Children Surviving*	*Children Ever Born*	*Children Surviving*
Mean	3.50	3.01	3.46	2.97	3.48	2.99
Std. Deviation	±2.017	±1.712	±1.877	±1.596	±1.940	±1.650
S. E. of Mean	±0.102	±0.086	±0.091	±0.077	±0.068	±0.058
Median	3.00	3.00	3.00	3.00	3.00	3.00
Mode	3	2	3	2	3	2
Minimum	0	0	0	0	0	0
Maximum	12	10	10	8	12	10

EXPLORATORY FERTILITY ANALYSIS

Several independent determinants influence the fertility performance and level of fertility of a population. These determinants can be stated as social, cultural, demographic, political, religious, economic, environmental, genetic and so on. The observed interplay between these is being discussed as exploratory fertility analysis.

Fertility Differentials by Demographic Characteristics

1. Fertility Differentials by Mothers' Age: In general, the number of children ever born is expected to be related to the current age of mother, i.e., the younger mothers are expected to have lesser number of children as compared to the older (Singh, 1986; NFHS-1, 1992-93). A similar picture is emerges out in the present study (Table 11; Figure 6, 7, 8, 9, 10, 11 and 12). Clustered box plot (Figure 6 and 7) shows a comparative picture of median number of children ever born and surviving, and its dispersion among the mothers of different age groups in different ecological zones.

Table 11
Fertility Differentials (Mean Number of Children Ever Born and Surviving) Among Middle and High Altitude Kinnaura as per Current Age of Mother.

	Kinnaur					
	Middle Altitude		*High Altitude*		*Pooled*	
Mothers' Age	*Children Ever Born*	*Children Surviving*	*Children Ever Born*	*Children Surviving*	*Children Ever Born*	*Children Surviving*
16-19	1.00	1.00	3.00	2.75	1.50	1.50
20-24	1.57	1.45	3.43	2.90	1.60	1.53
25-29	2.38	2.09	3.20	2.80	2.36	2.05
30-34	2.98	2.66	3.73	3.10	2.98	2.60
35-39	3.78	3.15	3.87	3.30	3.53	3.08
40-44	3.96	3.51	3.34	2.88	3.84	3.28
45-49	4.19	3.64	3.35	2.98	4.28	3.71
50-55	4.88	4.03	3.14	2.69	4.80	4.06
56+	6.09	4.97	3.37	2.89	5.56	4.49

Independent Sample t-Test

Variables	*Levene's Test for Equality of Variances*		*t Test*			
	F	*p-value*	*t*	*df*	*p-value*	*Significance*
Children ever born	1.16	0.280	0.333	800	0.739	Ns
Children surviving	0.89	0.345	0.311	818	0.756	Ns

Ns = Non-Significant.

A comparative panorama of average number of children ever born and surviving among the Kinnaura mothers of different age groups and different ecological zones (middle and high altitude) is presented in Figures 8 and 9. The difference between middle and high altitude in this aspect is apparent from the line graph and it can be seen that as the age of mother increases the average number of children ever born

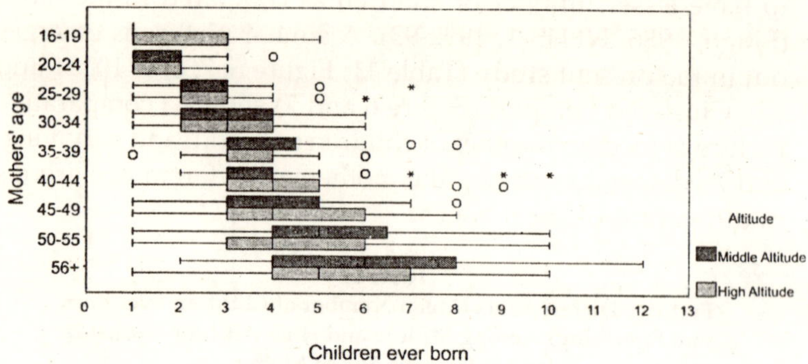

Figure 6: Clustered Box Plot Showing Comparative Median and Dispersion of Number of Children Ever Born Among Kinnaura Mothers of Different Age Group in Middle and High Altitude.

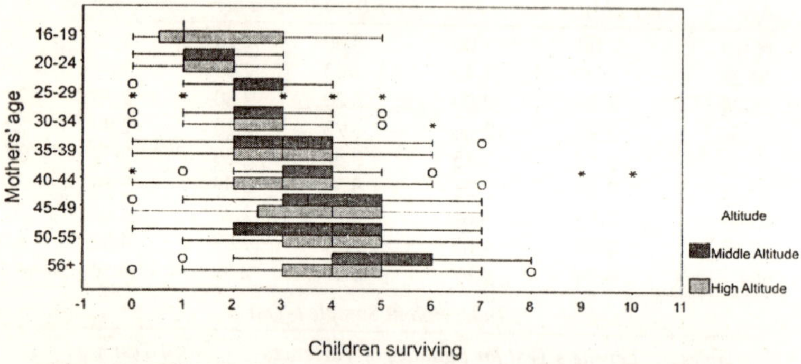

Figure 7: Clustered Box Plot Showing Comparative Median and Dispersion of Number of Children Surviving Among Kinnaura Mothers of Different Age Group in Middle and High Altitude.

and surviving also increases especially among the mothers belonging to middle altitude. The graph is almost flat or horizontal for mothers belonging to high altitude indicating that the average number of children ever born and surviving does not change with the increasing age of mothers.

Furthermore, Figures 10, 11 and 12 present average numbers of children ever born and surviving among the Kinnaura mothers (pooled), mothers belonging to middle and high altitude respectively. It is apparent that there is a greater degree of similarity between Kinnaura mothers (pooled) and those belonging to middle altitude. However, the mothers' in

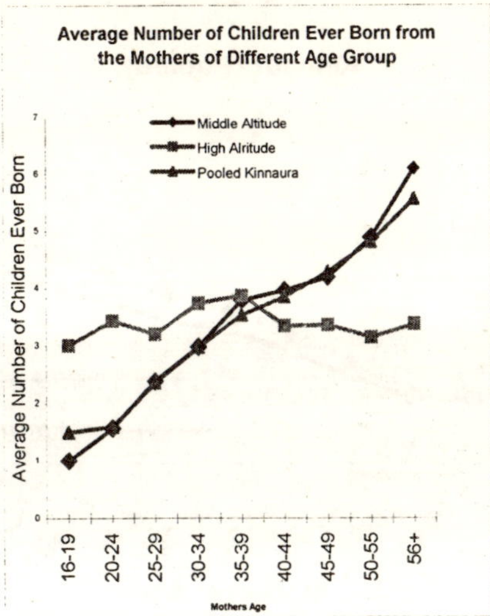

Figure 8: Line Graph Showing Comparison of Average Number of Children Ever Born from the Kinnaura Mothers of Different Age Groups and Different Ecological Zones.

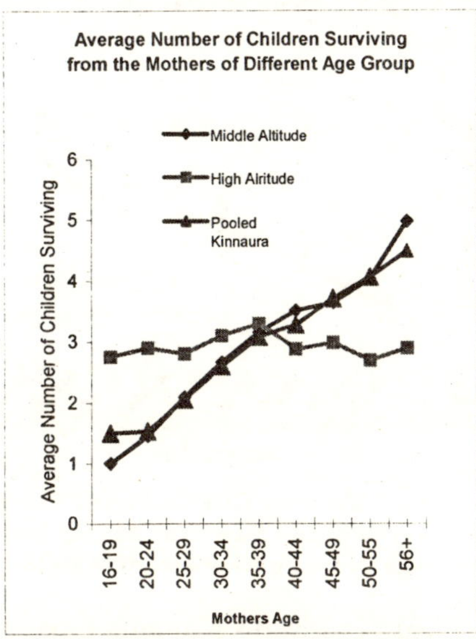

Figure 9: Line Graph Showing Comparison of Average Number of Children Surviving Among the Kinnaura Mothers of Different Age Groups and Different Ecological Zones.

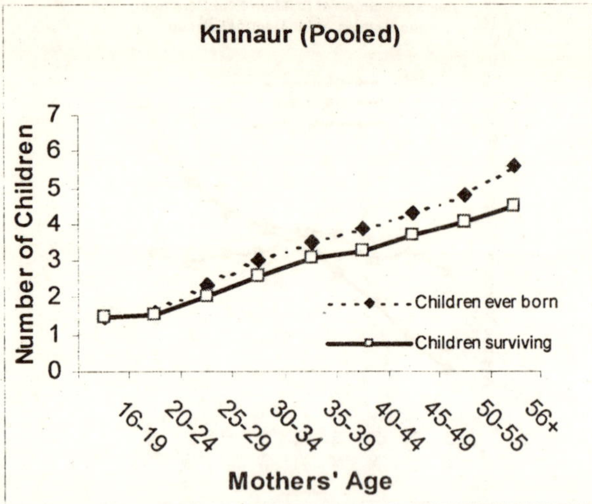

Figure 10: Line-Graph Showing Distribution of Average Number of Children Ever Born and Surviving Among Kinnaura Mothers' of Different Age Group

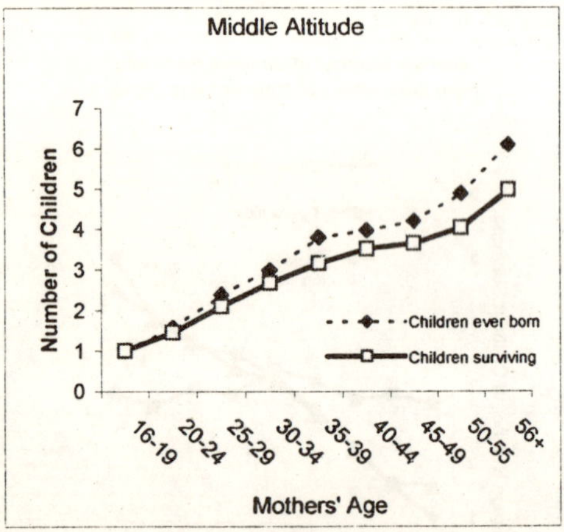

Figure 11: Line-Graph Showing Distribution of Average Number of Children Ever Born and Surviving Among Mothers' of Different Age Group in Kinnaura of Middle Altitude

younger ages in high altitude Kinnaur have higher average number of children ever born and surviving (Figure 12) as compared to mother belonging to middle altitude who achieve it much later.

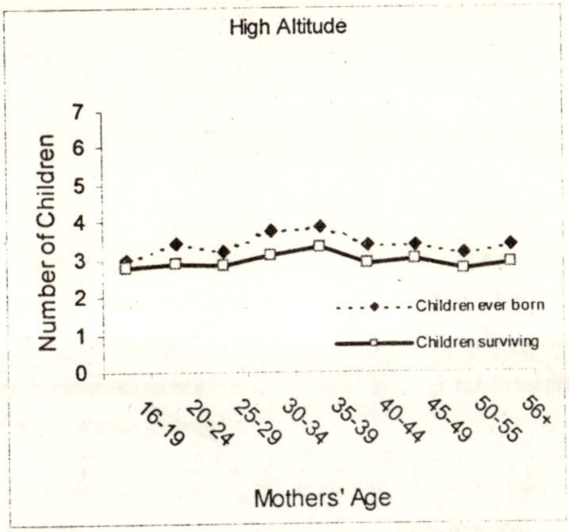

Figure 12: Line-Graph Showing Distribution of Average Number of Children Ever Born and Surviving Among Mothers' of Different Age Group in Kinnaura of High Altitude.

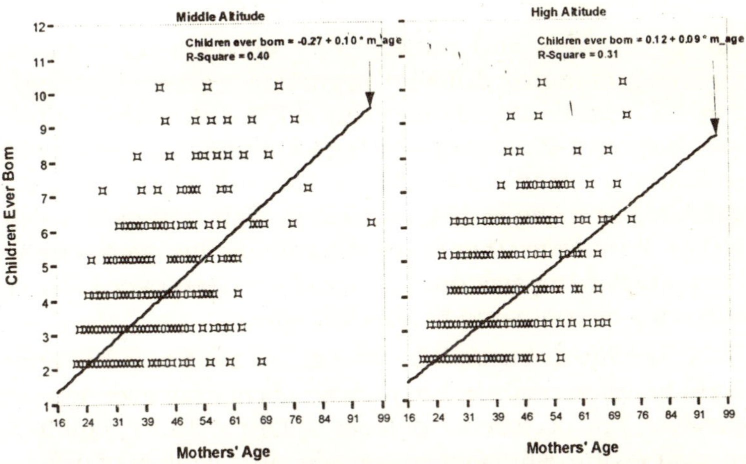

Figure 13: Scattered Plot Diagramme Alongwith Regression Line Showing Positive Correlation Between Mothers' Age and Number of Children Ever Born Among Kinnaura of Middle and High Altitude.

To find out the exact correlation between age of mothers and number of children ever born and surviving among them with respect to different ecological zones, scattered diagramme are plotted as shown in Figure 13 and 14. It is clear from these diagramme that there is significant positive correlation between

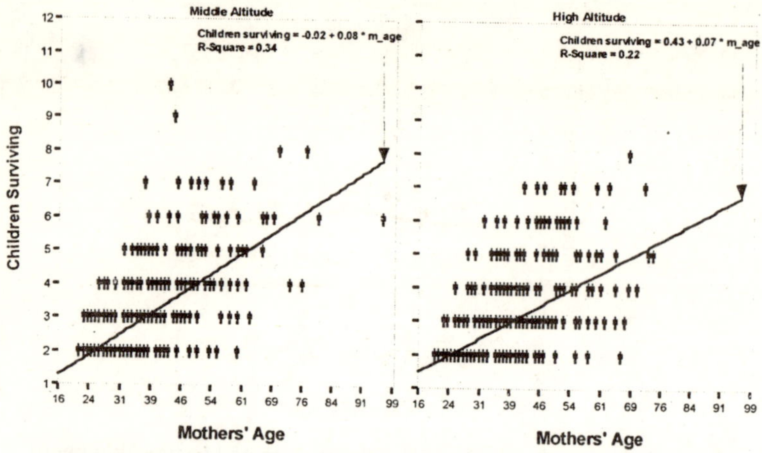

Figure 14: Scattered Plot Diagramme Alongwith Regression Line Showing Positive Correlation Between Mothers' Age and Number of Children Surviving Among Kinnaura of Middle and High Altitude.

age of mothers and number of children ever born and surviving, though in different magnitude in different ecological zones. In middle altitude the value of R^2 for number of children ever born is 0.40, whereas in high altitude this value is 0.31 similarly in middle altitude the value of R^2 for number of children surviving is 0.34, whereas in high altitude this value is 0.22. It indicates that in middle altitude the age of mothers have greater impacts on number of children ever born and surviving as compared to high altitude.

2. *Fertility differentials by Mortalities Experienced by Woman:* Fertility differentials (mean number of children ever born and surviving) by occurrence of foetal, infant and early childhood mortalities are estimated among Kinnaura women of different backgrounds (Table 12). The pooled data shows that those women who have had experienced abortion had lower average number of children ever born as compared to those women who hadn't, and is true for stillbirths as well. But in case of women who had experienced premature delivery in their reproductive life span, they had higher number of children ever born than the women who hadn't. Similar fertility differentials were observed in case with the women who had

experienced neonatal mortality (within 28 days), but incase with the women who had experienced post neo-natal mortality, the situation is reversed. The women who had experienced early childhood mortality they had lesser number of children ever born.

The mean number of children surviving is higher among the women who hadn't experienced any abortion, stillbirths, post neo natal mortality and early childhood mortalities. Simultaneously, the average number of children surviving is higher among the women who had experienced premature delivery and neo natal mortality.

Table 12

Fertility Differentials (Mean Number of Children Ever Born and Surviving) Among Kinnaura by Foetal Mortality, Infant Mortality and Childhood Mortalities Experienced by Women.

		Kinnaura		
		Middle Altitude	*High Altituds*	*Pooled*
Experience of Foetal/ Infant and Early Childhood Mortalities		*Mean Number of Children Ever Born*		
FOETAL MORTALITY				
Abortion				
	Not experienced	3.50	3.48	3.50
	Experienced	3.50	3.16	3.29
Still Births				
	Not experienced	3.58	3.47	3.65
	Experienced	3.20	2.33	3.46
Premature Delivery				
	Not experienced	3.47	3.47	3.46
	Experienced	4.04	2.87	3.94
INFANT MORTALITY				
Neo-Natal (within 28 days)				
	Not experienced	3.50	3.46	3.48
	Experienced	4.00	3.00	3.80
Post Neo-Natal (29 days to 364 days)				
	Not experienced	3.50	–	3.47
	Experienced	2.00	–	2.00
CHILD MORTALITY				
	Not experienced	3.50	–	3.47
	Experienced	2.00	–	2.00
		Mean Number of Children Surviving		

Contd...

		Kinnaura		
		Middle Altitude	*High Altituds*	*Pooled*
Experience of Foetal/ Infant and Early Childhood Mortalities		*Mean Number of Children Ever Born*		
FOETAL MORTALITY				
Abortion				
	Not experienced	3.01	2.98	3.01
	Experienced	3.02	2.83	2.84
Still Births				
	Not experienced	3.04	2.98	3.13
	Experienced	2.30	2.16	2.42
Premature Delivery				
	Not experienced	3.01	2.97	2.99
	Experienced	3.04	2.75	3.06
INFANT MORTALITY				
Neo-Natal (within 28 days)				
	Not experienced	3.01	2.97	2.98
	Experienced	3.33	2.75	4.00
Post Neo-Natal (29 days to 364 days)				
	Not experienced	3.01	-	2.98
	Experienced	1.00	-	1.00
CHILD MORTALITY				
	Not experienced	3.01	-	2.99
	Experienced	2.00	--	2.00

As clearly seen from the Table 12, in middle altitude the average number of children ever born is higher (4.04) among the women who had experienced premature delivery and neo-natal (within 28 days) mortality. But in case of those women who had experienced abortion, they had average number of children ever born equal to those who hadn't. The average number of children ever born is less among the women, who had experienced stillbirths; post neo natal (29 to 364 days) mortality and child mortality. Further in middle altitude the mean number of children surviving is greater among the women who had experienced abortion, premature delivery and neo natal mortality, but simultaneously lesser among the women who had experienced, still births, post neo natal mortality and early childhood mortalities (Table 12).

Fertility differentials (mean number of children ever born and surviving) among the Kinnaura women of high altitude shows that the average number of children ever born and surviving is always less among the women who had experienced any kind of foetal, infant and child mortalities.

Fertility Differentials by Socio-Cultural Practices

To measure the impact of prevalent socio-cultural practices on the fertility performance of Kinnaura women, only marriage and family types were considered in present investigation.

1. Fertility Differentials by Type of Marriage: As evident from Table 13, the pooled data show that the mean number of children ever born is highest (5.00) among the polygyny & polyandrous marriage followed by polyandrous (4.29) polygynous (3.95) and monogamous (3.33) families.

A similar picture is observed in case of average number of children surviving, which is highest (4.66) among the 'polyandry & polygynous' marriages, followed the polyandrous (3.68), polygynous (3.38), and monogamous (2.86) marriages.

Table 13
Fertility Differentials (Mean Number of Children Ever Born and Surviving) Among Kinnaura by Type of Marriage.

	Kinnaura		
	Middle Altitude	*High Altitude*	*Pooled*
Type of Marriage	*Mean Number of Children Ever Born*		
Monogamy	3.38	3.41	3.33
Polyandry	4.23	3.69	4.29
Polygyny	4.00	4.00	3.95
Polygyny & Polyandry	4.00	3.00	5.00
	Mean Number of Children Surviving		
Monogamy	2.91	2.96	2.86
Polyandry	3.58	2.95	3.68
Polygyny	3.31	3.80	3.38
Polygyny & Polyandry	4.00	3.00	4.66

In middle altitude the mean number of children ever born is highest among polyandrous marriages, followed by polygynous and polygynous & polyandrous marriages. Here too, the lowest average number of children ever born is among the women who belong to monogamous family. Further, in middle altitude the mean number of children surviving is highest (4.00) among polygynous & polyandrous marriages, followed by polyandrous (3.58), polygynous (3.38) and monogamous (2.91) marriages.

In high altitude the mean number of children ever born and surviving is highest among the polygynous marriages and lowest among monogamous marriages.

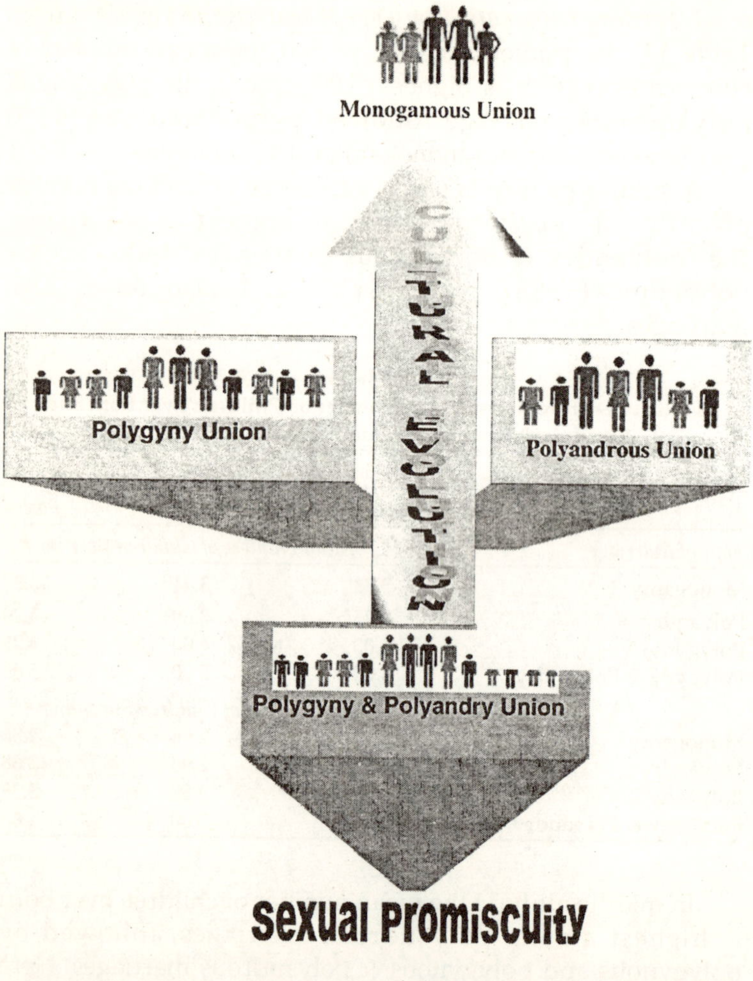

Figure 15: Evolution of Form of Marriage (Cultural Evolution) and Average Number of Children Ever Born Among Kinnaura Mothers.

2. *Fertility Differentials by Family Structure:* To find out the impact family structure on the fertility performance of Kinnaura women, mean number of children ever born and surviving were estimated among them. As evident from Table 14, the pooled data shows that mean number of children ever born and surviving is highest among the women who belong to extended family followed by Nuclear and Joint despite of their belongingness to middle and high altitude.

Table 14
Fertility Differentials (Mean Number of Children Ever Born and Surviving) Among Kinnaura.

	Kinnaura		
	Middle Altitude	*High Altitude*	*Pooled*
Family Structure	*Mean Number of Children Ever Born*		
Nuclear	3.68	3.66	3.51
Joint	3.15	3.15	3.20
Extended	3.45	3.15	3.71
	Mean Number of Children Surviving		
Nuclear	3.12	3.14	3.02
Joint	2.80	2.67	2.84
Extended	2.95	2.77	3.06

3. *Fertility Differentials by Family Structure and Type of Marriage:* Multivariate analyses leads to minimize the biasness of a variable and gives clear picture of impact of various variables on a particular characteristics. Here is the analysis of average number of children ever born and surviving, keeping in the view of belongingness of woman to a particular structure of family and the type of marriage currently being practiced by that family. Table 15 clearly shows that belongingness of a woman to either joint or extended family alongwith 'polygyny & polyandry' or polygyny type of marriage practice stressed women for higher fertility performance as they had average of 5 children ever born and 4 to 5 children surviving, followed by the combination of polyandry form of marriage and extended family type in such a condition the average number of children ever born is 4.86 and average number of children surviving is 4.05. The lowest number of children ever born and

surviving is observed in the combination of nuclear form of family and polygyny type of marriage. The combination of nuclear family and monogamy is in between with 3.43 average number of children ever born and 2.92 mean number of children surviving.

Table 15
Fertility Differentials (Mean Number of Children Ever Born and Surviving) Among Kinnaura of Different Family Type by Type of Marriage.

	Kinnaur			
	Pooled	*Nuclear*	*Joint*	*Extended*
Type of Marriage	*Mean Number of Children Ever Born*			
Monogamy	3.33	3.43	3.03	3.32
Polyandry	4.29	4.63	3.27	4.86
Polygyny	3.95	2.55	5.00	5.00
Polygyny & Polyandry	5.00	–	5.00	5.00
	Mean Number of Children Surviving			
Monogamy	2.86	2.92	2.70	2.73
Polyandry	3.68	3.97	2.93	4.05
Polygyny	3.38	2.44	4.09	4.00
Polygyny & Polyandry	4.66	–	5.00	4.50
	MIDDLE ALTITUDE			
Mean Number of Children Ever Born				
Monogamy	3.38	3.63	3.00	3.03
Polyandry	4.23	5.16	2.87	4.93
Polygyny	4.00	2.33	5.00	5.00
Polygyny & Polyandry	4.00	–	–	4.00
	Mean Number of Children Surviving			
Monogamy	2.91	3.07	2.69	2.68
Polyandry	3.58	4.41	2.68	3.86
Polygyny	3.31	2.16	4.00	4.00
Polygyny & Polyandry	4.00	–	–	4.00
	HIGH ALTITUDE			
Mean Number of Children Ever Born				
Monogamy	3.41	3.58	3.07	3.14
Polyandry	3.69	4.34	3.35	3.18
Polygyny	4.00	4.00	4.00	–
Polygyny & Polyandry	3.00	–	3.00	3.00
	Mean Number of Children Surviving			
Monogamy	2.96	3.07	2.66	2.87
Polyandry	2.95	3.57	2.58	2.50
Polygyny	3.80	4.00	3.50	–
Polygyny & Polyandry	3.00	–	3.00	3.00

Almost similar situation is observed in middle altitude, but in high altitude the situation is different. Here, the highest average number of children ever born is in the combination with polyandrous marriages and nuclear families. Simultaneously, the highest average number of children surviving is in nuclear family where polygyny is being practiced. The lowest average number of children ever born is associated with extended family where the form of marriage is 'polygyny & polyandry'. The combination of monogamy type of marriage and nuclear family is in between with 3.58 and 3.07 average number of children ever born and surviving respectively.

Table 16
One Way Analysis of Variance for Number of Children Ever Born: Middle Altitude

Family Types	*Nuclear*	*Joint*	*Extended*	*Monogamous*	*Polyandrous*	*Polygynous*
Nuclear		–	–	–	–	–
Joint			–	–	–	–
Extended				–	–	–
Monogamy					–	–
Polyandrous						–
Polygynous						

+p<0.05, – p>0.05

Table 17
One Way Analysis of Variance for Number of Children Ever Born: High Altitude

Family Types	*Nuclear*	*Joint*	*Extended*	*Monogamous*	*Polyandrous*	*Polygynous*
Nuclear		–	–	–	+	–
Joint			–	–	–	–
Extended				+	–	–
Monogamy					–	–
Polyandrous						
Polygynous						

+p<0.05, – p>0.05

One-way analysis of variance (ANOVA) test were applied for number of children ever born and surviving to find out the difference in means between pairs of groups (nuclear, joint and extended family and monogamous, polyandrous and polygynous family types), which reveals that in respect of most of the values there exist statistically non-significant differences (Tables 16, 17, 18 and 19).

Table 18
One Way Analysis of Variance for Number of Children Surviving: Middle Altitude

Family Types	*Nuclear*	*Joint*	*Extended*	*Monogamous*	*Polyandrous*	*Polygynous*
Nuclear		–	–	–	+	–
Joint			–	–	–	–
Extended				–	–	–
Monogamy					–	–
Polyandrous						–
Polygynous						

$+p<0.05$, $-p>0.05$

Table 19
One Way Analysis of Variance for Number of Children Surviving: High Altitude

Family Types	*Nuclear*	*Joint*	*Extended*	*Monogamous*	*Polyandrous*	*Polygynous*
Nuclear		+	–	–	+	–
Joint			–	+	–	–
Extended				–	–	–
Monogamy					–	–
Polyandrous						
Polygynous						

$+p<0.05$, $-p>0.05$

Fertility Differentials by Socio-economic Characteristics

There are several studies indicating that socio-economic status i.e. income, occupation, land holding etc. has great impact on fertility. Often negative relationship has been established between socio-economic condition and fertility. To find out the impact of socio-economic status on fertility among Kinnaura their living standards, income and land holding were taken into consideration, as described below.

1. *Fertility Differentials by Standards of Living:* Availability and accessibility to amenities such as drinking water, spacious residence with other essential facilities (i.e toilet), ownership

of house, refined source of lighting, fuel and owing the luxurious goods i.e. car, television, motorcycle etc. are relative indicators to measure the standards of living of individual/ household and society. An index was developed followed Kshatriya et. al. (2002) from possession of above listed facilities/items to find out the standard of living of Kinnaura household. This index is used to correlate with fertility performance of women.

Table 20

Fertility Differentials (Mean Number of Children Ever Born and Surviving) Among Kinnaura by Standard of Living (on the Basis of Owing of Luxurious Household Items).

	Kinnaura		
	Middle Altitude	*High Altitude*	*Pooled*
Living Standard	*Mean Number of Children Ever Born*		
Poor	3.07	4.20	3.16
Moderate	3.48	3.44	3.46
Better	3.58	3.44	3.57
	Mean Number of Children Surviving		
Poor	2.35	3.60	2.54
Moderate	2.95	2.95	2.94
Better	3.22	2.95	3.22

In general, the very first observation says that better living standard among Kinnaura leads to higher fertility performance, as evident from Table 20. This is true only to middle altitude Kinnaura for high altitude Kinnaura the situation is reversed, where higher mean number of children ever born and surviving is from the women who belong to families of poor standard of livings.

2. *Fertility Differentials by Income:* Income is widely acknowledged as a complex variable. Since it is being affected by different socio-economic and demographic variables. Thus, an attempt to separate out the particular role of income is often difficult. Though, there are analyses of average number of children ever born and surviving to find out the relationship between income and fertility among Kinnaura of different background, as shown in Table 21.

The pooled data of Kinnaur shows that there is no uniform relationship between fertility and income in studied population. If upper middle-income group (Rs. 100001/- to 1000000/- annual income) were not considered for a moment, the average number of children ever born is declining with the increase of income. While the highest (3.61) mean number of children ever born is recorded from the women who belong to the households having annual income in the range of Rs. 1 to 10 lakh. Further, the lowest mean number of children ever born, 2.60 were recorded from the women belonging to higher income (more than 10 lakh per annum) group.

Table 21
Fertility Differentials (Mean Number of Children Ever Born and Surviving) among Kinnaura by Annual Income

	Kinnaura		
Annual Income (in Indian Rs.)	*Middle Altitude*	*High Altitude*	*Pooled*
	Mean Number of Children Ever Born		
Below 12000	2.28	3.26	3.50
12001-50000	3.46	3.49	3.38
50001-100000	3.27	3.48	3.38
100001-1000000	3.68	3.44	3.61
More than 10 Lakh	4.00	4.00	2.60
	Mean Number of Children Surviving		
Below 12000	2.14	2.95	3.26
12001-50000	2.78	2.98	2.83
50001-100000	2.78	3.01	2.82
100001-1000000	3.27	2.94	3.17
More than 10 Lakh	4.00	3.50	2.60

In middle altitude the lowest mean number of children ever born 2.28 was recorded from the women belong to families of lowest income group (below Rs. 12000/-), and highest mean number of children ever born, 4.00 were recorded from higher income group (Rs. more than 10 lakh per annum). The mean number of children surviving increases with the raise of annual income.

In high altitude too, the lower income group had lowest average number of children ever born and surviving 3.26 and

2.95 respectively, and this increases with the increase of annual income, and highest mean number of children ever born (4.00) and surviving (3.50) were also recorded from the women belong to higher income groups.

Correlation and Regression Analyses of Various Fertility Differentials

To find out further correlation between number of children ever born and surviving with different determinants bivariate and multivariate regression analyses was done. For this purpose 2 dependent variables and 24 determinants were assigned independent scores, which are shown in the Table 22. which clearly indicates that the number of children ever born and surviving among Kinnaura is determined by the variables included, these variables accounts 83.8 percent in deciding the number of children ever born among the Kinnaura mothers (R^2=0.838), whereas these variables account 90 percent in the determining the number of children surviving among them (R^2=0.900). The further analyses indicate that these variables accounts in almost same proportion in middle and high altitude in shaping the number of children ever born and surviving. In middle altitude they accounts 93.5 per cent (R^2=0.935), whereas in high altitude they accounts slightly more 94.7 percent (R^2=0.947) as determining factors of number of children ever born among Kinnaura. In case of number of children surviving, these variables play slightly greater role as in middle altitude they accounts 96.7 per cent (R^2=0.967), whereas in high altitude they accounts 95.8 per cent (R^2=0.958).

Regression Analyses on Number of Children Ever Born and Surviving

All the 24 determinants as described in Table 22 are taken into consideration for bivariate linear regression analysis. The results of analyses are shown in Table 23, 24, 25 and 26, separately for children ever born and surviving, respectively for different ecological zones (middle and high altitude). It is evident from values of β_1 shown in Table 23 that in middle

Table 22
Score Assigned

Variables		Score 01	02	03	04
DEPENDENT VARIBLES					
Children Ever Born	Y1	1-3	4-6	7-9	10-12
Children Surviving	Y2	1-3	4-5	6-7	8-10
INDEPENDENT VARIBLES					
Mothers' Age	X1	<20	21-39	40-59	60+
Age at Marriage of Mother	X2	<18	19-20	27-34	35+
Mothers' Education	X3	Illiterate	Upto Primary	Upto High School	Higher Secondary+
Marriage Distance (in Km)	X4	0.0	1-100	101-200	201+
Family Structure	X5	Nuclear	Joint	Extended	
Type of Marriage Practiced	X6	Monogamy	Polyandry	Polygyny	Polyandry and Polygyny
After Marriage When Couple Start Living together?	X7	Right After	After Few Years		
Age At Marriage of Father	X8	<20	21-29	30-39	40+
Number of Live Birth Male Child	X9	1-2	3-4	5-6	7+
Number of Live Birth Female Child	X10	1-2	3-4	5-6	7+
Number of Surviving Male Child	X11	1	2	3	4+
Number of Surviving Female Child	X12	1-2	3-4	5-6	7+
Number of Child Deaths	X13	1	2	3	4+
Abortion Occurred	X14	Yes	No		
Stillbirth Occurred	X15	Yes	No		
Premature Delivery Occurred	X16	Yes	No		
Number of Pregnancy Experienced by Mothers	X17	1-2	3-4	5-6	7+
Source of Drinking Water	X18	Chasma	Tap Shared	Tap	Owned
Type of House	X19	Katcha	Semi Pucca	Pucca	
Source of Lighting	X20	Kerosene	Electricity		
Fuel Used	X21	Fire wood	Kerosene	LPG	Electricity
Toilet Used	X22	No Latrine	Ownpit	Own flush	
Living Standard	X23	Poor	Good	Well off	
Owing Agricultural Land	X24	Yes	No		

altitude the number of children ever born had significant positive correlation with mothers' age (X1), type of marriage (X6), after marriage when couple started living together (X7), number of live birth of male child (X9), number of live birth of female child (X10), number of surviving male child (X11), number of surviving female child (X12), number of child deaths (X13), number of pregnancy experienced by the mother (X17); whereas eight variables viz. age at marriage of mother (X2), mothers' education (X3), marriage distance (X4), family structure (X5), age at marriage of father (X8), experience of premature delivery by mother (X16), source of drinking water (X18), owing the agricultural land (X24) had negative correlation with the number of children ever born. In high altitude, most of the determinants had positive correlation, only six having negative correlation with the number of children ever born, these are marriage distance of spouses (X4), occurrence of still birth (X15), occurrence of premature delivery (X16), source of drinking water (X18), type of house (X19) and owing the agricultural land (X24). The comparative correlation between number of children ever born and different determinants as well as comparison between middle and high are shown in bar-diagramme Figure 16, which is self-explanatory.

In case of number of children surviving less number of determinants had negative correlation, in middle altitude number of such variables are found to be limited to 4 only, viz. age at marriage of mother (X2), marriage distance (X4), family structure (X5) and owing of agricultural land (X24). In high altitude except family structure three of four having same kind of correlation beside that three more variable viz. age at marriage of father, source of drinking water and type of house also had negative correlation with the number of children ever born, whereas rest of the variables showing positive correlation as apparent from Table 25 and 26. The comparison of extent of correlation between number of children surviving and different determinants as well as comparison between middle and high altitude is apparent from the bar diagramme (Figure 17).

Table 23

Bivariate Linear Regression Analyses on Number of Children Ever Born With Its Determinants Among Kinnaura of Middle Altitude.

Variables	*Regression Coefficients*				*t-Statistics*	*F-Statistics*		
			Unstandardized	*Standardized*				
	R	R^2	$\beta_0+\beta_1$	β_1	*t-value*	*F-value*	*df*	*P*
Y1 Vs X01	0.483	0.233	0.248+0.519	0.483	10.690	114.460	378	*
Y1 Vs X02	0.089	0.008	1.678-0.103	-0.089	1.743	3.030	382	ns
Y1 Vs X03	0.010	0.001	1.530-0.007	-0.010	-0.185	0.030	378	ns
Y1 Vs X04	0.105	0.011	1.951-0.214	-0.105	-2.071	4.290	384	†
Y1 Vs X05	0.084	0.007	1.641-0.073	-0.084	-1.649	2.710	384	*
Y1 Vs X06	0.169	0.028	1.247+0.231	0.169	3.350	11.220	384	*
Y1 Vs X07	0.168	0.028	0.824+0.679	0.168	3.341	11.161	384	*
Y1 Vs X08	0.011	0.001	1.538-0.011	-0.011	-0.218	0.048	382	ns
Y1 Vs X09	0.514	0.264	0.768+0.623	0.514	10.954	119.991	335	*
Y1 Vs X10	0.655	0.430	0.673+0.675	0.655	15.549	241.776	322	*
Y1 Vs X11	0.370	0.137	1.087+0.285	0.370	7.142	51.007	323	*
Y1 Vs X12	0.564	0.318	0.713+0.686	0.564	12.056	145.344	313	*
Y1 Vs X13	0.459	0.210	1.298+0.413	0.459	5.653	31.954	121	*
Y1 Vs X14	0.013	0.001	1.475+0.025	0.013	0.248	0.620	384	ns
Y1 Vs X15	0.063	0.004	2.733+0.467	0.063	1.017	1.035	259	ns
Y1 Vs X16	0.081	0.007	4.912-0.685	-0.081	-1.588	2.523	384	ns
Y1 Vs X17	0.878	0.771	-0.362+1.821	0.878	35.860	1285.919	384	*
Y1 Vs X18	0.045	0.002	3.873-0.132	-0.045	-0.890	0.791	384	ns
Y1 Vs X19	0.016	0.001	1.494+0.015	0.016	0.311	0.097	384	ns

Contd...

	Regression Coefficients							
			Unstandardized	*Standardized*	*t-Statistics*	*F-Statistics*		
Variables	R	R^2	$\beta_0+\beta_1$	β_1	*t-value*	*F-value*	*df*	P
Y1 Vs X20	0.089	0.008	0.471+0.529	0.089	1.750	3.062	384	ns
Y1 Vs X21	0.009	0.001	1.486+0.013	0.009	0.168	0.028	384	ns
Y1 Vs X22	0.043	0.002	1.463+0.032	0.043	0.837	0.700	384	ns
Y1 Vs X23	0.027	0.001	1.440+0.037	0.027	0.530	0.281	384	ns
Y1 Vs X24	0.057	0.003	1.669-0.134	-0.057	-1.125	1.237	384	ns

Y1=Children ever born.
*p<0.001,
†p<0.05
ns= Not significant

Table 24
Bivariate Linear Regression Analyses on Number of Children Ever Born with its Determinants Among Kinnaura of High Altitude.

	Regression Coefficients							
			Unstandardized	*Standardized*	*t-Statistics*	*F-Statistics*		
Variables	*R*	R^2	$\beta_0+\beta_1$	β_1	*t-value*	*F-value*	*df*	*P*
Y1 Vs X01	0.456	0.208	0.359+0.456	0.456	10.310	106.340	407	*
Y1 Vs X02	0.073	0.005	1.628-0.103	0.073	-1.490	2.220	416	ns
Y1 Vs X03	0.058	0.003	1.402+0.036	0.058	1.160	1.350	405	ns
Y1 Vs X04	0.105	0.011	1.722-0.129	-0.105	-2.140	4.590	416	†
Y1 Vs X05	0.081	0.007	1.395+0.065	0.081	1.650	2.720	416	ns
Y1 Vs X06	0.160	0.026	1.231+0.225	0.160	3.299	10.880	416	*
Y1 Vs X07	0.001	0.001	1.498+0.001	0.001	0.003	0.000	416	ns
Y1 Vs X08	0.094	0.009	1.665-0.094	0.094	-1.916	3.672	416	ns
Y1 Vs X09	0.517	0.267	0.709+0.656	0.517	11.560	133.640	368	*
Y1 Vs X10	0.623	0.388	0.667+0.669	0.623	14.801	219.064	347	*
Y1 Vs X11	0.390	0.152	1.023+0.309	0.390	7.927	62.832	351	*
Y1 Vs X12	0.532	0.283	0.740+0.639	0.056	11.392	129.775	329	*
Y1 Vs X13	0.423	0.179	1.410+0.326	0.423	12.155	27.445	127	*
Y1 Vs X14	0.101	0.010	1.017+0.250	0.101	2.059	4.240	416	†
Y1 Vs X15	0.046	0.002	4.809+0.475	-0.046	-0.589	0.347	167	ns
Y1 Vs X16	0.007	0.001	3.715-0.090	-0.007	-0.137	0.019	416	ns
Y1 Vs X17	0.916	0.838	-0.344+1.882	0.916	46.372	2150.318	416	*
Y1 Vs X18	0.046	0.002	3.771-0.125	-0.046	-0.939	0.881	416	ns
Y1 Vs X19	0.059	0.003	1.592-0.056	-0.059	-1.207	1.457	416	ns

Contd...

	Regression Coefficients							
			Unstandardized	Standardized	t-Statistics		F-Statistics	
Variables	*R*	R^2	$\beta_0+\beta_1$	β_1	*t-value*	*F-value*	*df*	*P*
Y1 Vs X20	0.051	0.003	0.898+0.302	0.051	1.045	1.091	416	ns
Y1 Vs X21	0.023	0.001	1.319+0.061	0.023	0.465	0.216	416	ns
Y1 Vs X22	0.046	0.002	1.426+0.041	0.046	0.940	0.883	416	ns
Y1 Vs X23	0.055	0.003	1.316+0.085	0.055	1.117	1.248	416	ns
Y1 Vs X24	0.097	0.009	1.835-0.324	-0.097	-1.980	3.921	416	†

Y1=Children ever born.
*p<0.001,
†p<0.05
ns=Not significant

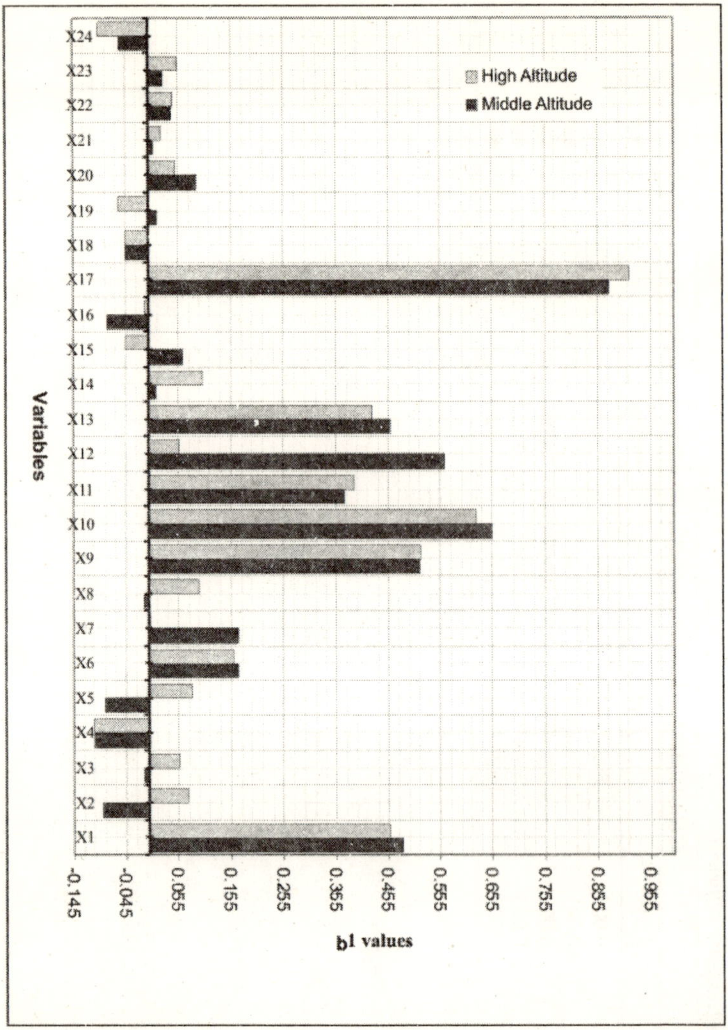

Figure 16: Showing Comparative Relationship (Through Values of â1) Between Number of Children Ever Born and Different Determinants as well as Variation in Middle and High Altitude.

To diagnose the possible factors affecting fertility bivariate and multivariate analyses was run in SPSS. Initially, a total of 24 possible variables were assumed to be predictor and included in the analyses, which accounts 83.8 per cent

Table 25

Bivariate Linear Regression Analyses on Number of Children Surviving With Its Determinants among Kinnaura of Middle Altitude.

	Regression Coefficients							
			Unstandardized	*Standardized*	*t-Statistics*		*F-Statistics*	
Variables	*R*	R^2	$\beta_0+\beta_1$	β_1	*t-value*	*F-value*	*df*	*P<*
Y2 Vs X01	0.496	0.246	0.101+0.543	0.496	11.002	121.044	372	*
Y2 Vs X02	0.043	0.002	1.513-0.052	-0.043	-0.842	0.708	376	ns
Y2 Vs X03	0.007	0.000	1.422+0.005	0.007	0.007	0.016	372	ns
Y2 Vs X04	0.136	0.018	2.012-0.286	-0.136	-2.665	7.103	378	†
Y2 Vs X05	0.001	0.000	1.442-0.001	-0.001	-0.018	0.000	378	ns
Y2 Vs X06	0.163	0.026	1.166+0.230	0.163	3.200	10.239	378	*
Y2 Vs X07	0.138	0.019	0.848+0.576	0.138	2.711	7.348	378	†
Y2 Vs X08	0.012	0.000	1.409+0.013	0.012	0.238	0.057	376	ns
Y2 Vs X09	0.428	0.183	0.793+0.535	0.428	8.575	73.535	329	*
Y2 Vs X10	0.607	0.368	0.601+0.659	0.607	13.639	186.024	341	*
Y2 Vs X11	0.470	0.221	0.831+0.375	0.470	9.566	91.500	323	*
Y2 Vs X12	0.654	0.428	0.418+0.841	0.654	15.268	233.118	313	*
Y2 Vs X13	0.152	0.023	1.340+0.141	0.152	1.646	2.709	115	ns
Y2 Vs X14	0.023	0.001	1.353+0.047	0.023	0.44	0.193	378	ns
Y2 Vs X15	0.122	0.015	0.843+0.315	0.122	1.956	3.827	255	ns
Y2 Vs X16	0.011	0.000	1.376+0.033	0.011	0.217	0.047	378	ns
Y2 Vs X17	0.690	0.476	0.334+0.508	0.690	18.497	342.141	378	*
Y2 Vs X18	0.006	0.000	1.428+0.006	0.006	0.107	0.012	378	ns
Y2 Vs X19	0.063	0.004	1.221+0.223	0.063	1.221	1.491	378	ns

Contd...

			Regression Coefficients					
			Unstandardized	*Standardized*	*t-Statistics*	*F-Statistics*		
Variables	R	R^2	$\beta_0+\beta_1$	β_1	*t-value*	*F-value*	*df*	*P<*
Y2 Vs X20	0.073	0.005	0.553+0.447	0.073	1.418	2.011	378	ns
Y2 Vs X21	0.053	0.003	1.201+0.083	0.053	1.040	1.082	378	ns
Y2 Vs X22	0.089	0.008	1.311+0.070	0.089	1.744	3.042	378	ns
Y2 Vs X23	0.083	0.007	1.178+0.117	0.083	1.616	2.612	378	ns
Y2 Vs X24	0.074	0.005	1.641-0.184	-0.074	-1.443	2.084	378	ns

Y2=Children surviving.
*p<0.001,
†p<0.05
ns=Not significant

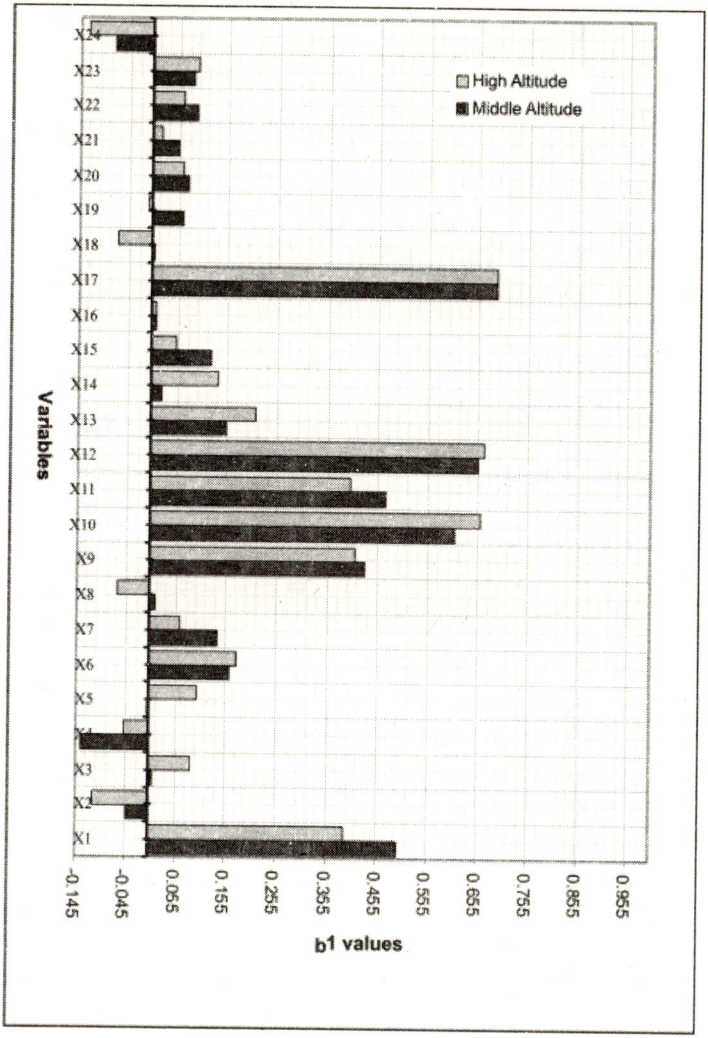

Figure 17: Showing Comparative Relationship (Through Values of β1) Between Number of Children Surviving and Different Determinants as well as Variation in Middle and High Altitude.

variability in number of children ever born among the Kinnaura mothers, whereas these same variables accounts for 90 per cent variability in case of number of children surviving. The further analyses indicate that these variables accounts in

Table 26
Bivariate Linear Regression Analyses on Number of Children Surviving with its Determinants among Kinnaura of High Altitude

	Regression Coefficients							
			Unstandardized	Standardized	t-Statistics	F-Statistics		
Variables	*R*	R^2	$\beta_0+\beta_1$	β_1	*t-value*	*F-value*	*df*	*P<*
Y2 Vs X01	0.389	0.151	0.424+0.394	0.389	8.405	70.651	398	*
Y2 Vs X02	0.111	0.012	1.615-0.116	-0.111	-2.242	5.028	407	†
Y2 Vs X03	0.085	0.007	1.274+0.054	0.085	1.699	2.885	396	ns
Y2 Vs X04	0.049	0.002	1.524-0.062	-0.049	-0.991	0.982	407	ns
Y2 Vs X05	0.097	0.009	1.289+0.080	0.097	1.965	3.863	407	†
Y2 Vs X06	0.176	0.031	1.116+0.251	0.176	3.607	13.010	407	*
Y2 Vs X07	0.062	0.004	0.828+0.586	0.062	1.261	1.591	407	ns
Y2 Vs X08	0.063	0.004	1.529-0.064	-0.063	-1.266	1.603	407	ns
Y2 Vs X09	0.409	0.167	0.774+0.531	0.409	8.487	72.027	359	*
Y2 Vs X10	0.659	0.435	0.482+0.733	0.659	16.174	261.601	341	*
Y2 Vs X11	0.400	0.160	0.901+0.327	0.400	8.169	66.736	351	*
Y2 Vs X12	0.666	0.444	0.412+0.832	0.666	16.184	70.360	329	*
Y2 Vs X13	0.211	0.045	1.266+0.162	0.211	2.336	5.457	118	†
Y2 Vs X14	0.136	0.019	0.758+0.342	0.136	2.769	7.668	407	†
Y2 Vs X15	0.052	0.003	1.138+0.195	0.052	0.665	0.443	164	ns
Y2 Vs X16	0.009	0.000	1.332+0.043	0.009	0.181	0.033	407	ns
Y2 Vs X17	0.689	0.475	0.365+0.508	0.689	19.165	367.303	407	*
Y2 Vs X18	0.067	0.005	1.540-0.066	-0.067	-1.355	1.836	407	ns
Y2 Vs X19	0.007	0.000	1.429-0.007	-0.007	-0.150	0.022	407	ns

Contd...

	Regression Coefficients							
			Unstandardized	Standardized	t-Statistics		F-Statistics	
Variables	*R*	*R^2*	$\beta_0+\beta_1$	β_1	*t-value*	*F-value*	*df*	*P<*
Y2 Vs X20	0.063	0.004	0.579+0.421	0.063	1.278	1.632	407	ns
Y2 Vs X21	0.019	0.000	1.265+0.051	0.019	0.385	0.148	407	ns
Y2 Vs X22	0.062	0.004	1.316+0.057	0.062	1.259	1.585	407	ns
Y2 Vs X23	0.093	0.009	1.099+0.148	0.093	1.886	3.558	407	ns
Y2 Vs X24	0.128	0.017	1.867-0.434	-0.128	-2.610	6.814	407	†

Y2=Children surviving.
*p<0.001,
†p<0.05
ns=Not significant

different proportion in middle and high altitude in shaping the number of children ever born and surviving. In middle altitude where these variable accounts 93.5 per cent (R^2=0.935), in high altitude they accounts slightly more 94.7 percent (R^2=0.947) as determining factors of number of children ever born among Kinnaura. In case of number of children surviving, these variables play greater role as in middle altitude they accounts 96.7 percent (R^2=0.967), whereas in high altitude they accounts 95.8 per cent (R^2=0.958). To find out intra-correlation between variables, zero-order correlations were analyzed, which shows that in 33 to 36 per cent cases the correlation is negative. The result of bivariate analysis indicates that some of the variables accounts for upto 69 per cent variability and having significant correlation with the number of children ever born and surviving independently of middle and high altitude such variables are: mother's age$_{(X1)}$, marriage distance$_{(X4)}$, number of live births male$_{(X9)}$ and female$_{(X10)}$ child as well as number of surviving male$_{(X11)}$ and female$_{(X12)}$ child, number of child deaths$_{(X13)}$ and number of pregnancy experienced$_{(X17)}$; Whereas some of the variables are found to be significant correlation in high altitude only, these variables are age at marriage of mother$_{(X2)}$, family type$_{(X5)}$, type of marriage$_{(X6)}$, after marriage when couples starting living together$_{(X7)}$, occurrence of abortion$_{(X14)}$ and owing of agricultural land$_{(X24)}$, yet only age at marriage of mother$_{(X2)}$, marriage distance$_{(X4)}$ and owing of agricultural land$_{(X24)}$.

From the above discussion it can be concluded that Kinnaura having moderate fertility, which is resulting into low young age dependency ratio and fostering the socio-economic development in the region. Out of 24 determinants, only 8 (as described above) are found to have significant correlation with the fertility among Kinnaura.

Chapter 10

MORTALITY

Mortality is one of three principal component of population change; the other two are fertility and migration. It is a continuous force of attrition, tending to reduce populations- a major negative force in the equilibrium processes of population dynamics. The level of mortality is taken into consideration to define fitness, survival and growth of a population. It is the other intrinsic component of the demographic transition theory. Mortality is also an excellent indicator of economic, social status and well being of peoples of a region.

Unlike fertility, man's effort to regulate this component has been relatively successful almost everywhere. Whereas industrialized countries reduced their death rate since 1650, the developing countries had done so from 1920 onward (Dorn, 1972). But, as a consequence, the population pressure has increased rapidly particularly in developing countries due to untamed fertility, creating a situation of disequilibrium. This does not imply that mortality must remain unchecked and left to take its own course and unnecessary and premature deaths may not be prevented, but that fertility must be curbed side by side. Besides that there are many regions in the world where mortality is still quite high.

Crude Death Rate (CDR)

The death rate or the crude death rate is the most common and widely used measure of mortality, describing the frequency with which deaths occur in a population at a specified time/period. It is well known that mortality has declined in this century. According to Population Reference Bureau (2003) the death rates for the world is 9. It is also comparable in more developed and less developed countries (10 and 8 respectively). In India too, the death rate has shown a progressive decline from 36.3 in 1921-30 to 10.1in 1992 (SRS, 1992). Currently estimated death rate of India is 8 (Population Reference Bureau, 2003). Interestingly, this rate is not much different from the death rates for certain developed countries as Finland (9), Ireland (8), United Kingdom (10), France (9), Netherlands (9), Switzerland (8) and Australia (7). On the other hand in many parts of the World, particularly in Africa and South Asia the death rates are quite higher than India (Mozambique in Eastern Africa, 28; Botswana in Southern Africa, 25; Afghanistan in South Central Asia, 18).

The SRS (2000) also had given similar estimation of death rate 8.5 for the year 2000 for India and its states, though it varies from 3.9 in Chandigarh to 10.5 in Orissa. The states like Himachal Pradesh and Kerala with 7.2 and 6.4 CDR respectively, are clearly more progressive. The estimation of death rate for bigger states shows that it is higher than national average for most of the states i.e. Bihar (8.8), Madhya Pradesh (10.3), Assam (9.6), Rajasthan (8.5), Uttar Pradesh (10.3) and Orissa (10.5). Data on CDR of individual tribe is not satisfactory, only few studies have been reported and it varies from a minimum of 9 in Hill Korwas to a maximum of 25 in Oraon of Bihar (Kshatriya, 2000).

Table 1
Crude Death Rates, Under–5 Mortality Rates, Infant Mortality Rates, Neonatal Mortality Rates, Post-neonatal Mortality Rates among Kinnaura of Middle and High Altitude, Kinnaur District, Himachal Pradesh, India.

Death Statistics	*Middle Altitude*	*High Altitude*	*Kinnaura (Pooled)*
Crude Death Rate	12.10	6.76	9.21
Under-5 Mortality Rate	104.16	66.66	83.33
Infant Mortality Rate	83.33	66.66	74.07
Neonatal Mortality Rate	41.66	66.66	64.81
Post-Neonatal Mortality Rate	20.83	–	9.25

The countries and states having high lands of the world such as Peru (Andes), Ethiopia and Nepal (Himalayas) had death rates of 7, 15 and 10 respectively (Population Reference Bureau, 2003). Bhasin and Nag (2002) estimated a death rate 15.7 for Himalayan high land Ladakh (Jammu and Kashmir State of India).

As evident from Table 1 the present study estimated a death rate of 9.2 for Kinnaura. The estimation of death rate for middle altitude population is just double (12.10) than high altitude (6.76). This may be because of comparative younger structure of population of high altitude. Sick and senile hardly stay at high altitude region, by the point of view of health care they migrate to middle or low altitude region, where better healthcare facilities are available, and ultimately reach to death; increasing the death statistics of middle altitude. On the other hand crude death rates are found to have positive correlation with crude birth rate and Total dependency ratio (Figure 1 and 2) but inverse correlation with old age dependency ratio (Figure 3).

Table 2

Distribution of Crude Death Rates (CDR), Infant Mortality Rate (IMR) and Under-5 Mortality Rates among Some Tribal and Non-Tribal Population Groups of India, Himalayan Region, Andes, Ethiopia and Other Major Parts of the World.

Region/ State/ Country	*Population Group*	*CDR*	*IMR*	*Under-5 MR*	*Source*
	Region and Population Specific Comparative Mortality Measures				
INDIAN HIMALAYAS					
Eastern Himalayas					
Sikkim					
	Buddhist	19.8	177.8	–	Bhasin and Bhasin (1995)
	Hindus	17.8	70.2	–	"
Meghalaya					
	Khasi			57.96	Adak (2001)
	Garo			79.01	"
	Mizo			31.91	"
Manipur					
	Mao	3.1	43.5		Maheo (1999)
	Total	5.6	23	–	SRS (2002)
Western Himalayas					
Jammu and Kashmir					

Contd...

Region/ State/ Country	*Population Group*	*CDR*	*IMR*	*Under-5 MR*	*Source*
Ladakh[HA]		15.7	221.2	132.8	Bhasin and Nag (2002)
	Bodhs	14.3	97.6	195.1	"
	Baltis	16.8	163.3	244.9	"
	Brokpas	21.7	200.0	300.0	"
	Arghuns	13.2	76.9	153.9	"
	Total	6.2	50	–	SRS (2002)
Himachal Pradesh					
	Brahman	12.9	125.4	–	Bhasin and Bhasin (1993)
	Rajput	11.8	113.3	–	"
	SC	26.0	263.2	–	"
	Total	7.2	–	60	SRS (2002)
Central Himalaya					
Uttaranchal (or erstwhile UP)					
Johari Bhotia		12.79	152.8	–	Kapoor (1996)
Rang Bhotia		16.11	212.0	–	"
Marchha Bhotia		13.12	158.7	–	"
Marchha Bhotia		8.22	142.8	–	Chachra and Bhasin (1998)
Dharchula Bhotia		18.12	120.0	240.0	"
Johar Bhotia		10.01	150.0	350.0	"
Raji		29.0	192.0	–	Samal, et.al. (2000)
Raji		47.6	344.8	724.1	Patra (2001)
Jaunsaris		11.85	81.00	–	Kshatriya, et.al. (1997)
Total		6.9	50	–	SRS (2002)
Country/ State Specific Comparative Mortality Measures					
INDIA		9.7	67.6	94.9	1998-99 NFHS-2 (2000)
Delhi		7.8	46.8	55.4	"
Haryana		8.1	56.8	76.8	"
Himachal Pradesh		8.3	34.4	42.4	"
Jammu & Kashmir		8.3	65.0	80.1	"
Punjab		8.4	57.1	72.1	"
Rajasthan		10.2	80.4	114.9	"
Madhya Pradesh		10.2	86.1	137.6	"
Uttar Pradesh		10.2	86.7	122.5	"
Bihar		11.2	72.9	105.1	"
Orissa		12.9	81.0	104.4	"
West Bengal		8.3	48.7	67.6	"
Arunachal Pradesh		12.4	63.1	98.1	"
Assam		9.4	69.5	89.5	"
Manipur		9.0	37.0	56.1	"
Meghalaya		9.9	89.0	122.0	"
Mizoram		7.3	37.0	54.7	"
Nagaland		6.9	42.1	63.8	"
Sikkim		6.3	43.9	71.0	"
Goa		10.1	36.7	46.8	"
Gujarat		8.0	62.6	85.1	"
Maharashtra		9.0	43.7	58.1	"
Andhra Pradesh		10.7	65.8	85.5	"
Karnataka		7.9	51.5	69.8	"

Contd...

Region/ State/ Country	*Population Group*	*CDR*	*IMR*	*Under-5 MR*	*Source*
Kerala		6.0	16.3	18.8	"
Tamil Nadu		10.8	48.2	63.3	"
Indian States	Minimum	6.0	16.3	18.8	"
	Maximum	12.9	89.0	137.6	"
INDIA					
	Scheduled Caste	–	83.0	119.3	
	Scheduled Tribe	–	84.2	126.6	
	Other backward Caste	–	76.0	103.1	
	Kinnaura (Pooled)	9.21	74.07	83.33	Present study (2006)
	Middle Altitude	12.10	83.33	104.16	"
	High Altitude	6.76	66.66	66.66	"

HA= High Altitude
PTG= Primitive Tribal Group
SC= Scheduled Caste
ST=Scheduled Caste

Infant Mortality Rate (IMR)

Infant mortality rate (IMR) is one of the important measures of mortality. As it estimates the mortality in that segment of population, where occurrence of death is very high. This indicator of mortality has taken great attention because of its direct relationship with fertility. Where infant mortality rate is high, the fertility rate is also high. Infant mortality rate is also considered as an indicator of human development.

In the present study infant mortality rate has been observed 74.07 for Kinnaura as a whole, for middle altitude it is computed as 83.33, while for high altitude, it is slightly lower 66.66 (Table 1).

The comparison of infant mortality rates of present study population with Indian States reflects that IMR is high among present study population as this indicator varies from lowest 16.3 for Kerala and highest is recorded as 89 for Meghalaya state (Table 2). Further this estimation for Himachal Pradesh is 34.4 and for Jammu & Kashmir it was estimated to be 65 by 1998-99, NFHS-2 (2002). If the comparisons of present findings made exclusively with Himalayan populations, portrays that

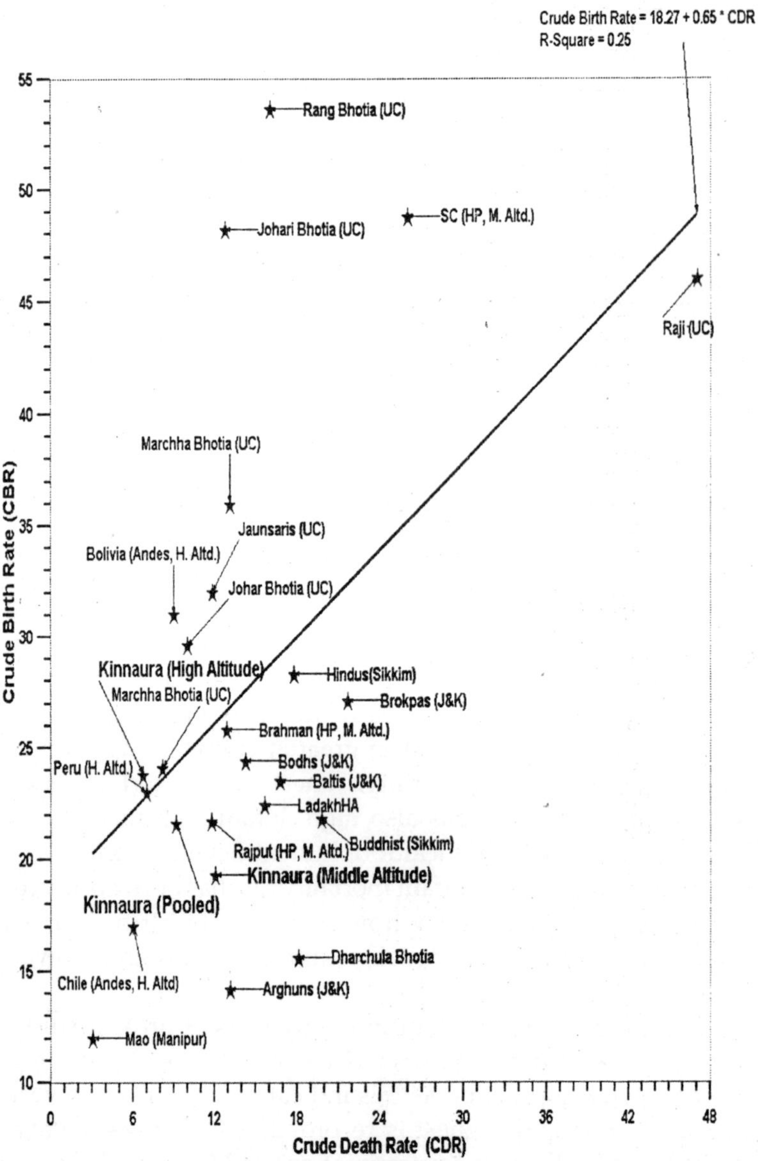

Figure 1: Bivariate Scattered Plot Diagramme Showing Correlation between Crude Birth Rate and Crude Death Rate among Different Population.

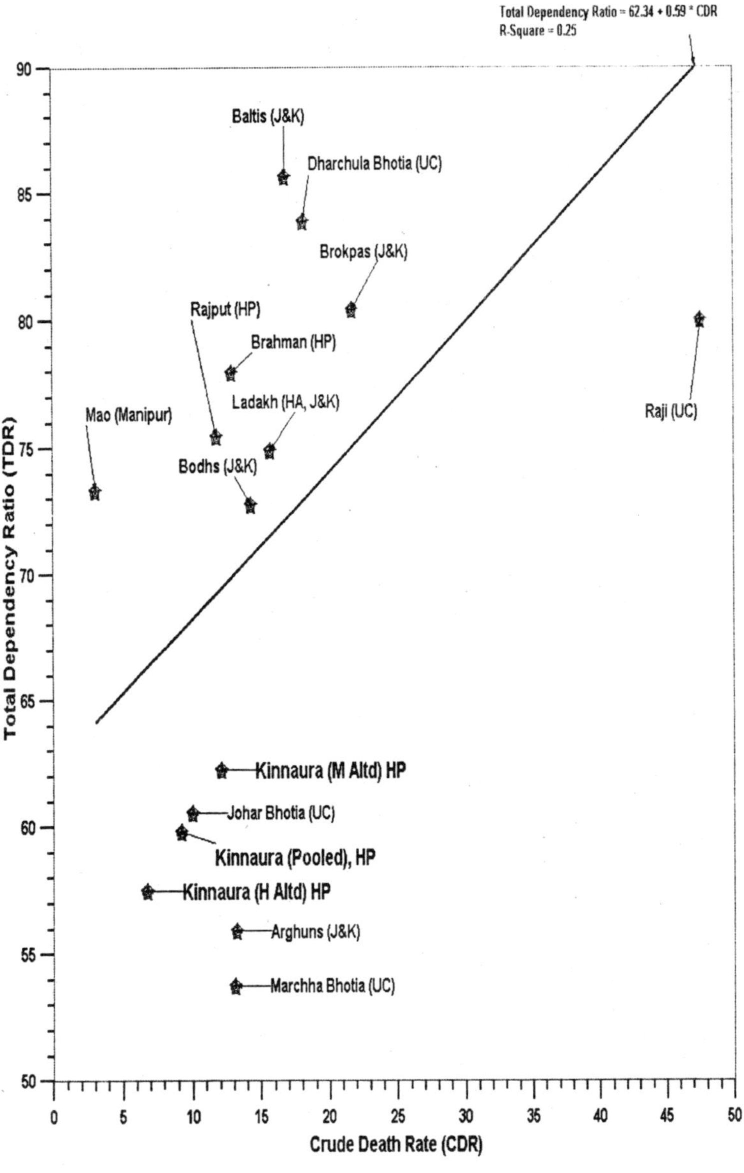

Figure 2: Bivariate Plot Diagramme Showing Correlation and Regression between Total Dependency Ratio and CDR.

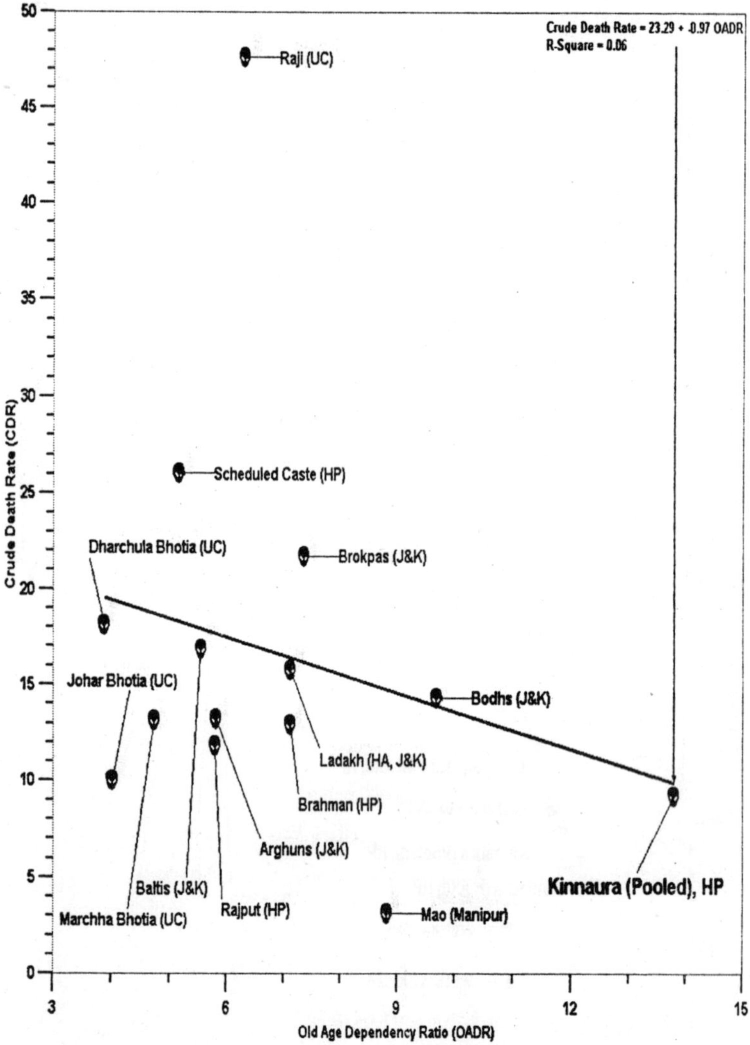

Figure 3: Bivariate Scattered Plot Diagramme Showing Inverse Correlation between CDR and Old Age Dependency Ratio

the IMR is less among Kinnaura than other studied population, simultaneously it is strongly correlated with young age dependency ratio, which accounts 40 percent variability in IMR (Figure 4). Furthermore the IMR among Kinnaura are higher than National average (67.6), yet it should be reduced, which is possible through development of better health care services specially routine pediatric services to remote areas, fully immunization of infants, promotion for female education, prevention of childhood infections and finally through effective mother and child nutrition Programmes.

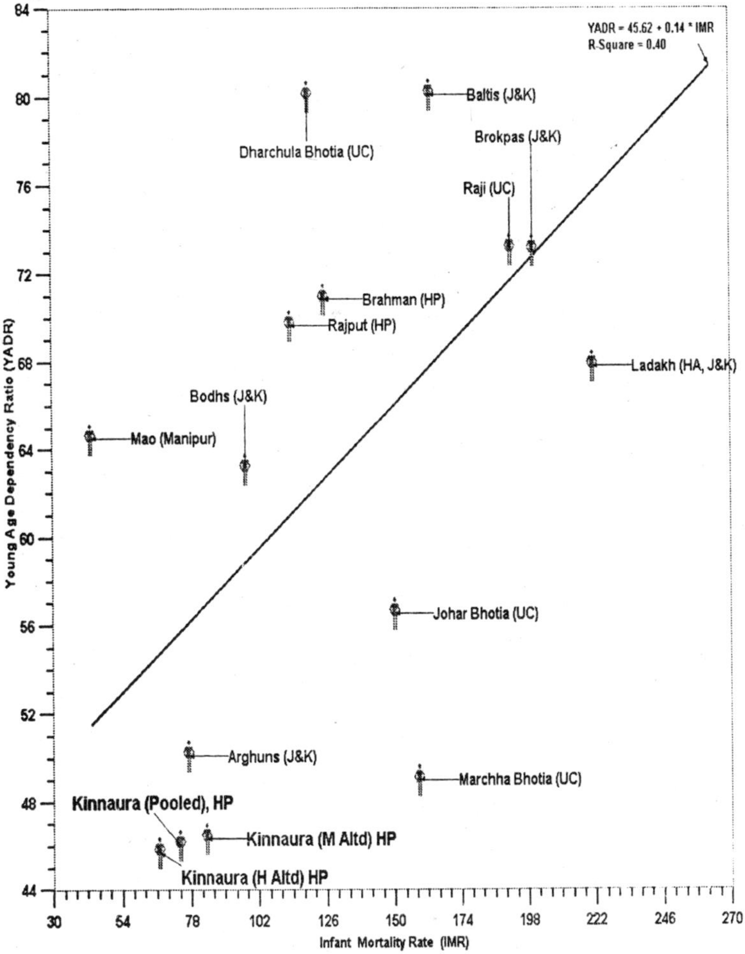

Figure 4: Bivariate Scattered Plot Diagramme Showing Correlation and Regression between Young Age Dependency Ratio and Infant Mortality Rate among different Himalayan Population

FOCUS GROUP DISCUSSION

Village	–	Reckong Peo
Participants	–	Pradhans of Mahila Mandal

Pradhans of Mahila Mandal were gathered to participate in a programme. Most of them were tribal women. Availing this opportunity a FGD of these women is conducted. Dr. S. Koley helped as recorder. The total number of participant was 15. They belong to different villages. Their age varies from 30-45 years.

Regarding health problems a majority of the women (80%) were of the opinion that most common morbid conditions are ARI (Acute respiratory infection), water borne diseases and STD (sexually transmitted diseases). They also opined that malaria, filaria were uncommon. The reason for ARI in their opinion was climatic condition of the region. According to 75% women, water borne disease can be controlled by treatment of water, whereas 70% women suggested that STD could be controlled by safe sexual intercourse. Regarding new born care, 88% women spelt that people were quite aware regarding immunization, but still effective education and awareness programme might lead to better result and decrease infant mortality. They felt that better education especially among girls has resulted in increased awareness. The quantitative findings corroborate this view of these women as almost cent percent girls of 10-14 years are enrolled for education or none of this age group is found to be illiterate.

Neonatal Mortality Rate and Post-Neonatal Mortality Rate

The infant mortality varies markedly from very early to the latter part of the first year of life. For this reason infant mortality rate is divided into two parts (i) neonatal mortality (infant deaths upto 28 days of life), and (ii) post-neonatal mortality (infant deaths from 29 days to 364 days of life).

Neonatal Mortality Rate: In general, the neonatal mortality is attributed to endogenous or antenatal causes, whereas post-neonatal mortality is attributed to exogenous or environmental causes. The latter groups of course are mostly the function of unhygienic weaning practices, and several other factors, including economic, educational characteristics of parents. In most of the developed societies/regions, it is post neo-natal deaths that have been reduced most, with the result that a majority of all infant deaths are neonatal. And by and large, in the developing countries, the post-neonatal deaths account for most of the infant deaths. But, in country like India, and most of the states of Indian republic, neonatal deaths are either slightly higher or nearly similar to the post neonatal deaths, because of the exogenous causes account for significant proportion of neonatal deaths too.

Post-Neonatal Mortalities: As evident from Table 1, the post-neonatal mortality in Kinnaura is 9.25. For middle altitude it is higher 20.83. The high altitude population didn't experienced post-neonatal mortality, preceding two years of investigation.

Table 3
Distribution of Neonatal and Post-neonatal Mortalities among Some Tribal and Non-Tribal Population Groups of India and Himalayan Region.

Region/ State/ Country	*Population Group*	*Neonatal Mortality*	*Post neonatal Mortality*	*Source*
INDIAN HIMALAYAS				
Eastern Himalayas				
Meghalaya				
	Khasi	17.2	24.8	Adak (2001)
	Garo	33.9	18.1	"
	Mizo	3.5	19.5	"
Sikkim				
	Buddhist	66.7	111.1	Bhasin and Bhasin (1995)
	Hindus	35.1	35.1	"
Western Himalayas				
Jammu and Kashmir				
Ladakh				Bhasin and Nag (2002)
	Bodhs	24.4	73.2	"
	Baltis	81.6	81.6	"
	Brokpas	100.0	100.0	"
	Arghuns	–	76.9	"
INDIA		43.4	24.2	1998-99 NFHS-2 (2000)
Delhi		29.5	17.4	"
Haryana		34.9	21.9	"
Himachal Pradesh		22.1	12.3	"
Jammu & Kashmir		40.3	24.7	"
Punjab		34.3	22.8	"
Rajasthan		49.5	30.9	"
Madhya Pradesh		54.9	31.2	"
Uttar Pradesh		53.6	33.1	"
Bihar		46.5	26.4	"
Orissa		48.6	32.3	"
West Bengal		31.9	16.8	"
Arunachal Pradesh		41.8	21.3	"
Assam		44.6	24.9	"
Manipur		18.6	18.4	"

Contd...

Region/ State/ Country	*Population Group*	*Neonatal Mortality*	*Post-neonatal Mortality*	*Source*
Meghalaya		50.7	38.3	"
Mizoram		18.8	18.2	"
Nagaland		20.1	22.0	"
Sikkim		26.3	17.6	"
Goa		31.2	5.5	"
Gujarat		39.6	23.0	"
Maharashtra		32.0	11.7	"
Andhra Pradesh		43.8	22.1	"
Karnataka		37.1	14.4	"
Kerala		13.8	2.5	"
Tamil Nadu		34.8	13.3	"
Indian States	Minimum	13.8	2.5	"
	Maximum	54.9	38.3	"
Kinnaur		64.81	9.25	Present study (2006)
Middle altitude		41.66	20.83	"
High Altitude		66.66	-	"

The comparison of neonatal and post-neonatal mortality among different tribes and Indian states are presented in the Table 3, clearly indicates that the both mortality indicator are found quite higher among present study population.

Under 5-Mortality Rate

Under 5-mortality is another important measure of mortality, as almost all deaths in childhood occur before the age of 5 years. UNICEF (1991) has promoted it as main pointer of the state of children, as well as human and economic progress in a region. Furthermore, because in low mortality populations, mortality risks between ages 1 and 5 years are low, that the infant mortality rate can be used as a reasonable single index of child mortality, but in the population with higher mortality, relatively high proportion of deaths occur between age 1 and 5 years as well, so the under-5 mortality, is a more important index of overall child mortality, although the main infant mortality rate also remain a crucial measure (UN, 1992).

As evident from Table 1, the present study gives 83.33 under 5-mortalty for Kinnaura of Kinnaur district Himachal Pradesh, as a whole this rate is higher for middle altitude Kinnaura (104.16) as compared to high altitude (66.66).

The under-5 mortality rate for the developed countries in 1991 has been estimated as only 17; but those for the developing and least developed countries have been observed much higher 101 and 180, respectively (UNICEF, 1993). The NFHS-2 (2000) gives under 5-mortality for the period of 1998-99 for India and its different region/states/population groups indicates decline in under 5-mortalities as it stated 94.9 for India, which varies from 137.6 in Madhya Pradesh to 18.8 in Kerala. The State of Himachal Pradesh lies in the middle with a rate of 42.4. The under 5-mortality rate for scheduled tribe, scheduled caste and backward class of the country has reported to be 126.6, 119.3 and 103.1 respectively (Table 2). Further it is evident that the Under-5 mortality rate varies from 31.91 among the Mizo of Meghalaya (Adak, 2001) to 724 among Rajis of Uttaranchal in Himalayan region. Some population groups with high Under-5 mortality rates are Brokpas (300) and Baltis (244.9) of Ladakh region and Johar Bhotia (350) of Uttaranchal, whereas in the present study it has to be found as 83.33, which is higher for middle altitude Kinnaura (104.16) as compared to high altitude (66.66). In this way, Kinnaura shows relatively moderate under-5 mortality as compared to tribes and other states of India. The variation in child mortality among middle and high altitude of Kinnaura is due to mainly disparity in young age dependency ratio of two ecological zones, as young age population increases (especially <15 years of age) the infant and child mortality also increases, it is also evident from Figure 4 & 5.

FOCUS GROUP DISCUSSION

Village	–	Pangi
Participants	–	Women

The group consisted of Kinnaura women, 3 of them were lactating, 3 were pregnant and 5 having children below five years of age. The theme of discussion was pre-natal and post-natal care.

Out of this group 82% women told us that as and when they conceived, they try to contact Anganwadi worker or female health worker of the village. But in case of first pregnancy 64% of them did not consulted any health provider timely. 27% of the group consulted the above stated workers after six months, because in first

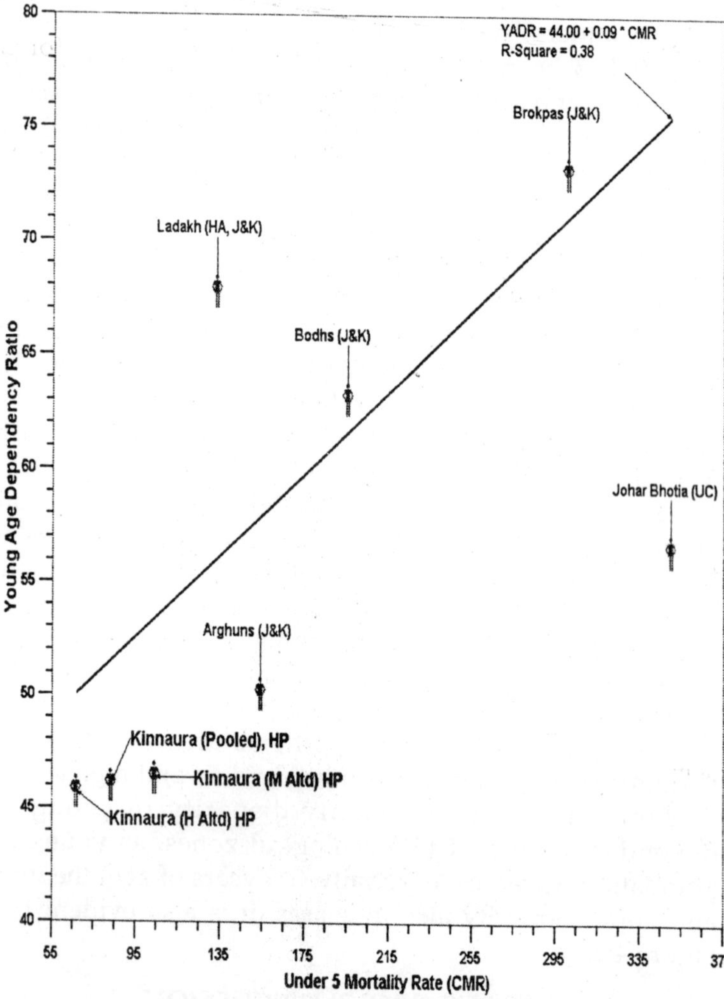

Figure 5: Bivariate Scattered Plot Diagramme Showing Correlation and Regression between Young Age Dependency Ratio and Under 5-Mortality Rate among different Himalayan Population.

pregnancy they are shy and tried to hide the fact. But from second pregnancy onwards they didn't hesitate to tell the fact and received the essential doses of TT (tetanus toxoid). The geography of the region is so adverse that none of them were scared in last trimester form doing heavy work such as fetching water, carrying firewood etc. All of them delivered at home. The reason behind home delivery is inaccessible habitation. The houses are scattered on steep valley, only stair like narrow zigzag footpath is the way to reach up to road-head. The public vehicle is available only two times in a day. During the acute labour pain even in daytime it is not possible to carry a pregnant women to the health center because path from the house leading to road is almost vertical and far. In such a condition home delivery is preferred. None of the women ever faced the problem of obstructed delivery, or had heard about it from other women in the village. On being asked as to how they would tackle this problem if they encounter one, 18% of group replied that in that case they would do something to transport the lady to district hospital. 64 per cent women have opinion that they would make a telephone call for ambulance service, or request doctor to make a home visit.

During present investigation 820 households of 30 villages were visited but only one case of obstructed labour was reported in village Shalkher, where doctor of civil hospital came at home for conducting the delivery. During pregnancy fever, giddiness, vomiting is common problem faced by every women of the present group who experienced pregnancy. Among common problem of women they reported white discharge and excessive bleeding.91% of the group are aware regarding immunization of child. Blade is used to cut the cord of newborn; the cord stump is tied with thread or mother's hair. According to these women nothing should apply on cord stump. 81% of the group have opinion that breast-feeding should started as early as possible. All of them are agree that colostrums should not be discarded. Simultaneously weaning should be started from the age of 4-6 months. 45% of the group prefer to give branded baby food like 'Cerelac', whereas rest can't afford and give whatever they are eating at home e.g. rice, roti (country bread), pulse etc.

Age Specific Death Rate (ASDR)

Initially there is inverse relation between age and occurrence of death. The early days of human life is more susceptible to death as compared to childhood and adulthood. The occurrence of death in human beings varies sharply with age. Hence, to understand the overall death rates, age specific death rates are also studied, as these can separate the component of mortality from the effect of age composition of a population. In the present study population, the death rate of children of less than one year has been observed relatively high 60.15 (Table 4).

It can be noticed here that the age pattern of the mortality risks, in general, does not vary greatly with the level of mortality. Mortality risks are high in the period immediately after birth, and then decline, often rapidly to a minimum between ages 6-14 years, then rise gradually to about 40 years, after which it rises very rapidly to high levels in old age.

Table 4
Age-specific Death Rates for Kinnaura of Middle and High Altitude, Kinnaur District, Himachal Pradesh, India.

Kinnaura	*<1 Year*	*1-5*	*6-14*	*15-29*	*30-44*	*45+*
Middle Altitude	65.57	5.29	–	2.65	4.02	40.46
High Altitude	55.56	–	–	1.31	5.50	18.95
Kinnaura (Pooled)	60.15	2.61	–	1.98	4.80	30.18

In case of the present study populations, the curve for age specific death rates has been formed more or less as inverted J-shaped, as shown in Figure 6, indicating relatively high mortality during infancy than old ages. However certain variation can be noticed in middle and high altitude population.

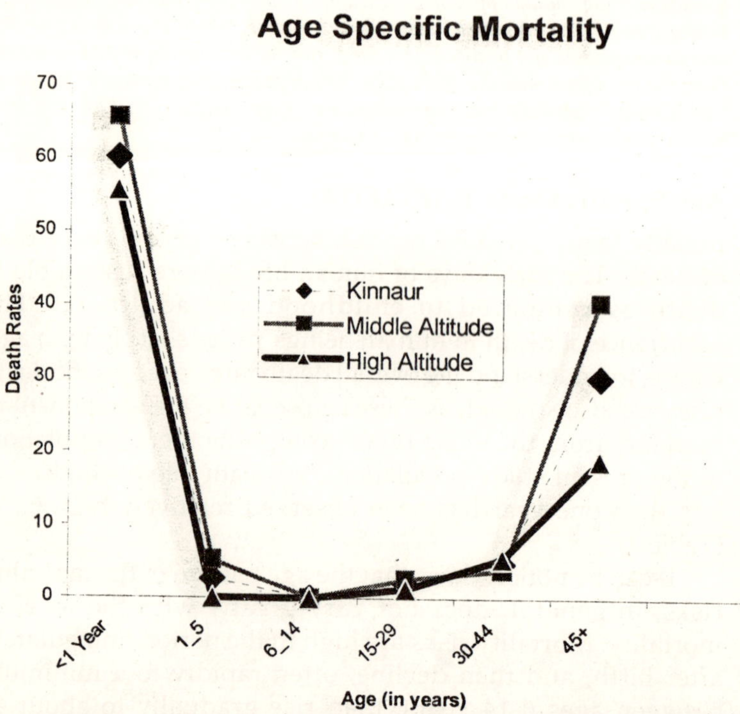

Figure 6: Line Graph Showing inverted J-Shape Curve of Age Specific Mortalities among Kinnaura of Middle and High Altitude.

Table 5
Mean Live Birth, Average Child Survival, Total Child Deaths, Percentage of Child Loss, Child Loss and Survival Ratio among Kinnaura of Middle and High Altitude, Kinnaur District, Himachal Pradesh, India.

	Number of Mothers	*Children Ever Born*	*Children Surviving*	*Mean Live Birth*	*Average Children Surviving*	*Total Child Deaths*	*Average Child Loss*	*% of Child Loss*	*Child Loss Ratio*	*Child Survival Ratio*
Kinnaura										
Middle Altitude	386	1379	1186	3.50	3.07	193	0.43	12.28	0.14	0.86
High Altitude	417	1475	1267	3.46	3.04	208	0.42	12.12	0.15	0.85
Kinnaura (Pooled)	803	2854	2453	3.48	3.05	401	0.43	12.22	0.15	0.85

In developing countries/regions, including India the curve of age specific death rates is usually U-shaped, representing high mortality in childhood and old age. On the other hand in the developed countries, where mortality has declined in the past, the curve appears to be J shaped, since the mortality has reduced to a greater extent at the infancy and early childhood age.

EXPLORATORY CHILD MORTALITY ANALYSIS

Alike fertility, mortality, especially child mortality is determined by a number of biological, demographical, socio-cultural and socio-economic determinants. Here is an analysis of these determinants, according to child loss and survival ratio.

Child Loss and Survival

As stated in Table 5, the average live birth per women among Kinnaura as a whole was estimated 3.48, while the children surviving per women were 3.05. Thus an average of 0.43 children per women seems to have died by the time of survey. In terms of proportion of child loss, it is 12.22 per cent. In middle and high altitude it does not vary too much.

Differentials in Child Loss and Survival by Current Age of Women: Differentials in child loss and survival by current age of women among different groups of Kinnaura have been given in Table 6. It is clear from the Table that overall child loss ratio or the proportion of child loss increases with the advancement of age of woman, although the increase was not exactly uniform. The reverse was noticed when the proportions of survivors (child survival ratios) by age of women were studied.

Differentials in Child Loss and Survival by Socio-Cultural Practices

Socio-cultural practices like type of marriages practiced viz. monogamy, polyandry, polygyny and polygyny & polyandry; type of family i.e. nuclear, joint and extended etc. has direct or indirect relation with child mortality. Here an attempt has been paid to find out the role of these variables in case of child loss and survival.

Table 6
Child Mortality Differentials (Child Loss and Survival Ratio) among Middle and High Altitude Kinnaura by Current Age of Mothers

	Kinnaura					
	Middle Altitude		*High Altitude*		*Pooled*	
Current Age of Mothers	*Child Loss Ratio*	*Child Survival Ratio*	*Child Loss Ratio*	*Child Survival Ratio*	*Child Loss Ratio*	*Child Survival Ratio*
16-19	0.000	1.000	0.000	1.000	0.000	1.000
20-24	0.076	0.924	0.000	1.000	0.043	0.957
25-29	0.119	0.881	0.143	0.857	0.130	0.870
30-34	0.110	0.890	0.145	0.855	0.128	0.872
35-39	0.168	0.832	0.097	0.903	0.129	0.871
40-44	0.114	0.886	0.173	0.827	0.145	0.855
45-49	0.132	0.868	0.134	0.866	0.133	0.867
50-55	0.174	0.826	0.135	0.865	0.154	0.846
56+	0.184	0.816	0.203	0.797	0.193	0.807

Table 7
Mortality Differentials (Child Loss and Survival Ratio) among Kinnaura by Type of Marriage.

	Kinnaura		
	Middle Altitude	*High Altitude*	*Pooled*
Type of Marriage		*Child Loss Ratio*	
Monogamy	0.136	0.144	0.140
Polyandry	0.154	0.135	0.142
Polygyny	0.172	0.053	0.145
Polygyny & Polyandry	0.000	0.091	0.067
		Child Survival Ratio	
Monogamy	0.864	0.856	0.860
Polyandry	0.846	0.865	0.858
Polygyny	0.828	0.947	0.855
Polygyny & Polyandry	1.000	0.909	0.933

Child Mortality Differentials by Type of Marriage: The pooled data shows (Table 7) that child loss ratio is lowest 0.067 in polygynous & polyandrous marriages. In general, child loss ratio increased from monogamous to polyandrous and polygynous marriages, respectively in order from 0.140 to 0.142 and 0.145.

In case of middle altitude Kinnaura almost similar pattern of child loss ratio is noticed, here the ratio of child loss is lowest with monogamous (0.136), increased with polyandrous (0.154) and polygynous (0.172) form of marriages. In high altitude the child loss ratio increased in reverse order from polygyny (0.053) to polyandry (0.135) and monogamy (0.144) form of marriages. The contrary was noticed when the proportions of survivors (child survival ratios) by type of marriage were studied.

Table 8
Mortality Differentials (Child Loss and Survival Ratio) among Kinnaura by Type of Family

	Kinnaura		
	Middle Altitude	*High Altitude*	*Pooled*
Family Type	*Child Loss Ratio*		
Nuclear	0.151	0.127	0.139
Joint	0.110	0.116	0.112
Extended	0.145	0.197	0.174
	Child Survival Ratio		
Nuclear	0.849	0.873	0.861
Joint	0.890	0.884	0.888
Extended	0.855	0.803	0.826

Child Mortality Differentials by Type of Family: The difference in child loss and survival ratio as per family type is given in Table 8. The pooled data shows that child loss ratio is lowest in joint family (0.112), followed by nuclear (0.139) and extended (0.174) family type. There is by and large, no variation in middle and high altitude in terms of order of family type and child loss ratio. The reverse trend is noticed when the proportions of survivors (child survival ratios) by type of family is considered.

Mortality Differentials by Family and Marriage Types: As it is already established that alike other vital events mortality is also determined by too many factors. Here is an analysis of mortality differentials, keeping in view two cultural practices (i.e. type of marriage and family) together. As evident from

Table 9, the child loss ratio is highest in extended families where the current practice of marriage is polygyny (0.200), followed by joint family and polygyny (0.182). The lowest child loss ratio was noticed in extended family type along with 'polygyny & polyandry' form of marriages (0.100).

Table 9
Mortality Differentials (Child Loss and Survival Ratio) among Kinnaura by Family Type and Form of Marriage Practiced Currently.

	Kinnaura			
Type of Marriage	*Pooled*	*Nuclear*	*Joint*	*Extended*
		Child Loss Ratio		
Monogamy	0.140	0.123	0.108	0.179
Polyandry	0.142	0.142	0.102	0.167
Polygyny	0.145	0.043	0.182	0.200
Polygyny & Polyandry	0.067	–	0.000	0.100
		Child Survival Ratio		
Monogamy	0.860	0.757	0.892	0.821
Polyandry	0.858	0.858	0.898	0.833
Polygyny	0.855	0.957	0.818	0.800
Polygyny & Polyandry	0.933	–	1.000	0.900
		Middle Altitude		
		Child Loss Ratio		
Monogamy	0.136	0.153	0.101	0.116
Polyandry	0.154	0.145	0.065	0.216
Polygyny	0.172	0.071	0.200	0.200
Polygyny & Polyandry	0.000	–	–	0.000
		Child Survival Ratio		
Monogamy	0.864	0.847	0.899	0.884
Polyandry	0.846	0.855	0.935	0.784
Polygyny	0.828	0.929	0.800	0.800
Polygyny & Polyandry	1.000	–	–	1.000
		High Altitude		
		Child Loss Ratio		
Monogamy	0.144	0.127	0.115	0.229
Polyandry	0.135	0.140	0.129	0.132
Polygyny	0.053	0.000	0.100	–
Polygyny & Polyandry	0.091	–	0.000	0.167
		Child Survival Ratio		
Monogamy	0.856	0.873	0.885	0.771
Polyandry	0.865	0.860	0.871	0.868
Polygyny	0.947	1.000	0.900	–
Polygyny & Polyandry	0.909	–	1.000	0.833

In middle altitude the highest child loss ratio (0.200) were computed for combination of polygyny form of marriage with extended and joint family type; while lowest was recorded among joint family and polyandry form of marriage. Simultaneously, in high altitude child loss ratio is highest (0.229) in extended family, where monogamy is being practiced, while lowest was recorded in joint family, where prevalent form of marriage is polygyny. There is no child loss were recorded, in those nuclear families where the form of marriage is polygyny. The contrary was noticed when the proportions of survivors (child survival ratios) by type of marriage were studied.

Differentials in Child Mortality by Economic Characteristics: Three important economic characteristics viz. standards of living, annual income and land holding are considered for exploratory mortality analysis and see the difference between economic characteristics, cultural practices and Geo-climatic condition (altitude).

Differentials of Child Mortality by Standards of Living: Table 10 shows that the ratio of child loss is highest among poor (0.197). Naturally, the child loss is lowest among rich people, who had better standard of living, who had moderate living standard; the ratio of child loss among them is also moderate.

Table 10
Mortality Differentials (Child Loss and Survival Ratio) among Kinnaura by Standard of Living (on the Basis of Owing of Luxurious Household Items/Services).

		Kinnaura	
	Middle Altitude	*High Altitude*	*Pooled*
Standard of Living		*Child Loss Ratio*	
Poor	0.233	0.152	0.197
Moderate	0.152	0.150	0.151
Better	0.100	0.097	0.099
		Child Survival Ratio	
Poor	0.767	0.848	0.803
Moderate	0.848	0.850	0.849
Better	0.900	0.903	0.901

In middle altitude, the ratio of child loss is higher (ranked by all categories) as compared to high altitude. The reverse was noticed when the proportion of survivors (child survival ratios) by standard of living is considered.

Differentials of Child Mortality by Annual Income: The mortality differentials by annual income is evident from Table 11. The findings are in accordance with the results obtained on the relationship between mortality differentials and living standard, with one exception of child loss ratio being less among those households, where annual income is less than Rs. 12000/- per annum.

Table 11

Mortality Differentials (Child Loss and Survival Ratio) among Kinnaura of Different Religious Background by Annual Income

	Kinnaura		
Annual Income (in Indian Rs.)	*Middle Altitude*	*High Altitude*	*Pooled*
		Child Loss Ratio	
Below 12000	0.063	0.067	0.067
12001-50000	0.198	0.140	0.162
50001-100000	0.148	0.181	0.164
100001-1000000	0.112	0.133	0.121
More than 10 Lakh	0.000	0.000	0.000
		Child Survival Ratio	
Below 12000	0.938	0.933	0.933
12001-50000	0.802	0.860	0.838
50001-100000	0.852	0.819	0.836
100001-1000000	0.888	0.867	0.879
More than 10 Lakh	1.000	1.000	1.000

CORRELATION AND REGRESSION ANALYSES OF DIFFERENT MORTALITY DIFFERENTIALS

Bivariate and multivariate regression analyses are under taken to find out the determinants of differential mortality. For this purpose 1 dependent and 24 independent variable are assigned scores, independently, which is shown in the Table 12.

Multiple Regression Analyses on Child Loss Ratio

It is found that the child loss ratio among Kinnaura is poorly determined by the variables included in correlation and regression analyses, the pooled data show that these variables accounts only for by 6.6 per cent variability in deciding the child loss ratio among the Kinnaura mothers (R^2=0.066), whereas the further analyses indicate that these variables accounts in greater and different proportion in middle and high altitude in determining the child loss ratio. In middle altitude where these variable accounts 14.5 percent (R^2=0.145), in high altitude they accounts slightly less, only 11 percent (R^2=0.110) in variability determining factors of child loss ratio among Kinnaura mothers.

Bivariate Regression Analyses on Child Loss Ratio

All the 24 determinants as described in Table 12 are taken into consideration for bivariate linear regression analysis. The results of analyses are shown in Table 13 and 14 separately for different ecological zones middle and high altitude. It is evident from values of β_1 that the correlation between child loss ratio and different determinants is poor, insignificant and negative in most of the cases. Further it is apparent from Table 13 that in middle altitude the child loss ratio had significant negative correlation only with 4 variables i.e. the number of children surviving, number of live birth of female child, number of surviving female child and the occurrence of premature delivery. In high altitude, the scenario is different; none of the determinants included in analyses had significant correlation with child loss ratio out of 24 variables 11 having negative correlation while 13 having positive correlation. The comparison of middle and high altitude is apparent in bar-diagramme (Figure 7), values of β_1 are plotted to show the comparative correlation of various determinants with the child loss ratio, simultaneously extent of variation in different ecological zones.

As it is apparent from above discussion, infant and child mortality (IMR & CMR or under-5 mortality) plays significant role in overall mortality or CDR (Crude Death Rate) in any population. For further elucidation of the fact and to find out the determinants of child mortality among Kinnaura (the present study population), bivariate and multivariate regression analysis were undertaken, keeping the child loss ratio as dependent variable, whereas 24 variables were identified as independent variables. The multiple regression analysis indicates that despite of middle and high altitude these 24 predictors accounts only 6 per cent variability in child loss ratio, though independent analysis for middle and high altitude shows variation as in middle altitude, as these variables accounts 14.5 percent and whereas in high altitude 11 per cent variability in child loss ratio. To see the individual effects and correlations of each of the predictors bivariate analysis was run, which indicates that mothers' education$_{(X3)}$, number of surviving female child$_{(X12)}$, abortion occurred$_{(X14)}$, number of pregnancy experienced by mother$_{(X17)}$ are only predictors found to have significant inverse correlation with child loss ratio among the Kinnaura of middle altitude only. None of the predictors are found to have significant correlation among the Kinnaura of high altitude. In the light of above discussion it could be concluded that similar to fertility; the mortality has also declined among Kinnaura.

Table 12
Score Assigned

		Score			
Variables		*01*	*02*	*03*	*04*
DEPENDENT VARIBLES					
Y3 Child loss ratio	Y3	0.00-0.25	0.26-0.50	0.51-0.75	0.76-1.00
INDEPENDENT VARIBLES					
Number of Pregnancy Experienced by Mothers	X1	1-2	3-4	5-6	7+
Children Ever Born	X2	1-3	4-6	7-9	10-12
Children surviving	X3	1-3	4-5	6-7	8-10
Mothers' Age	X4	<20	21-39	40-59	60+
Mothers' Age at Marriage	X5	<18	19-20	27-34	35+
Mothers' education	X6	Illiterate	Upto Primary	Upto High	Higher School Secondary +
Age at Marriage of Father	X7	<20	21-29	30-39	40+
Marriage Distance	X8	0.0	1-100	101-200	201+
Family structure	X9	Nuclear	Joint	Extended	
Type of marriage practiced	X10	Monogamy	Polyandry	Polygyny	Polyandry and Polygyny
Number of live birth male child	X11	1-2	3-4	5-6	7+
Number of live birth female child	X12	1-2	3-4	5-6	7+
Number of surviving male child	X13	1	2	3	4+

Contd...

Variables		*Score* 01	02	03	04
Number of surviving female child	X14	1-2	3-4	5-6	7+
Abortion occurred	X15	Yes	No		
Still birth occurred	X16	Yes	No		
Premature delivery occurred	X17	Yes	No		
Source of drinking water	X18	Chasma	Tap Shared	Tap Owned	
Type of House	X19	Katcha	Semi Pucca	Pucca	
Source of lighting	X20	Kerosene	Electricity		
Fuel used	X21	Fire wood	Kerosene	LPG	Electricity
Toilet used	X22	No Latrine	Ownpit	Own flush	
Living standard (on the basis of total of item owned)	X23	Poor	Good	Well off	
Owing Agricultural Land	X24	No Latrine	Ownpit	Own flush	

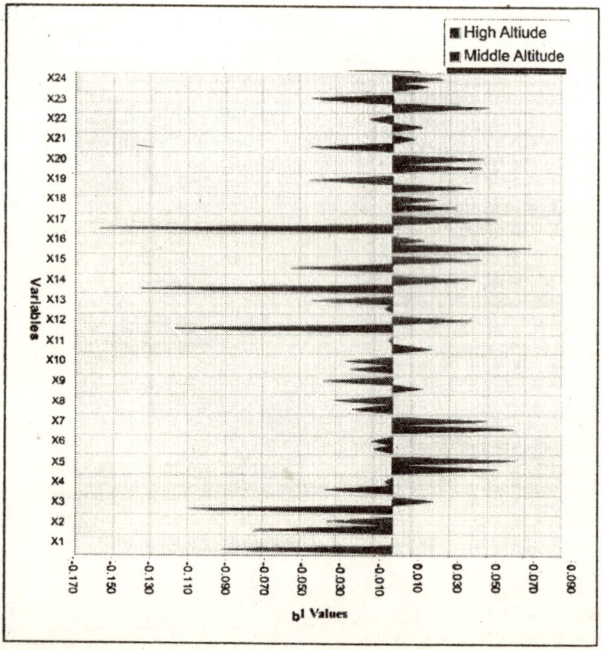

Figure 7: Showing Comparative Correlation of Various Determinants with the Child Loss Ratio, as well as Variation in Middle and High Altitude

Table 13

Bivariate Linear Regression Analyses on Child Loss Ratio with its Determinants Among Kinnaura of Middle Altitude.

			Regression Coefficient s					
			Unstandardized	Standardized	t-Statistics	F-Statistics		
Variables	R	R^2	$\beta_0+\beta_1$	β_1	t-value	F-value	df	P<
Y1 Vs X01	0.091	0.000	1.339-0.052	-0.091	-1.790	3.206	385	0.074
Y1 Vs X02	0.074	0.005	1.317-0.060	-0.074	-1.443	2.083	384	0.150
Y1 Vs X03	0.109	0.012	1.350-0.086	-0.109	-2.131	4.541	378	0.034
Y1 Vs X04	0.036	0.001	1.301-0.031	-0.036	-0.697	0.486	386	0.486
Y1 Vs X05	0.056	0.003	1.141+0.051	0.056	1.106	1.224	391	0.269
Y1 Vs X06	0.010	0.000	1.236-0.006	-0.010	-0.192	0.037	386	0.848
Y1 Vs X07	0.064	0.004	1.125+0.053	0.064	1.261	1.589	391	0.208
Y1 Vs X08	0.021	0.000	1.291-0.034	-0.021	-0.421	0.177	393	0.674
Y1 Vs X09	0.016	0.000	1.205+0.011	0.016	0.323	0.104	393	0.747
Y1 Vs X10	0.022	0.001	1.252-0.024	-0.022	-0.443	0.197	393	0.658
Y1 Vs X11	0.021	0.000	1.179+0.018	0.021	0.377	0.142	335	0.707
Y1 Vs X12	0.117	0.014	1.359-0.096	-0.117	-2.107	4.439	322	0.036
Y1 Vs X13	0.004	0.000	1.202-0.002	-0.004	-0.074	0.005	323	0.941
Y1 Vs X14	0.135	0.018	1.389-0.129	-0.135	-2.414	5.828	313	0.016
Y1 Vs X15	0.054	0.003	1.388-0.088	-0.054	-1.066	1.137	393	0.287
Y1 Vs X16	0.073	0.005	0.944+0.156	0.073	1.185	1.405	265	0.237
Y1 Vs X17	0.157	0.025	1.928-0.363	-0.157	-3.140	9.860	393	0.002
Y1 Vs X18	0.034	0.001	1.164+0.027	0.034	0.668	0.446	393	0.505
Y1 Vs X19	0.042	0.002	1.162+0.031	0.042	0.836	0.699	393	0.404
Y1 Vs X20	0.047	0.002	0.774+0.226	0.047	0.924	0.853	393	0.356
Y1 Vs X21	0.043	0.002	1.370-0.051	-0.043	-0.857	0.735	393	0.392
Y1 Vs X22	0.016	0.000	1.206+0.010	0.016	0.308	0.095	393	0.758
Y1 Vs X23	0.043	0.002	1.100+0.055	0.051	1.010	1.019	393	0.313
Y1 Vs X24	0.019	0.000	1.183+0.037	0.019	0.385	0.148	393	0.701

Table 14
Bivariate Linear Regression Analyses on Child Loss Ratio with its Determinants Among Kinnaura of High Altitude.

			Regression Coefficient s					
			Unstandardized	Standardized	t-Statistics	F-Statistics		
Variables	R	R^2	$\beta_0+\beta_1$	β_1	t-value	F-value	df	P<
Y1 Vs X01	0.000	0.000	1.227+0.000	0.000	0.007	0.000	416	0.994
Y1 Vs X02	0.035	0.001	1.275-0.031	-0.035	-0.719	0.517	416	0.473
Y1 Vs X03	0.022	0.000	1.252-0.019	0.022	-0.450	0.202	407	0.653
Y1 Vs X04	0.004	0.000	1.246-0.004	-0.004	-0.077	0.006	416	0.939
Y1 Vs X05	0.065	0.004	1.128+0.061	0.065	1.348	1.817	425	0.178
Y1 Vs X06	0.011	0.000	1.250-0.006	-0.011	-0.218	0.048	414	0.828
Y1 Vs X07	0.050	0.003	1.152+0.045	0.050	1.041	1.083	425	0.299
Y1 Vs X08	0.031	0.001	1.293-0.035	-0.031	0.637	0.406	425	0.524
Y1 Vs X09	0.037	0.001	1.275-0.027	-0.037	-0.755	0.571	425	0.450
Y1 Vs X10	0.025	0.001	1.271-0.032	-0.025	-0.518	0.268	425	0.605
Y1 Vs X11	0.002	0.000	1.218-0.003	-0.002	-0.048	0.002	368	0.962
Y1 Vs X12	0.042	0.002	1.174+0.038	0.042	0.774	0.600	347	0.439
Y1 Vs X13	0.043	0.002	1.259-0.029	-0.043	-0.809	0.654	351	0.419
Y1 Vs X14	0.044	0.002	1.166+0.044	0.044	0.796	0.633	329	0.427
Y1 Vs X15	0.047	0.002	1.027+0.107	0.047	0.967	0.935	425	0.334
Y1 Vs X16	0.017	0.000	1.116+0.050	0.017	0.225	0.051	171	0.822
Y1 Vs X17	0.055	0.003	0.763+0.237	0.055	1.140	1.301	425	0.255
Y1 Vs X18	0.024	0.001	1.194+0.021	0.024	0.494	0.244	425	0.622
Y1 Vs X19	0.044	0.002	1.295-0.038	-0.044	-0.907	0.823	425	0.365
Y1 Vs X20	0.048	0.002	0.764+0.236	0.048	0.985	0.970	425	0.325
Y1 Vs X21	0.012	0.000	1.149+0.028	0.012	0.245	0.060	425	0.807
Y1 Vs X22	0.012	0.000	1.250-0.010	-0.012	-0.247	0.061	425	0.805
Y1 Vs X23	0.051	0.003	1.362-0.060	-0.043	-0.886	0.786	425	0.376
Y1 Vs X24	0.027	0.001	1.146+0.083	0.027	0.561	0.314	425	0.575

Chapter 11

NATURAL SELECTION

Survival of the fittest is the basis of natural selection. It is a prime process of evolutionary change in a population. Natural selection is one of the major evolutionary factors that bring about changes in the gene frequencies in a population through the action of differential fertility and mortality. In this way fertility and mortality are not only components of population structure, but also being used in measuring micro evolutionary dynamics. The fertility and mortality can cause a major disruption of gene frequencies from those predicted by the Hardy-Weinberg theorem. Therefore, the quantum of change of differential genetic transmission becomes a significant indicator of the amount of potential evolutionary change within a group, which is actually the production of reproductive viability expressed in form of differential fertility and mortality.

Crow (1958) has devised an index to measure the maximum amount of differential mortality and fertility in a population, which is known as Index of Total Selection. Further, incorporating the embryonic mortality component Johnston and Kensinger (1971) modified this index. The later investigator has taken into account the embryonic mortality but has not analyzed the post-natal mortality separately. The relative contribution of death in the age group 0-5 years (childhood mortality) and from 5 years to reproductive age (juvenile mortality) is significantly high. In order to elucidate the specific contribution of these components, the post natal mortality in Johnston and Kensinger's (1971) methodology has been further fragmented by Basu et.al. (1988) to explicate childhood mortality and index of juvenile mortality.

Differential fertility and differential mortality vary not only according to biological factors but also determined by socio-cultural, religious, ethnic and environmental factors. Several studies conducted in different parts of the world including India have noted the influence of socio-cultural factors on total selection intensity and its components (Spuhler, 1962 and 1976; Barrai and Fraccaro, 1964; Cruz-Coke et al., 1966; Reddy and Lakshmanudu, 1979; Bharti, 1981; Mukhopadhyay, 1981, 1989; Basu et al. 1988; Khongsdier, 1990, 1994; Sarkar, 1997; Patra and Kapoor, 1997, 1998; Kapoor and Patra, 1998). In a review of Indian data, Reddy and Chopra (1990), observed variation of total selection intensity between rural and urban, socio-economically backward and advance group. Bhasin and Kshatriya (1990) found inter and intra religious variations of the index and its components among different populations of Assam, and Khonsindier (1994) observed inter and intra religious variations of the index among populations of Meghalaya. Kapoor et al. (2003) were computed index of total selection for 24 Himalayan populations revealed that the contribution of fertility component (I_f) in determining total index of selection (I_t) are stronger than mortality component (I_m), simultaneously they observed that both I_f and I_m are strongly associated with I_t and accounts for 76 per cent and 67 per cent variability in I_t respectively.

Among Kinnaura a total of 813 mothers interviewed, out of them 160, who had already completed their fertility (above 45 years of age) constitute sample size for analysis of Natural Selection. These 160 mothers had conceived a total of 809 pregnancies, which resulted in 793 live births. Out of these 793 live births 664 survived upto their reproductive ages. Mean number of live birth per mother has been found to be 4.89 with a variance of 3.794. The results of reproductive performance are presented in Table 1 and the indexes of total selection based on differential fertility and mortality data have been computed

Table 1
Demographic Variables Utilized in Calculating Index of Total Selection for Middle and High Altitude Kinnaura.

Altitudes	*Fertility Performance of the Mother with Completed Fertility (aged45+)*					
	Number of Mothers with Completed Fertility (age 45+)	*Total Number of Pregnancies*	*Number of Children Ever Born (Live Births)*	*Number of Children Surviving*	*Mean Live Births (from Mothers aged 45+)*	*Variance of Live Births*
Middle Altitude	74	394	381	317	5.14	4.049
High Altitude	86	415	412	347	4.79	3.533
Kinnaur (Pooled)	160	809	793	664	4.89	3.794

using the methodologies of Crow (1958) and Johnston and Kensinger (1971) is presented in Tables 2 and 3. The mean number of live birth is higher among middle altitude Kinnaura (5.14) as compared to high altitude Kinnaura (4.49). The index of total selection intensity (I_t) is calculated according to Crow is always lower than that of Johnston and Kensinger index (I_2), perhaps because of inclusion of embryonic deaths in the latter. It is also evident that differential mortality contributes more than differential fertility to the total selection intensity.

The present findings are also compared with other Indian tribes as well as non-tribes, of Himalayan region and other parts of the country. It reveals that this index (Crow, 1958) among Kinnaura is moderate than the other population groups; among Himalayan population the highest was reported for Galong (I_t= 1.07) of Arunachal, whereas the lowest was reported from Ahom (I_t=0.218) of Manipur. In western Himalayas the index was found highest for Baltis (I_t= 1.02) of Jammu & Kashmir and lowest was reported among Bodhs (I_t= 0.263) of Himachal Pradesh; while for total of Kinnaura the index is computed I_t=0.384, which varies from I_t=0.370 high altitude to I_t=0.386 in middle altitude. In this way, Kinnaura shows similarity with Muklom (I_t=0.315) of Arunachal Pradesh, Khamti (I_t=0.312) and Sonawal Kachari (I_t=0.360) of Assam, Swangal (I_t=0.339) of Himachal Pradesh, Ladakhi (I_t= 0.34) as a whole, Dogra Rajput (I_t= 0.313) of Jammu and Kashmir and Halba (I_t=0.388) of Madhya Pradesh. The over all Indian scenario shows that the Kota (I_t=1.367) having highest selection intensity while Ahom (I_t=0.218) having lowest index of total selection.

The proportions of survivors from birth to reproductive age were found higher for high altitude Kinnaura (0.842) as compared to middle altitude Kinnaura (0.832). Contrary to that the proportions of pre-reproductive deaths were found to be higher among middle altitude Kinnaura (0.168) as compared to high altitude (0.158). On the whole, the proportion of survivors from birth to reproductive age was found to be (0.837) and the proportion of pre-reproductive deaths (0.163). However, the proportion of embryonic (pre-natal) deaths

Table 2
Selection Intensities (Based on Live Births and Pre-Reproductive Mortalities-Crow, 1958); among Kinnaura of Middle and High Altitude.

Kinnaura	*Proportion of Pre-reproductive Deaths*	*Proportion of Survivors from Birth to Reproductive Age*	*Index of Selection due to Mortality*	*Index of Selection due to Fertility*	*Total Index of Selection*	*Percentage of*	
						Fertility Component	*Mortality Component*
	P_d	P^a_s	I_m	I_f	I_t		
Middle Altitude	0.168	0.832	0.202	0.153	0.386	47.67	52.33
High Altitude	0.158	0.842	0.187	0.154	0.370	49.46	50.54
Kinnaura (Pooled)	0.163	0.837	0.194	0.159	0.384	49.48	50.52

Table 3
Selection Intensities (Based on Live Births and Pre-Reproductive Mortalities- Johnston and Kensinger, 1971); among Kinnaura of Middle and High Altitude.

Kinnaura	*Proportion of Pre-reproductive Deaths*	*Proportion of Survivors from Birth to Reproductive Age*	*Proportion of Embryonic (prenatal) Deaths*	*Proportion of Survivors to Birth*	*Index of Selection due to Embryonic Mortality*	*Index of Selection due to Post-natal Mortality*	*Index of Selection due to Fertility*	*Total Index of Selection*	*Percentage of* Fertility Component	*Percentage of* Post natal Mortality Component	*Percentage of* Embryonic Mortality Component
	P_d	P^a_s	P_{ed}	P^a_b	I^a_{mc}	I^a_{mc}	I^a_f	I_z			
Middle Altitude	0.168	0.832	0.033	0.967	0.034	0.202	0.153	0.433	45.54	46.58	7.87
High Altitude	0.158	0.842	0.007	0.993	0.007	0.187	0.154	0.380	48.81	49.28	1.92
Pooled	0.163	0.837	0.020	0.980	0.020	0.194	0.159	0.412	47.91	47.19	4.90

Table 4
Indices of Natural Selection Among Different Population Groups (Tribes and Non-Tribes) of Himalayan Region and Other Parts of India.

Region	*Population*	*Crow's Index (1958)*			*Johnston & Kensinger' Index (1971)*				*Reference*
		I_m	I_f	I_t	I_{mc}	$I_{mc/Pb}$	$I_{f/ybPs1}$	I_z	
HIMALAYAN REGION									
Eastern Himalayas									
Arunachal Pradesh									
	Muklom	0.107	0.188	0.315	0.021	0.107	0.188	0.342	Sarkar (1997)
	Apatani Guchi	0.435	0.190	0.710	–	–	–	–	Padmanabham (1982)
	Apatoni Guth	0.440	0.312	0.889	–	–	–	–	"
	Singapos	0.437	0.406	1.020	–	–	–	–	Padmanabham (1981)
	Galong	0.750	0.180	1.070	–	–	–	–	Chakraborty & Ahmed (1989)
Min		0.107	0.180	0.315					
Max		0.750	0.406	1.070					
Mean		0.433	0.255	0.800					
Assam									
	Semsa	0.471	0.098	0.616	0.038	–	0.098	0.677	Ghosh &Limbu (2002)
	Khamti	0.179	0.113	0.312	0.005	0.179	0.113	0.319	Sarkar et.al. (1994)
	Sonawal Kachari	0.192	0.141	0.360	–	–	–	–	Deka (1978)
	Bengali Muslim	0.430	0.310	0.860	–	–	–	–	Chakraborty (1989)
	Oraon	0.990	0.131	0.243	0.102	0.099	0.131	0.370	Sengupta & Phukan (1997)
Min		0.179	0.098	0.243					
Max		0.990	0.310	0.860					
Mean		0.452	0.158	0.478					
Meghalaya									
	Hajongs	0.443	0.131	0.631	0.032	0.443	0.131	0.684	Barua (1983)
	Jaintias	0.456	0.125	0.638	0.107	0.456	0.125	0.814	Deka (1989)
	Phar	0.236	0.134	0.401	0.202	0.236	0.134	0.681	Khongsdier (1990)

Contd...

Region Population	Crow's Index (1958)			Johnston & Kensinger' Index (1971)				Reference
	I_m	I_f	I_t	I_{me}	$I_{me/Pb}$	$I_{f/pbPs1}$	I_2	
War Khasi (Christian)	0.147	0.185	0.359	0.093	0.147	0.185	0.486	Khongsdier (1994)
War Khasi (Non-Christian)	0.180	0.225	0.446	0.084	0.180	0.225	0.568	Khongsdier (1994)
Dalu	0.499	0.231	0.847	0.032	0.499	0.231	0.897	Patra and Kapoor (1997)
Min	0.125	0.359	0.359	0.320	0.147	0.125	0.486	
Max	0.231	0.847	0.847	0.202	0.499	0.231	0.897	
Mean	0.171	0.553	0.553	0.091	0.326	0.171	0.688	
Manipur								
Hmar	0.072	0.250	0.340	0.028	0.072	0.250	0.379	Varte (1998)
Ahom	0.083	0.119	0.218	0.074	0.083	0.119	0.308	Sengupta & Chakraborty (1998)
West Bengal								
Sherpa	0.206	0.173	0.415	–	–	–	–	Reddy & Chopra (1990) cf. Gharami et.al. (2003) *Western Himalayas*
Himachal Pradesh								
Bodh	0.105	0.143	0.263	–	–	–	–	Chaudhury (1982)
Shipi	0.227	0.207	0.482	–	–	–	–	"
Swangal	0.157	0.157	0.339	–	–	–	–	"
Min	0.105	0.143	0.263	–	–	–	–	
Max	0.227	0.207	0.482	–	–	–	–	
Mean	0.163	0.169	0.361	–	–	–	–	
Jammu and Kashmir								
Ladakh Region[HA]	0.387	0.387	0.340	0.103	0.387	0.340	1.049	Bhasin & Nag (2002)
Bodhs	0.201	0.327	0.594	0.076	0.201	0.327	0.714	"
Baltis	0.624	0.243	1.020	0.127	0.624	0.243	1.277	"
Brokpas	0.506	0.168	0.759	0.057	0.506	0.168	0.860	"
Arghuns	0.265	0.455	0.828	0.120	0.256	0.455	1.048	

Contd...

Region Population	Crow's Index (1958)			Johnston & Kensinger' Index (1971)				Reference
	I_m	I_f	I_t	I_{me}	$I_{mc/Pb}$	$I_{f/pbPs1}$	I_2	
ashmir Region								
Kashmiri Pandit	0.059	0.214	0.286	0.000	0.059	0.214	0.286	"
Kashmiri Muslim	0.154	0.556	0.795	0.000	0.154	0.556	0.795	"
Jammu Region								
Dogra Rajput	0.074	0.223	0.313	0.017	0.074	–	0.223	"
Min	0.059	0.168	0.286	0.000	0.059	0.000	0.223	
Max	0.624	0.556	1.020	0.127	0.624	0.556	1.227	
Mean	0.283	0.321	0.616	0.062	0.282	0.329	0.781	
Central Himalayas								
Uttaranchal (erstwhile UP)								
Bhoksa	0.282	0.058	0.356	–	–	–	–	Garg et.al. (1980)
Bhotia (Migratory)	0.277	0.158	0.479	0.091	0.277	0.158	0.606	Kapoor and Patra (1998)
Bhotia (Settled)	0.167	0.142	0.330	0.095	0.167	0.142	0.456	"
Raji	0.585	0.174	0.862	0.0625	0.585	0.174	0.979	Patra (2001)
HPA[b]								
Barbatiya	0.243	0.443	0.794	0.076	0.261	0.593	0.930	Kapoor et.al. (2003)
Tibetan	0.142	0.324	0.512	0.060	0.151	0.392	0.603	"
Khampa	0.207	0.369	0.653	0.131	0.235	0.505	0.871	"
Harkotiya	0.114	0.244	0.386	0.081	0.123	0.294	0.498	"
Bodh	0.148	0.226	0.407	0.098	0.163	0.285	0.546	"
Kuthalia Bora	0.223	0.330	0.627	0.076	0.240	0.435	0.751	
Brahman Group								"
Brahman	0.059	0.312	0.389	0.039	0.062	0.343	0.444	"
Brahman	0.178	0.278	0.505	0.098	0.195	0.359	0.652	"
Brahman	0.111	0.249	0.388	0.058	0.118	0.292	0.468	"
Brahman	0.065	0.283	0.366	0.045	0.067	0.316	0.428	"
Brahman	0.125	0.239	0.395	0.041	0.131	0.280	0.452	

Contd...

Region Population	Crow's Index (1958)			Johnston & Kensinger' Index (1971)				Reference
	I_m	I_f	I_t	I_{me}	$I_{mc/Pb}$	$I_{f/pbPs1}$	I_2	
Rajput Group								
Rajput	0.148	0.263	0.450	0.065	0.157	0.322	0.544	"
Rajput	0.155	0.219	0.408	0.085	0.168	0.274	0.528	"
Rajput	0.083	0.262	0.367	0.056	0.088	0.300	0.444	"
Rajput	0.096	0.297	0.422	0.088	0.104	0.354	0.546	"
Rajput	0.140	0.180	0.345	0.061	0.149	0.218	0.428	"
Rajput	0.163	0.246	0.449	0.049	0.171	0.301	0.521	"
SC (Shilpkar Group)								
Shilpkar	0.193	0.326	0.582	0.062	0.205	0.413	0.680	"
Shilpkar	0.089	0.263	0.376	0.082	0.097	0.310	0.489	"
Shilpkar	0.103	0.251	0.380	0.055	0.109	0.291	0.455	"
Shilpkar	0.145	0.631	0.446	0.022	0.148	0.308	0.478	"
Shilpkar	0.114	0.208	0.346	0.047	0.119	0.243	0.410	"
Shilpkar	0.130	0.255	0.418	0.067	0.139	0.307	0.513	"
SC of Himachal Pradesh	0.108	0.244	0.379	0.073	0.116	0.290	0.479	"
Min	0.059	0.180	0.345	0.022	0.062	0.218	0.410	
Max	0.243	0.631	0.794	0.131	0.261	0.593	0.930	
Mean	0.137	0.289	0.450	0.067	0.147	0.334	0.548	
INDIAN PLAIN								
Madhya Pradesh								
Kol	0.504	0.122	0.688	0.036	0.504	0.122	0.749	Gharami et.al. (2003)
Ladiya SC	0.396	0.089	0.521	–	–	–	–	Gharami and Mandal (2001)
Muria	0.217	0.173	0.492	0.014	0.272	0.173	0.514	Basu et.al. (1988)
Madia	0.310	0.191	0.558	-	0.308	0.191	0.558	"
Bhattra	0.277	0.281	0.633	0.002	0.275	0.281	0.637	"
Halba	0.200	0.148	0.388	0.016	0.209	0.148	0.410	"

Contd...

Region Population	Crow's Index (1958)			Johnston & Kensinger' Index (1971)				Reference
	I_m	I_f	I_t	I_{me}	$I_{me/Pb}$	$I_{f/pbPs1}$	I_2	
Min	0.200	0.089	0.388					
Max	0.504	0.281	0.688					
Mean	0.317	0.167	0.546					
Karnataka								
Koranga	0.008	0.280	0.340	–	–	–	–	Chandrasekar et.al. (1998)
Andhra Pradesh								
Manne Kolam	0.544	0.306	1.012	–	–	–	–	Murthy and Ramesh (1978)
Chenchu	0.500	0.200	0.810	–	–	–	–	Sirajuddin and Basu (1984)
Hill Kolam	0.344	0.284	0.728	–	–	–	–	Murthy and Ramesh (1978)
Kolam	0.444	0.295	0.870	–	–	–	–	"
Sugalis	0.375	0.162	0.606	–	–	–	–	Reddy and Reddy (1985)
Yanadi	0.113	0.408	0.566	–	–	–	–	Vasulu (1987)
Min	0.113	0.162	0.566					
Max	0.544	0.408	1.012					
Mean	0.386	0.275	0.765					
Tamil Nadu								
Kota	0.445	0.638	1.367	–	–	–	–	Reddy & Chopra (1990) cf. Gharami et.al. (2003)
Present Study								
Kinnaura (Pooled)	0.194	0.159	0.384	0.020	0.194	0.159	0.412	Present Study (2006)
Kinnaura ^{MA}	0.202	0.153	0.386	0.034	0.202	0.153	0.433	"
Kinnaura ^{HA}	0.187	0.154	0.370	0.007	0.187	0.154	0.380	"

HPA=Himalayan population with Asian affinities
HA=High Altitude
MA=Middle Altitude
SC=Scheduled Caste
UP= Uttar Pradesh

varied from 0.0 to 0.048 (Table 3). It has been noticed that the total index of selection is higher among middle altitude Kinnaura as compared to high altitude Kinnaura, irrespective of methodologies used. However, all the estimates (as per Crow's formulation) below of 1.18 reported by Sphuler (1976) for various populations.

Table 5

Regression and Correlation of Fertility (I_f) and Mortality (I_m) Component with the Index of Total Selection (I_t) among Populations of Different Himalayan States (Dependent Variable I_t).

States	*R*	*R^2*	*df*	*F*	*p- value*	*b_1*	*SE*	*t*
				Independent Variable I_f				
Arunachal Pradesh	0.460	0.211	4	0.804	0.436	1.396	1.557	0.897
Assam	0.744	0.553	4	3.711	0.150	2.206	1.145	1.926
Himachal Pradesh	0.872	0.761	5	12.733	0.023	2.745	0.769	3.568
Jammu and Kashmir	0.243	0.059	7	0.376	0.562	0.497	0.812	0.613
Meghalaya	0.172	0.030	5	0.122	0.745	0.656	1.881	0.349
Uttaranchal	0.619	0.384	3	1.246	0.381	2.944	2.638	1.116
Pooled	0.464	0.216	33	8.793	0.006	1.084	0.366	2.965
				Independent Variable I_m				
Arunachal Pradesh	0.883	0.779	4	10.583	0.047	1.185	0.364	3.253
Assam	0.167	0.028	4	0.086	0.788	-0.130	0.443	-0.294
Himachal Pradesh	0.958	0.918	5	44.984	0.003	1.603	0.239	6.707
Jammu and Kashmir	0.636	0.404	7	4.075	0.090	0.860	0.426	2.019
Meghalaya	0.933	0.870	5	26.741	0.007	1.107	0.214	5.171
Uttaranchal	0.969	0.938	3	30.298	0.031	1.325	0.241	5.504
Pooled	0.540	0.291	33	13.142	0.001	0.655	0.181	3.625

The correlation and regression analysis (Table 5) between total index of selection (I_t) and fertility (I_f) & mortality (I_m) components for pooled data of populations of Indian Himalayan States (Figure 1 and 2) shows that I_f and I_m accounts 21.6 per cent and 29.1 per cent variability, respectively; in the crow's total index of selection (I_t) alongwith strong association which is significant at 1% level; this indicates that mortality plays greater role in natural selection incomparison to fertility among populations of Indian Himalayas. Furthermore, the individual analysis for states (Figure 3 and 4) exhibit great variation, the least variability of fertility component (I_f) was noticed in Meghalaya (3 per cent) followed by Jammu and Kashmir (5 per cent), whereas, the highest was noticed in

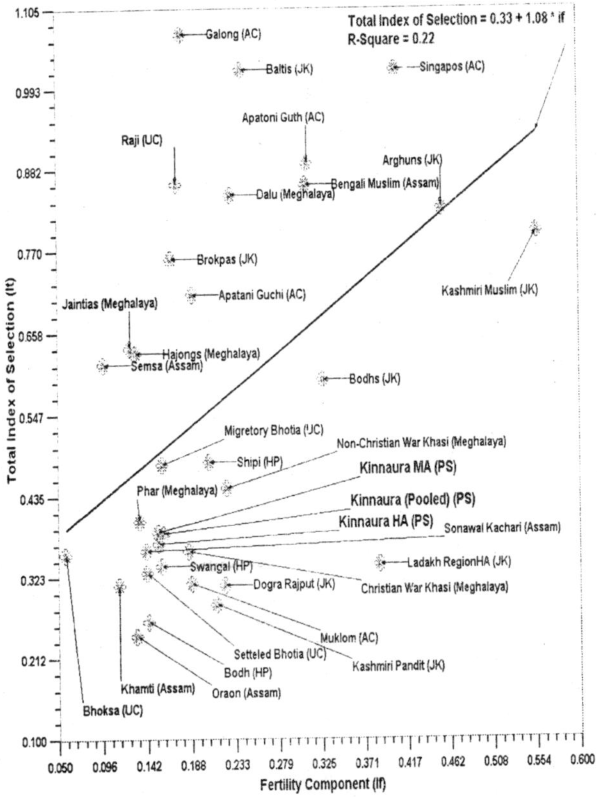

Figure 1: Bivariate Scattered Plot Diagramme Showing Regression and Correlation between Fertility Component and Total Index of Selection among Himalayan Populations.

AC= Arunachal Pradesh, JK= Jammu and Kashmir, UC= Uttaranchal, HP= Himachal Pradesh, PS=Present Study

Himachal Pradesh (76 per cent) followed by Assam (55.3 per cent), Uttaranchal (38.4 per cent) and Arunachal (21.1 per cent). In the same way the least variability of mortality component (I_m) on the Crow's total index of selection (I_t) were found to be in the state of Assam (2.8 per cent) followed by Jammu and Kashmir (40.4 per cent), whereas the highest was noticed in Uttaranchal (93.8 per cent) followed by Himachal Pradesh (91.8 per cent), Meghalaya (87 per cent) and Arunachal (77.9 per cent). In the light of above discussion, the findings of present

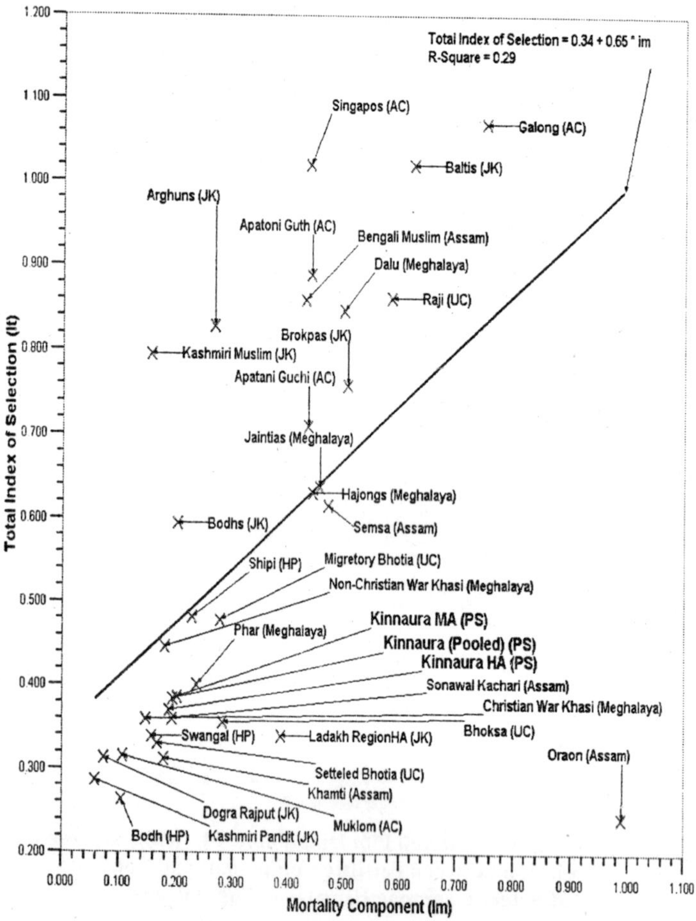

Figure 2: Bivariate Scattered Plot Diagramme Showing Regression and Correlation between Mortality Component and Total Index of Selection among Himalayan Populations.

study indicates that Kinnaura having moderate value of component of fertility (I_f), mortality (I_m) and mortality playing greater role in natural selection over fertility as it is true to all majority of Himalayan Populations. The present findings are not showing any great variation with previous one (Chaudhury, 1982) but more or less supporting it, the average (0.361) of total index of selection is near to present findings (0.384).

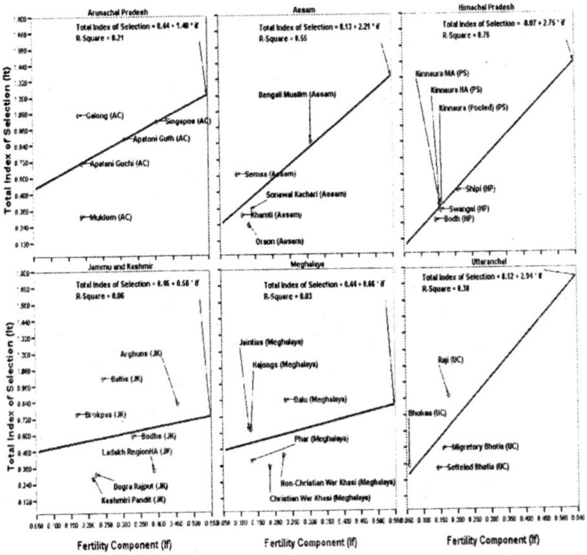

Figure 3: Bivariate Scattered Plot Diagramme Showing Regression and Correlation between Fertility Component and Total Index of Selection among Populations of different Himalayan States.

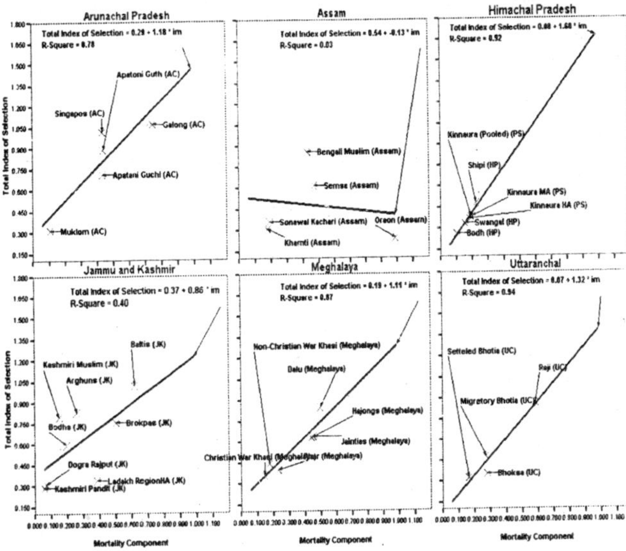

Figure 4: Bivariate Scattered Plot Diagramme Showing Regression and Correlation between Mortality Component and Total Index of Selection among Populations of Different Himalayan States.

Chapter 12

FAMILY PLANNING

Family Planning is not merely the use of contraception for limited family size. Rather it is a mode of planning family size as per requirement of time and space. According to WHO Expert Committee (1971) 'the family planning is a way of thinking and living that is adopted voluntarily, upon the basis of knowledge, attitudes and responsible decisions by individuals and couples, in order to promote the health and welfare of the family group and thus contribute effectively to the social development of a country'. In this chapter knowledge about contraceptives, current use of contraceptives, trend and determinants of family planning practices, fertility differential among users and non-users will be discussed in the light of other studies.

KNOWLEDGE ABOUT CONTRACEPTIVES

Lack of knowledge has been a major obstacle in the way of use of contraceptive methods. In the present study all the respondents, a total of 820, including 330 male and 490 females, were asked about various family planning methods, if a respondent did not recognize the name of a method/technique, a short description was given to them regarding the same. As evident from Table 1, most of the respondents, 90 to 99 per cent of either sex, are aware of modern male and female contraceptive methods and sterilizations techniques, while only 41 per cent people were found having knowledge of safe period. 13.2 per cent have knowledge of abstinence and 4.3

per cent are aware regarding withdrawal. Males are more aware of these methods as compared to females (Figure 1). Females in the present study are found a little more knowledgeable about sterilizations techniques and oral pills as compared to male respondents. In case of other spacing methods like Nirodh (Condom) and Cu-T males are found to be more knowledgeable. There is no significant difference between middle and high altitude Kinnaura regarding the knowledge about the contraceptive methods/techniques for family planning. Furthermore, out of 820 households, there were 667 eligible couples, 93 to 99 per cent of them were found to have knowledge regarding Modern FP methods

Table 1
Distribution of Kinnaura who are aware Regarding Various Family Planning Techniques.

	Kinnaura					
	People (N=820)		*Male (N=330)*		*Female (N=490)*	
Family Planning Methods	N	%	N	%	N	%
			Male Contraceptives			
Vasectomy	809	98.7	323	97.9	486	99.2
Nirodh	784	95.6	319	96.7	465	94.9
			Female Contraceptives			
Tubectomy	809	98.7	323	97.9	486	99.2
IUD/Cu-T	748	91.2	330	91.8	445	90.8
Oral Pills	779	95.0	312	94.5	467	95.3
			Natural Methods			
Rhythm/Safe Period	336	41.0	141	42.7	195	39.8
Abstinence	108	13.2	53	16.1	55	11.2
Withdrawal	35	4.3	19	5.8	16	3.3

The present findings corroborate the RHS (2001). The district wise distribution of Kinnaura respondents and currently married women aged 15-44 years of Districts of Himachal Pradesh by Knowing Contraceptive Methods are presented in the Table 2 for further elucidation of the facts. In general sterilization methods (vasectomy and tubectomy) are known to 90 to 100 percent respondents of Himachal Pradesh whereas the IUD/Loop, oral pills and condom are known to 55 to 98 percent people.

Table 2
Percentage Distribution of Kinnaura Respondents and Currently Married Women Aged 15-44 Years of Districts of Himachal Pradesh by Knowing Contraceptive Methods.

Population/ Region/ District	*Male Sterili-zation*	*Female Sterili-zation*	*IUD/ Loop*	*Oral Pills*	*Condom*	*Source*
			Percentage Knowing			
		Currently Married Women (15-44 years)				
Himachal Pradesh	98.3	99.0	80.9	83.1	82.1	1998-99 RHS (2001)
Bilaspur	96.7	98.1	64.4	67.2	66.7	"
Chamba	98.7	98.6	74.6	78.5	76.6	"
Hamirpur	100	100	72.0	74.2	76.9	"
Kangra	99.7	99.4	89.5	88.3	87.8	"
Kullu	96.6	97.7	69.7	68.5	67.2	"
Lahul & Spiti	90.0	91.6	56.8	62.9	63.4	"
Mandi	95.9	98.0	77.7	78.3	75.3	"
Shimla	98.3	99.3	83.6	87.2	81.8	"
Sirmaur	98.5	99.0	88.1	87.9	89.5	"
Solan	98.1	98.9	69.2	74.7	76.0	"
Una	99.7	99.7	96.3	97.0	97.0	"
Kinnaur	99.7	99.4	89.5	88.3	87.8	"
		All Respondents (male/female)				
Kinnaura	98.7	98.7	91.2	95.0	95.6	Present study (2006)
Middle Altitude	98.5	98.5	93.7	95.4	94.7	"
High Altitude	98.8	98.8	89.0	94.6	96.5	"

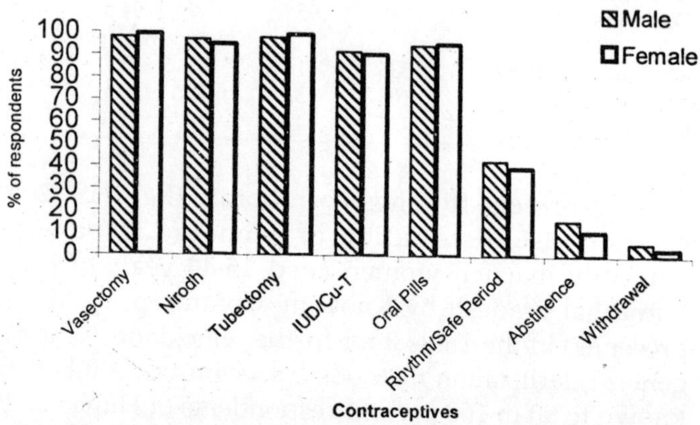

Figure 1: Comparative Bar-Diagram of Knowledge of Various Family Planning Methods among Male and Female Kinnaura.

CURRENT PRACTICE OF CONTRACEPTIVES

Tables 3, 4 and 5 present the current use of family planning methods among Kinnaura. It can be seen from the tables that half of the eligible couples have undergone sterilization. More than one fourth (27.8 per cent) of the couples have adopted vasectomy, whereas slightly less than one fourth (24.8 per cent) have adopted tubectomy. The use of temporary methods vary from 3 to 5 per cent; 4.8 percent are using condom, 5.1 per cent use Cu-T and 3.3 per cent take OP (oral pills), while 31.2 per cent couples were not using any method at the time of investigation (Figure 5.43).

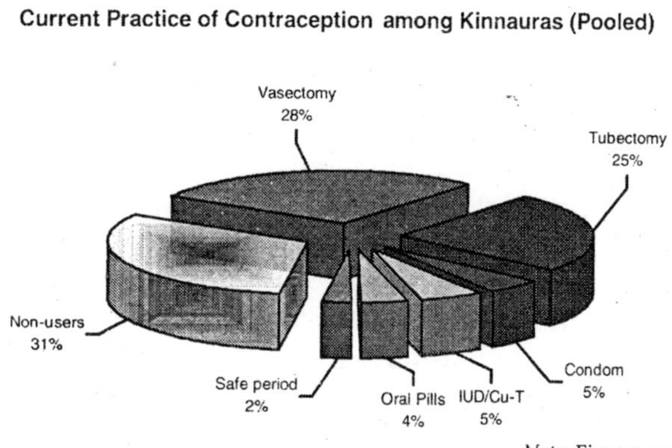

Note: Figures are rounded

Figure 2: Current Practice of Contraception among Kinnaura

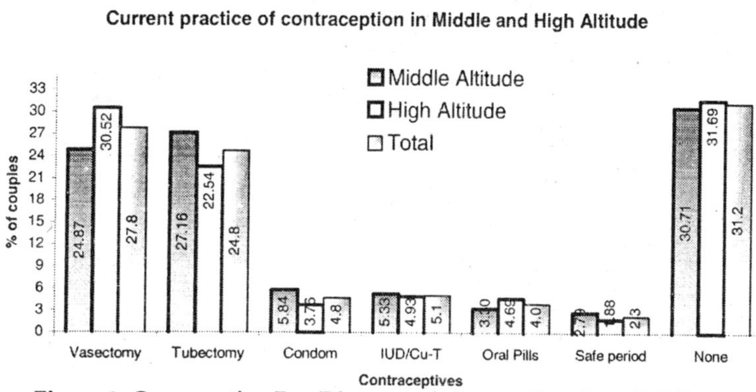

Figure 3: Comparative Bar-Diagram of Current Practice of Different Type of Contraceptives among Kinnaura of Middle and High Altitude

CURRENT PRACTICE OF CONTRACEPTION BY GEOGRAPHICAL AND SOCIO-CULTURAL BACKGROUND

As evident from Table 3, Vasectomy is so called more popular in high altitude as compared to middle altitude, during focus group discussions (FGDs) the vasectomy adopters were expressed that they were adopted it because of compulsion of different government authorities. Special provisions and privileges for vasectomy adopters motivated them to adopt it. In middle altitude the prevalence of tubectomy adopters is higher as compared to high altitude as well as higher to vasectomy adopters of middle altitude region. In case of temporary and natural methods like condom, IUD (Cu-T) and safe period, the middle altitude couples are pioneer, whereas in case of oral pills reverse is observed. Practicing or living or belonging to a particular family type, having least role in current use of contraception, but the adoption of vasectomy is greater in proportion in nuclear family (30.1 per cent) as compared to Joint (25.9 per cent) and extended families (23.3 per cent); simultaneously the use of IUD and safe period is higher in joint families (>7 per cent) whereas use of condom is higher in extended families (8.8 per cent) as compared to rest two types respectively.

Further, as apparent from Table 3, vasectomy is adopted in greater proportion by monogamous couples (28.2 per cent) as compared to others, whereas tubectomy and Cu-T is popular among polyandrous couples as compared to others.

CURRENT PRACTICE OF CONTRACEPTION BY SELECTED DEMOGRAPHIC CHARACTERISTICS

Current Age of Wife

Current age of spouses is a principal determinant of contraception practice. In the present study the current age of wife is computed against current use of family planning methods, As stated in Table 4, it is apparent that adopting sterilization as a permanent technique of family planning boost-up as per progression of age of wife, simultaneously, the use of temporary and natural methods decreases accordingly. The

Table 3
Current Use of Contraception% Percent Distribution of Kinnaura Couples by Contraceptive Method Currently Used, according to Selected Background.

	Kinnaur							Total	
Background Characteristics	*Vasectomy*	*Tubectomy*	*Condom*	*IUD/ Cu-T*	*Oral Pills*	*Rhythm/ safe period*	*None*	*N*	*%*
Altitude									
Middle Altitude	24.9	27.2	5.8	5.3	3.3	2.8	30.7	394	100
High Altitude	30.5	22.5	3.8	4.9	4.7	1.9	31.7	426	100
Total	27.8	24.8	4.8	5.1	4.0	2.3	31.2	820	100
Family Type									
Nuclear	30.1	27.1	3.4	4.7	3.4	0.8	30.5	472	100
Joint	25.9	21.7	4.8	7.4	4.8	7.9	27.5	189	100
Extended	23.3	21.4	8.8	3.8	5.0	–	37.7	159	100
Total	27.8	24.8	4.8	5.1	4.0	2.3	31.2	820	100
Marriage Type									
Monogamy	28.2	23.5	5.1	5.1	4.2	2.5	31.4	688	100
Polyandry	25.0	32.4	3.7	6.5	3.7	1.9	26.9	108	100
Polygyny	28.6	19.0	–	–	–	–	52.4	21	100
Polyandry and Polygyny	33.3	66.7	–	–	–	–	–	3	100
Total	27.8	24.8	4.8	5.1	4.0	2.3	31.2	820	100

proportion of non-users (any method) decreases sharply as per advancement of age of wife, and it reaches to lowest (12.5 per cent) at age group 35-39, but again the proportion of non-users (any method) increased sharply with greater strength as per increase of age of wife as well as couples, as evident from V-shaped line graph (Figure 4).

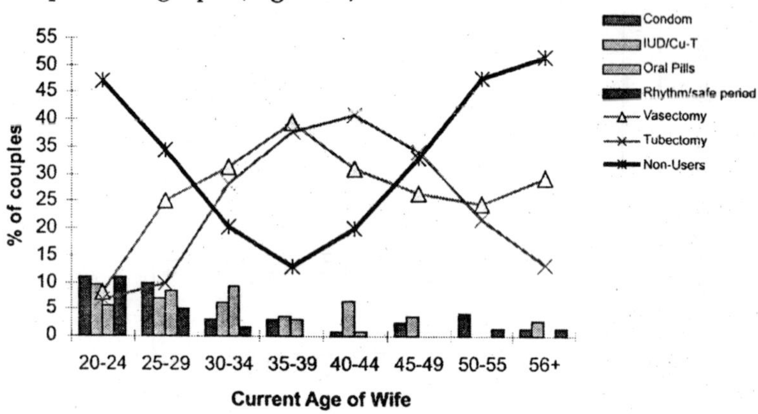

Figure 4: Current Practice of Contraception by Current Age of Wife

After How Many Children Method is being Used

In the present study, it was investigated that after how many children, the respective couple have started using current contraceptive. As evident from Table 4 that there are twenty nine couples having one child, out of these 17.2 per cent of them have undergone vasectomy, 10.3 per cent have adopted tubectomy, 27.6 per cent are using condom, again 17.2 per cent are using IUD (Cu-T), and similar proportion is taking Oral Pills (OP); whereas 10.3 per cent of them are not using any method. After 2 children adoption of permanent technique, i.e. sterilization increased more than two folds; simultaneously, the use of temporary methods decreases accordingly, as also evident from Figure 5; and this trend continues with the number of successive children. After four children the majority of contraceptive users are adopted vasectomy, almost same height of the graph of tubectomy adopters reaches after six children, which is optimum height of the graph. After 6 children, the proportions of non-users become negligible.

Table 4
Percent Distribution of Kinnaura Couples by Contraceptive Method Currently Used, according to Selected Demographic Characteristics.

Background Characteristics	*Kinnaur*							*Total*	
Current Age of Wife	*Vasectomy*	*Tubectomy*	*Condom*	*IUD/ Cu-T*	*Oral Pills*	*Safe Period*	*None*	*N*	*%*
20-24	8.3	6.9	11.1	9.7	5.6	11.1	47.2	72	100
25-29	25.0	10.0	10.0	7.1	8.6	5.0	34.3	140	100
30-34	31.3	28.1	3.1	6.3	9.4	1.6	20.3	128	100
35-39	39.4	37.9	3.0	3.8	3.0	–	12.9	132	100
40-44	30.9	40.9	0.9	6.4	0.9	–	20.0	110	100
45-49	26.6	34.2	2.5	3.8	–	–	32.9	79	100
50-55	24.6	21.7	4.3	–	–	1.4	47.8	69	100
56+	29.4	13.2	1.5	2.9	–	1.5	51.5	68	100
Total	28.2	25.1	4.7	5.2	4.1	2.4	30.2	804	100
After How Many Children the Method is being Used									
After 1 Child	17.2	10.3	27.6	17.2	17.2	–	10.3	29	100
After 2 Children	30.5	25.7	7.8	9.0	9.0	1.2	16.8	167	100
After 3 Children	36.0	40.9	4.8	6.5	2.2	1.1	8.6	186	100
After 4 Children	55.6	33.3	–	4.4	1.1	1.1	4.4	90	100
After 5 Children	45.7	39.1	–	6.5	4.3	–	4.3	46	100
After 6 Children	40.5	54.8	–	–	4.8	–	–	42	100
After 7 Children	45.5	27.3	–	18.2	–	9.1	–	11	100
Total	37.8	34.4	5.2	7.3	5.0	1.0	9.3	579	100

Contd...

Background Characteristics				*Kinnaur*				*Total*	
Current Age of Wife	*Vasectomy*	*Tubectomy*	*Condom*	*IUD/ Cu-T*	*Oral Pills*	*Safe Period*	*None*	*N*	*%*
Age of Youngest Living Child									
<One month	11.8	11.8	5.9	–	–	5.9	64.7	17	100
1-11 Months	10.1	7.9	10.1	9.0	3.4	3.4	56.2	89	100
1-2 Years	22.4	8.6	11.2	6.9	11.2	7.8	31.9	116	100
3-4 Years	21.8	12.8	11.5	14.1	11.5	3.8	24.4	78	100
5 Years	31.3	31.3	–	3.1	15.6	–	18.8	32	100
5+ Years	36.6	38.5	1.6	2.9	0.8	0.3	19.3	374	100
Total	28.5	25.9	5.4	5.5	4.7	2.4	27.6	706	100

CASE STUDY

Cu-T Failure

Angzin (wife) and Ramala (husband) both are educated. Angzin is a high school passed young lady of 26 years whereas Ramlal is 32 year old an art graduate. After giving birth to first child they decided to opt for Cu-T as spacing device for preventing undesired pregnancy, and in February 2001, the female health worker Rinchin Zangmo placed Cu-T in to her uterus. Even after adopting Cu-T from March to November, she was having regular menstruation from March through November. In December, however, menstruation stopped. .

After five months in April 2002, couple came to know that the wife had actually conceived and was carrying five-month pregnancy. The village Sumra is one of the remotest villages at the border of Tibet as well as at the border of neighboring district Lahul and Spiti, but has a Government Ayurvedic Health Center. Since the Ayurvedic doctors are possibly not trained to handle gynaecological problems, pregnancy could not be diagnosed, and even she was left without any essential pre-natal care.

Ultimately she gave birth to a premature baby (female) in July 2002 at home, and at the time of recording this case study the newborn was 3-month-old. However both were fine. Ironically, they didn't inform doctor regarding failure or missing of Cu-T. The health worker visited the village and had given vaccines to the newborn.(Note: The Names used are imaginative).

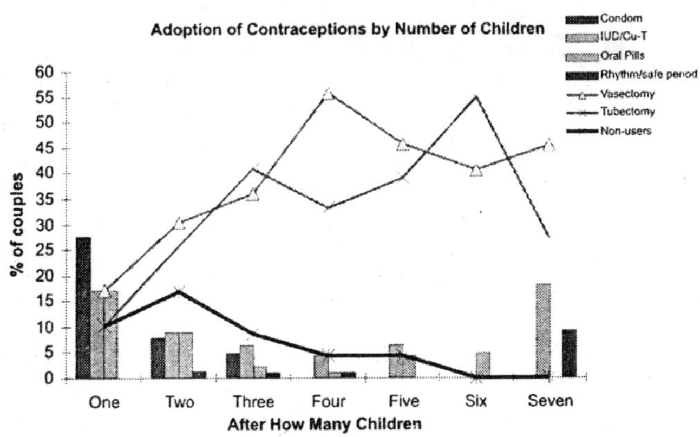

Figure 5: Adoption of Contraception by Number of Children (After How Many Children Method is Being Used)

Current Use of Contraceptives by Age of Youngest Living Child

Here is analysis, from present study, how increasing age of youngest living child affects the current use of contraceptives. As apparent from Table 4, there are eleven couples, at the time of investigation, who having child of less than one month of age, and 23.6 per cent of such couples have adopted sterilization equally for male and female, 5.9 per cent are using condom and the same proportion (5.9 per cent) are using safe period. At the same time 64.7 per cent of such couples are non-users. Figure 6 shows that the adoption of vasectomy and tubectomy increases gradually as per progression of age of youngest living child, simultaneously the proportion of non-user decreases sharply.

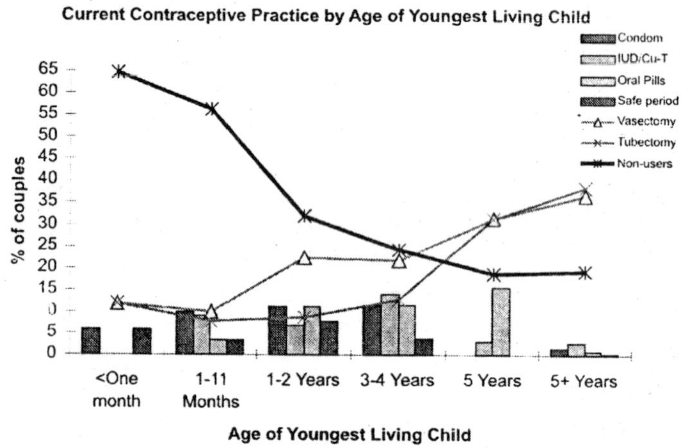

Figure 6: Current Contraceptive Practice by Age of Youngest Living Child

Current Practice of Contraception by sex preference for children, Number of children surviving and ever died

Usually, in some societies, preference for particular sex is predominant. Couples delayed the use of contraceptives in expectation of child of preferred sex, which spontaneously leads to bigger family size. Experience of infant and child mortalities also adversely affects the use of contraception. Therefore in the present study, the sex preference of children, number of children of either sex or particular sex and number of children ever died among various kinds of contraceptive users is studied as displayed in Table 5. It can be seen from Table that in the present study different contraception practice have differential association with number of surviving children (daughter, son and both) and children ever died.

Total number of surviving daughters: It is evident from the Table 5 that 12.8 to 21.2 per cent of any kind of modern contraceptive users has no daughter at all, among vasectomy adopters 17.5 per cent, and among tubectomy adopters 21.2 per cent fall under this category. Those who have adopted vasectomy 36 per cent of them having one daughter, 27.2 per cent having two daughters and 11.8 per cent have three daughters; almost similar prevalence can be seen for tubectomy adopters. Those who are using modern temporary method (i.e. Condom, Cu-T, Oral Pills and Safe Period) majority (40 to 51 per cent) of them have one daughter, while those have two daughters they vary between 15 to 18 per cent.

Total number of surviving sons: Son preference is very common in most of the societies; hence people hardly adopt any permanent method of family planning, without having at least one son. This hypothesis is absolutely proved in the present study as only 9.2 and 9.9 per cent vasectomy and tubectomy adopters have no surviving sons, respectively, at the time of investigation, whereas 36 to 40 per cent of them having one or two sons and 10 to 15 per cent having three sons. Simultaneously, among temporary method users one fifth to one third (19 to 33 per cent) have no son, in the same way one fourth of non-users also have no son. In case of have at least one son the use of contraceptives rises very sharply, as among tubectomy and vasectomy adopters 36 to 40 per cent have at least one son, in the same way 43.6 per cent of condom users, 50 per cent of Cu-T users, 60.6 per cent of oral pills users and 42.1 per cent of safe period users having at least one son (Table 5).

Total Number of Surviving Children among different contraceptive users is displayed in Table 5.75 as well as in Figure 5.48 shows that most of the contraceptive users having 1 to 4 children. There are also some aged couples (1.3 to 2.5 per cent), who had lost their children after adopting vasectomy and tubectomy. Further among vasectomy and tubectomy adopters, the proportion of one-child-bearing couple is negligible (3.9 to 4.4 per cent), whereas the proportion of 2 to 4 children bearing couple is 79.4 to 72.5 per cent respectively.

Table 5
Percent Distribution of Kinnaura Couples by Contraceptive Methods Currently being Used, according to Number of Children Surviving and Ever Died.

	Kinnaur							*Total*	
BACKGROUND CHARACTERISTICS	*Vasectomy*	*Tubectomy*	*Condom*	*IUD/Cu-T*	*Oral Pills*	*Safe period*	*None*	*N*	*%*
Number of Surviving Daughter									
None	17.5	21.2	12.8	21.4	21.2	36.8	25.4	176	21.5
One	36.0	31.5	51.3	40.5	45.5	26.3	36.3	296	36.1
Two	27.2	25.1	15.4	16.7	18.2	15.8	16.8	178	21.7
Three	11.8	13.3	12.8	9.5	3.0	15.8	12.5	99	12.1
Four	4.8	3.9	–	4.8	9.1	–	6.3	40	4.9
Five	2.2	4.9	5.1	4.8	–	–	1.6	23	2.8
Six	0.4	–	–	2.4	3.0	5.3	1.2	7	0.9
Nine	–	–	2.6	–	–	–	–	1	0.1
Total	100	100	100	100	100	100	100	820	100
Number of Surviving Son									
None	9.2	9.9	33.3	19.0	21.2	36.8	26.6	144	17.6
One	40.4	36.0	43.6	50.0	60.6	42.1	39.1	331	40.4
Two	36.4	36.0	15.4	19.0	15.2	21.1	21.1	233	28.4
Three	10.1	15.3	2.6	9.5	3.0	–	6.3	76	9.3
Four	3.1	2.0	5.1	2.4	–	–	5.1	27	3.3
Five	0.9	1.0	–	–	–	–	2.0	9	1.1
	100	100	100	100	100	100	100	820	100

Contd...

BACKGROUND CHARACTERISTICS	Kinnaur							Total	
	Vasectomy	Tubectomy	Condom	IUD/Cu-T	Oral Pills	Safe period	None	N	%
Total Children Surviving									
None	1.3	2.5	2.6	2.4	6.1	5.3	7.8	33	4.0
One	3.9	4.4	20.5	9.5	15.2	31.6	22.7	99	12.1
Two	27.2	22.7	35.9	38.1	39.4	36.8	24.2	220	26.8
Three	32.5	35.5	25.6	23.8	24.2	10.5	12.9	209	25.5
Four	19.7	14.3	–	7.1	3.0	10.5	13.7	115	14.0
Five	9.6	10.3	–	16.7	6.1	–	7.8	72	8.8
Six	3.9	8.9	10.3	–	6.1	–	5.1	46	5.6
Seven	1.8	1.5	2.6	2.4	–	–	4.3	20	2.4
Eight	–	–	–	–	–	5.3	1.2	4	0.5
Nine	–	–	2.6	–	–	–	–	1	0.1
Ten	–	–	–	–	–	–	0.4	1	0.1
Total	100	100	100	100	100	100	100	820	100
Children Ever Died									
One	66.7	66.2	33.3	30.0	80.0	33.3	58.3	154	61.6
Two	19.8	23.1	33.3	50.0	10.0	50.0	27.8	62	24.8
Three	6.2	7.7	16.7	10.0	–	16.7	8.3	19	7.6
Four	7.4	–		10.0	10.0	–	2.8	10	4.0
Five	–	3.1	16.7	–	–	–	1.4	4	1.6
Six	–	–	–	–	–	–	1.4	1	0.4
Total	100	100	100	100	100	100	100	250	100
	(81)	(65)	(6)	(10)	(10)	(6)	(72)		

The total number of surviving children among different temporary method (i.e. condom, Cu-T, oral pills and safe period) users shows that negligible proportion (2 to 6 per cent) of such couples used the method without having any issue, most of such couple having one to three children.

Children Ever Died: In the present study, a total of 250 spouses had experienced child loss, 178 (69 per cent) of them were current users of any method of family planning, as majority of child loss is experienced by aged couples, who had

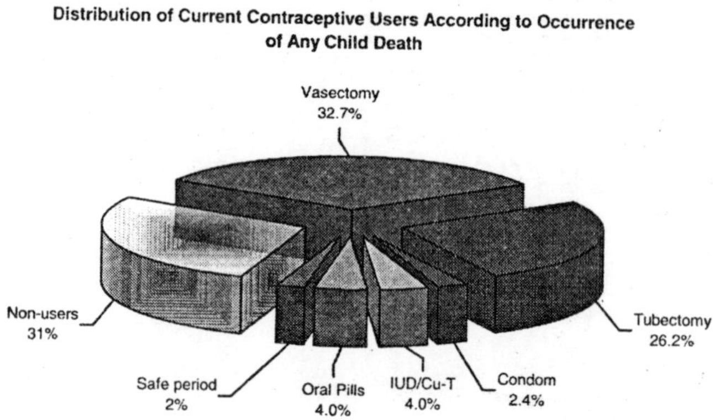

Figure 7: Pie-Diagram Showing the Distribution of Current Contraceptive Users According to Children Ever Died

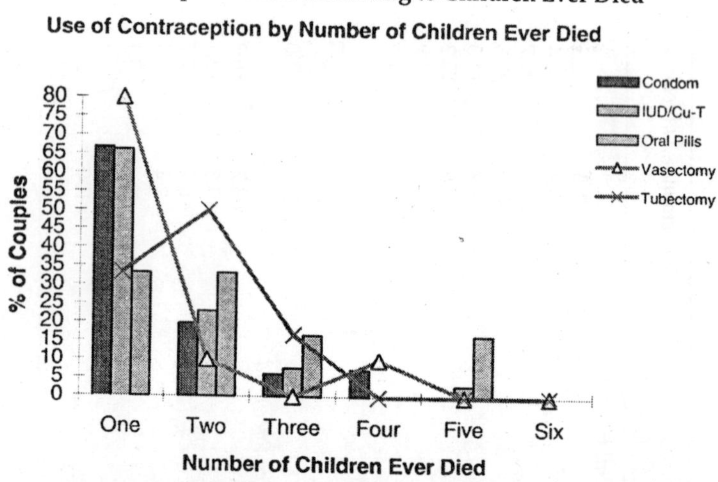

Figure 8: Current Practice of Contraception Among Couples Who Experienced Offspring Mortalities

adopted permanent methods, they had undergone for either vasectomy (32.7 per cent) or tubectomy (26.2 per cent) (Figure 7). In case of vasectomy adopters the highest child loss reported was 4, whereas among tubectomy adopters, the highest child loss was 5, but most of permanent method adopters (66 per cent from each) were lost one child, 19.8 per cent of vasectomy adopters and 23.1 per cent of tubectomy adopters had lost 2 children respectively, only 6 to 7 percent among these permanent method adopters had lost 3 and 4 children, 3.1 per cent of tubectomy adopters had also experienced loss of 5 children. Among temporary method adopters most of couples experienced 1-3 child. As the number of child loss increases the proportion of adoption of any family planning method decreases (Figure 8).

Table 6
Percentage Distribution of Kinnaura Respondents and Currently Married Women using Contraceptive Methods (Aged 15-44 Years) in Districts of Himachal Pradesh

	Percentage Using					
Population/ Region/ District	*Male Sterili-zation*	*Female Sterili-zation*	*IUD/ Loop*	*Oral Pills*	*Condom*	*Source*
	Currently Married Women/Husband					
Himachal Pradesh	7.6	43.0	2.6	2.3	6.9	1998-99 RHS (2001)
Bilaspur	12.2	45.2	1.2	1.5	4.1	"
Chamba	21.5	20.6	2.6	1.2	6.8	"
Hamirpur	7.6	45.6	1.1	2.5	3.6	"
Kangra	2.7	45.2	2.1	1.7	8.6	"
Kullu	19.8	35.5	3.7	2.4	5.8	"
Lahul & Spiti	15.6	26.2	4.6	2.4	7.8	"
Mandi	4.7	53.1	2.5	2.2	4.3	"
Shimla	6.4	46.5	3.6	3.5	6.7	"
Sirmaur	3.0	40.7	2.2	2.1	9.9	"
Solan	6.6	44.5	2.9	2.7	6.3	"
Una	3.0	39.1	3.4	2.6	11.7	"
Kinnaur	25.3	28.3	3.8	4.4	4.5	"
	All respondents (male/female)					
Kinnaura	27.8	24.8	5.1	4.0	4.8	Present study (2006)
Middle altitude	24.9	27.2	5.3	3.3	5.8	"
High Altitude	30.5	22.5	4.9	4.7	3.8	"

In the state of Himachal Pradesh (Table 6) the male sterilization vary form 2.7 to 25.8 percent; the highest male sterilization was reported from Kinnaur District and lowest from Kangra District. In Kinnaur District the female sterilization was reported 28.3 per cent, though in the state, it varies from 46.5 per cent in Shimla district to 20.6 per cent in Chamba District. The use of different spacing methods (IUD/ Loop, OP and Condom), in Himachal Pradesh varies from 1 to 11.7 percent. The comparison of current use of contraception among Kinnaura is compared with other studies i.e. RHS-2001 for Kinnaur District; RHS-2001 for Himachal Pradesh and NFHS-3—2007 for Himachal Pradesh is displayed through Figure 9 corroborate the present finding.

CASE STUDY

Vasectomy+Tubectomy

On the advice of female health worker (FHW), Rinchin Zangmo (imaginative name), in December 1996, the respondent had undergone for NSV (Non-scalpel vasectomy) in Yangthang camp. Initially the surgery was successful and he returned home after surgery. On 3rd day after the operation he opened the bandage to change it, but unfortunately the binding thread came out. He understood the problem and decided to consult physician. So he visited Community Health Center (CHC), Pooh, where he consulted Dr. Tanzin, who referred him to district hospital, Reckong Peo, for sperm test. After diagnostic tests in district hospital, doctors concluded that the NSV had failed and suggested for tubectomy. After two months, his wife (Sonam Kunjam) underwent for tubectomy. Prior to tubectomy, however, she was using Cu-T, which was not user friendly. At the time of tubectomy, she was carrying two month pregnancy which was to be aborted before tubectomy.

Correlation and Regression Analysis with Fertility

It is apparent that current use of family planning (FP) practices reduces fertility; to understand the extent of impact of current use of family planning practices on fertility, correlation and regression analyses was executed keeping current use of FP practices as independent variable and children ever born, number of children surviving, number of male and female child ever born, number of surviving male and female child and number of child deaths as dependent

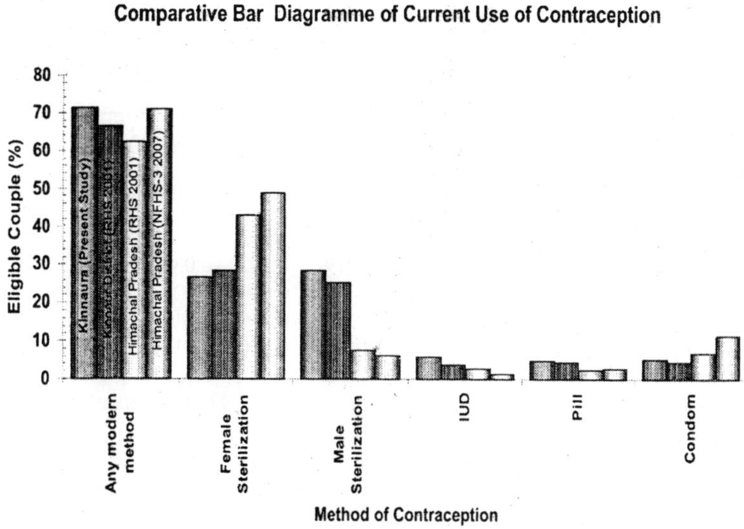

Figure 9: Comparative Bar Diagramme of Current Use of Contraception

variable. For the purpose of bivariate regression analyses independent score were given to each of dependent and independent variables as described in Chapter 9 Table 22. The current practice of family planning also assigned score in the same manner 1 for non-users, 2 for Oral Pills/Condom/ Natural Methods, 3 for IUD and 4 for Sterilization. The result of bivariate analysis shows poor correlation as indicated by â values (Table 7). In middle altitude except one variable (number of surviving male child) rest of the fertility indictors and mortality indictors had negative correlation with current use of FP practices, whereas in high altitude only three fertility indicators viz. number of children ever born, number of children surviving and number of surviving male child had shown negative correlation and rest of the fertility as well as mortality indictors had positive correlation with poor or negligible variability.

For further elucidation of facts scattered plot diagramme is drawn as shown in Figure10 and 11 based on data provided in NFHS-3, 2007 which corroborate the present findings. Crude birth rate and under-5 mortality rate have negative correlation with current use of any contraception.

Table 7
Correlation and Regression Analyses on Current Use of Family Planning Practices (Independent Variable) and Fertility Indicators (Dependent Variables).

Predictors	*R*	R^2	β_1	*t value*	*<p value*
			Middle Altitude		
Children Ever Born	0.060	0.004	-0.060	-1.185	0.237
Number of Children Surviving	0.050	0.002	-0.050	0.967	0.334
Male Child Ever Born	0.039	0.002	-0.039	-0.714	0.476
Female Child Ever Born	0.021	0.000	-0.021	-0.380	0.704
Number of Surviving Male Child	0.019	0.000	0.019	0.349	0.727
Number of Surviving Female Child	0.010	0.000	-0.010	-0.173	0.863
Number of Child Deaths	0.118	0.014	-0.118	-1.296	0.197
			High Altitude		
Children Ever Born	0.031	0.001	-0.031	-0.626	0.532
Number of Children Surviving	0.017	0.000	-0.017	-0.336	0.737
Male Child Ever Born	0.035	0.001	0.035	0.673	0.501
Female Child Ever Born	0.027	0.001	0.027	0.494	0.622
Number of Surviving Male Child	0.014	0.000	-0.014	-0.259	0.796
Number of Surviving Female Child	0.009	0.000	0.009	0.167	0.868
Number of Child Deaths	0.111	0.012	0.111	1.255	0.212

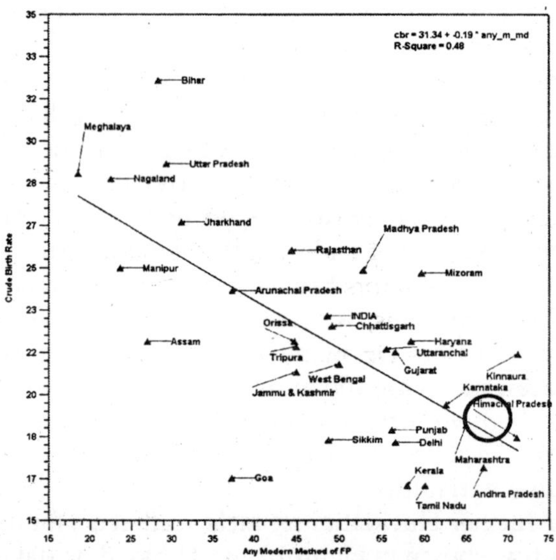

Source: NFHS-3, 2007, present finding is also plotted in circle.

Figure 10: Scattered Plot Diagramme Showing Correlation between Crude Birth Rate (CBR) and Current Use of Any Modern Method of FP

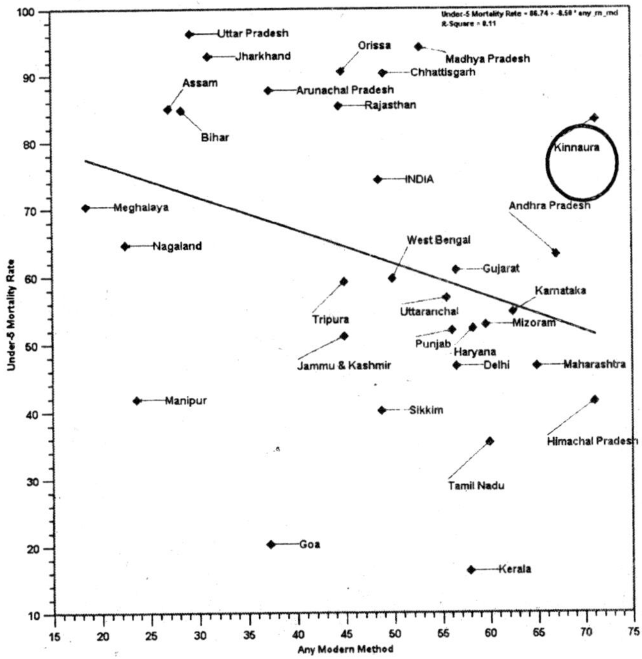

Source: NFHS-3, 2007, present finding is also plotted in circle.

Figure 11: Scattered Plot Diagramme Showing Correlation between under-5 Mortality Rate and Current Use of any Modern Method of FP

Chapter 13

HEALTH SEEKING BEHAVIOUR & HEALTH INFRASTRUCRE

Availability, accessibility and affordability lead to utilization of particular services/goods, as tribal people live in divergent geo-climatic set-ups. Geographical isolation, least developed transportation system, un-affordability etc. affects the availability and accessibility of health services, which ultimately causes poor utilization of health care delivery system, and simultaneously it is also difficult to health providers to reach these people. Here is an analysis of accessibility and availability of health institutions, services provided by these institutions, knowledge of people regarding occurrence of different health problems, their beliefs, perceptions and finally their attitude, practice and health seeking behaviour among the Kinnaura; which ultimately leads to influence the vital events and population structure and characteristics.

AVAILABILITY OF HEALTH INSTITUTIONS

In Kinnaur district, there is one district hospital, assisted by community health centers (CHCs), primary health centers (PHCs) and sub-centers (PHSCs) at periphery level. There is also a civil hospital in a border village (Chango). The Indian System of medicine (Ayurveda) is also developed horizontally in the district as there is Ayurvedic and Homeopathic district hospitals at the district headquarter, assisted by Ayurvedic health centers at periphery. The private practiceners are situated only in lower Kinnaur and their number is limited to two or three only.

Table 1
Distribution of Kinnaura by the Distance (within 5 Km) from Health Institutions.

	Middle Altitude	*High Altitude*	*Kinnaura (Pooled)*	
	%		N	%
Health Institutions	*First Health Institution within 5KM*			
District/Civil Hospital	52.8	1.4	214	26.1
CHC	0.3	22.8	98	12.0
PHC	29.9	15.7	185	22.6
PHSC	16.2	41.1	239	29.1
Ayurvedic Health Centre	0.3	19.0	82	10.0
Private practiceners/Quake	0.5	–	2	0.2
Total	100.0	100.0	820	100.0
	2nd Health Institution within 5KM			
District/Civil Hospital	9.3	1.5	22	6.3
CHC	0.5	60.9	82	23.6
PHC	0.9	1.5	4	1.1
PHSC	0.5	20.3	28	8.0
Ayurvedic Health Centre	0.5	15.0	21	6.0
Private practiceners/Quake	88.4	0.8	191	54.9
Total	100.0	100.0	348	100.0

The details of availability of various kind of health institution to people, within 5 km of their residence is given in Table 1, as evident from the Table that majority of people approximately, one third (29.1 per cent) have easy access to PHSC as it is within 5 km to their residence. 26.1, 22.6, 12.0 and 10.0 per cent have access to district hospital, PHC, CHC/ Civil Hospital and Ayurvedic health centers respectively. Only 0.2 per cent has responded that private practitioners are near to them. In middle altitude more than half (52.8 per cent) of the households have access (within 5 km) to district hospital, around one third (29.9 per cent) have access to PHC; whereas in high altitude majority of the households (41.1 per cent) have access to PHSC, followed by CHC (22.8 per cent), PHC (15.7 per cent) and Ayurvedic health centers (19.0 per cent). Out of the 820 households interviewed, 348 (around 42 percent) had such a unique location that they had more than one health institution within 5 km of their residence. The middle altitude Kinnaura had more such benefits.

Table 2
Distribution of Kinnaura by the Health Institution Preferred by them Available in their Periphery.

	Kinnaura		*Pooled*	
Health Institutions	*Middle Altitude*	*High Altitude*	*N*	*%*
	%			
District/Civil Hospital	84.8	5.4	357	43.5
CHC	–	36.4	155	18.9
PHC	12.7	16.0	118	14.4
PHSC	0.8	32.9	143	17.4
Ayurvedic Health Centre	–	9.4	40	4.9
Private practiceners/Quake	1.8	–	7	0.9
Total	100.0	100.0	820	100.0

PREFERENCE TO PARTICULAR HEALTH INSTITUTION

Availability of facilities and services in an area is a developmental aspect of the region, out of available facilities, which one is preferred most or least depends on so many factors, especially in case of health facilities it depends on availability of health care providers, his/her skill and knowledge, attitude towards the people, commitment and devotion to services, distance of services from residence, quality of services being provided etc. Table 2 shows the analysis, that among available health institution, which is preferred by Kinnaura.

Opinion about others: Opinion were gathered, regarding which health institutions, were mostly preferred by the people of the area is displayed in Table 3, showing that majority of people (42.6 per cent) preferred district hospital, followed by CHC (19.4 per cent), PHSC (18.4 per cent), PHC (14 per cent), Ayurvedic health center (5 per cent) and private practitioners (0.6 per cent). As district hospital is situated in middle altitude, most of middle altitude Kinnaura (83 per cent) prefer to seek health services from district hospital, whereas in high altitude none of the people have preference to district hospital.

Table 3
Distribution of Respondents According to their Opinion on 'Which Available Institution is Mostly Preferred by the People'.

			Kinnaura (Pooled)	
Health Institutions	*Middle Altitude%*	*High Altitude*	*N*	*%*
District/Civil Hospital	83.0	5.2	349	42.6
CHC	0.3	37.1	159	19.4
PHC	13.2	14.8	115	14.0
PHSC	2.3	33.3	151	18.4
Ayurvedic Health Centre	–	9.6	41	5.0
Private practiceners/Quake	1.3	–	5	0.6
Total	100.0	100.0	820	100.0

REASON OF PREFERENCE TO PARTICULAR HEALTH INSTITUTION

The information were gathered regarding, why a particular health institution is preferred by the respective respondents, through open ended multiple response type questions, the results were displayed in Table 4, indicates that there are 5 major reasons prevailing to choose a particular health institution.

Table 4
Distribution of Kinnaura by Reasons of 'Preference to Particular Health Institution/Services' Available in their Periphery *(Multiple Responses)*.

	Kinnaura			
	Middle Altitude	*High Altitude*	*Pooled*	
Reasons	*%*		*N*	*%*
Nearest/No alternate	40.4	79.3	497	60.6
Better facility/quick recovery	75.4	48.8	505	61.6
Availability of providers/No queue	63.2	62.7	516	62.9
Free of cost medicine/services	64.7	68.5	547	66.7
Availability of Lab./diagnostic facilities	54.3	21.4	305	37.2

SERVICES PROVIDED BY GOVERNMENT HEALTH INSTITUTIONS

Table 5 displaying the information of prevalence of the respondents' according to their knowledge regarding the services available or being provided by the nearest health institution, as evident from Table the pooled data shows that most of the people are knowledgeable about the services being provided by the health institutions, though the specific services are less known as 94.1 per cent respondents have knowledge that general health care services are being provided by their nearest health institution, followed by 75.1, 73.3 and 69 per cent who are quite knowledgeable about immunization, antenatal care, post natal care including family planning and welfare and finally laboratory and diagnostic services are being provided respectively by their nearest health institution.

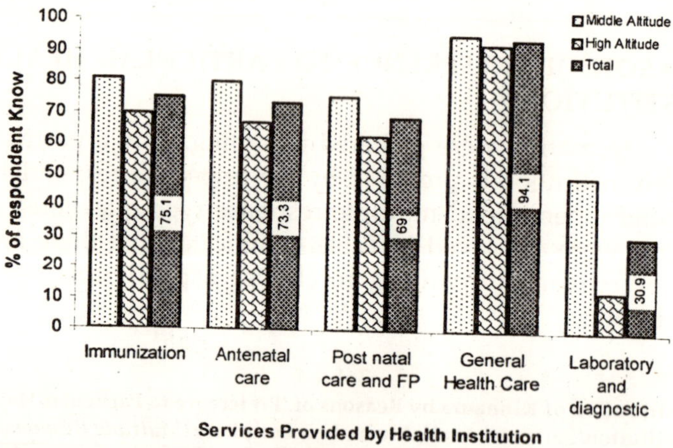

Figure 1: Distribution of Middle and High Altitude Kinnaura by Knowledge of Services Provided by 1st Nearest Health Institution

Table 5
Distribution of Kinnaura by Knowledge of Services Provided by 1st Nearest Health Institutions *(multiple responses)*.

	Kinnaura					
Services Provided by Health Institutions	*Middle Altitude*		*High Altitude*		*Pooled*	
	N	%	N	%	N	%
Immunization	318	80.7	298	70.0	616	75.1
Antenatal care	315	79.9	286	67.1	601	73.3
Post natal care and FP	298	75.6	268	62.9	566	69.0
General Health Care	377	95.7	395	92.7	772	94.1
Laboratory and diagnostic	198	50.3	55	12.9	253	30.9

Furthermore, the prevalence of middle altitude Kinnaura is higher in comparison to high altitude in respect of knowledge of services provided by the nearest health institution as displayed in Figure 1.

KNOWLEDGE OF HEALTH PROBLEMS

The health problems, which occurred in the study area, are varied from village to village or one kind of locality or altitude to the other; but the common type of health problems are stated in Table 6. It is evident from the pooled data that the highest percentage (94.3 per cent) of people were knowledgeable about the occurrence of acute respiratory infections (ARI), upper respiratory infections (URI) and infections of ear, nose and throat (ENT), followed by 84 per cent, 50.7 per cent, 54.4 per cent, 37.3 per cent, 21.3 per cent people who were quite knowledgeable regarding the occurrence of Gastrointestinal disorders/oral diseases; Arthritis/Body pain/factures; UTI/STD/RTI and Skin diseases/Leprosy etc. In respect of knowledge of occurrence of various kind of health problem the prevalence of knowledgeable people is greater in high altitude as compared to middle altitude.

Table 6
Distribution of Kinnaura by Knowledge of Occurrence of Current Health Problem in their Periphery (Multiple Responses).

	Kinnaura					
	Middle Altitude		*High Altitude*		*Pooled*	
Health Problems	N	%	N	%	N	%
Gastrointestinal/ oral diseases etc.	289	73.4	400	93.1	689	84.0
ARI/URI/ENT	357	90.6	416	97.7	773	94.3
UTI/STD/RTI	81	20.6	225	52.8	306	37.3
Arthritis, Body pain, factures	158	40.1	258	60.6	416	50.7
Liver, Jaundice, BP, stone case, heart problem	224	56.9	222	52.1	446	54.4
Skin diseases, Leprosy	40	10.2	135	31.7	175	21.3

HEALTH SEEKING BEHAVIOUR AND BELIEFS

Health seeking behaviour of people are swayed by the knowledge they had, education they attained, culture they belong to, religious background, availability and feasibility of health facilities in the area, their traditional beliefs and so on. Tribal people in general had different kind of health seeking behaviour, their knowledge, attitude and practice (KAP) has great influence of their traditional beliefs and superstitions they inherited associated to occurrence of health problems. In the present study some important aspects of health seeking behaviour such as-who takes decision to consult the doctor or health provider? Have you ever visited PHC/PHSC? Simultaneously, their attitude towards available health facilities/services likewise- Are you satisfied with the services provided by the health institution? Was the medical facility readily available? And finally their traditional practices and believes e.g.- Did you seek the help of traditional healer? Which method is better, traditional or modern? Belief on evil spirits etc were analyzed thoroughly as exhibited in Table 7.

Decision of Consulting the Doctor/Health Providers

It is evident from the Table 7 that in the slightly more than one third (34.9 per cent) households the decision to consult health provider were taken by the head of household, the analyses states clearly that in case of absence of the head of household the seeking of treatment would be delayed even in emergency situations. Almost in equal prevalence of households (36 per cent), the decision to consult health provider were being taken collectively. Simultaneously, in one fifth (20 per cent) households the decision to consult doctor/health provider were taken by other than member or head of the households, these 'other people' had very intact, deep and great impact on health seeking behaviour of these tribal people, They are- traditional healers, lamas, priests of the temple etc.

In this aspect the data analyzed separately for middle and high altitude, shows that there is clear-cut variation in middle and high altitude Kinnaura as in middle altitude in 40.6 per cent families the decision to consult the health provider were taken by head of households whereas in high altitude, this is true for lesser proportion (29.6) of families. Here in high altitude collective decisions were being taken by 43.9 per cent of the families.

Visiting of Health Centers

The pooled data (Table 7) shows that 97.4 per cent of the respondent had visited their nearest health centers, as evident from Table the prevalence of visiting health center is slightly higher in high altitude (98.4 per cent) as compared to middle altitude (96.4 per cent), it leads to conclude that the prevalence of morbidity is higher in high altitude as compared to middle altitude.

Satisfaction from the Services being Provided by Health Centers

Majority of the respondents' (86 per cent) are found satisfied with the services being provided to them by the nearest health centers. As stated in Table 7 indicates that the greater proportion of people of high altitude (91.5 per cent) are satisfied with the services being provided to them whereas the component of dissatisfaction is greater in middle altitude as 20.1 per cent are dissatisfied with the services being provided to them.

Availability of Medical Facility

In the aspect of availability of medical facilities to these tribal people, it is found that 77 per cent of the respondents found access to medical facilities, while rest 23 per cent says that the required medical facilities are not available to them. The comparison of middle and high altitude Kinnaura shows that in middle altitude somewhat lesser proportion (79.9 per cent) of them get medical facilities readily available than high altitude Kinnaura as 82.6 per cent of them found medical facilities readily available.

Seeking the help of Traditional Healer

In general, Kinnaura were found better in position in various aspects and measures of development and living standards as compared to other Tribal groups of the country, but surprisingly, more than half (54.3 per cent) of them were still seeking health care from traditional healers. Further there is variation in this aspect among middle and high altitude Kinnaura (Table 7) as the tendency to seek the help of traditional healer is found more among high altitude Kinnaura (65.5 per cent) as compared middle altitude (42.1 per cent).

Table 7
Distribution of Kinnaura by Health Seeking Behaviour and Beliefs

	Kinnaura			
	Middle Altitude	*High Altitude*		*Pooled*
Behaviour/ Perception/Believe	%		N	%
Who takes decision to consult Dr.?				
Head of household	40.6	29.6	286	34.9
Wife	8.1	1.9	40	4.9
Elderly males	5.8	1.2	28	3.4
Collectively decision	27.4	43.9	295	36.0
Any other	18.0	23.5	171	20.9
Total	100.0	100.0	820	100.0
Have ever visited PHC/PHSC?				
Not visited	3.6	1.6	21	2.6
Visited	96.4	98.4	799	97.4
Total	100.0	100.0	820	100.0
Do you satisfied by the services?				
Not satisfied	20.1	8.5	115	14.0
Satisfied	79.9	91.5	705	86.0
Total	100.0	100.0	820	100.0
Was the medical facility readily available?				
No	29.2	17.4	189	23.0
Yes	70.8	82.6	631	77.0
Total	100.0	100.0	820	100.0
Did you seek the help of traditional healer				
No	57.9	34.5	375	45.7
Yes	42.1	65.5	445	54.3
Total	100.0	100.0	820	100.0
Is traditional method better				
No	97.0	61.7	645	78.7
Yes	3.0	38.3	175	21.3
Total	100.0	100.0	820	100.0
Beliefs on evil spirit				
No	65.0	58.5	505	61.6
Yes	35.0	41.5	315	38.4
Total	100.0	100.0	820	100.0

Better Method of Health Care

The information were gathered, to seek the opinion of study population group, in respect of comparison of traditional method of health care and modern system of health care which one is better. Slightly more than one fifth (21.3 per cent) of the respondents have opinion that traditional methods are better, the rest says modern system of health care is better than the traditional. In addition to that variation can also be observed among middle and high altitude Kinnaura, on the aspect, as more people of high altitude (38.3 per cent) consider that traditional methods of health care are better as compared to middle altitude, where only 3.0 per cent of the people had this kind of opinion rest 97 per cent considered modern system of health care are better.

Beliefs on Evil Spirit

Tribal population has many superstitions regarding the causation of disease. Poor exposure to outer world, lack of technical and scientific approach to causation of health problems, they are insisted to find out the cause of problems through supernatural spirits. Therefore, they believe that health problems are caused due to possession on benevolent and malevolent spirits, evil eyes, break of taboo and so on. In the present study it is found that 38.4 per cent of Kinnaura believe in evil spirit. Again, there are slight differences among middle and high altitude Kinnaura as lesser proportion of middle altitude Kinnaura (35 per cent) believe in evil spirits as compared to high altitude (41.5 per cent).

PROBLEM SPECIFIC PREFERENCE TO HEALTH PROVIDERS

It is a very common and universal fact that people choose a particular treatment/procedure and provider for specific problem or in other words the preference to opt a particular health provider vary according to the problem. In the present study it is found that in case of illness of children, adult male and female as well as gynae problems, antenatal care, family planning and Immunization services of children and pregnant women approximate 55.7 per cent to 77.7 per cent people prefer to seek the treatment/services from Government Doctor. Further, less than 1 percent prefers to seek the treatment/ services from private doctor or quake and from ANM or LHV

Table 8
Distribution of Kinnaura by Health Seeking Behaviour for Various Health Problems/Services.

	Health Problem/Services						
	Child Illness	*Adult Male Illness*	*Adult Female Illness*	*Antenatal Care*	*Gynae Problems*	*Family Planning*	*Immunization*
				Kinnaur			
Preferred providers				%			
Government Doctor	73.4	74.1	73.7	76.1	77.7	55.7	59.3
Private Dr./ quake	0.5	0.5	0.5	–	0.2	–	–
Lama	6.2	6.4	6.4	2.9	2.3	0.5	0.5
ANM/LHV	2.2	1.6	2.1	4.0	2.1	28.1	24.4
Lama/ANM/LHV	0.6	0.6	0.6	0.3	0.6	0.1	0.1
Govt. Dr./Lama/ ANM/LHV	14.4	14.2	14.1	14.3	14.5	15.6	15.6
All type of providers	2.7	2.7	2.7	2.4	2.6	–	–
Total %	100.0	100.0	100.0	100.0	100.0	100.0	100.0
Number	785	818	818	795	815	796	787
			Middle Altitude				
Government Doctor	95.4	96.4	95.7	93.2	96.4	66.8	74.3
Private Dr./ quake	1.1	1.0	1.0	–	.5	–	–
Lama	0.5	0.5	0.5	0.5	0.5	–	–
ANM/LHV	1.1	–	1.0	4.2	0.3	29.8	21.9
Lama/ANM/LHV	–	–	–	–	–	–	–
Govt. Dr./Lama/ANM/LHV		1.6	1.8	1.5	1.8	2.1	3.4
3.7							
All type of providers	0.3	0.3	0.3	0.3	0.3	—	—
Total %	100.0	100.0	100.0	100.0	100.0	100.0	100.0
Number	372	392	393	380	389	382	374
High Altitude							
Government Doctor	53.5	53.5	53.4	60.5	60.6	45.4	45.8
Private Dr./ quake	–	–	–	–	–	–	–
Lama	11.4	11.7	11.8	5.1	4.0	1.0	1.0
ANM/LHV	3.1	3.1	3.1	3.9	3.8	26.6	26.6
Lama/ANM/LHV	1.2	1.2	1.2	0.5	1.2	0.2	0.2
Govt. Dr./Lama/ ANM/LHV	25.9	25.6	25.6	25.8	25.8	26.8	26.4
All type of providers	4.8	4.9	4.9	4.3	4.7	–	–
Total %	100.0	100.0	100.0	100.0	100.0	100.0	100.0
Number	413	426	425	415	426	414	413

or Lama; whereas 0.5 to 6.4 per cent, 1 to 28 per cent, 14 to 15.6 per cent prefer to seek the treatment/services respectively from Lama only, ANM or LHV and multiple providers including Government Doctor, Lama, ANM and LHV; while slightly more than 2 per cent opt all type of providers for these health problems/services, as also evident from Table 7. For Health services like antenatal care, family planning and immunization nobody prefer traditional healer Lama. Approximately one fourth (24.4 to 28.1 per cent) of study population prefer Auxiliary Nurse Midwives (ANM) or Female health worker/ Lady Health Visitor/Supervisor (LHV) for family planning and immunization services.

In middle altitude more than 90 per cent people prefer Government Doctor in case of child and adult (male/female) illness, as well as services of antenatal care and gynae problems. Simultaneously, 29.8 per cent and 21.9 per cent respectively prefer to seek the services from female health worker/ supervisor (ANM/LHV) for family planning and immunization. Whereas in high altitude, only 45 to 60 per cent people opt Government Doctor exclusively for all kind of treatment and services as described above and displayed in Table 8. The rest of the people opt successive option as first they prefer the nearest and most feasible option, which is usually Lama or traditional healer, then go to health workers and lastly on the failure of these option they prefer Government Doctor. In none of the case nobody of high altitude Kinnaura prefer private practitioners or quakes as there is no private practitioners or quake in the high altitude region of the study area. Slightly more than one fifth opt female health workers (ANM/LHV) for family planning and immunization services.

EPILOGUE

The enchanting Himalayas and its habitants are vast in size, variant in shape and unique in cultural paradigm. The enormous expansion of Himalayas has countries like Nepal and Bhutan at its lap and part of India and China on its extreme. The highest peak of earth Mount-Everest is blessed to Nepal. The similar other mountain system on earth are Andes of South America and Ethiopia of African continent. The vastness of Indian Himalayas can be imagined by number of states established in its land. The total number of states including union territories in Indian republic is 35 and out of these 12 states are in Himalayas, although most of them are smaller states. The whole Himalayan region is full of tremendous natural resources. There are variety of flora and fauna. The rivers originates from Himalayas are life line for many countries. These rivers are not only the source of drinking and irrigation water but many hydroelectric power projects are established on these rivers are source of energy to many of us. In this point of view the conservation of such a lively mountain system should be given priority.

The population dynamics of Himalayas is also similarly divergent as its size, shape and altitude. At the one end in northeastern states there is highly fertile population like Khasi, Garo, Jantia, Naga etc. who are equally conflicting in their cultural practices. The Khasi and Jantia are still matrilineal alike Kinnaura are still polyandrous.

Population Characteristics of an area or group leads to understand the micro differences within the selected universe. The people of the high-altitude regions of the world have long fascinated both scientists and laymen. Comparative study of Middle and High altitude population gives an understanding of problems and perspectives of population dynamics of such a population and region, which is least explored, and contradictorily reported. Though sizeable section of human populations live at altitudes above 3,000 meters indicating the success of man's adaptation to the environmental conditions of mountains especially to the reduced partial pressure of oxygen; the hypoxic stress affects all the biological system, namely growth, body structure, work capacity, demographic performance and nutritional needs (Singh et.al. 1989). Most of the world's population (33.5% or 1.88×10^9 people) lived within 100 vertical meters of sea level. The population living at 2,000-2500 m are 1.3×10^8 (Cohen and Small, 1998), between 20 and 30 million people all over the world live permanently at elevations of 3,000 m or higher and are exposed to a harsh environment, known as high altitude, which comprise a constellation of stresses, namely, hypobaric hypoxia, cold, rugged terrain, high dosage of ultraviolet radiation, iodine deficiency, limited resources etc. (Gupta, et.al., 1989). Singh (1989) tried to define high, moderate and low altitude in the western Himalayas, according to him high altitude is above 2,500m moderate altitude is between 2,000 and 2,500m and low altitude is below 2,000m. In the present study the delimiter line for deciding high altitude is 2,500m keeping in mind that there is not a single factor, but one should consider other variables also in deciding the delimiter for high altitude; and below that is considered as middle altitude as also suggested by Pawson and Jest (1978).

In country like India, apart from the population explosion, the demographic diversity is also striking. This is because of the dynamics of population components within and across states, regions. Populations (caste, communities and tribes) are influenced by the physical environment, biological, economical, social and cultural factors. Demographic diversity in India show variable picture, there are states like Bihar, MP, Rajasthan, UP, Orisa and three daughter states Chhatisgarh, Uttaranchal and Jharkhand (BIMARU) which show relatively poor picture in various demographic indicators. There are other states which are comparatively progressives (i.e. Kerala, Tamilnadu, Himachal Pradesh, Andhra Pradesh etc.) demographic indicators provide valuable information about the differential relationship with various factors stated above so that one can assess as to which state is lagging behind in demographic transition. In the view of above, present study has been conducted to study the population characteristics of Middle and High altitude Kinnaura of district Kinnaur, Himachal Pradesh.

The present Kinnaur district is lying between 77° 45' and 79° 00' 35" East Longitude and between 31° 05' 50" and 32° 05' 15" North Latitude, the altitude ranges from 1200 meter to 6816 meter. This is basically greater Himalayan region, in Indian Himalayas, and , one of the districts of Himachal Pradesh State of Indian Republic.

There were strong reasons behind the selection of area like— The district is located in the greater Himalayan region. The whole greater Himalayan region was in complete seclusion for many years and recently developed its link to the outer world. Kinnaura of this area are polyandrous and patriarchal; the mode of property inheritance among them is primogeniture. Remote areas of Himalayas, like district Kinnaur has hardly been explored scientifically for its population characteristics.

The principal indicators of population characteristics viz. literacy rate, population composition, dependency ratio, fertility and mortality measures alongwith exploratory analysis and selection intensity are computed in the investigation among the Kinnaura of Kinnaur district of Himachal Pradesh State of Indian Republic. The findings of the study are compared with the similar findings of Indian National Population, different States, tribal and non-tribal population of Himalayas. It has been found that middle and upper Kinnauras show similar results with minor differences in various demographic measures. The results on various dimensions of population characteristics of Kinnauras are impressive, particularly in the context of tribal populations of India.

SUMMARY OF RESULTS

Variables		*Kinnaura (Pooled)*	*Middle Altitude*	*High Altitude*	*Himachal Pradesh*	*India*
Population		4991	2497	2512	6077900[c]	1027015247[c]
	Male	2488	1233	1255	3087940[c]	531277078[c]
	Female	2503	1246	1257	2989960[c]	495738169[c]
Sex Ratio		1006	1011	1002	968[c]	933[c]
Dependency Ratio						
	Young age	46.01	46.34	45.71	52[c]	62[c]
	Old age	13.80	15.90	11.79	15[c]	13[c]
	Total	59.81	62.24	57.49	67[c]	75[c]
Index of Aging		29.99	34.32	25.79	29[c]	21[c]
Crude Literacy Rate (%)						
	Male	79.42	81.10	77.77	86.02[c]	75.85[c]
	Female	65.92	68.48	63.48	68.08[c]	54.16[c]
	Total	72.62	74.41	70.62	77.13[c]	65.38[c]
Mean Age at Marriage						
	Male	22.80	23.5	22.55	26.7[n]	24.9[n]
	Female	19.58	19.25	19.93	22.1[n]	19.7[n]
Type of Marriage						
	Monogamy	83.9	84.8	83.1		
	Polyandry	13.2	10.9	15.3		
	Polygyny	2.6	4.1	1.2		
	Polyandry & Polygyny	0.4	0.3	0.5		
Mean Age at Menarche		15.11	15.19	15.03		
Mean Age at Menopause		45.45	44.58	46.66		
Fertility Indicators						
	CBR	21.64	19.36	23.89	19.9[n]	24.8[n]
	GFR	67.72	58.73	76.79		
	TFR	2.55	2.13	2.92	2.14[n]	2.85[n]
	GRR	1.25	1.04	1.43		
	Child women Ratio	356.60	346.26	358.62		
	GMFR	110.57	95.82	125.31		
	TMFR	2.55	2.13	2.92		
	MGRR	1.25	1.04	1.43		
Mortality Indicator						
	CDR	9.21	12.10	6.76	7.2[s]	8.5[s]
	Under-5 mortality rate	83.33	104.16	66.66	42.4[n]	94.9[n]

Contd...

Variables	*Kinnaura (Pooled)*	*Middle Altitude*	*High Altitude*	*Himachal Pradesh*	*India*
IMR	74.07	83.33	66.66	60[s]	68[s]
Selection Intensity					
Mortality Index (I_m)	0.194	0.202	0.187		
Fertility Index (I_f)	0.159	0.153	0.154		
Total Selection (I)	0.384	0.386	0.370		

Sources:

[c] Census of India, 2001

[n] National Family Health Survey-2 (NFHS-2), 1998-99

[s] Sample Registration Survey (SRS), 2000

It can be seen that Indian population in general and tribal populations in particular are at different stages of demographic transitions, primarily because of their placement, economy, social and cultural practices, and their differential involvements in different development programs. Interestingly, pattern of early child bearing is common among both tribal and non-tribal populations of rural India. It has been further observed that fertility level of tribal groups are high and comparable to the more progressive southern states of 1970s. It has been reported (Human Development Report, 1994) that CBR and TFR dips in relation to developmental activities, level of living and literacy across various social groups. Regarding mortality measures, it has been found that literacy rate especially among women is a most important predictor variable that contributes to low CDR and IMR. Moreover mortality variables do not vary significantly by income as much as they are affected by the level of education among women. It can be observed that despite concerted efforts of various State Governments as well as Government of India, the tribal groups of India are lagging behind. However, ever since independence, there is dramatic change in all the demographic indicators affecting tribal health together with a shift in morbidity profile (Kshatriya, 2000). Although changes are slow, but obvious, many tribal groups of India are participating in developmental activities and consciously coming in the fold of mainstream and are hardly distinguishable from the immediate non-tribal neighbors. And Kinnauras of Himachal Pradesh are one of those many tribal groups who are demographically more progressive. In the present study, Kinnauras are found to be more close to Indian National population than with other tribal groups of India. Economy, level of living, female literacy, awareness among users and placement of health providers along with their acceptability, availability and affordability can be said to be the most important variables among many others that have shaped the course of population characteristics of Kinnaura substantially.

REFERENCES

Abelson, A. Altitude and fertility: Biology and cultural effects. In: proceedings of the Indian Statistical Institute, Golden Jublee International Conference on Human Genetics and adaptation, vol. 2, Human Adaptation, (Eds.) A. Basu K. C. Malhotra. Calcutta: Indian Statistical Institute, (1984a).

Abelson, A. E., Baker, T.S. and Baker, P.T.: Altitude migration and fertility in the Andes. *Soc. Biol.*, 21: 12 (1974).

Abelson, A.E.: Altitude and fertility. *Human Biology.*,48: 83-92 (1976).

Adak, D. K. and Gharami, A.K.: A Study on the Population Composition of the Ladiya of Madhya Pradesh, India. *South Asian Anthropologist;*1 (2): 83-89. (2001).

Adak, D.K. and Gharami, A.K.: Sexual Maturity and its Biological Proximates: A Study among the Ladiya of Madhya Pradesh, India. *Anthropologie,*40/2, 141-144 (2002).

Adak, D.K., Gharami, A.K., Singhai, T., Jain, M.K.: A Study on menarche and fertility among the Ladiya of Sagar District, Madhya Pradesh. *J. Hum. Ecol.,* 12: 279-281. (2001).

Adak, D.K.: A Study of the phenomenon of demographic transition among the Ladiya of Madhya Pradesh, India. *Anthropologie,* (39), 2-3: 241-242. (2001).

Adelman, I.: An econometric analysis of population' growth. *Am. Econ. Rev..* 53: 314 (1963).

Agarwala, R.D.: Influence of infant and child mortality on fertility in India. *Paper Presented at the Seminar on Infant Mortality in Relation to Level of Fertility, Bangkok.* CICRED, Series, Paris (1975).

Agarwala, S. N.: *Age at Marriage in India.* Kitab Mahal, Bombay. (1962)

Agarwala, S.N.: *A Demographic Study of Six Urbanizing Villages.* Asia Publishing House, Bombay (1970).

Agarwala, S.N.: Raising the marriage age of women: A mean at lower birth rate. *Eco.Pol. Weekly*, 1: 797 (1966).

Ahmad, S.: Effect of education on marital fertility in four Muslim populations. *Genus*. 41: 23 (1985).

Aitken, A. And Stoeckel, J.: Dynamics of the Muslim-Hindu differential in family planning practices in rural East Pakistan. *Soc. Biol.*, 18: 268 (1971).

Annapurna, M. : A study of genetical demography on the Bagata tribe of Chintapalli block villages in Visakhapatnam district of coastal Andhra Pradesh (Unpublished, Andhra University) (Cited by Bhattacharyya et.al., 1991) (1972).

Appleman, P. : Thomas Robert Malthus: An Essay on the Principle of Population (ed.).New York: Nortan. (1976).

Arnold, F. et .al.: *The value of Children: A Cross National Study*. Vol. 1 East West Population Institute, Honolulu, Hawaii (1975).

Arnold, F., and Zhaoxiang, L.: Sex preference, fertility and family planning in China. *Pop. Dev. Rev.*, 12: 221 (1986).

Ashley-Montague, M.F.: Adolescent Sterility. *The Quarterly Review of Biology*, 14: 13-34. (1939).

Babu, B.V. and Naidu, J.M.: A demographic profile of four Andhra Caste populations. *Ind. Jr. Phys. Anthrop and Hum.Genet.*, 15 (3): 97-102. (1989).

Bajpai S.C.: Kinnaur in the Himalayas, Mythology to modernity, New Delhi: Concept Publishing Company (1981).

Baker, E.R.: Body weight and the initiation of puberty. *Clin. Obstet. Gyneco.*, 28: 573-579. (1985)

Baker, P. T. and Dutt, J.S.: Demographic variable as measure of biological adaptation : A case study of high altitude human population. In the structure of human population, (Eds.) G.A. Harison and A. J. Boyce. Oxford : Clarendon press, (1972).

Baker, P. T. and Weiner, J. S.(Eds.): The biology of human adaptability. Oxford: Clarendon Press, (1966).

Baker, P. T.: Human adaptation to high altitude. *Science*, 165: 1149-56 (1969).

Baker, P. T.: The adaptive fitness of high altitude populations. In *The Biology of High-Altitude Peoples*, (Ed.). PT. Baker. Cambridge University press, Cambridge. 317. (1978)

Baker, P.T. : Introduction. In *Human Biology of Asian Highland Populations in the Global Context* , (Eds.) A. Basu and R. Gupta, 9 Indian Anthropological Society Occasional Papers, The Indian Anthropological Society, Calcutta (1989).

Baker, P.T. and Little, M.A. (Eds.): *Man in the Andes: A Multidisciplinary Study of High altitude Quenchua*. Dowden, Hutchinson and Ross, Stroudsburg (1976).

Bali, K. and Elford, J. : 'Health in Zangskar'. In Crook, J. and Osmaston, H. (Eds) *Himalayan Buddhist Villages: Environment , resources, Society and Religious Life in Zangkar, Ladakh.* Bristol: University of Bristol Press. 405-431 (1994).

Banerjee, U.K. and Banerjee, S.: The Mystic Kinnaur in the Himalayas: Its People and Forests. *J. Hum. Ecol. Special Issue N., .6*: 221-224 (1997).

Bangham, C.R.M. and Sacherer, J. M.: Fertility of Nepalese Sherpas at moderate altitudes: Comparision with high altitude data. *Ann. Hum. Biol.*, 7: 323 (1980).

Bangladesh Fertility Survey, 1975: *A Summary of Findings*. International Statistical Institute, The Hague, Netherlands (1979).

Barua, S. : Selection intensity among the consanguineous and non-consanguineous groups of a Muslim population of 24 Parganas. *Man in India*, 56: 359-364 (1976).

Barua, S. : The Hajongs of Meghalya: A Bio-cultural Study. *Hum. Sci.*, 32: 19-20 (1983).

Barua, S.: The Hajongs of Meghalaya: A Biodemographic study. *Human Biology*, 30: 1-13 (1985).

Basu, A and Gupta, R. (Eds.) : Human Biology of Asian Highland Populations in the Global Context. *Indian Anthropological Society, Culcutta; Occassional Papers* . (1989).

Basu, A. and Gupta R.: Comments on high altitude hypoxia, culture and human fecundity/fertility: A comparative study. *Am. Anthrop.* 86: 994 (1984).

Basu, A., Gupta, R. and Bhattacharya, K.K.: A demographic study of Mirpur: A village in coastal Midnapore District, West Bengal. *J. Biosoc. Sci.*, 12: 227 (1980).

Basu, A., Gupta, R. and Mukhopadhyay, B.: Anthropopological demography of populations of the eastern Himalayas. In: *the People of South Asia*. J.R. Lukacs (Ed.). Plenum Press, New York (1984).

Basu, A.: A demographic study of the Kota of Nilgiri Hills. *J. Ind. Anthrop.Soc.*, 7: 29 (1972).

Basu, A.: Selection intensity in the Pahiras. *Eugen. Quart.*, 14: 214 (1967).

Basu, S. & Gupta, P.: Trend of menarche and menopause among the ibred Muslim Shia Dawoodi Bhoras of Udaipur, Rajasthan, 4th Annual Conference of the Indian Society of Human Genetics (Abstract) pp 8. (1977).

Basu, S. : *Health Need Assessment of Tribal Populations of District Midnapore, West Bengal.* Unpublished Ph.D. Thesis submitted to the University of Delhi, Delhi (1998).

Basu, S., Kshatriya, G. and Jindal, A.: Fertility and Mortality Differentials among the Tribal Population Groups of Bastar District, Madhya Pradesh, India. *Human Biology*,60 (3): 407-416 (1988).

Basu, S.K. : Genetics, socio-cultural and health care among the tribal groups of Jagdalpur and Konta tehsil of Bastar district, M.P. pp 87-105. In : *Anthropology, Development and Nation Building.* A.K. Kalla and K.S. Singh (Eds.). Concept Publishing Company, New Delhi (1986).

Basu, S.K. and Kshatriya, G.K. : Index of opportunity of natural selection among the tribal population groups of Madhya Pradesh. *J. Ind. Anthropol. Assoc.*, 25: 264-271 (1990)

Beall, C. M. : Growth in a population of Tibetan origin at high altitude. *Ann. Hum. Biol.*, 8: 31-38, (1981a).

Beall, C. M., and A. B. Reichsman : Hemoglobin levels in a Himalayan high altitude population. *Am. J. Phys. Anthrop.*, 63: 301-06, (1984).

Beall, C. M., and M. C. Goldstein: Tibetan fraternal polyandry : A test of sociobiology theory. *American Anthropologist*, 83: 5-12, (1981).

Beall, C. M., P. T. Baker, T. S. Baker, and J. D. Hass : The effect of high altitude on adolescent growth in southern Peruvian Americans. *Human Biology* 49: 109-24, (1977).

Beall, C. M.: Ages at menopause and menarche in a high altitude Himalayan population. *Ann. Hum. Biol*, 10: 365-70, (1983).

Beall, C. M.: Aging and growth at high altitudes in the Himalayas. In the people of South Asia, (Ed.) R. J. Lucas. New York: Plenum Press, (1984).

Beall, CM: Ages at menopause and menarche in a high altitude Himalayan population. Ann. Hum. Biol., 20: 365 (1983).

Bean. R and Wood, C.: Ethnic variations in relation- ship between income and fertility. *Demography*, II: 629 (1974).

Bebarta, P .C. : Recent studies in fertility. *Sociological Bulletin.* 10: 27. (1961).

Bebarta, P.C.: Attitude of women towards family planning -A study of differences on family types in six villages of Delhi. *J. Ind. Stud. Soc. Sci. Bombay*, 1: 78 (1967).

Becker, G.: An economic analysis of fertility. In: *Demographic and Economic Change in Developed Countries.* A.J. Coale (Eds.). Universities National Bureau Committee for Economic Research. Princeton University Press, Princeton (1960).

Belitz, B.: A map on recent menarcheal age research in Europe. *Arztl. Jugendkd.,* 68: 81-92. (1977).

Belmaker, E.: Sexual maturation of Jerusalem Schoolgirls and its association with socio-economic factors and ethnic group. *Ann. Hum. Biol.*, 9: 321-328 (1982).

Berelson, B.: Beyond family planning. *Stud. Fam. Plann.*, 38: 1 (1969).

Berelson, B.: Social science research on population. *Pop. Dev. Rev.*, 1.: 219 (1976).

Betrand, J.T., Betrand, W.E. and Bermeo, D.: Correlates of contraceptive use among urban poor in Colombia. *J. Biosoc. Sci.*, 13: 431 (1981).

Bhalla, V. & Chopra, S.R.K.: Gene differentiation in Hill Rajputs (Kanets) of upper Satluj Valley (H.P.). Indian Journal of Physical Anthropology and Human Genetics, 5 (1), 1-6 (1979).

Bhalla, V., Bhatia, K. and Tanwar, S.: Genetic polymorphism in Cis-Himalayan populations, III : A1 A2 BO, Mn, blood groups, ABH secretion and colour blindness in Hill Rajputs and Kolis of Sainj valley (H.P.) *Journal of the Indian Anthropological Society*, 15, 18-3 (1980).

Bhalla. S.R., Kapoor, AK. and Singh, LP.: Variation in the age at menarche due to physical exercise and altitude. *Z. Morph. Anthrop.*, 73: 323 (1983).

Bhasin, M.K. : People of India, An Investigation of Biological, Ethno-Economic and linguistic Groups. Kamla-Raj Enterprises. Delhi (1994).

Bhasin, M.K. and Kshatriya, G.K.: Fertility and mortality differentials in the population groups of Sikkim. *J. Hum. Ecol.(India),* 30:267 (1990).

Bhasin, M.K. and Nag, S. : A Demographic Profile of the people of Jammu and Kashmir 1. Population structure. *J. Hum. Ecol.,*13 (1-2): 1-55 (2002).

Bhasin, M.K. and Nag, S. : A Demographic Profile of the people of Jammu and Kashmir 2. Estimates, Trends and Differentials in Fertility. *J. Hum. Ecol.,*13 (1-2): 57-112 (2002).

Bhasin, M.K. and Nag, S. : A Demographic Profile of the people of Jammu and Kashmir 3. Estimates, Trends and Differentials in Mortality. *J. Hum. Ecol.,*13 (1-2): 113-140 (2002).

Bhasin, M.K. and Nag, S. : A Demographic Profile of the people of Jammu and Kashmir 4. Selection intensity. *J. Hum. Ecol.,*13 (1-2): 141-146 (2002).

Bhasin, M.K. and Nag, S. : A Demographic Profile of the people of Jammu and Kashmir 5. Family Planning. *J. Hum. Ecol.,*13 (1-2): 147-166 (2002).

Bhasin, M.K. and Nag, S. : A Demographic Profile of the people of Jammu and Kashmir 6.Regression Analyses. *J. Hum. Ecol.,*13 (1-2): 167-176 (2002).

Bhasin, M.K. and V. Bhasin: Ecology People, and Health: The Indian Scenario. *The Anthropologist,* 4 (1): 1-41 (2002).

Bhasin, V. and Bhasin, M.K.: A cross-cultural fertility differential in Sikkim. *J. Hum. Ecol.,* 11 (6): 429-444 (2000).

Bhasin, V. and Bhasin, M.K.: Ecology, population dynamics among Transhumance of Himalayas. A case study of Gaddis of Himachal Pradesh. *J. Hum. Ecol.,* 4: 171 (1993).

Bhasin, V.: Ecology and Status of Women among Tribals of India. *J. Hum. Ecol.* 15 (4): 237-249 (2004).

Bhasin, V.: *Habitat, Habitation and Health in the Himalayas: A comparative Study of the People of Sikkim and the Gaddis of Himachal Pradesh.* Kamla–Raj Enterprises. Delhi (1990).

Bhasin,V. and Nag. S. : Population Dynamics, Problems and Prospects of High Altitude. *The Anthropologist,* 4 (1): 43-72 (2002).

Bhatnagar, N.K.: Decline of fertility and family planning. An appraisal. p. 145.In: *Studies on Fertility in India.* R. S. Kurup (Eds.).

Monograph Series No. 7. The Gandhigram Institute of Rural Health and Family Planning, Gandhigram, India (1975).

Bhatnagar, N.K.: Status of women and family planning in India. *J. Family Welfare*, 18: 21 (1972).

Bhatt, G.S.: Anthropology, Women and Polyandry. *The Eastern Anthropologist*.50: 3-4, 433-443 (1997).

Bhattacharyya, S. K., Bhattacharyya, S. and Das, N.K.: Menarche and Menopause among the Mahar of Maharashtra. *Man In India*, 71: 491-495. (1991).

Bhattacharyya, S. K., Dutta, P.C. and Bhattacharyya, S. : The migrant Oraon in Andaman Islands: Some demographic aspects. *Jr. Indian Anthrop. Soc.*, 20: 86-92. (1985).

Bhattacharyya, S., Chatterjee, S. and Bhattacharyya, S.K. : Menarcheal age in some endogamous groups of Bengal. *Jr. Indian Anthrop. Soc.*, 12: 60-68. (1977).

Bhende, A. A. and Kanitkar, T.: Principles of Population Studies, Himalayan Publishing House, Mumbai-4 (2001).

Birdsall, N.: Analytical approaches to the relationship of population growth and development. *Pop. Dev. Rev.*, 3: 63 (1977).

Biswas, N.: Age at menarche among Punjabi girls of Delhi. *Anthropologist*, 14: *IS3* (1967).

Blake, J.: Are babies consumer durables? A critique of the economic theory of reproductive motivation. *Population Studies*. 22: 5 (1968).

Blake, J.: Demographic science and the redirection of population policy. p. 41. In: *Public Health and Population Change*. M. Sheps and J.C. Ridley (Eds.). University of Pittsburgh Press, Pittsburgh (1965).

Blake, J.: Reproductive ideals and educational attainments among White Americans, 1943-60. *Population Studies*, 21: 159 (1967).

Bogue, D.J.: *Principles of Demography*. John Wiley and Sons, New York (1969).

Boldsen, J. L.: Season of birth and recalled age at menarche. *J. Bios. Sci.* 24: 167-173. (1992).

Bradshaw, B.S.: Fertility differences in Peru: A reconsideration. *Population Studies*, 23: 5 (1969).

Bravo-Casas, G.A.: Socio-economic factors affecting fertility decline in Colombia. p. 116. In: *Demographic Transition and Socio-Economic*

Development. Proceedings of the United Nations. UNFPA Expert Group Meeting, Istanbul, 1979. United Nations, New York (1979).

Brig, H. : World Population Projection for the Twenty-first Century: Theoretical Interpretations and Quantitative Simulations. New York: St. Martin's Press. (1995).

Brown, D.E., Koenig, T.V., Demorales, A.M. et.al.: Menarche age , fatness, and fat distribution in Hawaiian adolescents. *Am. J. Phys. Anthropol.* 99:239-247. (1996).

Bruch,Thomas K.: Expaining Human Fertility: One Theory or Many Theories? *http://www.sscl.uwo.ca/sociology/popstudies/dp/dp00-3.pdf*

Buck, A.A., Sasaki, T.T., Anderson, R.I., Hitchock, J. C. and Leigh, G.R.: *Health and Diseases in Four Peruvian Villages: Contrast in Epidemiology.* The Johns Hopkins University Press, Baltimore, Maryland (1968).

Busfield, J. : Age at Marriage and Family Size: Social Causation and Social Selection Hypothesis. *J. Biosoc. Sci.* 4 : 117. (1972).

Cain M.: *Women's Status and Fertility in Developing Countries: Son Preference and Economic Security.* Centre for Policy Studies Working Paper No. 110. Population Council, New York (1984).

Cain, M.: The economic activities of children in a village in Bangladesh. *Pop. Dev. Rev.*, 3: 201 (1977).

Caldwell, I.C.: Fertility and household economy in Nigeria. *Journal of Comparative Family Studies,* 7: 193 (1976).

Caldwell, I.C.: Perspective of fertility and mortality in Africa. p. 32. In: *Population Dynamics: Fertility and Mortality in Africa.* Proceeding of the Expert Group Meeting on Fertility and Mortality Levels and Trends in Africa and their Policy Implications. Monrovia, Liberia. 1979 United Nations Economic Commission for Africa (1981).

Caldwell, J.C., Reddy, P.H. and Caldwell, P. : The Causes of Demographic Change in Rural South India : A Micro Approach. *Population and Development Review.* 8 (4) 689-727. (1982).

Caldwell, J.C., Reddy, P.H. and Caldwell, P.: The determinants of fertility decline in rural South India: A micro-approach. *Pop. Dev. Rev.*, 8: 689 (1984).

Caldwell, J.C.: Mass education as a determinant of the timing of the fertility decline. *Pop. Dev. Rev.*, 6: 225 (1980).

Census of India, 1971. *Series I, India, Part -II -A* (ii), *.S'ocial Cultural Tables.* Office of the Registrar General and Census Commissioner, New Delhi (1976).

Census of India, 1981: *Series-8, Jammu and Kashmir District Census Handbook, Parts XIII-A and B. Village and Townwise Primary' Census Abstract, Kargil District.* Director of Census Operations, Jammu and Kashmir (1981).

Census of India, 1981: *Series-8, Jammu and Kashmir Parts XIII. Census Atlas.* Director of Census Operations, Jammu and Kashmir (1990).

Census of India, 1991. *Series 1. India Paper-2 of* 1992, *Final Population Totals, Brief Analysis of Primary Census Abstract.* Office of the Registrar General and Census Commissioner, New Delhi (1992).

Census of India,2001. *Series-3, Himachal Pradesh, Paper 1 of 2001, Provisional Population Totals,* Director of Census Operations Himachal Pradesh. (2001).

Census of India. 1981.*Series I. India Paper 5 of 1984. (Age Tables Based on 5 Percent Sample Data.* Office of the Registrar General and Census Commissioner, New Delhi (1984).

Chachra, S.P. and Bhasin, M.K.: Anthropo-demographic Study among the Caste and Tribal Groups of Central Himalayas: 1. Population Structure. *J. Hum. Ecol.* 9 (5) : 405-416 (1998a).

Chachra, S.P. and Bhasin, M.K.: Anthropo-demographic Study among the Caste and Tribal Groups of Central Himalayas: 2. Fertility Differentials and Determinants . *J. Hum. Ecol.* 9 (5) : 417-429 (1998b).

Chachra, S.P. and Bhasin, M.K.: Anthropo-demographic Study among the Caste and Tribal Groups of Central Himalayas: 3. Mortality Differentials and Determinants . *J. Hum. Ecol.* 9 (5) : 431-439 (1998c).

Chachra, S.P. and Bhasin, M.K.: Anthropo-demographic Study among the Caste and Tribal Groups of Central Himalayas: 4.Selection Intensities. *J. Hum. Ecol.* 9 (5) : 441-443 (1998d).

Chakravarti, I. and Sinha, A.K.: Declining age of menarchi, in West Bengal. *J. Ind Med. Assoc.*, 82: 10 (1991).

Chakravarti, S.K.: Selection Potential among Bengalee Muslims of Cachar. *J. Ind. Anthrop. Soc.* 11:177. (1976).

Chandra, R.: Highlanders of North Western Himalayas. Inter India Publications, Raja Garden New Delhi. (1992).

Chandrasekhar, S.: *infant Mortality. Population Growth and Family Planning in India.* George Allen and Unwin Ltd., London, (1972).

Chang, G.C., Warren, F.D. and Pendleton, B.F.: Testing and clarifying a macromodel of socio-economic change and fertility. *Soc. Biol.,* 26: 30 (1979).

Chaudhury, R.H.: Female status and fertility behaviour in metropolitan urban area of Bangladesh. *Population Studies.* 31: 261 (1978).

Chaudhury, R.H.: *Social Aspects of Fertility: With Special Reference to Developing Countries.* Vikas Publsihing House Pvt. Ltd., New Delhi (1982).

Chaudhury, S. : Selection Intensity of the Dakshnarahi Kayasthas in Metropolitan Calcutta. *J. Ind. Anthropol. Soc.* 11: 176. (1976).

Chengal Reddy, P. and M. Lakshanudu : Indices of opportunity of selection in Mala Madiga and other Indian Populations. *J. Ind. Anthropol. Soc.* 14: 245-252. (1979).

Clegg, E.J. : Fertility and early growth . In *The Biology of high altitude people.* (Ed.) P.T. Baker. Cambridge : Cambridge University Press. (1978).

Clegg, E.J., Harrison, G.A. and Baker, P.T.: The impact of High altitude on human populations. *Hum. Biol.,* 42: 486 (1970).

Clegg, E.J., Pawson, I.G., Ashton, E.H. and Flinn, R.M.: The growth of children at different altitudes in Ethiopia. *Philosophical Transactions of the Royal Society, Londo,* B 264: 403-37 (1972).

Cleland, J. and Rodriguez, G.: The effect of parental, education on marital fertility in developing countries. *Population Studies.* 42: 419 (1988).

Coale, A.I.: Factors associated with the development of low fertility: A historic summary. *Proceedings of the World Population Conference.* Vol. 2. 205 (1965).

Cochrane, S.R.: Effects of education and urbanization on fertility. In: *Determinants of Fertility in Developing Countries.* 2. *Fertility Regulation and Institutional Influence.* R.A. Bulatao and R.D. Lee (Eds.). with P.E. Hollerbach and J. Bongaarts. Reports of the National Research Council Committee on Population and Demography. Academic Press, New York (1983).

Cohen, J.E. and Small, C. : Hypsographic demography: The distribution of human population by altitutde. *Applied Physical*

Science, Social Sciences; Proc. Natl. Acad. Sci. USA, 95: 14009-14014 (1998)

Collver, A.O. and Langois, E.: The female labour force in metropolitan areas: An international comparison. *Eco. Dev. Cult. Change.* 10: 367 (1962).

Collver, A.O.: Women's work participation and fertility in metropolitan areas. *Demograph*, 5: 55 (1966).

Coombs, L.C.: Preferences for sex of children among U.S. couples. *Fam. Plann. Persp.*, 9: 259 (1977).

Coon, C.S.: Some problems of human variability and natural selection in climate and culture. *Am. Nat.*, 89: 257 (1955).

Crane, C.G., Hornabrook, R.W. and Kelly, A. : Anaemia on the coast and highlands of New Guinea. *Hum. Biol. Oceania*, 1 : 234-242 (1972).

Crow, F.J.: Some possibilities of measuring selection intensities in man. *Hum. Bioi..* 30: I (1958).

Crow, J.F.: The equality of people: Human evolutionary changes. *Biosciences*, 16: 863 (1966).

Cruz-Coke, R., A. P. Cristoffanni, A. Aspillaga, and F. binanacani : Evolutionary forces in human population in an environmental gradient in Arica. *Human Biology*, 38: 421-38, (1966).

Cruz-Coke, R.: A genetic description of high altitude population. In the biology of high altitude peoples, (Ed.) P. T. Baker. Cambridge: Cambridge University Press, (1978).

Cruz-Coke, R.: Genetic characteristics of high altitude populations in Chile. *Paper presented as PAHO/WHO IBP Meeting of investigators on Population Biology of Altitude.* Washington D.C. (1967).

Daland, G.A. and Castle, W.B.: A simple and rapid method of demonstrating sickling of red blood cells : the use of readucing agent. *J. Lab. Clin. Med.*3:1085- 8 (1948).

Dandekar, K.: Effect of education on fertility. *World Population Conference, Belgrade*, 1965. Vol. 4. United Nations, New York (1966).

Danker, H. : Menarcheal age in Europe. *Yearbook of Physical Anthropology* 29: 81-112. (1986).

Danker-Hopfe, H. and Delibalta, K.: Menarcheal age of Turkish girls in Bremen? *Anthropol. Anz.*, 48:1-14 (1990).

Danker-Hopfe. D.: Menarcheal age in Europe. *Am. J. Phys. Anthrop. (Year Book)*, 29: 81 (1986).

Das Gupta, M.: Selective discrimination against female children in rural Punjab, India. *Pop. Dev. Rev.*. 13: 77 (1987).

Das, B. M. :Outline of physical Anthropology. Kitab Mahal, Allahabad. (1999).

Das, F.A. and Saikia, J.R.: Some aspects of fertility of the Garo women of Pochimbosti Garo Village in Sibsagar District, Assam; *J.Hum.Ecol., 10 (4): 273-277* (1999).

Das, P.B. & Das, B.M.: Age at menarche of Kalita girls in Assam. *Man In India*, 47. (1966).

Das, S. K., P. P. Mazumder, and A. Basu : Demography and demographical genetics of two isolated mountain villages of northern Sikkim. Journal of the Indian Anthropological society 17: 155-62, (1981).

Datta, S. : Differential fertility in West Bengal in 1956. *Artha Vijana*, 3: 67 (1961).

Davis, K. : Institutional patterns favouring high fertility in under developed areas. *Eug. Quart.*,2: 33 (1955).

Davis, K.: Population Policy: Will current programme succeed? *Science*, 158: 730 (1967).

Davis, K.: The theory of change and response in modern demographic history. *Population Index*, 29: 345 (1963).

Day, L.H.: Natality and ethnocentrism: Some relationship suggested by an analysis of Catholic -Protestant differentials. *Populaiton Studies*, 22: 27 (1968).

De Jong, G.F.: Patterns of human fertility .p. 32. In: *The Structure of Human Populations*. G.A. Harrison and A.J. Boyce (Eds.). Clarendon Press, Oxford (1972).

De Jong: The impact of High altitude on human populations. *Hum. Biol.*, 42: 486 (1968).

De Jung, G.F. Demography and research with high altitude population, *Soc. Biol.*17:114 (1970).

De Pranab Jyoti: The Kinnaura Stratification: An Appraisal Past and Present, *J. Anthrop.Surv.India* 52: 85-94 (2003).

Demery, L. and Renselaar, J.V.: The demographic consequences of employment and income distribution planning. Paper No.2.

Seminar on Population Employment and Development in ASEAN Countries, Bangkok, 1978. Report and Background Papers, International Labour Office, Regional Office for Asia and the Pacific, Bangkok (1979).

Dixon, R.B.: Women's rights and fertility. *Reports on Population / Family Planning No.17.* The Population Council, New York (1975).

Do, K.A., Treolar, S.A., Pandey, N., et.al. : Predictive factors of age at menopause in a large Australian twin study. *Hum.Biol.* 70: 1073-1091 (1998).

Donayre, J. : Population growth and fertility at high altitude. In *Life at high altitude.* A. Hurtado (Ed.) Scientific Publication No. 140. Washington D.C.: Pan American Health Organization (1966)..

Dorn, H.F.: Mortality p. 437. In : *The Study of Population: An Inventory and Appraisal.* P.M. Hauser and O.D. Duncan (Eds.). University of Chicago Press, Chicago, (1972).

Doyanre, J. : Population growth and fertility at high altitude. In life at high altitude, (Ed.) by A. Hurtado. Scientific Publication No. 140Washington D. C : Pan American Health Organization, (1966).

Driver, E.D.: Fertility differentials among economic strata in central India. *Eug. Quart.,* 7: 15 (1960).

Driver, E.D.: *Fertility Differentials in Central India.* Princeton University Press, Princeton (1963).

Duarah, A.: A Study of certain aspects of Demography among the Adis of Mirbuk Villages, Pasighat, NEFA. Dissertation (Unpublished) submitted to Dibrugarh University (Cited by Kar and Mahanta, In *Indian Jr. of Phys. Anthrop. Hum. Genet.,* 1975). (1989).

Durand, J.: Demography's Three Hundredth Anniversary, Population Index, 28, 4, 333-334 (1962).

Dutt, J.S.: Altitude and fertility: The confounding effect of childhood mortality- A Bolivian example. *Social Biology,* 27: 101-13 (1980).

Dwight W., Read and Steven A. Le Blanc: Population Growth Carrying Capacity and Conflict. *Current Anthropology,* 44, I: 59-85 (2003).

Dyson, T. and Moore, M.: On kinship structure, female autonomy and demographic behaviour in India. *Pop. Dev. Rev..* 9: 35 (1983).

Early, J.D.: Low forager fertility: Demographic characteristics or methodological approach? *Hum. Biol.,* 57: 387 (1985).

Eaton, J.W. and Mayer, A.G. : Social Biology of Very High Fertility among the Hutterities: The Demography of a Unique Population: *Hum. Biol.* 25 (3): 206-264. (1953).

Eberstadt, N.: Recent declines in fertility in less developed countries and what 'Population Planners, may learn from them. *World Development*, J8: 39 (1980).

Ehrlich, P. and Ehrlich, A. : The Population Explosion. New York: Simon and Schuster, and London: Hutchinson. (1990).

Ehrlich, P.: Population Bomb. New York: Ballantine (1968); London: Pan. (1971).

Ekanem, I.: A further note on the relation between economic development and fertiliy. *Demography*, 9: 383 (1972).

Ekvall, R. B. : Demographic aspects of Tibetan nomadic pastoralism. In population growth : Anthropological implication, (Ed.) B. Spooner. Cambridge : Massachusetts Institute of Technology, (1972).

El-Badry, M.A.: A study of differential fertility in Bombay. *Demography*, 4: 626 (1967).

Encyclopædia Britannica Atlas: *Encyclopædia Britannica.* 2003 Ultimate Reference Suite CD-ROM, (2003).

Encyclopædia Britannica: *Encyclopædia Britannica* 2003 Ultimate Reference Suite CD-ROM. (2003).

ESCAP: Population Data Sheet, Population and Development Indicators for Asia and the Pacific, 2001; Economic and Social Commission for Asia and Pacific, Bangkok (2001).

Espenshade, T .J.: Estimating the economic cost of children in less developed countries: Some methodological issues. *Paper Presented at the Session on Value and Cost of Children to Parents at the Seventh General Conference of the International Union for the Scientific Study of Population, Mexico City* (1977).

Farooq, G.M. and Tuncer, B.: Fertility and economic social development in Turkey: A cross sectional and time series study. *Population Study*, 28: 263 (1974).

Fedrick, J.: Encephalus: Variation with Marital Age, Parity, Social Class and Religion in England, .Scotland and Wales. *Ann. Hum. Genet.* 34: 31-37. (1970).

Fernando, D.F.S.: Social and demographic determinants of fertility in Sri Lanka. *J. Biosoc. Sci.*, 14: 59 (1982).

Fisher, R.A. : *The Genetical Theory of Natural Selection.* Oxford University Press, London (1930).

Flinn, M. V.: Correlates of reproductive success in a Carribean village *Hum. Eco.*, 14: 225 (1986).

Flint, M.P.: Menarche and menopause of Rajput women. Unpublished Ph.D. thesis, University of New York, New York, USA. (Cited by Bealls, 1983) (1974).

Flint, M.P.: Secular trends in menopause age. *J. Psychosom. Obstet. Gynaecol.*, 18: 65-72. (1997).

Freedman, D., Thornton, A. and Wallisch, L.: Age at first birth and family size: Evidence from longitudinal study. *Soc. Biol.*, 28: 217 (1981).

Freedman, R. and Coombs, L.C.: *Cross Cultural Comparisons: Data on Two Factors in Fertility Behaviour.* Occasional Paper of the Population Council, New York, p.13 (1974).

Freedman, R.: Expected family size and family size values in West Germany. *Population Studies*, 13: 136 (1959).

Freedman, R.: The sociology of human fertility: A trend report and bibliography. *Curr. Sociol.*, 10. 11: 35 (1963).

Frisancho, A.R. and Baker, P.T. : Altitude and growth of a high altitude Peruvian Quencha population. *Am. J. Phys. Anthrop.*, 32: 279 (1970).

Frisancho, A.R. and Cossman, A.J. : Secular trend in neonatal mortality in the mountain sates. *Am. J. Phys. Anthrop.*, 33: 103 (1970).

Frisancho, A.R., Klayman, J.E. and Matos, J.: Symbiotic relationship of high fertility, high childhood mortality and socio economic status in an urban Peruvian population. *Hum. Biol.*, 48: 101 (1976).

Frisancho, A.R.: Ecological interpretations of postnatal growth at high altitude. In: *Environmental and Human Population Problems at High Altitude.* P.T. Baker and C. Jest (Eds.). CNRS, Paris (1981).

Gaisie, S.K.: Mortality, socio-economic differentials and modernization in Africa. p.441. In.: *Population Dynamics: Fertility and Mortality in Africa, Proceedings of the Expert Group Meeting on Fertility and Mortality Levels and Trends in Africa and Their Policy Implications, Monrovia; Liberia,* 1979. United Nations Economic Commission for Africa (1981).

Gange, T.B., McCullough, I.M., Weitz, C.Z. Dutt, J.S., and Abelson, A.: Demographic studies and human population biology. p.45.

In: *Human Population Biology: A Transdisciplinary Science.* M.A. Little and I.D. Hass (Eds.). Oxford Univeristy Press, New York, (1989).

Gautam, R. K. and Jyoti, R.: Primitive Tribe in Post-Modern Era with special reference to Baigas of Central India. In *The Primitive Tribes in Contemporary India.* (Ed.) S. K. Choudhary [In Press] (2005).

Gautam, R. K. and Sharma A. N.: Evaluation of Awareness regarding Sickle Cell among Sicklers and Non-Sicklers of Mehra (Jhariya) of Mandla district, Madhya Pradesh, Central India. *South Asian Anthropologist;*3 (2): 107-110. (2003).

Gautam, R. K. and Sharma A. N.: The Nicobarese of Harminder Bay, Little Andaman, India. *South Asian Anthropologist;* 4 (1): 1-11 (2004).

Gautam, R. K. and Sharma, A. N.: Anthropological Approach to the Development of few Isolated Tribes of Andaman Islands. In *Tribal Development in Andaman Islands* (Ed) A.N. Sharma; Sarup and Sons, New Delhi-110002 p.81-88 (2003).

Gautam, R. K. and Sharma, A. N.: Occurrence of Sickle Gene and Malaria Among the Mehra (Jhariya) Caste of Mandla District, Madhya Pradesh, India. *Anthropologist,* 4 (4): 281-283 (2002).

Gautam, R. K. and Tekhre, Y.L. : Determinants Contraceptive acceptance among Males of District Kullu Himachal Pradesh, India. *South Asian Anthropologist.* 5 (1): 45-59 (2005).

Gautam, R. K.: A comparative study of welfare and developmental issues of Baiga Chak, Dindori District, Madhya Pradesh and Nicobarese of Andaman and Nicobar Islands. In *Tribal Development in Andaman Islands* (Ed) A.N. Sharma; Sarup and Sons, New Delhi-110002 p.43-51 (2003).

Gautam, R. K.: Living Fossils of Human Being: The Primitive Tribes of Andaman and Nicobar Islands. In *The Primitive Tribes in Contemporary India.* (Ed.) S. K. Choudhary. [In Press] (2005).

Gautam, R. K.: SARS. *Dharna (Hindi Magazine of National Institute of Health &Family Welfare),* 9: 44-53 (2004)

Gautam, R.K., Adak, D.K., Gharami, A.K. and Dutta, T.: Body Mass Index in Central India: Inter District Variation. *Anthropol. Anz.,* [In Press] (2005).

Gautam, R.K., Misra, A.M. and Sharma, A.N.: Traditional Health Care Practices among Sicklers and Non-sicklers of Mehra (Jhariya) a

Scheduled Caste Population of Mandla District, Madhya Pradesh. *Anthropologie,* [In Press] (2005).

Gautam, R.K., Sharma, A.N., Gharami, A.K. and Gupta, A.: Trend and Determinants of Family Planning Practices among the Tribals of Andaman and Nicobar Islands: With special reference to Nicobarese of Harminder Bay, Little Andaman, India. *In the proceeding of National Seminar on Tribal Health In India: Perspective and Challenges,* Department of Anthropology, Pondicherry University [In Press] (2005).

Gautam, R.K.: Sickle Cell Aneamia : Anuvansic Bimari. *Dharna (Hindi Magazine of National Institute of Health &Family Welfare),* 10: 36-45 (2005).

Germain, A.: Status and role of woman as factor in fertility behaviour: A policy analysis. *Stud. Fam. Plann.,* 6: 192 (1975).

Gharami, A. K. and Adak, D. K.: Opportunity for Natural Selection among the Ladiya of Madhya Pradesh. *Anthropologist,* 2 (4): 261-262. (2000).

Gharami, A.K. and Mandal, B. K.: Genetic Demography of the Ladiya of Sagar District, Madhya Pradesh. *Anthropologist,* 3 (3): 213-214. (2001).

Gharami, A.K., Sharma, A.N., and Adak, D.K.: Selection intensity among the Kol of Madhya Pradesh. *South Asian Anthropologist,* 3 (2): 197-201. (2003).

Ghosh, A.K. : Selection intensity in the Kota of Nilgiri Hills, Madras. *Soc.Biol.* 17:224-225. (1970).

Ghosh, A.K. and Limbu, D. K.: The Semsa— A Bio-Demographic Study. In Tribal studies in North East India (edn.) by Sengupta, S.; A Mittal publication, 129-145. (2002).

Ghosh, B.: Recent study in socio and economic determinants in fertility: A review and a critique. *J. Family Welfare,* 21: 38 (1975).

Gill, M.S.: 'Marriage and Polyandry'. In *Himalayan Wonderland.* New Delhi: Vikas Publishing House. 140-152. (1972).

Gogoi, D. : Menarche and Menopause among women of a Ahom village in Upper Assam. *The Bulletin of the Department of Anthropology, Dibrugarh University.* (1972).

Goldstein, M.C., Tsarong, P. and Beall, C.M. : High altitude hypoxia, culture and human fecundity/fertility: A comparative study. *Am. Anthrop.,* 85: 28 (1983).

Goldstein, M.C., Tsarong, P. and Beall, C.M: High at. titude hypoxia, culture and human fecundity/fer- tility: A comparative study. *Am. Anthrop.*, 85: 28 (1983).

Goldstein, M.C.: High altitude Tibetan Population in the remote Himalaya: Social Transformation and its demographic, economic and ecological consequences, *Mountain & Research and Development*, 1:5.(1981).

Goldstein, M.C.: Pahari and Tibetan Polyandry Revisited. Ethnology, 17 (3): 325-327 (1978).

Goldstein, M.C.: When Brothers Share a Wife. Natural History, 96 (3): 109-112 (1987)

Goldstein. S.: The influence of labour force participation and education on fertility in Thailand. *Population Studies*, 26: 419 (1972).

Gonzales, G.F. and Villena, A.: Body mass index and age at menarche in Peruvian children living at high altitude and at sea level. *Hum. Biol.*, 68: 265-275. (1996).

Goody. I.R., Duly. C.I., Beeson, I. and Harrison. G.: Implicit sex preference: A comparative study. *J. Biosoc. Sci.*, 13: 455 (1981).

Gould. K.H.: Comments. *Curr. Anthrop.*, 13: 249 (1972).

Government of India: India Country Report, fifth Asian and pacific population conference on population and poverty in Asia and pacific, Bangkok. 11-17 December 2002. (2002).

Government of India: Report of Reproductive & Child Health Project Proposal & Implementation Plan, Vol.-I, Directorate Of Health Services, Ministry Of Health & Family Welfare, New Delhi, March 1997. (1997).

Grabill. W. H. Kiser. C. V. and Whelpton. P. K.: *The Fertility of American Wolnen*. John Wiley and Sons, New York (1958).

Graff H.I.: Literacy, education and fertility, past and present: A critical review. *Pop. Dev. Rev.*, 5: 105 (1979).

Grahn, D., and Kratchman, J.: Variation in neonatal death rate and birth weight in the United States and possible relations to environmental radiation, geology and altitude. *Am. J. Hum. Genet.*, 15: 329-52 (1963).

Gray, R. : Biological factors other than Nutrition and Lactation which may Influence Natural Fertility: A Review. In *Natural Fertility,*

H. Leridon and J. Marken (eds.), Ordina Editions, Leige. (1979).

Gray, R.H. and Doyle, P.E.: The epidemiology of conception and fertility. In *Obstetrical Epidemiology,* S.L.Barron and A.M. Thompson, eds. London, England: Acedemic Press, 25-59. (1983).

Grey, R.H., Doyle, P.E.: The epidemiology of conception and fertility. In *Obstetrical Epidemiology,* S.L.Barron and A.M. Thompson (eds.). London, England: Academic Press, 25-29 (1983).

Gunasundaramma, K. and Reddy, V.R.: Age at menarche among the Balijas of Tirupati, South India, 4th Annual Conference of Indian Society of Human Genetics (Abstract) pp34 (1977).

Gupta, R. : Altitude and demography among the Sherpas. *J. Biosoc. Sci.,* 12:103 (1980).

Gupta, R. : Culture and demography among the high altitude Sherpas. *Paper presented at the Seminar on Population Structure among Tribes.* Tribal Research Center, Tamil University, Ooty, India (1985).

Gupta, R. : Selection intensity in the Sherpa. *Curr. Anthrop.,*21: 136 (1980).

Gupta, R., Basu, A., Pawson, I.G., Bharati, P., Majumder, P.P., Bhattacharya, S. K., Bhattacharya, K. K., and Das, I.K.: Altitude and Human Biology: A comparative study of Himalayan, Andean and Ethiopian Data. *J. Indian Anthropo. Soc.,* 22: 101 (1987).

Gupta, R., Basu, A., Pawson, I.G., Bharati, P., Mukhopadhyay, B., Mukhopadhyay, S., Roy, S.K., Majumder, P.P., Bhattacharya, S.K., Bhattacharya, K.K., and Das, S.K.: Altitude and Human Biology: A comparative Study of Himalayan, Andean and Ethiopian Data. In *Human Biology of Asian Highland Populations in the Global Context,* (Eds.) A. Basu and R. Gupta. The Indian Anthropological Society, Calcutta; 1-80. (1989).

Gupta, R., Das, S.K. and Bhattacharya, S.K. : Altitude and haematology among the Sherpas and Lepchas of the eastern Himalayas. Garcia de orta, Ser. Anthropobiol., 3 : 3-10 (1984).

Hall. R.L.: The demographic transition: Stage four. *Curr. Anthrop.,* 13: 212 (1972).

Harrington. I.A.: The effect of high infant and child- hood mortality on fertility: The West African Case. *Demography,* 3: 22 (1971).

Harris, C.W., Shields, J.L. and Hannon, J.P. : Acute altitude sickness in females. *Aerospace Medicine* 37: 1163-67 (1966).

Harrison, G.A., Kuchemann, C.F., Moore, M.A.S., Boyce, A.J. Baju, T., Mourant, A.E., Godber, M.J., Glasgow, B.G., Kopec, A.C., Tills, D., and Clegg, E.J.: The effects of altitudinal variation in Ethiopian populations. *Philosophical Transactions of the Royal Society of London,* 256 B: 147 (1969).

Harrison, G.A.: Population genetics – gene frequency changes. p. 208. In: *An Introduction to Human Evolution, Variation, Growth and Adaptability.* G.A. Harrison, J.M. Tanner, D.R. Pilbeam, P.T. Baker. Oxford University Press, Oxford (1990).

Hartman, B. : Reproductive Rights and Wrongs: The Global Politics of Population Control and Contraceptive Choice. New York: Harper. (1987).

Hashmi, S.S.: The people of Karachi: Demographic characteristics. *Monographs in Economics of Development No.* 13. Pakistan Institute of Development Economics, Karachi (1965).

Hasnain, N: Tribal India. Palka Prakashan, Delhi (2001).

Heath, D. and Williams, D.K.: *Man at High Altitude.* Churchill Livingstone, Edinburgh (1981).

Heer, D.M. : Fertility differences in Andean countries: A reply to W.H. James. *Population Studies,* 21:71-73 (1965).

Heer, D.M. : Fertility differences in Andean Countries: A reply to W .H. James. *Population Studies,* 1.1 : 71 (1967)

Heer, D.M. and Smith, D. : Mortality levels, desired family size and population increase. *Demography,* 5: 104 (1968).

Heer, D.M. and Turner, E.S.: A real difference in Latin American fertility. *Population Studies,* 18:279 (1965).

Heer, D.M. and Wu, H.: The effect of infant and child mortality and preference for sons upon fertility and family behaviour and attitudes in Taiwan. p. 253. In: *Population and Development in South East Asia.* J.F. Kantner and L. Mcs. Caffrey (Eds.). Lexington, D.C. Heath, Mass. (1975).

Heer, D.M.: Economic Development and fertility. *Demography,* 3: 423 (1966).

Heer, D.M.: Fertility differences between Indian and Spanish speaking parts of Andean countries. *Population Studies,* 9:71 (1964).

Hillman, R.W., Slator, P.and Nelson, M.O.: Season of brth, parental age, menarcheal age and body form; some inter-relation in young women. *Hum. Biol.,* 42: 370 (1970).

Hoff, C.J. : Reproduction and viability in a highland Peruvian Community. *Occasssional Papersin Anthropology*, I: 85160. The Pennsylvania State University, University Park (1968).

Hoff, C.J. and Abelson, A.E. : Fertility. p. 128 In: *Man in the Andes: A Mulit-Disciplinary study of High Altitude Quencha.* (Eds.) P. T. Baker and M.A. Little, Dowden, Hutchson and Ross, Stroudsburg (1976).

Hoff: C.J.: Is there significant hypoxic depression of fertility among Andean natives? A reply to Goldstein, Tsarong and Beall. *Am. Anthrop.*, 86: 417 (1984).

Howell, N. : *Demography of the Dobe/kung.* Academic Press, New York (1979).

Hunt, E. Jr., and Newcomer, N.W.: The timing and variability of menarche, cumulative fertility and menopause : Asymmetrical and parsimonious bioassay model. *Hum. Biol.* 56: 47-62. (1984).

Husain I. Z. : Educational status and differential fertility in India. *Soc. Biol.*, 17: 132 (1970).

Inoue, S.: Choice of policy measures to affect fertility: A computer microsimulation study. *Polulation Bulletin of the United Nations, No.10.* United Nations, N.Y. (1978).

Jaffe, A.J.: *People, Jobs and Economic Development.* The Free Press, Glencoe, Illinois (1959).

Jain, A.K. and Visaria, P. : Infant Mortality in India: Differentials and Determinants, Sage Publication, New Delhi (1988).

Jain, A.K.: The effect of female education on fertility: A simple explanation. *Demography*, 18: 577 (1981).

Jain, S.P .: Some aspects of mortality. p. 319. In: *Populatlon in India's Development:* 1947-2000. A. Hose, P. B. Desai and A. Mitra (Eds.). Vikas Publishing House, New Delhi (1974).

Jain, S.P. : *A status Study on Population Research in India* Vol. II. *Demography.* Tata McGraw Hill Pub Co., New Delhi (1975).

James, W.H. : The effect of high altitude on fertility in Andean countries. *Population Studies*, 20:97 (1966).

Johnston, F.E. and Kensinger, K.M.: Fertility and mortality differentials and their implications for microevolutionary change among the Cashinahua. *Hum. Biol.*, 43: 356 (1971).

Jones, G. W .: Fertility levels and trends in Indonesia. *Population Studies*, 31: 29 (1977).

Jones, G.W.: The Continuing Demographic Transition. New York: Oxford University Press and Oxford: Clarendon Press. (1997).

Kapoor, A.K. : Ecology and Development in Himalayas. In S.K. Chada, (Ed.). *Fragile Environment.* Anmol Publication, New Delhi. (1993).

Kapoor, A.K. and Kapoor, S.: The Secular Growth Trend among Himalayan Populations. *Anthrop. Kozl.* 29: 85-88. (1985).

Kapoor, A.K. and Patra, P.K.: Selection Intensity in a High Altitude Tribe of Central Himalayas. *Ind. Anth.* 28 (2): 81-87. (1998)

Kapoor, A.K. and Singh, D. : *Rural Development through NGOs.* Rawat Publications, Jaipur. (1997).

Kapoor, A.K. and. Kapoor, S: The effects of high altitude on age at menarche and menopause. *International Journal of Biometeorology,* 30, 1, 21-6 (1986).

Kapoor, A.K., Kshatriya, G.K. and Kapoor S.: Fertility and Mortality Differentials among Population Groups of the Himalayas. *Hum. Biol.*75 (5), 729-747 (2003).

Kapoor, A.K., Tiwari, S.C., Prasad, R.P.: Semi-Nomadism and Transhumance in Central Himalayas: A Pragmatic Perspective. *Man in India.* 70 (1): 47-60. (1990)

Kapoor, A.K.: Ecology and Tribal in Central Himalayas. In: *Ecology and Man in the Himalayas,* (eds.) A.K. Kapoor and Satwanti Kapoor. M.D. Publications Pvt. Ltd., New Delhi, pp. 69-90, (1994).

Kapoor, A.K.: Ecology, Demographic profile and Socio-economic Development of a Tribe of Central Himalayas. In P.K. Samal (ed.), *Tribal Development : Options (Proceedings of a National Seminar).* Pp. 118-138. Gynoday Prakashan, Nainital (1996).

Kapoor, A.K.: Enviroment Technology and Development- An Anthropological study of a Non-Governmental Organization (NGO) in Himachal Pradesh. *Man and Life.* 26 (3 & 4): 137-159 (2000).

Kapoor, A.K.: *Genetic Diversity among Himalayan Populations.* Vinod Publishers and distributers, Jammu. (1992)

Kapoor, A.K.: The Environment and Settlement Patterns of the Bhotia in the Central Himalayas. In: *Central Himalayan Panorama.* (Ed.). S.K. Biswas, Institute of Social Research and Applied Anthropology, Calcutta, (1) : 169-179. (1993)

Kapoor, S.: Research Planning and Development in the Himalayan Region. In A.K. Kapoor and D. Singh, (eds.) *Man and Development in the Himalayas, pp.* 197-211. Academic Foundation, Delhi. (1996)

Kaprio, J., Rimpela, A., Winter, T. et.al.: Common genetic influences on BMI and age at menarche. *Hum. Biol.* 6: 739-753. (1995).

Kar, R.K. and Mahanta, S.: Menarche and menopause among the Singpho women of Arunachal Pradesh. *Ind. Jr. Phys. Anthrop & Hum. Genet.*, 1: 51-57. (1975).

Kasarda, D.: Economic structure and fertility: A comparative analysis. *Demography,* 8: 307 (1971).

Kasarda, J.D., Billy, J.O.G. and West, K.: *Status Enhancement and Fe11ility.* Academic Press, Orlando, Florida (1986).

Kashiwazaki, H., Suzuki, T. and Takemoto, T.: Altitude and reproduction of the Japanese in Bolivia. *Hum. Biol.*, 16: 831 (1988).

Kaul, V.: Genetic Heterogeneity among the populations of Himachal Pradesh. In: Anthropology at the turn of the Century, Department of Anthropology, Panjab University, Chandigarh, pp. 139-148 (2000).

Kertzer, D.I. and Fricke, T.: Towards an Anthropological Demography. In Anthropological Demography, Towards and New Synthesis (edn.) by Kertzer, D.I. and Fricke, T.; The University of Chicago Press, Chicago and London (1999).

Ketker, S.L.: Determinants of fertility in a developing society: The case of Sierra Leone. *Population Studies.* 33: 479 (1979).

Khatoniar, A.: Demographic study of the Mikirs of Assam (Unpublished dissertation, submitted in Dibrugrah University, Dibrugarh) Cited by Kar and Mahanta In *Ind. Jr. Phys. Anthrop & Hum. Genet.* (1972).

Khongsdier, R.: Fertility and Mortality differentials among the war Khasi of Meghalaya. In Tribal studies in North East India (edn.) by Sengupta, S.; A Mittal publication, 147-159. (2002).

Kirchengast, S. : Relations between fertility, body shape and menopause in Austrian women. *J. Bios. Sci.* 24: 555-559 (1992).

Kirk, D.: Factors affecting Moslem natality. In: *Family Planning and Population Programme.* B. Berelson et. al. (Eds.). University of Chicago Press, Chicago (1966).

Kiser, C. V.: *Differential Fertility in the United States.* National Bureau of Economic Research, Princeton (1960).

Kotal, M and Baruah, P: A Biodemographic study smong the Digru Mishimi of Arunachal Pradesh. *South Asian Anthropologist;* 4 (1): 41-47. (2004).

Kshatriya, G.K. : Dimensions of tribal health: Few considerations. Paper presented at National Seminar on Tribal Health. Feb. 16th to 18th , 1999 organised by the Department of Anthropology, Doctor H.S. Gour University, Sagar (1999b).

Kshatriya, G.K. : Estimates of fertility and mortality among the Santals of Mayurbhanj district, Orissa. [*In Press*], (Cited from Kshatriya, 2000) , (1999a).

Kshatriya, G.K. : Tribal health study : Determinants of genetic and socio-cultural aspects of health vis-à-vis the role of health providers among the tribes of coastal, desert and Himalayan regions, *Final Report Submitted to Indian Council of Medical Research (ICMR), New Delhi* (2004).

Kshatriya, G.K. and Basu S. : Fertility and mortality trends in Dudh Kharia tribal population of Sundergarh district, Orissa. Paper Presented at the International Symposium on Human Genetics and Variation and XVIII Snn. Conf. Ind. Soc. Hum. Genet., Hyderabad. Jan. 1993. (1992-93).

Kshatriya, G.K., Singh, P. and Basu S. : Fertility and mortality in Bison Horn Madias of Dantewara tehsil of Bastar District of MP. *J. Hum. Ecol.*, 4, 93 (1993).

Kshatriya, G.K., Singh, P. and Basu, S.: Anthropo-demographic features and health care practices among the Jaunsaris of Jaunsar-Bawar, Dehradun, UP. *J. Hum. Ecol.*, 8: 347 (1997).

Kshatriya, G.K.: Ecology and Health with special Reference to Indian Tribes. *Human Ecology Special Issue No.*, 9: 229-245 (2000).

Kuroda, T.: An analysis of the change of fertility in Postwar Japan. *Archives of the Population Association of Japan {English Edition)*,.4: 24 (1963).

Lancaster, H. O. : Expectations of Life: A Study in the Demography, Statistics, and History of World Mortality. New York: Springer-Verlag. (1990).

Lang, S.D.R. and Lang, A.: The Kunde hospital and a demographic survey of the Upper Khumbu, Nepal. *New Zealand Medical Journal*, 74: 1 (1971).

Lannoy, R.: *The Speaking Tree A Study of Indian Culture and Society* Oxford University Press, London (1971).

Lapham, R.J. Wright. N.H., Quandt, M.D. and Quandt. S.: The influence or special mortality reduction programme on fertility: An initial look at some empirical data and measurements problems. p. 247 *Paper Presented at the Seminar on Infant Martality in Relation to the Level of the Fertility. Bangkok,* CICRED Series, Paris (1975).

Lasker, G.W.: Mixture and Genetic drift in ongoing human evolution, *American Anthropologist*, 54: 433-436. (1952).

Laurenson, L.F., Beton. M.A., Bishop, A.J. and Maacie-Taylor. C.G.N.,: Fertility at low and high altitude in Central Nepal *Soc. Biol.* 32: 65 (1985).

Lebedeva, L.M. and Musuraliev, M.S.: Some features or adaptation to hypoxia in female, at high altitude or the Pamir and low altitudes of Tien-Shan *J. Ind. Anthrop. Soc.*, 22: 226 (1987).

Leibenstein, II.: Conceptual framework for research on relaitons between socio-economic development and fertility decline. p 31. In *Demographic Transition and Socio-economic Development. Proceedings of the UN/UNFPA Experts Group Meeting. Istanbul. 1977.* Department or International Economic and Social Affairs, United Nations, New York (1979).

Leiberman, S.S.: *An Economic Approach la Differential Demographic Behaviour in Turkey* Ph.D. Dissertation (Unpublished). Harvard University (1977).

Levedeva, I.M. and Musuraliev, M.S.: Some features of adaptation to hypoxia in female at high altitudes of the Pamir and Low altitude of Tien-Shan. *J. Ind. Anthrop. Soc.*22: 226 (1987).

Lorimer, F. : The development of Demography. In: The study of population by Philip Ms. Hauser and Otis Dudley Duncan (Eds.), The University of Chicago Press, p. 129 (1959).

Lorimer, F., Fortes. M, Busia, K.A., Richards, A.I., Reinig, P. and Mortara, G.: *Culture and Human Fertility,* UNESCO. Paris (1954).

Luoto, R., Kapiro, J. and Uutela, A.: Age at natural menopause and socio-demographic status in Finland. *Am. J. Epidemiol.* 139: 64-76 (1994).

Lutz, W. : Distributional Aspects of Human Fertility: A Global Comparative Study. London: Academic Press. (1989).

Mabadevan, K.: *Infant and Childhood Mortality in India.* Mittal Publications, Delhi (1985).

MacMohan, B. and McKeown, T.: The Incidence of Hare tip and Cleft Palate Related to Birth Rank and Marital Age. *Am. J. Hum. Genet.* 5: 176-183 (1953).

Mahadevan, K.: *Sociology of Fertility Determinants of Fertility Differentials in South India.* Sterling Publishers, New Delhi. (1979).

Mahadevan, K: *Population Dynamics in Indian States Fertility and Family Formation and Mortality and Life Affecting Variables.* Mittal Publications, New Delhi (1989).

Majumdar, P. : Habitat, Society and Development in Ladakh. *Eastern Anthropologist;* 56: 2-4. (2003)

Majumder (Paul), G. : The Oraons of Barasat: A study on some aspect of demography. *J. Hum. Ecol.,* 14 (2): 133-136 (2003).

Malik, S.L. and Hauspie, R.: Age at menarche among high altitude Bods of Ladakh (India). *Hum.Biol.,* 58 (4): 541-548 (1986).

Malina, R.M.: Menarche in athletes: a synthesis and hypothesis. *Ann. Hum. Biol.* 10:1-24 (1983).

Malthus, T.R.: An Essay on the Principle of Population as It Affects the Future Improvement of Society, with Remarks on the Speculations of Mr. Godwin, M. Condorcet, and Other Writers. (Cited from Encyclopaedia Britannica, 2003) (1798).

Mamdani, M.: The idelogy of population control, p.39. In: *And the Poor Get Children:* K.L. Michaelson (Ed.). Monthly Review Press, New York (1981).

Mandelbaum, D.G.: *Human Fertility in India: Social Components and Policy Perspectives.* University of California Press, Berkeley (1974).

Mann, R.S. : Environment Ecology and Culture Paradigms, Case study of Ladakhi Tribe. In: studies on man, Issues and challenges, Kamal-Raj Enterprises, Delhi, India. 235-243 (2000).

Matsunaga, E.: Possible genetic consequences of family planning. . *Am. Med. Assoc.,* 198: 533 (1966).

May, D.A. and Heer, D.M.: Son survivorship, motivation and family size in India: A computer simulation. *Population Studies,* 22: 199 (1968).

Mazess, R.B. : Neonatal mortality and altitude in Peru. *American Journal of Physical Anthropology* 23: 209-14. (1965).

Mazur, D.P.: Fertility among ethnic groups in the USSR. *Delnography,* 4: 972 (1967).

Menard, S. W. and Mathiot, E. M. : Perspectives on Population: An Introduction to Concepts and Issues. New York: Oxford University Press. (1987).

Miklashevskaya, N.N., Solobyeva, V.S. and Godina, E.Z.: *Growth and development in high altitude regions of southern Kirghizia, USSR,* Miami: Field Research Project. (1973).

Miklashevskaya, N.N.: The effect of climatic factors on growth process in man. *Coll. Anthrop.,* 3: 173 (1979).

Miller, A.T. : Altitude. In: *Environmental Physiology.* N.B. Slonim (Ed.). C. V. Mosby, Saint Louis (1974).

Miller, A.T.: Altitude . In Environmental Physiology, (Eds.). N.B. Slonim. Saint Louis: C.V. Mosby (Cited by Gupta et.al., 1989) (1974).

Miller, B.D.: *The Endangered Sex: Neglect of Female Children in Rural North India.* Cornell University Press, Ithaca, New York (1981).

Minkler, M.: Fertility and female labour force participation in India: A survey of workers in the old Delhi area. *J. Family Welfare,* 17: 31 (1970).

Miro, C.A. and Martens, W.: Influences affecting fertility in urban and rural Latin America. *Milbank Memorial Fund Quarterly,* 46: 89 (1968).

Miro, C.A. and Potter, J.E.: Population policy: Research priorities in the developing world. *Report of the International Review Group of Social Science Research on Population and Development.* Frances Pinter (publishers), London (1980).

Misra, B.D.: *An Introduction to the Study of Populations.* South Asian Publishers Pvt. Ltd., New Delhi (1982).

Mitchel, J.C.: Cultural explanations of fertility differences. *J. Biosoc. Sci.,* 3: 60 (1971).

Mitra, A.: *India's Populations: Aspects of Quality and Control.* Abhinav Publications, New Delhi (1978).

Monge, C.: *Acclimatization in the Andes: Historical confirmation of climatic aggression in the development of Andean man.* Baltimore: John Hopkins Press, (Cited by Pawson, 1974), (1948).

Montagu, A. : *The Reproductive Development of the Female.* New York. (1948).

Morabia, A., and Costanza, M.C.: The World Health Organization Collaborative Study of Neoplasia and Steroid Contraceptives:

International variability in age at menarche, first livebirth and menopause. *Am. J. Epidemiol.*148: 1195-1205. (1998).

Morgan, S.P. and Rindfuss, P.R.: Household structure and the tempo of family formation in comparative perspective. *Population Studies*, 38: 129 (1984).

Mueller E.: The economic value of children. In: *Population and Development: The Search for Selective Interventions.* R.G. Ridker (Ed.). Johns Hopkins University Press, Baltimore (1976).

Mukherjee, D.P.: Some recent trends in population genetics in India. *ICMR Technical Report Series*, 20: 234 (1972).

Murty, G.B.: The Soliga of B.R. Hills: A demographic study. *The Journal of Family Welfare*, 34: 54-58 (1987).

Murty, J.S. and A. Ramesh : Selection intensities among the tribals populations of Adilabad district, Andhra Pradesh, India. *Soc. Biol.*, 25: 302-305 (1978).

Nag, M., White, B.N.F. and Peet, R.C.: An Anthropological approached to the study of the economic value of children in Java and Nepal. *Curr. Anthrop.*, 19: 293 (1978).

Nag, M.: Effect of Christianity on a few aspects of Khasi Culture. *Bull. Dept. Anthrop., Govt. of India.* 14: I (1965).

Nag, M.: *Factors Affecting Human Fertility in Non-Industrial Societies: A Cross Cultural Study*. Dept. of Anthropology, Yale University, Publication, No.66, Yale University, New Haven (1968).

Nag, M.: Family type and fertility. p. 160. In : *Proceedings of the IInd World Population Conference, New York*, 1965. Vol. II, United Nations, New York (1967).

Nag, M.: How modernization can also increase fertility. *Curr. Anthrop.*, 21: 571 (1980).

Nag, M.: Marriage and kinship in relation to human fertility. In.: *Population and Social Organization.* M. Nag (Ed.). Mouton, The Hague (1975).

Nag, M.: Sex, culture and human fertility: India and the United States. *Curr. Anthrop.*. 13: 231 (1972).

Nag, S.: *A Study of the Impact of Sex in Early Parities on Family Size and Other Associated Social and Bio-Demographic Factors Among the Lodhas, the Mundas, and the Santhals of Midnapore District (West Bengal).* M.Sc. Dissertation Department of Anthropology University of Delhi, (un- published) (1985).

Nag, M.H.: Trends in Moslem fertility and the application of the demographic transition model. *Soc. Biol.*, 30: 245 (1981).

Namboodiri, N.K.: The wife's work experience and child spacing. *Milbank Memorial Fund Quarterly*, 42: 65 (1964).

Narasimhan, R.L. and Chandra, H. : Sources of data on migration and recent trends. *India Journal of Labour Economics*, 41: 633-643 (1998).

Neel, J.V.: The study of natural selection in primitive and civilized human populations. *Hum. Biol.*, 30: 43 (1958).

Ness, I., Ciment, J.: Encyclopedia of Global Population and Demographics. Fitzroj Dearlorn Publication, Chicago (1999).

NFHS-1, 1992-93, *India*, National Family Health Survey, India. International Institute for Population Sciences. (1995).

NFHS-2, 1998-99. *Himachal Pradesh*, National Family Health Survey, India. International Institute for Population Sciences. (2002).

NFHS-2, 1998-99. *India*, National Family Health Survey, India. International Institute for Population Sciences, Mumbai, India. (2000).

O'Neill, B. and Balk, D. : World Population Futures. *Population Bulletin*,56,3: 4-40. (2001)

Oberai, A.S. and Singh, H.K.: *Migration, Urbanization and Fertility: The Care Study of the Indian Punjab*. ILO, Geneva, Population and Labour Policies Programmes Working Paper No.95 (1980).

Oppong, C.: Women's roles, opportunity costs and fertility. In: *Determinants of Fertility in Developing* Countries. Vol. 1. *Supply and Demand for Children* R.A. Bulatao and D.L. Ronald (Eds.). Report of the National Research Council Committee on Population and Demography, Panel on Fertility Determinants. Academic Press, New York (1983).

Osteria, T.S.: Nutritional status and menarche in a rural community in the Philippines. *Philip. J. Nutr.*, 36: 150-156. (1983).

Osteria, T.S.: Nutritional Status and menarche in a rural community in the Philippines. *Philip. J. Nutr.*, 36: 150-156 (1983).

Paddaiah, G. : A study of genetic demography among the Koyas of Andhra Pradesh. 4th Annual Conference of Indian Society of Human Genetics (Abstract) pp60. (1977).

Padmanabha, P.S.B.S.V. : Selection Intensities among the Rural and Urban Naika of Gujarat. *Anthropologie*, 23: 101-103 (1985).

Pakrasi, K. and Malakar, C.: The relationship between family type and fertility *.Milbank Memorial Fund. Quarterly,* 45: 451 (1967).

Panda, M. and Stpathi, R. : Population Genetics of Kondh Tribe of Orissa. *South Asian Anthropologist,* 17 (2): 101-104 (1996).

Pandey, B.N., Mishra, S.K., Yadav, S. and Dash Sharma, P.: Foetal wastage and infant mortality in four endogamous population of Purnia District (Bihar). *J. Hum. Ecol.,* 11 (6): 477-481 (2000).

Pandey, G.D. : Fertility and Family Planning in Primitive Tribe. Serial Publications, Delhi (India). (2002).

Pandey, G.D. and Tiwari, R.S.: Socio-cultural characteristics and health seeking behaviour of the Hill Korwa. *The Journal of Family Welfare.* 39:44, (1993).

Papiha, S.S. Genetic Structure and Micro differentiation Among Populations of Kinnaur District, Himachal Pradesh, India. In *Genetic Micro differentiation in Human and other Animal Populations.* Y.R. Ahuja and James V. Neel , *Indian Anthropologist* 1: 80-93 (1985).

Parazzini, F., Negri, E. and La Vecchia, C.: Reproductive and general lifestyle determinants of age at menopause. *Maturitas*15: 141-149. (1992).

Park, C.B.: The fourth Korean child. The effect of son preference on subsequent fertility *.J. Biosoc. Sci.,* 10: 95 (1978).

Park, K.: Textbook of Preventive and Social Medicine 17th Edition. M/s Banarsidas Bhanot, Jabalpur. (2002).

Pathak, K.B. and Ram, F.: Techniques of Demographic Analysis. Himalayan publishing house, Delhi (1998).

Pathare, R.: The family planning programme. A sociological analysis. *Sociol. Bull..* 15: 44 (1966).

Patnaik, B.: Age at Menarche among Urban Upper Caste Women of Orissa. *Man In India,* 51: 3 (1971).

Patra, P.: Demographic Profile With Reference to Development Programmes among the Rajis: A Primitive Tribe of Uttaranchal. *Ph.D. Thesis* submitted to Department of Anthropology, University of Delhi, India (Un-published) (2001).

Pawson, I.G. and Jest, C.: The high altitude areas of the worldand their cultures. In *The Biology of High-Altitude Peoples,* PT. Baker (Ed.). Cambridge University press, Cambridge. 17-45 (1978).

Pawson, I.G.: Growth and development in high altitude populations: A review of Ethopian, Peruvian and Nepalese studies. *Proceedings of the Royal Society tondon,* B 194: 83 (1976).

Pawson, I.G.: The growth and development of high altitude children with special emphasis on population of Tibetan origin in Nepal. Unpublished Ph.D. thesis, The Pennsylvania State University, Pennsylvania, USA (1974).

Petersen, W.: *Population.* Macmillian, New York (1975).

Pick, J.B., Tellis, G.L. and Butler, E.W.: Fertility determinants in the oil region in Mexico. *Soc. Biol.* 37:45 (1990).

Piplai, C.: Menarcheal age of the Tamang women tea labourers of the Duars, Jailpaiguri district, West Bengal. *Hum. Sci.,* 32: 219 (1983).

Population Reference Bureau: 2002 World Population Data Sheet of the Population Reference Bureau, Demographic Data and Estimates for the Countries and Regions of the World (2002).

Population Reference Bureau: 2003 World Population Data Sheet of the Population Reference Bureau, Demographic Data and Estimates for the Countries and Regions of the World (2003).

Potts, M. and Selman, P.: *Society and Fertility.* Macdonald and Evans Ltd., London (1979).

Prakash, M and Malik, S.L.: Differences in fertility in high landers and lowlanders Bods of Himachal Pradesh. *J. Hum. Ecol.,* 1: 175-180 (1990).

Raha, M. K. : Polyandry: Development, Distribution, and Decline. *J. Indian Anthrop. Soc.* 37: 01-14 (2002).

Raha, M.K. and Mahato, S.N. : The Kinnaurese of the Himalayas, Anthropological survey of India, Department of Culture, Government of India, Calcutta. (1985).

Raj J. Jaya and Reddy, B.K.C.: A study of age at menarche, marriage and fertility among Kapus of Chittor, Andhra Pradesh. 4th Annual Conference of Indian Society of Human Genetics (Abstract) pp36. (1977).

Rakshit, S.: Reproductive life of some Maharashtrian Brahmin Women. *Man In India,* 42:139-159. (1962).

Ramamma, K. and Reddy, V.R.: Age at menarche, marriage and menopause among the muslim Women of Atmakur in South-eastern Andhra Pradesh. 4th Annual Conference of Indian Society of Human Genetics (Abstract) pp72. (1977).

Raman, M.V. and Pakrasi, K. : Ideal family size, sexpreference for children and contraceptive practice by women wanting no more children: A Calcutta study. p. 126 In: *The Calcutta Couples.* K. Pakrasi, A.R. Banerjee and A.K. Halder (Eds.). Editions Indian Calcutta (1980).

Ranjan, A. : Studies in Population of Madhya Pradesh, Monograph Series 2, Population Foundation of India, New Delhi (1999).

Rao, M.N. and Mathen, K.K.: *Rural Field Study of Population Control, Singur (1957-1969).* All India Institute of Hygiene and Public Health (1970).

Rao, V.V. and Murty, J.S. : Selection intensities and inbreeding among some caste groups of Andhra Pradesh, India. *Soc.Biol.* 31, 114-119. (1984).

Rao, V.V.R. and Aruna, T.: Menarcheal age of Chenchu women. *Man In India,* 56:65-70. (1975).

Reddy, B.M., and Chopra, V.P., : Opportunity for natural selection among the Indian populations. *Am. J.. Phys. Anthropol.* 83:281-296 (1990).

Reddy, B.S.: Menarcheal age among the rural women of Karnataka. *Ind. J. Phys. Anthop. Hum. Genet.,* 10: 159 (1984).

Reddy, P.C. and Lakshmanudu, M. : Indices of Opportunity of selection in Mala, Madiga and other Indian Population. *J.Ind.Anthrop.Soc.*14: 245-252 (1979).

Reddy, P.C. and Mukherjee, D.P.: Marriage distance in two scheduled caste of Chittor District, Andhra Pradesh. *Proc. Sec. Ann. Conf. Ind. Soc. Hum. Genet., Calcutta* (1997).

Reid, T.R.: The Sherpas: *National Geographic,* May 2003.

Rele, J.R. and Kanitkar, T.: Fertility differentials by religion in Greater Bombay: Role of explanatory variables. p. 371: In: *The Economic and Social Support of High Fertility.* L.T. Ruzicka (Ed.) Australian National Univeristy, Canberra (1976).

Rele, J.R. and Kanitkar, T.: Residence background and fertility in Greater Bombay. *Population Studies,* 28: 303 (1974).

Rele, J.R.: Fertility differential in India: Evidence from rural background. *Milbank Memorial Fund Quartely,* 41: 183 (1963).

Ridker, R.: Desired family size and the efficiency of current family planning programmes. *Population Studies.* 23: 279 (1969).

Riley, A.P.: Determinants of adolescent fertility and its consequences for maternal health, with special reference to rural Bangaldesh. *Ann. New York Acad. Sci.* 709: 86-100. (1994).

Riley, A.P.: Determinants of adolescent fertility and its consequences for maternal health, with special reference to rural Bangladesh. *Ann. New York Acad. Sci.* 709:86-100 (1994).

Roberts, D.F., Chinn, S., Girija, B. and Singh, H.D.: A Study of menarcheal age in India. *Ann. Hum. Biol.*, 4: 171 (1977).

Rosen, B.C. and Simmons, A.B.: Industrialization, family and fertility: A structural-Psychological analysis of the Brazilian case. *Demography*,8:1 (1971).

Ross, J.L.: Culture and fertility in Nepal Himalayas: A test of hypothesis. *Human Ecology* 12: 163-81 (1984).

Sahay, S. : Cultural determinants of maternal and infant mortality in Madhya Pradesh. *Man in India*, 81 (3 & 4): 363-375. (2001)

Salat-Baroux, J. : The menopause and its problems. *Sem. Hop.*, 56: 1343-1345. (1980).

Sample Registration Survey (SRS): Sample Registration System, Registrar General, India. *Bulletin*, 36 (1). (2002)

Sample Registration Survey (SRS): Sample Registration System, Registrar General, India. *Bulletin*, (1999).

Sample Registration Survey (SRS): Sample Registration System, Registrar General, India. *Bulletin*, (1992).

Sample Registration Survey (SRS): Sample Registration System, Registrar General, India. *Bulletin*, (1997).

Samuel, T.J.: Social factors affecting fertility in India. *Eugen. Rev.*, 57:5 (1965).

Sarkar, N.C. : Opportunity for Natural Selction among the Muklom of Arunachal Pradesh. *Curr. Anthrop.* 38 (1): 140-143 (1997).

Sarkar, N.C., Barua, S. and Varte, R. Th.: Opportunity of selection in the Champ of Lakhimpur District, Assam, India. *J. Hum. Ecol.* 5: 217-220 (1994).

Sarkar, S.S. and Chowdhury, J. : Differential fertility and natural selection. In : Proc. *Workshop on Med. And Hum. Population Genet. S. Roy (Ed.)* Central Family Planning Institute, New Delhi (1967).

Schultz, T.P.: *Fertility Determinants: A Theory of Evidence and an Application to Policy Evalution.* The rend corporation Santa Monica, California (1974).

Sen, T. : A Historical Study of Ages at Menarche, Marriage, Menopause and Family size in High –Caste Bengalees of Calcutta. *Man In India.* 74 (3): 241-250. (1994).

Sen, T.: Reproductive life of some Indian women. *Man in India,*33 : 31 (1953).

Shah, K.A.: The Age of menarche in Gujarati Collage Girls. *J. Ind.Med. Assoc.,* 30:347 (1958).

Sharma, K. : Age at menarche in North-West Indian females and a review of Indian Data. *Ann. Hum. Biol.,* 17: 159 (1990).

Sharma, K.: Fertility and mortality in Kondhs: A Tribal Community of Orissa. *Man in India,* 57:77 (1978).

Sharma, M.B. and Chaudhury, D.: Menarche and fertility: A correlation study among the Gond tribe of Maharashtra. *J. of Hum. Ecol.*6: 209-212. (1995).

Sharma, R.D., Koshy, A.K., Murty, M.S.R. and Nair, N.V. : Anthropology and Population Studies. In Mahadevan K and P. Krishna. (eds.), *Methodology for Population Studies and development* (eds.) Sage Publications, New Delhi. (1993).

Shryock, H.S. and Siegel, J.S.: The methods and materials of Demography. Academic Press, New York (1976).

Simondon, K. B., Simon, I. And F. Simondon : Nutritional status and age at menarche of Senegalese adolescents. *Ann. Hum. Biol.,* 24: 521-532. (1997).

Simondon, K.B., Simon, I. and Simondon, F.: Nutritional status and age at menarche of Selegalese adolescents. *Ann. Hum. Biol.,* 24: 521-532 (1997).

Singh, I.P., Kapoor, A.K. and Kapoor, S. : Morpho-Physiological and Demographic status of the western Himalayan Population. In *Human Biology of Asian Highland Populations in the Global Context* , (Eds.) A. Basu and R. Gupta, 9 Indian Anthropological Society Occasional Papers, The Indian Anthropological Society, Calcutta (1989).

Singh, K.P. : *Correlates of fertility Behaviour.* Concept Publishing Co., New Delhi (1986).

Singh, K.S., Bhalla, V., Kaul, V. : People of India National Series. X. The Biological variation in Indian Population (1994).

Singh, K.S.: People of India, National series, Identity, Ecology, Social Organization, Economy, Linkages and Development Process. A

Quantitative Profile. Anthropological survey of India, Oxford University Press. 7: 274, 578, 802 and 958 (1996).

Singh, K.S.: People of India, National series, The Scheduled Tribes. Anthropological survey of India, Oxford University Press. 3: 533 (1994).

Singh, L. : Reproductive performance of Bhotia Women of Mana village .*Anthrop. Anz.,* 42: 137-140. (1984).

Singh, L. and Ahuja, S.: An estimation of reproductive performance in the women of Punjab. *Anthropl. Anz.* 37: 266-270 (1980).

Singh, M., Singh, R.K. and Sinha, S.P.: Biology of the Pahariya and the Santhal Tribes of the Rajmahal Region of Bihar. *J. Hum. Ecol.,* 10 (3): 183-190 (1999).

Singh, S.P.: Variations in Adult Anthropometry, Child Growth and Development in the Western Himalays- A Review. In *Human Biology of Asian Highland Populations in the Global Context* , (Eds.) A. Basu and R. Gupta, 9 Indian Anthropological Society Occasional Papers, The Indian Anthropological Society, Calcutta (1989).

Sirajuddin, S.M. and Basu, A.: Population structure, consanguinity and its effect on fertility and mortality among Chenchu of Andhra Pradesh, *Hum. Sci.,* 33: 179 (1984).

Synder, D.W.: Economic determinants of family size in West Africa. *Demography.* 11: 613 (1974).

Sobrevilla, L.: Fertility at high altitudes. *WHO/PAHO/IBP Meeting of investigators on Population Biology of Altitude.* Washington D.C.: Pan American Health Organization (1967).

Sood, A.K., Kapilasharmi, M.C. & Ali, A.: Socio Demographic & Health Profile of Himachal Pradesh. *National Institute of Health and Family Welfare, New Delhi* (2003).

Spengler, J.J.: The economist and population question. *Am.Eco.Rev.,* 56: 1 (1966).

Spuhler, J. N. : The maximum opportunity for natural selection in some human population, p. 185. In: *Demographic Anthropology: Quantitative Approaches,* (Ed.) E.B.W. Zubrow. University of New Maxico Press, Albuquerque (1976).

Spuhler, J.N.: Empirical studies of quantitative human genetics. p. 241. In: *Proceedings of UN/WHO Seminar on the Use of Vital Health Statistics for Genetics and Radiation Studies.* United Nations, New York (1962).

Sri Lanka Fertility Survey, 1975.: A Summary of Findings. International Statistical Institute, The Hauge, Netherlands (1978).

Srinivasan, K. : A prospective study of the fertility of the group of married women in rural India. Design and Findings of the first round of enquiry. *Pop. Rev.,* 11:46 (1967).

Srivastva, J.N. and Saksena, D. N. : Infant mortality differentials in an Indian setting: Followup for hospital deliveries. *J. Biosoc. Sci.,* 13: 467 (1981).

Standing, G.: *Labour Force Participation and Development.* ILO, Geneva (1978).

Stanford, J. L., Hartge, P. Brinton, L.A., et.al. : Factors influencing the age at natural menopause. *J. Chron. Dis.,* 40: 995-1002 (1987).

Statistical Hand Book,2001. *District Kinnaur.* District Statistical Office, District Kinnaur, Reckong Peo, Himachal Pradesh, (2002).

Stinner, W.F. and Mader, P.D.: Sons, daughters both? An analysis of family sex composition preferences in the Phillipines. *Demography,* 12:67 (1975).

Stoeckel, J. and Choudhury, M.A.: Differential fertility in a rural area of Pakistan. *Milbank Memorial Fund Quarterly,* 47: 189 (1969).

Stycos, J.M.: Culture and differential fertility in Peru. *Population Studies,* 26: 257 (1963).

Stycos, J.M.: Female employment and fertility in Lima, Peru. *Milbank-Memorial Fund Quarterly,* 43: 42 (1965).

Stycos, J.M.: Social class and different fertility in Peru. In: *Population and Society.* C. Nam (Ed.). Houghton Mifflin Co., Boston (1968).

Taeuber, I.B.: Population and modernization in Turkey. *Population Index,* 24:101 (1958).

Talukdar, S.: selection intensity in two Bagdi groups of 24-Parganas. West Bengal. *J. Ind. Anthrop. Soc.,* 6: 131 (1971).

Talwalkar, M.A.: Association of infant mortality and high fertility: An empirical investigation. *IIPS Newsletter,* Vol. 21 (1980).

Talwar, I., Sharma, K. and Rawat, U. : Socio-economic differences in sexual maturity in Punjabi girls. p. 131. In: *Sports Science: Health Fitness and Performance.* L.A. Siddhu et.al. (Eds.). IASSPE, Patiala (1987).

Thakur, S. and Kishtwaria, J. : Pattern and Determinants of Migration – A Study of Kangra district of Himachal Pradesh. *J.Hum. Ecol.,* 14 (4): 281-285 (2003)

Thomas, F., Renaud, F., Benefice, E., De Meeus, T. and Guegan, J. : International Variability of Ages at Menarche and Menopause: Patterns and Main Determinants. *Hum. Biol.*, 73 (2) 271-290 (2001).

Thompson, W.S. and Lewis, D.T.: *Populations Problems*. McGraw Hill Book Company, New York (1965).

Tonfer, K. : The relationship of education to fertility in Turkey. *Canad.Stud.Pop.*, 11:135 (1984).

Treolar, S.A., Do, K.A., Martin, N.G.: Genetic influences on the age at menopause. *Lancet*, 35: 1084-1085. (1998).

Trovato, F. and Grindstaff, C.F.: Decomposing urban-rural fertility differential, Canada, 1971. *Rural Sociology*, 45: 448 (1980).

Tuncer, B. : A survey of economic and social correlates of Turkish fertility. p. 135. In: *Demographic Transition and Socio-Economic Development*. Proceeding of the UN/UNFPA Expert Group Meeting, Istanabul 1977. United Nations, New York (1979).

Tuncer, B. *A Study of the Socio-Economic Determinants of Fertility in Turkey*. Yale University, Economic Growth Center Discussion Paper No. 121 (1971).

Udry, R.J. and Cliquet, R.L.: A cross-cultural examination of the relationship between ages at menarche, marriage and first birth. *Demography*, 19: 53 (1982).

Ulijaszek, S.J., Evans, E and Miller, D.S.: Age at menarche of European, Afro-Caribean and Indo-Pakistani schoolgirls living in London. *Ann. Hum. Biol.*, 18: 167-175. (1991).

United Nation: The Population Debate: Dimensions & Perspectives, Papers of the World Population Conference, Bucharest, 1974, Vol. II, United Nations, New York. (1975).

United Nations Population Fund: The State of the World population 1993. UNFPA, New York (1993).

United Nations: Demographic Indictors of the Countries, as assessed in 1980, Department of International Economic and Social Affairs, New York (1982).

United Nations: *Human Fertility and National Development: A Challenge to Science and Technology*. Department of Economic and Social Affairs, United Nations, New York (1971).

United Nations: Measuring the impact of socio-economic factors on fertility in the context of decline: Problems and issues. p. 38. In:

Demographic Transition and Socio-economic Development. Proceedings of the UN/UNFPA Expert Group Meeting, Istanbul, 1977. Population Studies No. 65, United Nations, New York (1979).

United Nations: Population and Development. p. 61. In: *The World Population Situation in 1979. Department of International Economics and Social Affairs.* Population Studies No. 72, United Nations, New York (1980).

United Nations: *Socio Economic Differentials in Child Mortality in Developing Countries.* Department of International Economic and Social Affairs. United Nations, New York (1985).

United Nations: *The Determinants and Consequences of Population Trends.* Vol.-I, Population Studies, No. 50. United Nations, New York. (1973).

United Nations: *The Mysore Population Study.* No. 34, United Nations, New York. (1961).

United Nations: *Women's Employment and Fertility: A comparative Analysis of World Fertility Survey Results for 38 Developing Countries. United Nations,* New York (1985).

United Nations: World Population Prospects: The 1996 Revision. New York (1998).

Upadhyay, V.S. and Pandey, G.: History of Anthropological thought. Concept Publishing Company, New Delhi (1997).

Valsik, J.A., Stukovsky, R., and Bernatova, L.: Quelque facteurs geographiques et sociaux ayant une influence sur l'age de la puberte. *Biotypologie* 24: 109-123 (cited by Clegg, 1978) (1963).

Van-Keep, P.A.: Ideal Family Size in five European Countries. *J. Biosoc. Sci.,* 3: 259 (1971).

Varma, G.R., Babu, B.V. and Rohini, A.: A study on fertility and its socio-demographic determinants among rural population of West Godavari District, Andhra Pradesh. *J.Hum. Ecol.,* 10(3): 179-182 (1999).

Vig, O.P. and Ram, F.: Reproductive and Child health project, Rapid Household Survey, 1998-99. Society for Applied Research in Humanities, New Delhi & International Institute for Population Sciences, Mumbai. (2001).

Visaria, L.: Religious differential in fertility. p. 365. In: *Population in India's Development, 1947-2000.* A. Bose et.al. (Eds.). Vikas Publishing House, Delhi (1974).

Vlassoff, C. and Vlassoff, M.: Family type and fertility in rural India. A critical analysis. *J. Biosoc. Sci.*,15: 407 (1983).

Wallace, A.R.: *The Action of Natural Selection on Man.* Academic Reprints, Stanford (1871) [Republished in 1953].

Ward, M.P.: Report of IBP expedition to Bhutan. London: The Royal Society. (1969).

Wattal, P.K.: Population Problem in India: *A Census Study,* Simla: Minerva Book Shop, p. V. (1958).

Way, A.B.: Health, exercise capacity and effective fertility aspects of migration to sea level by high altitude Peruvian Quenchua Indians. Unpublished Ph.D. thesis, University of Wisconsin, Madison, USA. (1972).

Weeks, J.R. : Population: An Introduction to Concepts and Issues. Belmont, CA: Wadsworth, (1978); 7th edn. (1999).

Weihe, W.H. (Ed.) : *The Physiological Effects of High Altitude.* Pergamon Press, Oxford (1964).

Weiner: In: The impact of High altitude on human populations by Clegg et. al. (1970). *Hum. Biol.*, 42: 486 (1964).

Weintraub, R.: The birth rate and economic development: An empirical study. *Econometrica,* 4: 812 (1962).

Weitz, C.A., Pawson, I.G., Weitz, M.V., Lang, S.D.R. and Lang, A.: Cultural factors affecting the demographic structure of a high altitude Nepalese population. *Soc. Biol.*, 25: 179-95 (1978).

Weitz, M.V. Lang, S.D.R. and Lang A.: Fertility of Nepalese Sherpas at moderate altitudes: Comparision with high altitude data. *Ann. Hum. Biol.*, 8: 383 (1981).

Wells, S.: Man's great leap outward, *Hindustan Times* (Daily News) Dated 13.07.2003. (2003)

Westoff, C.F. and Potvin, R.H.: Higher education, religion and women's family size orientations. *Am. Social Rev.*, 31: 489 (1966).

Westoff, C.F. and Ryder, N.: *The Contraceptive Revolution.* Princeton University Press, Princeton (1977).

Westoff, C.F., Potter, R.G. and Sagi, P.C.: *The Third Child: A Study in the Prediction of Fertility.* Princeton University Press, Princeton (1963).

Whelpton, P.K., Campbell, A.A. and Patterson, J.F.: *Fertility and Family Planning in the United States.* Princeton University Press, Princeton (1966).

Whitehead, L.: Altitude, fertility and mortality in Andean countries. *Population Studies*, 22: 335 (1968).

Wiley, A. S. : A Role for Biology in the Cultural Ecology of Ladakh. *Human Ecology*, 25, 2, June, pp. 273-295. (1997).

Wiley, A. S. : The ecology of low natural fertility in Ladakh. Journal of Biosocial Sciences, 30, pp. 457-480 (1998).

Willis, R.J.: A new approach to the economic theory of fertility behaviour. *J. Pol. Econ. (Chicago)*, 81: 514 (1973).

Wilson, C. : *The Dictionary of Demography*. Basil Blackwell Reference Ltd., London. (1985).

Wonnacott, T.H. and Wonnacott, R.J. : Introductory Statistics, John Wiley and Sons, New York. (1990).

Wood, J.W., Holman, D.J., Weiss, K.M. et.al.: Hazards models for human population biology. *Yrbk.Phys. Anthropol.* 35: 43-87 (cited from Kapoor, et.al., 2003) (1992).

Wood, J.W., Johnson, P.L. and Campbell, K.L.: Demographic and endocraniological aspects of low natural fertility in high land New Guinae. *J. Biosoc. Sci.*, 17: 57 (1985).

World Bank: World development Indicators (2002).

Wright, S. : Size of population and breeding structure in relation to evolution, *Science*. 87: 430-431. (1938).

Wright, S.: Breeding structure of populations in selection to speciation. *Amer. Naturalist*, 74: 232-248 (1940).

Wyon, J.B. and Gordon, J.K.: *The Khanna Study: Population Problems in Rural Punjab*. Harvard University Press, Cambridge (1971).

Yankaver, A.: Cultural base of infant mortality in India. P. 268. In: *Population Studies*. K.C.W. Kammenyar (Ed.) Rand McNeilly and Co., Chicago (1970).

Yaukey, D. : Demography : The Study of Human Population. New York: St. Martin's Press (1985).

Zachariah, K.C. : A Historical Study of Internal Migration in the Indian Sub-continent 1901-1931. Bomabay: Asia Publishing House. (1968).

Zachariah, K.C.: *Anomaly of the Fertility Decline in Kerala: Social Change, Agrarian Reform or the Family Planning Programme?* Population and Human Resources Division Discussion Paper No. 817. World Bank, Washington, D.C. (1981).

INDEX

R

Y